Austria

WORLD BIBLIOGRAPHICAL SERIES

General Editors:
Robert L. Collison (Editor-in-chief)
Sheila R. Herstein
Louis J. Reith
Hans H. Wellisch

VOLUMES IN THE SERIES

1 *Yugoslavia*, John J. Horton
2 *Lebanon*, Shereen Khairallah
3 *Lesotho*, Shelagh M. Willet and David Ambrose
4 *Rhodesia/Zimbabwe*, Oliver B. Pollack and Karen Pollack
5 *Saudi Arabia*, Frank A. Clements
6 *USSR*, Anthony Thompson
7 *South Africa*, Reuben Musiker
8 *Malawi*, Robert B. Boeder
9 *Guatemala*, Woodman B. Franklin
11 *Uganda*, Robert L. Collison
12 *Malaysia*, Ian Brown and Rajeswary Ampalavanar
13 *France*, Frances Chambers
14 *Panama*, Eleanor DeSelms Langstaff
15 *Hungary*, Thomas Kabdebo
16 *USA*, Sheila R. Herstein and Naomi Robbins
17 *Greece*, Richard Clogg and Mary Jo Clogg
18 *New Zealand*, R. F. Grover
19 *Algeria*, Richard I. Lawless
21 *Belize*, Ralph Lee Woodward, Jr.
23 *Luxembourg*, Carlo Hury and Jul Christophory
24 *Swaziland*, Balam Nyeko
25 *Kenya*, Robert L. Collison
26 *India*, Brijen K. Gupta and Datta S. Kharbas
27 *Turkey*, Meral Güçlü
28 *Cyprus*, P. M. Kitromilides and M. L. Evriviades
29 *Oman*, Frank A. Clements
30 *Italy*, Emiliana P. Noether
31 *Finland*, J. E. O. Screen
32 *Poland*, Richard C. Lewański
33 *Tunisia*, Allan M. Findlay, Anne M. Findlay and Richard I. Lawless
34 *Scotland*, Eric G. Grant
35 *China*, Peter Cheng
36 *Qatar*, P. T. H. Unwin
37 *Iceland*, John J. Horton
38 *Nepal*, Dina Nath Wadhwa
39 *Haiti*, Frances Chambers
40 *Sudan*, M. W. Daly
41 *Vatican City State*, Michael J. Walsh
42 *Iraq*, A. J. Abdulrahman
43 *United Arab Emirates*, Frank A. Clements
44 *Nicaragua*, Ralph Lee Woodward, Jr.
45 *Jamaica*, K. E. Ingram
46 *Australia*, I. Kepars
47 *Morocco*, Anne M. Findlay, Allan M. Findlay and Richard I. Lawless
48 *Mexico*, Naomi Robbins
49 *Bahrain*, P. T. H. Unwin
50 *The Yemens*, G. Rex Smith
51 *Zambia*, Anne M. Bliss, J. A. Rigg
52 *Puerto Rico*, Elena E. Cevallos
53 *Namibia*, Stanley Schoeman and Elna Schoeman
54 *Tanzania*, Colin Darch
55 *Jordan*, Ian J. Secombe
56 *Kuwait*, Frank A. Clements
57 *Brazil*, Solena V. Bryant
58 *Israel*, Esther M. Snyder (preliminary compilation E. Kreiner)
59 *Romania*, Andrea Deletant and Dennis Deletant
60 *Spain*, Graham J. Shields
61 *Atlantic Ocean*, H. G. R. King
63 *Cameroon*, Mark W. Delancey and Peter J. Schraeder
64 *Malta*, John Richard Thackrah
65 *Thailand*, Michael Watts
66 *Austria*, Denys Salt with the assistance of Arthur Farrand Radley
67 *Norway*, Leland B. Sather
68 *Czechoslovakia*, David Short

VOLUME 66

Austria

Denys Salt

Compiler

with the assistance of
Arthur Farrand Radley

CLIO PRESS

OXFORD, ENGLAND · SANTA BARBARA, CALIFORNIA
DENVER, COLORADO

British Library Cataloguing in Publication Data

Salt, Denys
Austria. – (World bibliographical series; v. 66)
1. Austria – Bibliography
I. Title II. Series
016.9436 Z2101

ISBN 1–85109–009–6

Clio Press Ltd.,
55 St. Thomas' Street,
Oxford OX1 1JG, England.

ABC-Clio Information Services,
Riviera Campus, 2040 Alameda Padre Serra,
Santa Barbara, Ca. 93103, USA.

Designed by Bernard Crossland
Typeset by Columns Design and Production Services, Reading, England
Printed and bound in Great Britain by
Billing and Sons Ltd., Worcester

THE WORLD BIBLIOGRAPHICAL SERIES

This series will eventually cover every country in the world, each in a separate volume comprising annotated entries on works dealing with its history, geography, economy and politics; and with its people, their culture, customs, religion and social organization. Attention will also be paid to current living conditions – housing, education, newspapers, clothing, etc. – that are all too often ignored in standard bibliographies; and to those particular aspects relevant to individual countries. Each volume seeks to achieve, by use of careful selectivity and critical assessment of the literature, an expression of the country and an appreciation of its nature and national aspirations, to guide the reader towards an understanding of its importance. The keynote of the series is to provide, in a uniform format, an interpretation of each country that will express its culture, its place in the world, and the qualities and background that make it unique.

SERIES EDITORS

Robert L. Collison (Editor-in-chief) is Professor Emeritus, Library and Information Studies, University of California, Los Angeles, and is currently the President of the Society of Indexers. Following the war, he served as Reference Librarian for the City of Westminster and later became Librarian to the BBC. During his fifty years as a professional librarian in England and the USA, he has written more than twenty works on bibliography, librarianship, indexing and related subjects.

Sheila R. Herstein is Reference Librarian and Library Instruction Coordinator at the City College of the City University of New York. She has extensive bibliographic experience and has described her innovations in the field of bibliographic instruction in 'Team teaching and bibliographic instruction', *The Bookmark*, Autumn 1979. In addition, Doctor Herstein coauthored a basic annotated bibliography in history for Funk & Wagnalls *New encyclopedia*, and for several years reviewed books for *Library Journal*.

Louis J. Reith is librarian with the Franciscan Institute, St. Bonaventure University, New York. He received his PhD from Stanford University, California, and later studied at Eberhard-Karls-Universität, Tübingen. In addition to his activities as a librarian, Dr. Reith is a specialist on 16th-century German history and the Reformation and has published many articles and papers in both German and English. He was also editor of the *American Society for Reformation Research Newsletter*.

Hans H. Wellisch is a Professor at the College of Library and Information Services, University of Maryland, and a member of the American Society of Indexers and the International Federation for Documentation. He is the author of numerous articles and several books on indexing and abstracting, and has also published *Indexing and abstracting: an international bibliography*. He also contributes frequently to *Journal of the American Society for Information Science, Library Quarterly*, and *The Indexer*.

Tu felix Austria . . .

Contents

Contents

Contents

Introduction

Geography, Climate, Communications and Population

Austria is a small land-locked country in central Europe. After the Treaty of St. Germain (1919) following the defeat of the Dual Monarchy of Austria-Hungary in World War I the geographical area of the Austria that remained represented only about 12 per cent of the former Habsburg Empire. Indeed the French delegate at the Paris Peace Conference, Georges Clémenceau, is alleged to have said 'Austria – it's what's left'. Understandably, therefore, the present boundaries reflect history rather than geography: few of them follow natural features such as watersheds or rivers and the main geophysical divisions are shared with her neighbours. The present perimeter is 1,682 miles long, providing common frontiers with (number of miles in parenthesis): West Germany (509), Switzerland (104), Liechtenstein (22), Italy (267), Yugoslavia (215), Hungary (220), and Czechoslovakia (355).

The country can be divided into several geographical areas. The *Eastern Alps* (62.8 per cent of the land area) which form the backbone of the country on an east-west axis, split roughly in half geologically. To the north, are the *Limestone Alps*, the highest peak of which is the Dachstein at 9,824 feet. This area also incorporates the Salzkammergut Lake District and key mineral deposits as at Eisenerz, the iron ore mountain. To the south along this line is the *High Alpine core* (with the highest peak in all Austria, the Grossglockner, 12,454 feet) petering out only gradually to the east. Some frontiers at the western end of this backbone are relatively logical: to the west, Switzerland, along the Upper Rhine and the Rhaetian Alps, and to the north, the limestone line descending into Bavaria. However, one real anomaly stands out here – Berchtesgaden. This, as a bishopric, was secularized by Napoleon, along with Salzburg, and transferred to Bavaria. Nonetheless, in 1816 it was not incorporated into the Austrian Empire when Salzburg was, and, as can be seen from the map, the resultant salient remains something of an oddity. It continues to create considerable communication problems, and allowed Hitler, even before the *Anschluss* in 1938, to sit safely in his German Alpine retreat and look back to the north over his country of origin.

The High Alpine frontier is also bedevilled with anomalies to the south, because of the problem of South Tirol. It can be argued geographically that the present line provides a more 'natural' frontier, but historically the area down to Trient (Trento) was, after the 11th century, Tirolese, in fact the very name comes from Tirol Castle near Meran (Merano). In 1919 the region was given to Italy by the victorious Allies in recognition of the Italian agreement to enter the war on their side in 1916. Today, however, the majority of the population of Austrian stock is all but reconciled to the *status quo*.

The *Southern Alps* to the south-east (the Carnic and Karawanken Alps) are separated from Italy and Yugoslavia respectively by a watershed boundary, though the 1919 settlements severed the previous southern extensions of Carinthia and Styria in favour of Yugoslavia. If you have a sense of humour, and a car, you will appreciate the latter boundary which is the middle of the road running west-east. When driving along this road you are 50 per cent certain of technically violating the other country's territory.

To the southeast and east lie the *Pannonian foothills* (named after the Roman province). A logical frontier here is almost out of the question since the rich agricultural and wine-growing area was always the contact point between German-speaking Austria and Hungary. In 1919 the Allies sliced off a piece of Hungary and gave it to Austria as the province of Burgenland. This was the only sop Austria received to compensate for all the other massive losses.

Finally, there is the *Danube area* which has a granite massif to the northwest, part of the Bohemian Woods, and which thus merges with the Czechoslovak mountain ring around Prague. This, the foothills to the south and northeast, and the Vienna Basin (latterly with its oil) were the cradle of the Ostmark, the East March where Austria began. The northeastern frontier with Czechoslovakia lies, appropriately enough, along the River March (Morava). It was here in 1278 that the first Habsburg, Rudolph I, won the battle of the Marchfeld over his opponent

Ottokar II, one of the only three Bohemian-based rulers over Austria. Thus began the rule of the Habsburgs which lasted until 1918.

The River Danube flows for 224 miles through Austria. It provides, as in Roman times, a navigable through route from Germany to the Black Sea which will be vastly enhanced when the Europa Canal (Main-Danube Ship Canal) is completed. The Danube, it should also be noted, is an important source of electric power. Its main Austrian tributary, the Inn, actually rises in Switzerland. The railways hug the valleys until forced into tunnels, as at the Arlberg, Mallnitz and the Semmering (the original engineering triumph of 1854 and the first anywhere in the Alps). The Berchtesgaden salient, however, still provides an obstacle and the Vienna-Switzerland line is subjected to considerable diversions. The Federal road network has been improved immeasurably over the last twenty years by the construction of motorways, which are connected with the European system and which pass through spectacular tunnels and over viaducts. Notwithstanding this, finance for road construction is short and progress is slow. The main through road from Germany to Yugoslavia is perpetually strewn with wrecked cars. The owners of many of these vehicles are foreign workers (*Gastarbeiter*) who, with minimal driving experience, attempt to return home to Yugoslavia, Greece or Turkey.

The western areas enjoy what is technically known as a 'central European transitional' climate, a wet and temperate mix reflecting an Atlantic influence, with prevailing west and southwest winds. The eastern regions on the other hand are subject to a drier and more extreme 'continental Pannonian' climate. The Alps, of course, should be viewed quite separately and are characterized by 'high precipitation'. Even in summer there can be prolonged periods of rain and, moreover, perfect winter snow cannot be guaranteed every day, even though Austria is the home of central European skiing.

It is arguable that only Britain offers a greater variety of scenery, although the area of land under forest is clearly higher in Austria at 44 per cent. The vegetation in the uplands is mainly oak and beech, with fir above 4,000 feet giving way higher up to larch and pine. Game of all kinds, including chamois, is abundant but wild life is now protected by special legislation. Indeed it should be noted that in the saltsteppe areas around the Neusiedler See in Burgenland there is United Nations protection for rare bird species, such as the avocet, spoonbill and purple heron.

The population of Austria in 1985 was approximately 7.5 millions but in 1918 the inhabitants of the Habsburg Empire had totalled some 50 millions. Vienna remains the city with the largest population (1.5 millions) and in the country as a whole, for every 100 men (life expectancy 69.5 years) there are 113 women (76.6). About 98 per cent of all Austrians speak German as their first language. There are two official ethnic groups with guaranteed minority rights and language; the Slovenes in Carinthia and the Croats in Burgenland. In addition, there are enough Czechs and Hungarians in Vienna to support their own independent newspapers and there are still a substantial number of foreign workers in the country, about half of whom emanate from Yugoslavia. Some 84 per cent of the population is Roman Catholic and 6 per cent is Protestant – mainly Lutheran, although some are Calvinists.

The 1920 Constitution established a Federal Republic with eight partly self-governing provinces. Any area, however, had the right to promote itself to that status, and the city of Vienna did just that in 1922. The provinces are as follows:

Burgenland (Capital Eisenstadt; area in square miles 1,530; population 272,274) is a richly fertile province and it has some of the best wines in Austria. Eisenstadt houses the winter palace of the Esterházy family, patrons of Joseph Haydn, who was born locally of Croat minority stock. The summer palace, Esterháza, is also still in existence but it is now in Hungary, at Fertöd.

Carinthia (Kärnten) (Klagenfurt; 3,680; 536,727). This province is historically bound up with the Tirol through the family connections of its rulers. Its Lake District (including the Wörther See) is comparable scenically with the Salzkammergut and its Slovene minority problem (the Slovenes lost the 1919 plebiscite to join Yugoslavia and re-opened the matter unsuccessfully in 1945) has now quietened down as a result of tactful Federal handling.

Lower Austria (Vienna; 7,402; 1,439,137) has Vienna as its capital, which, of course, is also the Federal capital. Accordingly, there are now proposals in some quarters to establish a separate provincial capital for Lower Austria at, for example, Krems on the Danube, an important local centre.

Salzburg (Salzburg (city); 2,762; 441,842) was an independent archbishopric from the 8th century until it was secularized and transferred to Bavaria by Napoleon, joining the Austrian Empire only in 1816. Although Mozart was born here he strongly disliked the place. Much of the Salzkammergut (the salt caverns estate) is, surprisingly, in Upper Austria.

Styria (Steiermark: Graz; 6,324; 1,187,512). This province was earlier a Mark (March) under the control of the rich iron town of Steyr (now in Upper Austria) and hence its name. In the 16th and 17th centuries Graz was the capital of Inner Austria (Lower Austria, Styria and Carinthia). Graz's monumental civic architecture of the time is in Renaissance style, and is incidentally the work of Swiss-Italian masters. It was also the headquarters of the British Military Government of the province after World War II.

Tirol (Innsbruck; 4,822; 583,139). The cession of South Tirol in 1919 left East Tirol isolated. The main communication route between the chief town, Lienz, and the capital Innsbruck lay through Italy over the Brenner Pass, and a system of sealed trains had to be organized. A recent road tunnel avoiding the Brenner altogether, through the Felbertauern, is an important addition to the European road network.

Upper Austria (Linz; 4,625; 1,270,426). The biggest industrial complex in Austria is situated here and the province's industry played a major role in the German War effort 1939-45. Together with Lower Austria the region (site of the original Ostmark-East March), contains the greatest concentration of architectural glories in the whole country, including, for example, the baroque abbeys of Wilhering, St. Florian, Kremsmünster, Seitenstetten, Melk, and Göttweig.

Vienna (Vienna (city); 160; 1,515,666). Vienna became a city in 1221 but has been capital of the country since 1156. It is one of the world's greatest historical cities with a vibrant musical and theatrical life as well as museums, parks and coffee houses. All of these features make Vienna an international tourist attraction.

Vorarlberg (Bregenz; 1,004; 305,615). This is the smallest province but it very nearly ceased to exist, for in 1919, after promotion to provincial status, the majority of the inhabitants were in favour of the province being seceded to Switzerland. The possible break with Austria was frustrated, however, by the French representative at the Peace Conference of 1919, Prime Minister Clémenceau, who vetoed it on fears of upsetting the balance between the German and French-speaking elements in Switzerland. Bregenz is situated on Lake Constance (Bodensee) and the province borders the friendly principality of Liechtenstein which is ruled by a House of Austrian origin. The Vorarlberg dialect differs from that of Tirol to the east, which is separated from the province by the massive mountain barrier of the Arlberg. The recently-constructed motorway under the Arlberg has, however, eliminated the problems caused by transporting cars on flat wagons through the rail tunnel during the winter and has led to a marked improvement in communications both with Tirol and the rest of Austria.

A brief historical background from the earliest times to 1955

It was logical in geographical and economic terms that a nation state should exist in the area now known as Austria, at the crossroads between the Danube through route and the 'Amber Road' from Scandinavia to the Mediterranean. The key to its economic viability was salt – certainly worked by the Iron Age Indo-European Illyrians at Hallstatt near Salzburg and, from the 4th century BC, by the Celts. The Celts held off the Bajuvari from Bavaria and, initially, the Romans, but by the Christian era the latter had established three major provinces – Raetia, Noricum and Pannonia – as part of a unified system which extended from present-day Switzerland down the navigable Danube to Romania, with fortified points such as Vindobona, now Vienna.

After the Romans had finally withdrawn (ca. AD 400), the Bajuvari once again invaded the region and were joined by the Avars and Slavs from the east so that the area became an established meeting point between German and Slav languages and cultures. A situation of considerable turmoil and confusion then continued for 300 years until the great consolidator Charlemagne set an eastern limit to his vast responsibilities and created buffer states in the southeast. One of these (by 799) was the Avar Mark, better known as the Ostmark (East March), in the Danube areas of what is now parts of Upper and Lower Austria. Here the progressive spread of Christianity had found expression in abbeys such as St. Florian (named after the early Christian martyr), Kremsmünster and Melk – later to become important baroque masterpieces.

The Mark held for a hundred years until overwhelmed by the next eastern wave, the Magyars (Hungarians), but in 955 it was revived by the first Holy Roman Emperor, Otto I.

In 976 his successor, Otto II, set up a dynasty of Margraves, or Counts of the Mark (later Dukes), the Babenbergs from the present-day Bamberg (same name) in Franconia, north Bavaria. Accordingly, the year 976 is generally accepted as the beginning of Austria as a political entity: the name 'Ostarrichi' (Österreich, the East Realm) is documented in 996 and the Latinized 'Austria' followed.

The Babenbergs demonstrated very clearly to their successors, the Habsburgs, the need to adopt a prudent foreign policy, to arrange marriages with territory in mind, and to ensure that the succession was not disputed. The last Duke, Frederick II, died on the field of battle without male issue and the German King, the Earl of Cornwall, a son of John of England, installed Frederick's brother-in-law Ottokar II of Bohemia. (At least the Earl knew where Bohemia was, more than Shakespeare, who set *The Winter's Tale* there – 'a desert country near the sea'). The Babenberg Leopold V also entered English history by imprisoning Richard I Coeur de Lion on his return from the Holy Land, traditionally rescued by Blondel, and was excommunicated by the Pope for interfering with a sacrosanct Crusader.

Although popular with the Austrians Ottokar upset the balance of power as seen by the German Electors and their favourite Rudolph of Habsburg (the Habichtsburg, Hawks Castle, near Zürich) ousted him. Ottokar, like the last Babenberg, fell in battle.

The reign of Rudolph I (1276-82) ushered in an era of nearly 650 years of triumph and tragedy during which Austria expanded to form the largest empire in the world (during the 16th century) only to shrivel in 1918 to not much more than the original size of the Ostmark. She faltered only when neglecting the Babenberg precepts referred to above, particularly over succession squabbles: and she saw her first Holy Roman Emperor, Frederick III, crowned in Rome in 1452 (the last there) and filled the position of Holy Roman Emperor almost continuously from 1452 until that empire crumbled under Napoleon in 1806.

The 'basic' Austria expanded to the west (Tirol), the south (to the Adriatic) and the east (Bohemia and Hungary). Indeed, Rudolph IV (the Founder of Vienna University in 1365) could say that 'all roads leading from Germany to Italy belong to Us'. Later Maximilian I (1493-1519), whose superb monument graces his capital at Innsbruck, started three generations of territory-increasing marriages, and his son Charles V (1519-56) inherited most of Central and Southern Europe and subsequently gained possession of the inconceivable riches of the Spanish Main. 'Bella gerant alii tu felix Austria nube' runs the dedication to this book – 'let others wage war, you, fortunate Austria, marry!. The other classic statement is made on Frederick III's tomb in St. Stephen's Cathedral in Vienna: 'A.E.I.O.U.'. Of many interpretations perhaps the most challenging is 'Austriae est imperare orbi universo', (it is for Austria to rule the whole world). Charles V nearly did but his Empire was unwieldy and ultimately was split up. It had to face threats from within (the Reformation) and from without (the Turks); and the Habsburg dream to unite Europe into one Catholic force and sweep both these threats away evaporated with the Thirty Years' War and the jealousy of France.

The Spanish line died out in 1700 and it took two generations of European wars to persuade France to abandon its own claims to the Spanish Succession. Moreover, the Turkish threat to Austria which had ebbed now came to the fore again and the second major Turkish thrust was only narrowly repelled at the gates of Vienna, in 1683. Only the baroque in art and architecture offered a resolution to the spiritual and military conflict of the age, through exuberance and theatricality. Indeed, the doyen of British writers on taste, Sacheverell Sitwell, proclaims that the splendour of Austria's baroque abbeys and palaces is an artistic legacy of the nation which is even more important than her music.

The Austrian line died out in 1740, or rather there was no male heir, and only delicate diplomacy (the Pragmatic Sanction) resulted in European acceptance of a female successor. Even then the Emperorship passed to Bohemia for five years and was only restored as a result of the marriage of Francis of Lorraine and Maria Theresa, who never actually *ruled* as an Empress. However, to the Austrians, Maria is considered as the most remarkable ruler of the 18th century, even though she failed to curb the rise of Prussia and gained a frontier with Russia, in the partition of Poland, which later proved of doubtful political and military value.

Her son Joseph II (1765-90) flirted with reform in the Age of Enlightenment but managed to avoid a revolution in Vienna in the French style. However, under Francis II, the last Holy Roman Emperor, who became Francis I, Emperor of Austria, Austria became embroiled in the war with revolutionary France and with Napoleon I, who faced stiff popular resistance in the Tirol from the legendary hero Andreas Hofer. At the Congress of Vienna (1814-15) Austria did not regain its former possessions in the Netherlands and in Baden but she did regain Lombardy, Venetia, Istria and Dalmatia. Moreover, she became the principal power in the Holy Alliance (Austria, Prussia & Russia) and the German Confederation (a collection of small states excluding Prussia) and under her foreign minister, Metternich, became the dominant power in Europe. This, the 'Biedermeier', was an era characterized by industrial expansion, the repression of nationalism throughout the Empire and political conservatism as expressed in Francis I's tenet 'displace nothing of the edifice of the state: rule and change nothing'. Perhaps not surprisingly such a policy ran counter to powerful undercurrents all over Europe culminating in the Revolutions of 1848. Although the revolutions were suppressed the main strands of development of the Twilight Era (1848-1918) soon began to emerge.

Pan-Germanism, the political union of the German-speaking peoples of Germany and Austria, was one of these developments. Although an Austrian Archduke was elected Imperial Regent by the emergent German Parliament in 1849 neither country could agree over which should prevail in a possible union and it was left to the German Chancellor Bismarck to organize Austria's military defeat in 1866. An undercurrent, however, persisted which surfaced in 1918 and materially helped the success of Nazism. The North Italian provinces also presented the Empire with severe difficulties. Austria sucessfully defended Lombardy and Venetia in 1848-9, but lost both progressively in the wars that established Italian unification in 1859 and 1866. In the latter she was fighting on two fronts and Prussia's victory at Königgrätz (Sadowa) allowed Bismarck to dictate the Peace.

In addition the ethnic minorities of the Empire presented intractable problems in a nationalistic age. Hungary had seen her revolution strangled by Russian intervention and Königgrätz enabled her to insist on the Ausgleich (Compromise) of 1867 which created the Dual Monarchy and gave encouragement to all her sister minorities. Hungary's armies were the first to desert in 1918 – the culmination of resistance to the Habsburg administration which the victorious Allies were to recognize in 1919.

Francis Joseph, catapulted onto the throne in 1848, reigned for sixty-eight years and during this time he saw his world progressively disintegrate. His brother Maximilian was executed by the Mexicans when he tried to revive the glory of Charles V; his son killed himself at Mayerling; and his wife fell to a madman. In addition, his nephew, then heir, Francis Ferdinand married morganatically and was the victim of a political assassination which ultimately led to defeat in World War I and the dismemberment of a 642-year old Empire. Francis Joseph had signed the Declaration of War: as baffled and frustrated as his subjects. His grand-nephew and successor Charles I withdrew from power in 1918 and died in Madeira, in poverty.

Both Austria and Hungary emerged from the Peace Treaties severely truncated and for the Slavs to north and south there were two new independent federations: Czechoslovakia and Yugoslavia. What rankled most was the loss to Italy of the South Tirol without even a plebiscite (as in Vorarlberg or the Slovene-speaking parts of Carinthia) under the secret arrangements by which Italy had entered the War on the Allied side. Lloyd George's protests (and later Churchill's) were in vain.

The Revolution of 1918 was modest compared with Germany's, though working-class solidarity revived a Pan-German spirit which proclaimed in the new constitution that Austria was a 'component part of the German Republic' and that 'German Austria is a democratic republic'. These sentiments, however, waned as the Left, which under Chancellor Renner had held off its more extreme factions, lost progressively to the Right, even under the severe inflation. The socialists formed a private army, the *Schutzbund* or Defence League, to be rivalled by two brands of Right-wing *Heimwehr* or Home Defence Force (which were later combined into one, the Vaterländische Front or Fatherland Front). However, the Left failed ignominiously in an attempted coup in 1934, in the very Vienna which it had nurtured as a socialist stronghold.

The Right, initially clinging to parliamentary democracy, but under pressure from both Nazi Germany and, even more persuasively, from Fascist Italy, felt induced to operate a brand of corporative state without a Parliament. Both Dollfuss (who was murdered by it) and Schuschnigg were, however, undermined by Nazism. Adolf Hitler, an Upper Austrian drop-out steeped in the lessons of pre-1914 Viennese politics and still technically Austrian until 1932, forced Schuschnigg to legalize the operations of the National Socialists and marched into Austria before Schuschnigg's last-minute plebiscite, designed to avoid *Anschluss*, could be held. Hitler's own plebiscite indicated 99.23 per cent support for the *Anschluss* (the 'Yes' box was physically four times larger than the 'No' box on the voting slip). Schuschnigg's final broadcast still rings in the ears of those who heard it: 'I yield to force: God save Austria!'.

In the ensuing War Austrians were assimilated into the German army: there *was* no Austria. The Allies declared that she would be judged later by the extent of resistance, and there was indeed some, partly fostered clandestinely by the Allies, and well-documented by the Austrians: its chief success, perhaps, was the preparation of a Provisional Government ready to receive the Russians when they arrived before the other Allies in 1945. Karl Renner, the first Chancellor in 1918, found himself re-installed, despite his championing of the Nazi *Anschluss* in 1938 on simple Pan-German grounds. He repeated his 1918 feat of containing the extreme Left but, as then, lost the first elections, held in November 1945.

The Allies occupied the country in four zones under a Quadripartite Allied Commission (as distinct from a *Control* Commission as in Germany). The Jeep patrols in Vienna manned by an American, British, French and Russian soldier in each provided good press photo-coverage as models of inter-Allied understanding, but they masked the realities. No true progress could be made in the reconstruction of Austria by the Austrians until the New Control Agreement of 1946, a British initiative which effectively stifled the Russian veto. The American–inspired Marshall Plan was also indispensable to economic recovery. The actual State Treaty ending hostilities was not signed until May 1955, after Stalin's death, when the Austrians themselves astutely exploited a Russian hint. The Allies gave them independence and the Austrians added neutrality.

The Austrian National Day is on 26 November, when the last Russian left in 1955. An open competition to replace Haydn's National Anthem tune, long shared with pre-War Germany and now re-adopted by West Germany, was won by an up-and-coming young Salzburger – Wolfgang Amadeus Mozart.

Post-1955 Developments and the Contemporary Situation

The political scene is dominated by the fact that Austria is the only Western country to have seen the Russians withdraw from territory occupied in World War II without being guaranteed the right of re-entry by treaty. Austria regained her territorial boundaries lost under Hitler and her post-World War I constitution as well as her social and political structure.

The Right, from 1955, was the largest party in Parliament (though not necessarily in the partly-independent provincial Assemblies with their own local elections): at first in coalition with the Left until 1966 and then outright, with an absolute majority, until 1970. The Left then dominated for thirteen years until reduced to leading yet another coalition until 1983, this time with the small Freedom Party (only founded in 1955).

The Austrians have thus become experts in coalitions and have devized special rules, for example on policy trade-offs and the proportional allocation of posts in government and nationalized industries. These developments provide a real chance of responsibility to any long-term minorities.

In the economic sphere the greatest advance has been the introduction of the Social Partnership, an intricately inter-woven system of representative chambers and trade union bodies whose outstanding success is the Parity Commission for Wages and Prices. The economy remains delicately balanced between harmonizing with West German trends, being a member of EFTA (European Free Trade Association), an associate member of the EEC (European Economic Community) and maintaining a unique relationship with Comecon (Council for Mutual Economic Aid).

The transit trade with Comecon, along with tourism, largely redresses an adverse balance of trade of some 2 billion Schillings per annum. State industries account for some one-sixth of the total industrial output and workforce.

The tourist industry, astonishingly, shows that throughout the country as a whole there is an overnight occupancy of twice as many visitors as locals, 2 per cent from the United States, 4.5 per cent from Britain, 15 per cent from France and the Benelux countries, and 65 per cent from West Germany. This is essentially due to Austria's pioneering position in skiing, since the world's first organized downhill race, the Arlberg Kandahar, was held at St. Anton in 1911, a joint venture between the Tirolese Hannes Schneider and the English 'Lowlander', Henry Lunn. Austria has since maintained its fair share of world champions and these have included, of course, Toni Sailer and Franz Klammer.

Internationally, Austria's independence and neutrality have favoured her predominance as a centre for over 50 organizations and as the third United Nations base after New York and Geneva. One in twelve soldiers on UN missions are Austrian. Austrians also continue to fill key positions in the Council of Europe and the United Nations, such as the latter's Secretary-General, Dr. Kurt Waldheim, 1972-81. Since 1905 sixteen resident Austrians have won Nobel Prizes, surely a record for a country the size of Austria.

The traditional image of Austria has also been retained: the coffee-house with newspapers on a bamboo frame; the Heuriger; culinary delights such as the Wiener Schnitzel, Tafelspitz,

Kaiserschmarrn and the Sachertorte; the Vienna Boys' Choir; the Opera; and the Spanish Riding School (although the only element that is really Spanish from 1572 is the white Lipizzaner stallions). Even the etiquette remains traditional. Your hostess's hand is there to be kissed: woe betide you if you forget those flowers. Respect for learning and the hierarchy is fanatical: 'Yes, Herr Doktor' and 'certainly, Frau Minister'. The aim is always, however, to stay relaxed (gemütlich), admitting a tendency to easy-going muddle (Schlamperei – stoutly preferred to Prussian hyper-efficiency) but determined at least to muddle through constructively (durchwursteln).

Austria's cultural achievement is unique and indisputable. In literature and drama the Middle Ages saw the first attributed poem in the German language, by the nun Ava, and the outstanding Minnesinger Walther von der Vogelweide. In the early 19th century, under intense Habsburg repression, the greatest Austrian dramatist, Grillparzer, wrote his Shakespearean-type tragedy *King Ottokar's Rise and Fall*. If the climate favoured his depiction of Ottokar as the villain and Rudolph of Habsburg the hero, the great patriotic speeches still move many good Austrians deeply. There followed: the popular Viennese dialect theatre of Raimund and Nestroy; Hofmannsthal's libretti for Richard Strauss; Rilke's lyrics; Schnitzler's social commentaries; Kafka's explosions (although a Czech he spent most of his time in Vienna and wrote in German); and now the émigré Canetti's Nobel Prize-winning novels. Austria has held a pre-eminence in medicine and science (another seven Nobel Prizes); psychoanalysis (Freud and Adler); philosophy (Wittgenstein); and economics (Menger, the founder of the modern school, and Hayek).

Austria's musical achievements are internationally recognized (Mozart; Beethoven and Brahms – the two Germans who lived in Vienna because they liked it there; Schubert; the 'Waltz Kings', Johann Strauss I and II; Bruckner; Mahler; Wolf; the whole Operetta school; the 'moderns', Schönberg, Berg, Webern, Josef Marx; and now von Einem). The list of world-class executants and conductors is too long to catalogue.

A word, too, on film, particularly in the 1930's when there was a whole gamut of nostalgic masterpieces recalling the social tensions of the Twilight, leading up to the world success of Ophüls' 'La Ronde' created by the closest observer of those tensions, Schnitzler.

It is, however, in the field of art and architecture that Austria's contribution has perhaps been most marked, from the Gothic altars of Pacher to the late 19th-century Secession (the Austrian counterpart of the German Jugendstil and the French Art Nouveau). It can perhaps be noted that one of the greatest recent successes of the Edinburgh International Festival was its theme 'Vienna 1900', with, naturally, that elusive Scot Mackintosh, who worked there, but full homage to its local painters Klimt, Schiele and Kokoschka and its architects Olbrich and Otto Wagner, not forgetting Loos, who broke away to found the school of Functionalism, which has had a lasting influence. The supreme visual achievement remains, however, the baroque of Fischer von Erlach at the Vienna Karlskirche, Hildebrandt at the Upper Belvedere, and Prandtauer at Melk.

Are the Austrians indeed still living in the past? Are they too introspective, too masochistic (even this latter term is an Austrian invention, from the characters of the late 19th-century novelist, Sacher-Masoch)? Or, on the contrary, is it the Austrians' constructive traits, which have been so well identified as 'tolerance, magnanimity, independence and creativity', which are paramount? Perhaps the most imaginative answer comes from '*The Book of Austria*' (1948), compiled by a group of resolute Austrians led by Ernst Marboe, which was a symbol of the Austrian revival after World War II. They looked back to the Ostmark as the Babenbergs left it, and concluded that it was then that 'the national characteristics of the Austrian people were formed. There lay, buried and dormant, but ready to germinate, instincts and talents of diametrically opposed races. Gothic imagination, Hellenic vitality, Celtic sense of form and Slavonic intensity of feeling, bound together by the visions of the East and embodied now in the Austrian character, were ready to grow and bear artistic fruit'.

Arthur Farrand Radley
London
December, 1985

Introduction

The bibliography

This bibliography in no way claims to be fully comprehensive. It is, however, hoped that the material included will provide a sufficiently broad and representative spectrum, both of a general and specialized nature, to enable the English-speaking reader to form a coherent and authentic impression of this key Central European country. There are relatively few original works in English about post-1945 Austria and for this reason a higher proportion of publications in the vernacular (in this case German), without translation, are featured than would perhaps be the case in other bibliographies in this series. Indeed, in some instances foreign books have been chosen, not simply in the absence of an adequate English work, but because they are noticeably superior to any English equivalent. Furthermore, foreign illustrated art books, guides, maps, dictionaries and bibliographies may well prove useful to the English-speaking reader with minimal or no knowledge of German. However, the problem does not arise in the field of history, since the literature for all but the very early periods is extensive in most major European languages and a rigorous process of selection has therefore had to be applied. Even so, the historical content remains substantial, for Austria's present is closely interwoven with her past and especially the 650 years of Habsburg rule, with its European, and at one time world-wide, ramifications. Indeed, the importance of Austria's complex history demands its thorough coverage.

The criteria for inclusion has been that the subject of an entry should be relevant, representative, readable, of more than ephemeral interest wherever possible and accessible through normal, or in certain areas, specialized channels. Some works have been included particularly on grounds of their exhaustive bibliographical contents, thus allowing the specialist, if he so desires, to research further into his particular area of interest, and the general reader to broaden his knowledge of the subject in less specific terms. Notwithstanding this, if certain sections appear only sparsely represented this is simply a reflection of the output and availability of published work.

The arrangement of the sections follows the standard format of this series in that the order of entries is alphabetical by author, or, where none is declared, by the institution or authority responsible for the publication, or by title. In the sections on music and literature, however, apart from general works, entries have been grouped chronologically under the composers and writers concerned. In the latter field textual criticism has been separated from individual writings, which have been selected for their importance and typicality and, wherever possible, in English translation: where none exists, the work is given in its original form.

Some personal views and predilections will inevitably be apparent to the reader, though none are intended to distort the relevance, or balance, of the work as a whole. Any omissions, errors, or misjudgements due to ignorance, oversight, or prejudice must remain my full responsibility.

Acknowledgements

The compilation of this bibliography would not have been possible without consultation with, and assistance from, many and varied individuals and institutions. First and foremost, I am greatly indebted to Arthur Farrand Radley, a good friend of Austria, who has written the introduction to this work and whose penetrating insights and sense of personal commitment to this collaborative enterprise inform so many of the pages that follow. Of the libraries consulted I wish to express my thanks to: the British Library and its various components, whose vast combined resources have proved invaluable and whose professional staff have, without exception, been most helpful; the Austrian Institute and especially its librarian Hannelore Schmidt for her expertise in handling a host of enquiries and for patiently accepting long delays in the return of books on loan; the Central Library of the Royal Borough of Kensington and Chelsea; the Imperial War Museum; the Royal Institute of International Affairs; the Royal Botanic Gardens at Kew; the London City Business Library; the Austrian Trade Commission; the London School of Economics and Political Science; the libraries of the School of Slavonic and East European Studies and the Institute of Germanic Studies, both of London University; the Victoria and Albert Museum; the Wellcome Institute of the History of Medicine; the BBC External Services library; and others in Austria itself.

As regards individual contributions I am grateful to: Dr. J. D. Warren of the Department of Modern Languages of Oxford Polytechnic for helpful recommendations on Austrian literature; Dr. John Leslie of Bristol University School of History for the use of his history reading lists; Alastair Macdonald for his succinct interpretations of certain historical items; Michael Watts for a number of practical suggestions; Irene Thornley for professional librarianship advice on the general approach; Sue Dunkerly for initial book searches; Dr. Robert Neville of Clio Press for much editorial guidance and constructive criticism; Georgina L. Neville for compiling the index; and RoseMary Arbus and Rosemary Graydon for their masterly typing of an intricate manuscript. Many Austrian friends, both in England and their homeland, have given me encouragement and support in this project, which, it is hoped, will in some small way advance the further study of and interest in this charming and hospitable country. To all the above I owe a debt of gratitude. The bibliography must now speak for itself.

Denys Salt
London
December, 1985

Glossary

Political Parties and Formations

FPÖ Freedom Party of Austria

KPÖ Communist Party of Austria

SPÖ Socialist Party of Austria

VPÖ People's Party of Austria

Heimwehr Home Defence Force composed of two right-wing groups of uniformed armed militia, based in the town and the countryside, and associated with the Christian Socials during the First Republic. It favoured a corporative State and drew strongly on monarchist, patriotic and religious feelings.

Schutzbund Defence League. A para-military left-wing organization formed by the Social Democrats in 1923. In the 1934 uprising it was defeated by the Federal Army and driven underground.

Vaterländische Front Fatherland Front. An authoritarian, patriotic Catholic movement set up by Dollfuss in 1933 as a unified para-military force, replacing the two *Heimwehr* groups.

Concepts and Definitions

Anschluss Union. The absorption of Austria within the Third Reich following Hitler's invasion of the country on 11 March 1938.

Ausgleich Compromise. The arrangement made on Hungary's initiative in 1867 which established the Dual Monarchy of Austria-

	Hungary, under which Francis Joseph I remained Emperor of Austria and operated independently as King of Hungary, thus ruling two separately defined territories and administrations under Imperial control.
Biedermeier	A style of living and interior decoration which flourished during the period between the end of the Napoleonic wars and the European revolutions of 1848–the 'Metternich Age'. It was characterized by middle-class domesticity and a rising prosperity.
Crown Lands	Upper and Lower Austria, Styria, Carniola, Carinthia and Tirol, under the Habsburgs.
Gastarbeiter	Foreign immigrant worker, mainly Yugoslav.
Heuriger	A hostelry, part open-air, part indoor, devoted to the tasting and later consumption of this year's wine. Most are to be found in the wine-growing villages which surround Vienna. Simple meals are often served and the totally Viennese atmosphere is completed by musicians and a singer who move from table to table with local folk-songs.
Inner Austria	Under the Vienna Treaty of 1396 the line of Emperor Leopold III split into two branches, the Tirolean and the Styrian, which resulted in three complexes of Austrian territory, of which Inner Austria comprised Styria, Carinthia, Carniola and the Adriatic possessions.
Jugendstil	Youth style. The German equivalent of Art Nouveau. An elaborate style of ornamentation in reaction to conservative classicism in the 19th century, characterized in Austria by the Secession movement.
Junktim	Trading off political concessions in one field against others in a non-related field.
Ostmark	Eastern March. The name given to a buffer state created by Charlemagne to secure the eastern defences of his Empire. Revived by the Babenbergs in 976 as the foundation of

	Austria and used again initially by Hitler after the *Anschluss*.
Proporz	A system of proportional allocation of posts in Government, administration and the nationalized industries during the coalition governments from 1945 to 1966, as officially recognized by the Parties at that time but still continuing in a modified form.
Protektion	The watchful eye kept by a senior official over the progress of a junior.
Pragmatic Sanction	An Imperial ordinance or realistic guarantee promulgated by Charles VI, issued as a fundamental law settling the Austrian succession in the absence of a male heir. It thus allowed his eldest daughter, Maria Theresa, to succeed to the Habsburg domains.
Ringstrasse	An architectural style of mid-19th century neo-classicism used initially in the monumental buildings along the Vienna Ring, a surrounding circle cleared by demolition of the City's fortifications.
Secession	An artistic movement breaking away from neo-classicism in architecture, painting and sculpture at the turn of the century.
Successor States	The territorial groupings formed by the Allies after World War I from parts of the dismembered components of the Austro-Hungarian Empire. Normally applied to Czechoslovakia, Yugoslavia and Hungary.

Some Culinary Terms

Apfelstrudel	Thinly sliced apples with nuts, raisins and roasted breadcrumbs spread on wafer thin pastry, then baked.
Kaiserschmarrn	A sweet omelette served with stewed fruit.
Knödel	Dumplings with an enormous variety of fillings, unsweetened and sweetened.
Palatschinken	Thin dessert pancakes.
Sachertorte	A chocolate cake served with whipped cream and named after the proprietor of a fashionable hotel in Vienna in the late 19th century.

Salzburger Nockerl	A soufflé of eggs, sugar, butter and flour.
Schlagobers	Sweetened whipped cream.
Tafelspitz	Boiled beef with a variety of sauces served separately.
Wiener Schnitzel	Fillet of veal, dipped in flour, egg and breadcrumbs, then fried.

Austrian rulers

House of Babenberg

Margraves		Leopold I	**976-994**
		Henry I	**994-1018**
		Adalbert	**1018-1055**
		Ernest	**1055-1075**
		Leopold II	**1075-1095**
		Leopold III	**1095-1136**
		Leopold IV	**1136-1141**
		Henry II	**1141-1156**
Dukes		Henry II	**1156-1177**
		Leopold V	**1177-1194**
		Frederick I	**1194–1198**
		Leopold VI	**1198-1230**
		Frederick II	**1230-1246**
		Various claimants	**1246-1253**
		Ottokar II Přemysl (of Bohemia)	**1253-1276**

House of Habsburg

Dukes		Rudolph I	**1276-1282**
	co-rulers	Rudolph II	**1282-1283**
		Rudolph III	**1282-1307**
		Albert I	**1282-1308**
	co-rulers	Leopold I	**1308-1326**
		Frederick I	**1308-1330**

Austrian rulers

	co-rulers	Otto	**1330-1339**
		Albert II	**1330-1339**
	sole ruler	Albert II	**1339-1358**
	co-rulers	Rudolph IV	**1358-1365**
		Frederick II	**1358-1362**
		Albert III	**1358-1395**
		Leopold III	**1358-1386**
	co-rulers	William*	**1386-1398**
		Leopold IV*	**1386-1398**
Dukes of Austria			
Upper and Lower Austria		Albert IV	**1398-1404**
		Albert V	**1404-1439**
		Ladislaus	**1440-1457**
		Albert VI*	**1457-1463**
Styria, Carinthia, Tirol, Carniola		William* (v.s.)	**1398-1406**
	co-rulers	Leopold IV* (v.s.)	**1398-1411**
		Ernest	**1406-1411**
	sole ruler	Ernest	**1411-1424**
	co-rulers	Albert VI* (v.s.)	**1424-1463**
		Frederick III	**1424-1452**
Archdukes of Austria			
Holy Roman Emperors		Frederick III	**1452-1493**
		Maximilian I	**1493-1519**
		Charles V	**1519-1556**
		Ferdinand I	**1556-1564**
		Maximilian II	**1564-1576**
		Rudolph II	**1576-1611**
		Matthias	**1611-1619**
		Ferdinand II	**1619-1637**
		Ferdinand III	**1637-1657**
		Leopold I	**1658-1705**
		Joseph I	**1705-1711**
		Charles VI	**1711-1740**
Archduchess		Maria Theresa	**1740-1780**

House of Habsburg-Lorraine

Holy Roman Emperors	Francis I of Lorraine	**1745-1765**
	Joseph II	**1765-1790**
	Leopold II	**1790-1792**
	Francis II	**1792-1806**
Emperors of Austria	Francis I	**1804-1835**
	Ferdinand I	**1835-1848**
	Francis Joseph I	**1848-1916**
	Charles I	**1916-1918**

First Republic

Presidents	Karl Seitz (acting)	**1920**
	Michael Hainisch	**1920-1928**
	Wilhelm Miklas	**1928-1938**
Chancellors	Karl Renner	**1918-1920**
	Michael Mayr	**1920-1921**
	Johannes Schober	**1921-1922**
	Ignaz Seipel	**1922-1924**
	Rudolf Ramek	**1924-1926**
	Ignaz Seipel	**1926-1929**
	Ernst Streeruwitz	**1929**
	Johannes Schober	**1929-1930**
	Carl Vaugoin	**1930**
	Otto Ender	**1930-1931**
	Karl Buresch	**1931-1932**
	Engelbert Dollfuss	**1932-1934**
	Kurt Schuschnigg	**1934-1938**

Second Republic

Presidents	Karl Renner	**1945-1950**
	Leopold Figl (acting)	**1950-1951**
	Theodor Körner	**1951-1957**
	Julius Raab (acting)	**1957**
	Adolf Schärf	**1957-1965**
	Josef Klaus (acting)	**1965**
	Franz Jonas	**1965-1974**
	Bruno Kreisky (acting)	**1974**
	Rudolf Kirchschläger	**1974-**

Austrian rulers

Chancellors

Karl Renner	**1945**
Leopold Figl	**1945-1953**
Julius Raab	**1953-1961**
Alfons Gorbach	**1961-1964**
Josef Klaus	**1964-1970**
Bruno Kreisky	**1970-1983**
Fred Sinowatz	**1983-**

The Country and Its People

1 **Austria: land of enchantment.**
Andreas Albrecht, Josef Brettenthaler, Karl Heinz Burmeister, Georgine Veverka, Hanns Jäger-Sunstenau, translated from the German with the collaboration of Donald Gutch, Antony Kemp, Carol Renner, Alison Thielecke, and Margaret Wasmeier, edited by Otto Hietsch. Salzburg, Austria: Helmut Schmid, 1979. 305p. maps.

A volume brimming over with confidence. It is the product of the Bavarian University of Regensburg, and was originally in German until an expatriate Austrian Professor of English summoned his largely English assistants to revise the text specifically for an English readership, 'enlarging the cultural background and adding polish and sparkling wit and verbal dexterity'. After a brisk introduction each province is tackled in German alphabetical order (Vorarlberg before Wien) and the narrative sustains momentum in a most readable series of historical essays. One of the most helpful features is the insertion at most material points of genuinely apt quotations from contemporary sources, including English translations of poems where the editor's intention to 'preserve the historical flavour of metre and diction' has in fact come off remarkably well. It could almost be said that preoccupation with the past and *genus loci* has pre-empted anything more than a cursory study, in most areas, of contemporary problems: but then the enchantment might have lost its spell.

2 **Austria: facts and figures.**
Vienna: Federal Press Service, 1984. 239p. map.

This is a most valuable and authoritative documentary source on Austrian life today and is normally updated at roughly five-year intervals. It is introduced by a brief outline of the Austrian landscape, climate, vegetation and population. A section on each of the nine provinces follows, while separate chapters are devoted to: history; government and politics; the economy; social services; sport and recreation; education and science; the arts; and the media. The publication is attractively illustrated and can be warmly recommended as a definitive background reference work.

3 **Das andere Österreich.** (The other Austria.)
Christian Brandstätter, Traute Franke, translated from the German by Günter Treffer. Vienna: Molden, 1981. 168p.

This attempt at portraying, through contrasting illustrations (past and present), the inter-relationship between traditional Austria and the country's modern economy is largely directed at those who tend to know only the half of Austria which is so regularly and rather cosily portrayed in guidebooks and promotional material. The 'other Austria' is a product of a flourishing, hard-headed and stable economy. Indeed Austria is one of the three countries in the world with the lowest inflation rates and the nation plays an important international role in scientific research and technological achievement. The 312 superb colour photographs in this handsome presentation juxtapose the traditional with the modern very successfully and range over an extraordinarily wide field. The captions are in German with English and French translations.

4 **Impressions of Austria.**
Humbert Fink, Hella Pflanzer, Reiner Schiestl. Innsbruck, Austria: Pinguin-Verlag, 1984. 118p.

This collection of photographs and ink drawings represents the very personal choice of three art specialists anxious to portray the less familiar regions of the Austrian countryside in an impressionistic idiom. The romantic and traditional are happily blended in their selections, and their contributions conclude with an excellent chronology of the main events in the country's history. An enjoyable presentation which is true to its title.

5 **The case of Austria.**
Robert A. Kann. *Journal of Contemporary History*, vol. 15, no. 1 (1980), p. 37-52.

Professor Kann claims that although Austria was the only successor state of the Habsburg Empire to rid itself of totalitarian government, imperial nostalgia is very much alive today. He notes the continuing veneration for titles, with all their gradations, and the loving care and attention paid to imperial architecture; and sees present-day Austria as a modest political entity but also as a nation determined to preserve its links with the power and grandeur of the past.

6 **Area handbook for Austria.**
Edited by Eugen K. Keefe. Washington, DC: Foreign Area Studies, American University, 1976. 247p. 7 maps. bibliog.

This is one of a country series of handbooks prepared by the American University of Washington for the military and others seeking a quick and accurate compilation of the social, economic, political and military institutions and practices of a particular country. All the information presented is drawn from openly published material and is both authoritative and comprehensive. Separate sections deal with: background history; physical environment; social security; the arts and education; the political situation; the economy; and national security. The bibliography is selective but fully relevant and represents a reliable and informative reference aid.

7 **Steiermark.** (Styria.)

Johannes Koren, translated from the German into English by Jacqueline Schweighofer, and into French by Fred Geets, Brigitte Kellermayr-Monghal. Innsbruck, Austria: Pinguin-Verlag, 1984. 127p. map.

This is basically a picture-book on the largest province in the southeast of Austria, with a series of telling photographs mainly by Kurt Roth and A. M. Begsteiger. There is also, however, a penetrating introduction by a prize-winning journalist, the son of a veteran archaeologist who was for long the president of the provincial Diet and who has also contributed to the volume. The result is an authoritative survey of the cultural and economic past and present of an area which has made major contributions to Austrian national life, which has produced five Nobel Prize winners in chemistry, medicine and physics, and which has strong British connections through being part of the British zone of occupation under the four-power agreements from 1945 to 1955.

8 **The book of Austria.**

Ernst Marboe, translated from the German by G. E. R. Gedye. Vienna: State Printing & Publishing House, 1958. rev. ed. 542p. maps. bibliog.

In the words of the author, '*The Book of Austria* is intended for everybody, for non-Austrians, foreigners who have found something in this country which appeals to them of which they would like to retain the memory, but also for Austrians of all classes and ages.' It was produced in the immediate post-World War II period as a statement of faith in the reconstituted country. The contributions owe much to the various national and municipal Collections in Vienna and the whole work is translated by a leading English writer on Austrian affairs, who also witnessed the Hitlerite occupation first-hand, the *Guardian* correspondent G. E. R. Gedye. The text glows with enthusiasm on all aspects of Austrian history, life, and the contribution of the nine provinces, and is copiously illustrated with contemporary documents and scenic views. No one compendium provides a better or warmer conspectus of the Austrian scene: it is Austria by the Austrians, written at a time when they had become themselves again.

9 **Austria: people and landscape.**

Stella Musulin. London: Faber & Faber, 1971. 248p. maps.

History and legend intermingle freely in this friendly introduction to Austria by a Viennese-born author, who manages to capture the atmosphere and flavour of each of the provinces she describes. Musulin also has a flair for 'discovering' some of the lesser-known areas of the country, which have considerable charm but are less well known to visitors, as, for example, the Mühlviertel in Upper Austria. There is a light-hearted foreword by the famous English poet, the late W. H. Auden, who lived near Vienna.

10 **Those eternal Austrians.**

John F. Putnam. *National Geographic*, vol. 167, no. 4 (Apr. 1985), p. 410-49.

This lively, compressed summary of Austrian history, geography and life is based on a series of interviews with a wide range of present-day Austrian personalities, which combine to present a vivid picture of modern Austria and its nine provinces in all its facets. The excellent photographs by Adam Woolfitt capture both the Austrian spirit and purpose.

11 **Imago Austriae.** (Austria's image.)

Edited by Otto Schulmeister, Johann Christoph Allmayer-Beck, Erich Lessing, translated from the German by Stella Musulin. Vienna: Herder, 1967. 304p.

The careful selection of illustrations in this handsome work is intended to portray the country's most enduring characteristics by placing the art and landscape of its people in a historical setting and revealing those elements which have brought the country together and resulted in so many achievements through the centuries. This interplay of the forces which went into the making of the old and the new Austria is well captured in a mosaic of pictures, all combining to present a character study of the Austrians by recalling their origins and development without indulging in over-sentimental nostalgia. The text of the commentary matches the high quality of the pictorial presentation.

12 **Austria.**

Sacheverell Sitwell, Toni Schneider. London: Thames & Hudson, 1959. 212p.

Sitwell's contribution is an introduction essay to Toni Schneider's well-annotated photographs of landscapes, buildings and life in the Austria of 1958. He stresses that all lies in the shadow of the Holy Roman Empire and the Habsburgs, and highlights the chief architectural delights, mainly baroque abbeys and palaces in each of the Austrian provinces: a nostalgic study of a lost period of greatness in which architecture was at least as important as the more famous musical heritage. A concluding chapter by Hans Bernard provides a short description of the geography and population of modern truncated Austria and then expands on this for each of the nine provinces.

13 **Sixty years Republic.**

Austria Today, no. 4 (autumn 1978), p. 1-89.

The whole of this issue is in commemoration of the sixtieth anniversary of the proclamation of the first Austrian Republic in 1918. It consists of a series of articles by distinguished contributors reviewing past developments in all areas of activity. The subjects covered include: political history; the Church; medicine; science; agriculture; technology; the arts; literature; music; and sport.

14 **Modern Austria.**

Edited by Kurt Steiner, Fritz Fellner, Hubert Feichtlbauer. Palo Alto, California: Society for the Promotion of Science and Scholarship, 1980. 507p. bibliog.

There are few books in English on post-war Austria, so this comprehensive and up-to-date survey of Austrian national life today is particularly welcome. The contributors, all Austrians living either in their homeland or the United States are acknowledged experts in their particular field and write for a US readership. There are separate chapters on: geography; demography; economy; government; politics; education; religion; the law; foreign policy; literature; music; art; the media; and defence policy. This can be regarded as a valuable and reliable background reference work for anyone interested in present-day Austria. The bibliography is extensive but contains mostly works in German.

15 **Austrians – how they live and work.**

Eric Whelpton. Newton Abbot, England: David & Charles, 1970. 176p. map. (How They Live and Work Series).

Despite basing his material largely on official publicity handouts, this well-known travel writer manages to present his facts in an original and personal style and there is much solid information in this useful introduction to Austrian life and customs. In his preface he rightly emphasizes the individual character of local traditions and the strong feelings of independence and regional patriotism in the nine provinces. The volume covers: constitution; political parties; currency and taxation; social security; housing; health; pensions; industry; trade unions; employment practices; education; transport; food and drink; sport; and the media. The whole work concludes with some sensible practical hints for travellers.

16 **The land and people of Austria.**

Raymond A. Wohlrabe, Werner Krusch. Philadelphia, New York: Lippincott, 1956. 117p. map. (Portraits of the Nations Series).

Straightforward and fairly basic in both its treatment and content, this brief outline of Austria and her people opens with a short historical sketch, followed by a separate section on the wars against the Turks, and chapters on each of the nine provinces. The work concludes with a summary of the main achievements of the Second Republic from 1945 to 1955, when the country gained its independence.

Geography

General

17 **Regional development in Western Europe.**
Edited by Hugh D. Clout. Chichester, New York, Brisbane, Toronto: John Wiley 1981. 2nd ed. 417p. maps.

The chapter on Austria (p. 335-346) in this collection of essays by twelve leading geographers is by David Burtenshaw of Portsmouth Polytechnic who investigates four main areas of the country: the Danube region; the frontier areas; the mountain regions; and urban agglomerations. He points to: the future linkage of the Danube and the Rhine with the proposed completion of the European Canal; the shift of population from the eastern provines to the western alpine regions; and the growing influence of provincial governments in determining the scope and nature of regional developments. A particular problem which faces Austria is that because she is not a member of the European Economic Community with its vast multinational investment potential, financial subvention from federal sources is necessarily restricted. Regional development in Austria, the author concludes, is very much the product of the country's geographical position and its history, and accordingly account has to be taken of its landscape, its resources for tourism, the needs of modern industry and the pressures on the towns.

18 **A geography of Europe: problems and prospects.**
Edited by George W. Hoffman. New York: Ronald Press, 1977. 4th ed. rev. 573p. maps. bibliog.

Austria (p. 305-367) is grouped with southern Germany, Switzerland and Liechtenstein in this survey by a panel of distinguished international geographers who examine the economic, social and political geography of each region against its physical and historical background. The authors also consider problems relating to agrarian and industrial change, environmental impoverishment and the supply of energy, which all apply to Austria.

19 **Die Ostalpen und das heutige Österreich.** (The Eastern Alps and present-day Austria.)
Norbert Krebs. Stuttgart, Germany: J. Engelhorn, 1928. 2 vols.

Although written over 50 years ago this two-volume standard work by Norbert Krebs, one-time Professor of Geography at Berlin University, is still a valid basic exposition. The national and provincial frontiers at the time of writing, although redrawn by Hitler during the Nazi period, were reconstituted immediately after World War II.

20 **Harms Handbuch der Geographie: Landeskunde Österreichs.** (Harms handbook of geography: regional studies of Austria).
Edited by Adolf Leidlmaier. Munich: Paul List, 1983. 242p. bibliog.

Although primarily designed for higher educational use this straightforward and up-to-date handbook of regional geography in a well-established series should serve as a useful basic reference tool for the general reader with a knowledge of German. Each of the nine provinces is covered, with individual sections on physical geography, population, the economy and cultural development. The work contains a number of sketch maps, diagrams and supporting statistical data.

21 **Central Europe: a regional and human geography.**
Alice F. A. Mutton. London: Longmans, 1970. 3rd ed. 488p. maps. bibliog.

In chapter 7 (p. 140-152) of this standard work the author provides a brief historical and economic survey of Austria which is followed by a regional review of the country's nine provinces (p. 153-184). Both chapters are clearly presented and are supported by a number of sketch maps and diagrams. The critical bibliography consists almost entirely of works in German. A useful outline in a very readable form.

22 **Italy, Switzerland and Austria; a geographical study.**
Henry Rees. London: Harrap, 1974. 385p. maps. bibliog.

Part 3 (p. 259-349) of this work deals with Austria, mainly from the economic point of view. There are single chapters on Tirol and Vorarlberg and shorter sections on the remaining provinces. Overall, this is a straightforward survey, with some emphasis on transport, energy resources and heavy industry.

23 **Geologie von Österreich: Zentralalpen.** (The geology of Austria: Central Alps.)
Alexander Tollmann. Vienna: Deuticke, 1977. 766p. maps. bibliog.

The author, Director of the Geological Institute at Vienna University, has produced a definitive and scholarly work on the geology of the central Alps based on twenty years research activity. Every aspect is studied and analysed and each chapter is prefaced with a brief outline of the state of current research in the particular field under discussion. The bibliography of seventy pages not only relates specifically to this region but includes comparative literature drawing parallels with geological data in other parts of the world. The second volume, now in preparation, will cover the eastern Alps.

Maps, atlases and gazetteers

24 **Guide to atlases.**
Gerard L. Alexander. Metuchen, New Jersey: Scarecrow Press, 1971. 900p.

This is an international list of all major atlases published since 1950 – world, regional, national and thematic. The section on Austria is on p. 280-285. There are language and publishers' indexes and the whole work is well cross-referenced.

25 **The Alps.**
Washington, DC: National Geographic, 1985. Scale: 1:1,057,000.

This relief map accompanies the article 'Those Eternal Austrians' (q.v.) featured in the April 1985 issue of this magazine and shows the full extent of the alpine chain stretching from the Dinaric and Julian Alps in Yugoslavia through southern France to northern Italy and therefore including the whole of Austria. On the reverse there are inset maps of the Salzkammergut, the Inn valley and south Tirol and eight suggested car tours.

26 **Art treasures in Austria: reference map.**
Vienna: Austria Information Office, 1983. Scale: 1:600,000.

A pictorial map, measuring 100cm × 60cm, with a simplified legend and showing the location of, and main access routes to, the country's art treasures, the most significant of which are shown in bold type. There are individual inset maps of all the provincial capitals. The reverse side includes brief details of the buildings concerned and the art treasures to be found. A most useful tourist map and guide.

27 **Austria.**
Vienna: Touring Club Austria, 1984. Scale: 1:200,000.

This series of four detailed road and railway maps covering the whole country has been produced by Touring Club Austria for the British Automobile Association. The maps cover the following areas: Vienna, Lower Austria, northern Burgenland; Upper Austria, Salzburg, Salzkammergut; Carinthia, southern Burgenland, Styria; and Tirol, Vorarlberg, South Tirol. The legend of conventional signs is in German, English and French.

28 **Austria.**
Brentford, England: Roger Lascelles, 1985. Scale: 1:300,000.

This facsimile of a German map (RV Reise und Verkehrsverlag, Berlin, 1984-5) is very clearly printed and features not only roads and railways, but also mountain road passes with heights, gradients, and dates when open as well as mountain railways and cable cars. There are town plans of all the provincial capitals. The legend is in English, French and German.

29 **Austria: administrative map.**
Paris: Supreme Headquarters Allied Expeditionary Force, 1945. Scale: 1:1,000,000.

This very clear map, prepared for military use by the Allied occupation forces after World War II, features the former administrative districts of Austria as part of the Third Reich with the Allied occupation zonal boundaries superimposed. A useful map for the history student of post-1945 Austria.

30 **Weltraumbildatlas.** (Pictorial atlas of the earth's surface.)
Edited by Johann Bodechtel. Braunschweig, GFR: Georg Westermann, 1978.

The country's physical features and environmental resources are brilliantly reproduced in a collection of satellite photographs, taken under the sponsorship of the European Space Agency. Nine such photographs illustrate Austria and each one is accompanied by an explanatory text and a small inset map, showing the precise area covered. Germany and Switzerland are also included.

31 **Geographisches Namenbuch Österreichs.** (Geographical gazetteer of Austria.)
Edited by Josef Breu. Vienna: Cartographical Institute of the Austrian Academy of Sciences, 1975. 323p. (Studies in Theoretical Cartography, vol. 3).

This is an invaluable guide, in German and English, to all the important geographical features and place-names in Austria. It is standardized according to United Nations requirements and contains a general pronunciation guide and a glossary of geographical terms.

32 **Atlas der Donauländer.** (Atlas of the Danube countries.)
Edited by Josef Breu. Vienna: Österreichisches Ost- und Südeuropa Institut, 1981.

The maps and accompanying legends are printed in German, English, French and Russian. There are four sections covering physical features, demography, economy and communications. Although the Danube itself flows through only three of the country's nine provinces, Austria is featured throughout.

33 **Catalogue of printed maps, charts and plans.**
British Museum, Department of Printed Books. London: the Trustees, 1974. 16 vols.

In this photolithographic edition of the British Library's collection Austria is well represented, particularly as regards the Habsburg Empire in the 19th century.

34 **Descriptio Austriae.** (A description of Austria).
Edited by Johannes Dörflinger, Robert Wagner, Franz Wawrik. Vienna: Tusch, 1977. 216p. maps. plans. charts.

This comprehensive and beautifully illustrated cartographic history of Austria and its neighbouring territories from the 2nd century AD to the early 1800's contains seventy maps, many in colour, and numerous charts and plans. The examples of early map printing are particularly well reproduced. The text is in German.

35 **Generalkarte von Mitteleuropa.** (General map of Central Europe).
Vienna: BEV, 1968. Scale: 1:200,000.

Austria is featured on twenty-three sheets of this series of official survey maps, which total 265 sheets in all.

36 **Geologische Karte der Republik Österreich und der Nachbargebiete.** (Geological map of Austria and neighbouring territories.)
Vienna: Herman Vetters, 1968. Scale: 1:500,000.

An improved and updated version of a 1930 issue in two sheets.

37 **Österreichische Karte.** (Map of Austria.)
Vienna: BEV, 1968-84. Scale: 1:50,000.

This series which is in colour, has replaced an earlier government provisional survey in black-and-white and covers 213 sheets. It is issued in three different formats: main communications; footpaths and mountain huts; provisional survey edition with hachures.

38 **School atlases in Germany, Austria and Switzerland.**
Written and translated by Wislaw Rybotycki. *Przeglad Powszéchny*, no. 10 (1979), p. 16-19.

A former cartographical specialist at the British Natural History Museum provides a brief historical account of the publication of school atlases from the time of the Habsburg Empire to the present day. Since World War II, Austria, using advanced printing techniques, has secured an expanding market in the production of atlases in a number of foreign languages.

39 **General Post- und Strassenkarte der österreichischen Monarchie**. (A general postal and communications map of the Austrian Monarchy).
Edited by de Trauer, Fr. Fried. Vienna: 1839. Scale: 1:500,000. On linen in folder.

This is an improved edition of a map issued in 1829, showing the administrative and political boundaries of the Austria-Hungarian Empire of the time. The main communication routes, major towns with population figures and distances are all clearly shown. An extremely valuable politico-historical map.

40 **International maps and atlases in print.**
K. Winch. London, New York: Bowker, 1976. 2nd ed. 866p. maps. bibliog.

Section 436 (p. 142-149) contains Austria and includes maps in several different languages of all categories: general; regional; specialist; physical relief; geological; town maps; official surveys; and atlases.

Tourism and travel guides

41 **Austria: a grand tour.**
Denver, Colorado: Oro Press, 1984. 99p. (Oro Travel Guide Series).

A suggested road itinerary of about 2,500 miles for American travellers through Austria, with an occasional retracing of one's steps. The itinerary is accompanied by practical information on accommodation, major sights of interest and geographical features. There are some excellent town maps and a full visual depiction of road signs.

42 **Austria: Michelin tourist guide.**
London: Michelin Tyre Company, 1982. 179p. maps.

This thoughtfully compiled compendium opens with a mass of practical and background information, including: notes on the democratic process in the nine provinces; a short bibliography mainly in English; and a German-English vocabulary. It continues with the scenic and cultural essentials, tour routes and selected places to stay. An intelligent layout enabling the visitor to make the right choice about what to see and how best to see it.

43 **Travelling on the Danube.**
J. Binder. Vienna: Danube Steamship Navigation Company, 1979. 179p.

Written by the Secretary-General of the Danube Steamship Company, this very readable and unpretentious guide is intended for passengers cruising on the company's ships on the Austrian stretch of the Danube, which covers some 230 miles. It contains a short history of the company itself, a number of colour plates and an itinerary map in sections. The writer offers a good description of Danubian scenery and the influences that have helped to shape it.

44 **Fodor's Austria.**
Eugene Fodor. London: Hodder & Stoughton, 1985. 370p.

The latest edition on Austria in this well-established series, while providing all the essential travel and guidebook information, includes four well-written chapters on the history of the country with special reference to post-World War II developments, music, food and wines. The section on Vienna, slightly revised, is available separately, from the same publisher (116p.).

45 **Austria.**
Monk Gibbon. London: Batsford, 1962. 216p. map.

This is one of the classic series of Batsford's guides by discerning authors with particular knowledge of the country. Details may have changed since this work was first published, but the basic judgements are of lasting value. A brief historical and geographical description of the country as a whole is followed by individual chapters on each province. The writer is particularly perceptive about the Austrian character.

46 **Youth Hostellers guide to Austria.**
Graham Heath. London: Youth Hostels Association, 1982. 29p. maps.

This is one of a series of guides for individual countries issued by the Association in conjunction with its more comprehensive but less detailed *Youth Hostellers Guide to Europe*. There is a fairly extensive array of facilities available through Austrian hostels, but intending visitors should also note the existence of a chain of huts organized by the Austrian Alpenverein (Alpine Club), particularly in the mountain areas of Tirol, Vorarlberg and Salzburg.

47 **Baedeker's Austria.**
Translated from the German by James Hogarth. London: Automobile Association, 1985. 301p. maps.

Karl Baedeker's first travel guide book appeared in Germany over 150 years ago. The 1985 edition on Austria is the first to be published in Britain, and in a changed and improved format, the arrangement is no longer by region, but simply alphabetical by place name. The work includes some excellent colour inset photographs to illustrate the area, town or particular attraction described in the text. There is also a mass of practical information to help the tourist and useful lists and details about monasteries, churches, museums, castles and gardens for the traveller with specialist interests. Also included is a most useful map in a loose folder.

48 **Nagel's encyclopaedia-guides: Austria.**
Geneva: Nagel, 1975. 4th rev. ed. 640p. 6 maps. (English Series).

The introductory section of this comprehensive travel guide deals in outline with the geography of the country, its history, present economy, the cultural scene and winter sports facilities. The main body of the work is an exhaustive coverage, province by province, of the main areas of tourist interest with detailed itineraries covering some scenic routes and linking places of particular cultural interest. The section on Vienna runs to almost one hundred pages. The final section provides practical information, which might, more logically, have been placed as an introduction rather than as a postscript. The maps at the end of the guide are clear and very well produced.

49 **Frommer's dollarwise guide to Austria and Hungary.**
Darwin Porter. New York: Simon & Schuster, 1985. 610p.

The Austrian section accounts for 524 pages of this reliable and helpful American guide in this successful series designed for the budget-conscious traveller with moderate tastes. Hotels, restaurants, guesthouses, inns, cafés and bars have all been well-researched and are listed here on personal recommendation. The detail is extremely impressive.

50 **The visitors guide to the Tirol.**
Alan Proctor. Ashbourne, England: Moorland Publishing, 1984. 144p. (Visitors Guide Series).

A useful feature of this handy illustrated guide is the listing of the main places of interest in each area in small inset boxes which immediately catch the eye without detracting from the explanatory narration which accompanies them. All cable cars and camp sites are included, together with a number of graded walks.

51 **Blue guide: Austria.**
Ian Robertson. London: A & C. Black, 1985. 410p.

Following the conventional pattern of this series – which has no connection with the Hachette Guide Bleue publications – some 40 itineraries are described backed up by a wealth of solid fact and helpful practical guidance. The 1985 edition has the added authority of introductory essays by Ernst Wangermann on history, Nicolas Powell on architecture and Mark Heller on skiing, with suggestions for further reading in each subject. Highlights are still asterisked with one, and more sparingly two, stars, but despite the subjectivity of this approach, the selections generally agree with the consensus of informed opinion. This is arguably the most reliable and comprehensive of the travel guides to Austria at present available to English readers.

52 **Blick auf Kärnten.** (A view of Carinthia.)
Edited and photographed by H. G. Trenkwalder. Klagenfurt, Austria: Verlag Carinthia, 1978-80. 3 vols.

This is a very complete photographic coverage of Carinthia in colour taken at close range from the air. Each of the three volumes, with a total of 425 photographs, features the whole province in different seasons, spring, summer and winter.

53 **Unknown Austria.**
Barbara Whelpton. London: Johnson Publications, 1966-69. 3 vols.

Sub-titled 'Motoring itineraries of lesser known general and archaeological features' each volume in this series by a well-known travel writer describes twelve such routes and is accompanied by thirty-two black-and-white illustrations. In the main it is a straightforward and eminently readable travel account although there are few details about hotel accommodation and road distances, and only outline maps and town plans. Architectural and geographical features are well-described and the discerning traveller will find much of unusual interest in this work which should lead him to a number of sites and places often neglected, or covered only cursorily by the average travel guide. Each volume contains an index of artists and architects mentioned in the text as well as a glossary of terms. The subject matter is divided as follows: Volume 1, Vorarlberg, Tirol, and Salzburg; Volume 2, Upper Austria, Lower Austria, and Vienna; and Volume 3, Styria, Burgenland, and Carinthia.

54 **Vienna – legend and reality.**

Ilsa Barea. London: Secker & Warburg, 1966. 367p.

Writing about her native city the author makes no claim to provide a straight account of its history and civilization but aims to 'sort out those elements that have gone into the making of Viennese society and attitudes, the influences which shaped its architecture, cultural atmosphere and speech'. This she does in an engaging manner, skilfully weaving into her story the threads of revolution and counter-revolution, the baroque legacy, Biedermeier domesticity and the city's imperial tradition.

55 **Vienna.**

Frederic V. Grunfeld. London, New York: Reader's Digest in association with Newsweek Books, 1981. 172p. (Wonders of Man Series).

This is unabashedly a 'coffee table' book which provides a brief guide to the city itself and a historical perspective from the earliest times. It is particularly strong on the literary side, with translations from key documents and works from leading Austrian authors, along with appreciations from distinguished foreign counterparts.

56 **Vienna.**

Martin Hürlimann, translated from the German by D. J. S. Thomson. London: Thames & Hudson, 1970. 252p. map. bibliog.

This conducted tour by a Swiss author who has treasured Vienna from his earliest days contains 166 well-annotated photogravure plates in addition to the text. It includes a comprehensive presentation of Viennese baroque architecture which is linked to a helpful historical summary and sidelights on Viennese social life.

57 **Vienna walks.**

J. Sydney Jones. New York: Holt, Rinehart & Winston, 1985. 288p. bibliog.

For the visitor to Vienna wishing to study the city on foot and from a particular historical angle this is a good guide. The author, who has lived in Vienna for the past ten years, has compiled a series of leisurely walks in Vienna and its surroundings based on three different themes – the Baroque, imperial and fin-de-siècle. Apart from reliable coverage of the architectural features of buildings and monuments, the work contains some useful information on some of the shops and restaurants passed along the routes. The two-page bibliography lists exclusively books in English.

58 **The coffee houses and palaces of Vienna.**
Sandy Lesberg. New York, London: Peebles Press International, 1976. 125p.

An illustrated guide for tourists, with a minimum of text, which presents palaces and coffee houses as symbols of the living past in which the spirit of Vienna still survives. The coffee houses, which date back to the second Turkish siege of Vienna in 1683, have a special political, literary and social significance in the history of Vienna, for they were often the scene of important chamber music concerts in Beethoven's days and of literary readings by leading authors such as Arthur Schnitzler at the turn of the century. The palaces speak for themselves.

59 **Vienna.**
Giovanna Magi, translated from the Italian by Merry Orling. Florence, Italy; Vienna: Bonechi Verlag Styria, 1982. 63p.

This is essentially a brief pictorial tourist guide to Vienna with 86 superb colour photographs on the lines of the rest of this series on Austrian towns. The main attractions of the inner city are featured with brief but adequate captions.

60 **Vienna, city of melodies.**
Charles Moore. Melksham, England: Uffington Press, 1977. 108p. map. (Venton Educational White Horse Library).

Under the sponsorship of the Austrian Tourist Office this work by an American travel writer provides a light-hearted but compressed picture of the key features of Vienna and Viennese life, including the inner city, the Spanish Riding School, music, art, cuisine, and coffee houses. A good introduction for those with no previous knowledge of the city.

61 **Where to find architecture and painting in the Vienna of 1900.**
Christian M. Nebehay. Vienna: Christian Brandstätter, 1984. 176p.

Published in both German and English, this handy book in pocket format guides the reader, with the help of detailed street plans, to the places where the leading figures of the Vienna art scene lived and worked at the turn of the century. The author is an acknowledged expert on the Jugendstil (Art Nouveau) period, and is the author of numerous books on the subject.

62 **Colourful Vienna.**
Text by Berta Sarne, photographs by Eric Holan, translated from the German by Andrew Smith. Vienna: Anton Schroll, 1984. 2nd ed. 104p.

What makes this book particularly helpful to the visitor is that it guides him in a logical progression on foot through the central areas and provides an unusual wealth of detail on the outlying districts. The illustrations, all in colour, provide a fuller and better coverage of buildings of the Secession and modern periods than most works of this kind.

63 **Vienna today: a complete and money-saving guide.**
Vienna: L. Englander, formerly United Nations World, 1985. 26th rev. ed. 213p. map.

Despite the publisher's name this is principally beamed on Americans, who could well save its modest price a thousand times over by heeding its 'money-saving' advice alone – 'furs remain one of the real bargains – no luxury tax is applied when you live outside Vienna'. The introduction is perceptive, 'a lazily enchanting capital' and the entries are chatty but highly informative. There is a most helpful glossary of menu terms, a discreet and selective guide to night-life and, among the end papers, a full introduction to the churches of all denominations published by the Roman Catholic Tourist office but not readily available elsewhere. Appropriately for Vienna there is a Freudian slip over the musician quoted as having written 'Die Meistersinger' in the Hadikgasse 72 – one Richard Wager: and his stay at the Imperial Hotel bears no mention that this was the Russian officers' hotel during the ten-year four-power occupation after World War II. Neither is this point made over 'the most colorful hotel', *Sacher*, which was the British equivalent, although it is at least highly recommended, whereas the American one, the *Bristol*, is not mentioned at all.

64 **Sounds of Vienna.**
Joseph Wechsberg. London: Weidenfeld & Nicolson, 1968. 297p.

This book by a notable Viennese author provides a revealing picture both of the social habits and customs of the Viennese and of the background of music, theatre, architecture and literature offered by their city. He particularly emphasizes its baroque character and the difficulty of separating legend from reality. There are detailed notes on the 136 half-tone illustrations and, in addition, the work contains a somewhat unusual feature, i.e., a number of translations in English of inscriptions on monuments, buildings and fountains.

65 **Vienna is different.**
Hans Weigel, translated from the German by Renate Welsh. Vienna: Jugend und Volk, 1985. 3rd ed. 80p. map.

What does one mean by different? Vienna is not on the Danube, the Theatre on the Wien (Theater an der Wien) is not on the river Wien, the Schottentor (Scots Gate) is not a gate at all, while the Ring (the main surrounding boulevard created in the 1870's) goes only three-quarters way round the circle. This is an apt title for an up-to-date and comprehensive work which is so refreshing and which captures the spirit of the capital so consummately. Weigel's introduction is typical of what one would expect the Viennese to write about themselves – some substantial truths emerge from a veneer of lightheartedness. 'In Vienna work is an unwelcome break from leisure. Most important is play – the play of thoughts augmented by wine at the Heuriger and by coffee at the coffee-house'. The photo-coverage which forms the bulk of the book is breathtaking and acutely observant. Moreover Ernst Hausner has done wonders on the design and each caption tells the reader just what he wants to know.

66 **Heritage and mission: Jewish Vienna.**
Compiled by Leon Zelman. Vienna: Vienna Tourist Board, 1983. 12p. map.

'This brochure' writes Dr. Zelman of the Jewish Welcome Service in an introductory letter, joining other messages from the Mayor of Vienna, a Rabbi and the president of the Jewish community, 'is intended to help you to get to know Jewish Vienna better'. It certainly succeeds in achieving this objective. There is a basic modicum of general tourist information but this is expanded with full details (in all likelihood not co-ordinated in this way before or elsewhere) concerning administration, synagogues, prayer rooms, schools, cemeteries and other subjects of various kinds, all pin-pointed in an excellent specialist map. The author has also dovetailed into this brochure a spirited exposé of different aspects of Viennese Jewry – its history through three main expulsions and its contributions to the defence of the realm and in the cultural field. The lists of names of those who have made their national and world mark in a wide variety of fields makes awe-inspiring reading and gives some substance to the claim that 'the blossoming of Austrian culture, reaching from the middle of the last century until the annexation of Austria in 1938, was for the most part determined by artists and scholars of Jewish origin'. It should be noted that there were then 180,000 Jews in Vienna but now there are approximately 8-10,000.

67 **Salzburg: a portrait.**
Diana Burgwyn. Salzburg, Austria: Alfred Winter, 1982. 163p. bibliog. maps.

It would be difficult to think of any aspect of Salzburg of interest to visitors which does not receive some mention, however briefly, in this book, which is as readable as it is comprehensive. Salzburg is a fascinating and unique city whose attraction derives as much from its geographical situation as from its historical associations and this is fully revealed in this compact and delightfully illustrated paperback. The bibliography lists books exclusively in English. This is a work which can be warmly recommended to intending visitors wishing to gain an all round view of this fine provincial capital. The author, an American, was at one time Assistant Director of the Salzburg Seminar in American Studies.

68 **Innsbruck.**
Translated from the Italian by John Sweet. Florence, Italy; Vienna: Bonechi Verlag Styria, 1981. 62p.

Another guide in the Bonechi series which eventually plans to cover all the major cities of Austria. There are 93 excellent colour illustrations and the text is clear and informative.

Travellers' Accounts

69 **Austria and the Austrians.**

W. Blumenbach. London: Henry Colburn, 1837. 2 vols.

Dedicated to Melbourne, the British Premier, this book was clearly intended to make the Austrian dominions better known both to the administration and the English people as a whole, and to act as a corrective to the prejudice and misinformation about the Habsburg Empire prevalent in England at the time. The account takes the form of a series of letters written to a close friend. With the eye of the artist and the pen of the journalist, the author presents a vivid detailed description, based on his personal experiences, of social and economic life. The first volume covers Vienna and a trip by the Danube to Pest, where he shows himself to be a strong supporter of the Hungarian national cause. The second volume, more general in character, is largely devoted to a powerful condemnation of the repressive absolutism of the Metternich régime. The author is also somewhat disparaging about the level of artistic achievement within the Empire, apart from music. There are excellent portraits of leading personalities and the aristocratic families whom he met on his travels. [See also Charles Sealsfield's *Austria as it is: by an eye witness* (q.v.)].

70 **Travels from Vienna through Lower Hungary, with some remarks on the state of Vienna during the Congress in the year 1814.**

Richard Bright. Edinburgh: Archibald Constable, 1818. 642p. maps.

Much of this work by a Scottish doctor consists of reprints of contemporary articles on a wide diversity of subjects, such as the mining industry in Hungary, agricultural and viticultural surveys, gypsies and their language and so on. However, this is simply the framework around which the author builds his story, based on close personal observation and expressed in powerful descriptive writing. Social conditions, festivals, visits to noblemen's estates, libraries and academic institutions (which interested him particularly) are all portrayed, sometimes with a minute attention to detail, always with style and sincerity.

71 **Austria-Hungary.**

Geoffrey Drage. London: John Murray, 1909. 864p. maps.

There is a great deal of factual information in this substantial work which was the product of twenty years of travelling within the Habsburg Empire. Practically every aspect of public administration is covered, while economic and commercial problems, political questions, and social and religious customs receive particular attention. Part of the material was gathered at this time for the use of the Royal Commission for Labour – hence the mass of statistical data and verbatim texts of treaties quoted in the appendixes.

72 **Austria: Vienna, Prague, Hungary.**

J. G. Kohl. London: Chapman & Hall, 1843. 532p.

This is a condensed translation of a five-volume work entitled *A Hundred Days in Austria* by the geographer and scientist extraordinary to the King of Bavaria. The three sections on Upper Austria, Lower Austria and Styria (pps. 88-170 and 386-415) reveal an acute observer of the landscape, local history and customs, all described in an easy-flowing readable style, and punctuated at times by flashes of wry humour.

73 **Descent of the Danube from Ratisbon to Vienna.**

James Robinson Planché. London: James Duncan, 1828. 320p.

This fascinating and delightfully written narrative is aptly sub-titled 'Anecdotes and recollections, historical and legendary, of the towns, castles, monasteries upon the banks of the river and their inhabitants and proprietors, ancient and modern'. It is probably the first full account in English of a journey down the Danube from Ratisbon, present day Regensburg in West Germany, to Vienna, most of it in Austria. The author was a prolific writer of plays and sketches and was hesitant about embarking on a travelogue until his travelling companion persuaded him: You have scribbled successfully for the stage – why should you fear to write for the passage boat!' A classic work.

74 **Austria as it is: by an eye witness.**

Charles Sealsfield. London: Hurst Chance, 1828. 228p.

Karl Postl, for that was the author's real name, began life as a priest in Moravia. A man of strong liberal views, an advocate of decentralization and violently opposed to Metternich's despotic rule, he emigrated to the United States, changed his name to Charles Sealsfield, became a close friend of the poet Longfellow and achieved considerable fame as a novelist. In the mid-1820's he returned to Europe on a visit where he was in fact suspected of being an Englishman. This fascinating account is largely a devastating diatribe against Metternich – 'never a man more detested and dreaded . . . dreadfully consistent in oppression.' He is dismissive of the Austrian aristocracy as an enemy of human freedom and castigates the bureaucrats for their 'gloom and dissoluteness'. However, this is also an excellent traveller's story with some humorous touches and it also provides a revealing commentary on contemporary social conditions, music, the theatre and education.

75 **Four boots to Brenner.**

G. R. Stratton. Eastbourne, England: Kematen, 1977. 66p. maps.

In 1971 two city office workers, with no previous climbing experience, inadequate map-reading skills and no knowledge of the German language, spent two weeks walking in one of the most difficult mountainous terrains of the Austrian Tirol. Although it cannot rank as a traveller's tale of any great merit, this amusing account of their adventures and mishaps, based on a diary kept by one of them, reveals some rare flashes of insight into the landscape and customs of the people they encountered on their journey.

76 **Vienna and the Austrians; with some account of a journey through Swabia, Bavaria, the Tyrol and Salzburg.**

Frances Trollope. Paris: A. & W. Galignam, 1838. 2 vols.

Frances Trollope was an inveterate traveller in Europe and was particularly interested in the social life and customs of the people in the countries she visited. This is an account of a year spent in the Habsburg Empire, mostly in Vienna, written in the form of 59 letters. She describes her frequent encounters with notable personalities, the sights of Vienna and the various ceremonial occasions she attended in an attractive and graceful style and with a good eye for detail. Unlike her contemporary, W. Blumenbach, who published his work *Austria and the Austrians* (q.v.) one year earlier, she does not venture on to the political scene, except to adopt a generally centralist stance by firmly suggesting that absolutism, to her mind, was a necessary and entirely appropriate form of rule for the Habsburg Empire and even exercised 'a benign influence through the equable administration of very mild laws'.

77 **Austria.**

Peter Evan Turnbull. London: John Murray, 1840. 2 vols.

The Habsburg Empire in the 1840's was almost unknown territory to the English. The author, who spent three years travelling within its boundaries, sets out in this two-volume work to provide his reader with a detailed review of political and social conditions based on personal observation and accounts from people of all rank and class with whom he came into contact. The first volume is essentially a narrative of his travels, written in a sober and restrained style with occasional flashes of humour. The second volume provides his impressions of Habsburg domestic and foreign policy, its civil administration, federal and municipal institutions, and includes separate chapters on religion, education and the law. There is also an extended account of a session of the Hungarian Diet which he attended and a study in depth of the Hungarian Constitution.

Flora and Fauna

78 **Fortschritte der Gefässpflanzensystematik. Floristik u. Vegetationsurkunde in Österreich (1961-71).** (Advances in the systematology of vascular plants: floristic and vegetational research in Austria.)
F. Ehrendorfer (et al.). Vienna: Verhandlungen der Zoologischen-Botanischen Gesellschaft. Band 14. 1974. p. 63-143. (Proceedings of the Zoological-Botanical Society in Vienna). bibliog.

This very extensive list of botanical publications which have appeared over the relatively short span of ten years under the auspices of the Zoological-Botanical Society in Vienna, covers 50 pages and includes no less than 394 authors. This publication reflects the wealth of research which characterizes the study of Austrian flora. A descriptive catalogue of both native and alien species of plants follows, with a systematic classification and Latin nomenclature and details of geographical location and distribution.

79 **Where to watch birds in Europe.**
John Gooders, in collaboration with Jeremy Brock. London, Sydney: Pan Books, 1978. 299p. maps. bibliog.

A useful reference book for birdwatchers which covers species likely to be found in each of the 27 countries listed. Details of access routes, local ornithological societies and seasonal variations in bird populations are included. The Austrian section concentrates mainly on the Neusiedler See, a lake lying near the Hungarian border and renowned for its wildfowl and marsh birds, but environmentally threatened by the proposal to put into operation the nearby nuclear power plant at Zwentendorf.

Flora and Fauna

80 **Bulbs: the bulbous plants of Europe and their allies.**
Christopher Grey-Wilson, Brian Matthew. London: Collins, 1981. 285p. bibliog.

This is the most up-to-date and comprehensive English guide to the bulbous flora of Europe. It is not simply a field guide but is helpful to both gardener and grower. The book is restricted to the Petaloid Monocotyledons and their closest allies, all of which have petals and petal-like structures. Full descriptions for most species are given in a standardized format and both common and scientific names in Latin are included. As regards distribution, a general area is denoted by a code number followed by a code letter ('A' for Austria) and a subsidiary one to pinpoint the location more exactly. The groupings are by genera and families and are not geographically set out, but the simple distribution code system enables the reader to identify bulbs common to Austria fairly readily.

81 **Floristic report on Austria, 1960-71.**
W. Guterman, H. Nilfield. Coimbra, Portugal: Memorias da Sociedade Broteriana 24 (1974), p. 9-23. bibliog.

This reprint of a report submitted to the European Flora Congress (Flora Europaea) in Coimbra, Portugal, in 1972 outlines the current state of botanical research in Austria and indicates that whereas in the 19th century many specialized geographical collections were made in those regions which now lie within the country's borders, this is no longer the case. However, it is hoped that the new floristic distribution mapping project may encourage a revival. The bibliography contained in this report is supplementary to that contained in Ehrendorfer's survey (q.v.) which covers the same period of research.

82 **Alpine flowers.**
Gustav Hegi, translated from the German by Winifred M. Deans. London, Glasgow: Blackie, 1930. 74p. illus.

Gustav Hegi is probably best known for his monumental seven-volume classification of central-European flowers, *Illustrierte Flora von Mittel-Europa* (Munich, 1907-36). This is an extract from that work and describes the most common alpine plants found in Austria, Switzerland and Bavaria with their German names, and vernacular variants where they exist. Wherever possible, English names with references are also given and plants found in the British Isles are asterisked. The terminology is kept as simple and non-technical as possible.

83 **From blossom time to autumn frost.**
István Homoki-Nagy. Budapest: Corvina Publishing House, 1956. 91p.

This well-known Hungarian film maker has produced a beautifully illustrated documentation of some of the wild life of Austria. There are excellent photographs of deer, wild boar, wolves and falcons. The text is informative and written for the general reader.

84 **Naturführer in Österreich.** (Nature guide to Austria.)
Franz Höpflinger, Herbert Schliefsteiner. Vienna; Graz: Styria Verlag, 1981. 480p. bibliog.

This is the most up-to-date comprehensive guide to Austrian flora and fauna at present available. The classification is according to internationally recognized standards, with German and Latin nomenclature, and the whole work is liberally illustrated. A simple system of symbols enables the reader to easily determine location, spread of distribution and special characteristics. The bibliography is selective and contains only works of major importance, all in German, although the specialist, for whom this book is intended, if only English speaking, should find his way around without much difficulty.

85 **Catalogus Florae Austriae.** (Classification of the flora of Austria.)
Erwin Janchen. Vienna: Springer Verlag, 1963-67. 3 vols.

The distinguished botanist, Erwin Janchen, under the sponsorship of the Austrian Academy of Sciences published four volumes of his systematic classification of Austrian flora by genera between 1956 and 1960, and supplemented these studies with three further volumes, also published by Springer, which appeared between 1963 and 1967. This was part of a continuation work which was uncompleted at the time of his death in 1970, but is still regarded as a major work of taxonomic scholarship.

86 **Neusiedler See: the limnology of a shallow lake in Central Europe.**
Edited by H. Löffler. The Hague; Boston, Massachusetts; London: Dr. W. Junk, 1979. 543p. bibliog. (Monographiae biologicae, vol. 37).

The Neusiedler See in the easternmost part of Austria, near the Hungarian frontier, is a lake of unique scientific interest and a well-known bird sanctuary. Ecological research in this area only started in the 1920's but has been intensified since World War II. In view of its importance it was designated a Biosphere Reserve by UNESCO in 1977 to ensure proper control of local building and to protect it against agricultural and fishing pressures which threaten to disturb the ecological balance. This deeply researched and well-documented study of the lake's animal and plant life, though technical in parts, makes fascinating reading, particularly the chapter on bird life (p. 439-474) which summarizes the current state of ornithological research in the area with numerous diagrams and some excellent colour photographs.

87 **The year of the greylag goose.**
Konrad Lorenz, translated from the German by Robert Martin. London: Eyre Methuen, 1981. 199p.

This beautifully illustrated book by the world famous zoologist and animal behaviourist, describes in words, but mostly pictures, a year in the life of a set of hand-reared geese. These were mainly greylags, a species which Konrad Lorenz has been studying at his research institute near Almsee, a lake in Upper Austria, for many years. He describes the work not as a scientific book but 'a kind of by-product of my scientific research.'

88 **Trees and bushes of Europe.**
Oleg Polunin, with drawings by Barbara Everard. London, New York: Oxford University Press, 1976. 208p.

Much of the interest and value of this botanical reference work lies in the excellent photographs and drawings, particularly of leaf shapes. The arrangement is by families in accepted botanical specification. The work covers both indigenous trees and plants as well as those introduced into Europe. There is also a useful section on the uses to which certain trees and shrubs are put by man. Distribution, and other features, are indicated by a system of symbols to which reference must be made to identify all the trees and bushes in Austria.

89 **Arbores fruticesque Europae: Vocabularium octo linguis redactum.**
(Trees and shrubs of Europe: a dictionary published in eight languages.)
Szaniszló Priszter. Budapest: Akadémiai Kiadó, 1983. 298p. bibliog.

This dictionary, printed in eight languages, (Latin, English, French, German, Hungarian, Italian, Spanish, and Russian), lists 1,200 trees and shrubs found in Europe. It provides their names based on a standard scientific nomenclature as in *Flora Europaea* (q.v.) and includes the vernacular names of the various species in different languages. Abbreviations are used to denote the various taxonomic categories, geographical areas of distribution and other features. There are alphabetical indexes in each language and a list of authors mentioned in the text with dates of birth and death. A valuable reference work for specialists and translators.

90 **European animals.**
Robert Francis Scharff. London: Constable, 1907. 258p. maps. bibliog.

This is a systematic investigation of the geological history of European animals with detailed descriptions of them and their geographical distribution. Chapter 7 covers the Alps and therefore Austria and her neighbours. The bibliography, although extensive, is mainly focused on geological, rather than natural, history.

91 **Flora europaea.** (European flora.)
Edited by T. G. Tutin. London: Cambridge University Press, 1964. 5 vols. maps.

This authoritative publication contains a classified description of all the major species of European flora, including those found in Austria. It includes glossaries of technical terms with simple descriptions designed as much for the layman as for the scholar. As the arrangement is botanical, rather than geographical, it is not possible for the reader to determine the full range of Austrian flora by a single reference to the index. Notwithstanding this, every plant, flower or tree can be researched individually and each description includes its exact location, or spread of distribution.

Prehistory and Archaeology

92 **The Danube in pre-history.**
Gordon V. Childe. Oxford: Clarendon Press, 1929. 479p. maps. bibliog.

In view of the broad scope of this scholarly and authoritative work, published over fifty years ago, its interest to today's student of Austrian history may appear tangential. However, this work could well provide a framework for further study of the subject, for the pre-history of the Danube is to some degree the pre-history of Austria. The volume represents a lucid guide and invaluable research and reference tool to the ancient highway of civilizations spread between northeastern Europe, the Aegean and the Ancient East. The detailed descriptions of objects and materials and their location with explanatory notes and marginal annotations are all placed in the wider context of European cultural trends and contribute to an impressive survey of the Danube basin in pre-historic times.

93 **Lexikon Ur- und Frühgeschichtlicher Fundstätten Österreichs.**
(Encyclopaedia of pre-historic site finds in Austria.)
Edited by L. Franz, A. R. Neumann. Vienna: Brüder Hollinek, 1965. 244p.

This encyclopaedia lists archaeological and pre-historical sites within the country's borders with dates and findings of excavations. The bibliographical references are extensive and there is a useful biographical index. The arrangement is by provinces.

94 **Quantifying Hallstatt: some initial results.**
Frank Roy Hodson. *American Antiquity*. vol. 42, no. 3 (July 1977), p. 394-412.

The Iron Age cemetery at Hallstatt is probably the most extensive of its kind in Europe and is a major source of information about the European Iron Age.

Professor Hodson, in this short monograph, attempts to determine from the grave finds the sex, age, status and relative date of burial of the victims based on 980 graves which were originally excavated between 1846 and 1863. He applies a mathematical specification of basic archaeological procedures and the graves are then graded and described by the objects they contain.

95 **Hallstatt: Bilder aus der Frühzeit Europas.** (Pictures from European pre-history.)
Erich Lessing. Vienna: Jugend und Volk, 1980. 283p. 5 maps. bibliog.

An international team of experts on archaeology, history and art have collaborated with the author in producing a beautifully illustrated and comprehensive survey of the Hallstatt Iron Age period from the 8th to the 5th century BC. The important excavations at this settlement and the nearby salt mines, trading links with the Danube area to the east and to central and western Europe, living conditions and burial rites, are all described in an explanatory text. Illustrations of tools, weapons, jewellery and other artefacts fill 160 pages. An authoritative and attractive presentation of a very important culture.

96 **Hallstatt.**
Friedrich Morton. Hallstatt, Austria: Musealvereine, 1953-54. 2 vols.

This comprehensive work has the added attraction of being written by one of the local experts who has not only provided a full historical account of Hallstatt in the Iron Age period but has also brought this up to date with detailed descriptions of the local scene in all its aspects from 1800 onwards. The illustrations, which have been carefully selected, tell their own story and should be of particular value to the non-German reader.

97 **Das Gräberfeld von Kapfenstein und die Römischen Hügelgräber in Österreich.** (The grave sites of Kapfenstein and the Roman barrows in Austria.)
Otto H. Urban. Munich: C. H. Becksche Verlagsbuchhandlung, 1984. 304p. map. bibliog. (Munich Contributions to pre-history, vol. 35).

The findings of a research survey undertaken by a Bavarian archaeology commission in 1981 into Roman gravesite remains in southern Styria are presented in a well-annotated report. This volume also contains a review, in tabulated form, of the current general state of research on excavations in this important area.

History

General

98 **The Austrian odyssey.**

Gordon Brook-Shepherd. London: Macmillan; New York: St Martin's Press, 1957. 302p. maps. bibliog.

For an understanding of the background to present-day Austria, it is illuminating to concentrate on the whole period from the Compromise with Hungary in 1867, when Austria became a separate kingdom under the Dual Monarchy, to 1955, the year of the signing of the State Treaty ending the four-power occupation after World War II. The author is well-qualified to do this having been a young correspondent in Vienna before World War II, a Colonel in the British Army there in 1945, and since then a journalist and a historian. An important ingredient in this book is the judgments given to him in personal interviews by Austrians of all political persuasions, while it also contains an unique evaluation, for an English work, of the nature and performance of the Austrian resistance to the Nazi régime during World War II.

99 **Vienna – the past in the present: a historical survey.**

Inge Lehne, Lonnie Johnson. Vienna: Federal Publishing Office, 1985. 200p. bibliog. maps.

This is, like Richard Rickett's *A brief survey of Austrian history* (q.v.), an excellent and perceptive attempt at a short synthesis, written by two scholars both teaching in Vienna and, like Rickett, born outside it – Lehne in the South Tirol and Johnson in the United States. Their introduction immediately sets the tone and the approach: 'enjoying Vienna involves finding some kind of middle ground between the commercial illusion of the cliché and the pessimistic blanket condemnation of the counter-cliché, an objective synthesis of the extremes'. Their coverage extends well outside the capital, however, and if the treatment of the periods up to the end of the Middle Ages is not as detailed as Rickett's they allow themselves in the process more opportunity for in-depth analysis of the later inward life of the capital and indeed the country, which they now see embodied in the current Austrian tendencies towards traditionalism and a sense of precedent. They are particularly strong on the 19th century: early-Biedermeier and late-Secession, where their perception is masterly. They are possibly less successful in the immediate post World War II period.

100 **Austrian History Yearbook.**
Edited by John Rath. Minneapolis, Minnesota: University of Minnesota, Center for Austrian Studies. 1964-. annual. bibliog.

Since 1983 this yearbook has been published by the Centre for Austrian Studies, University of Minnesota (it was formerly published by Rice University, Houston, Texas) in co-operation with the Conference Group for Central European History. This group sponsors a joint Austro-US committee for the promotion of studies of the history of the Habsburg Monarchy and is composed of a number of distinguished historians and an international group of correspondents, some of whom are resident in the United States and some in Austria. The handbook contains essays on politics, diplomatic history and military campaigns, biographies, extensive book reviews, commemorative articles on leading personalities, and accession lists of the committee's libraries. It also contains a normally comprehensive bibliography of books, articles, dissertations, essays and *Festschriften* on Austrian history which have appeared, either in unpublished or published form during the year in question. This yearbook is tangible proof of the great interest in Habsburg affairs in present day US scholastic circles.

101 **A brief survey of Austrian history.**
Richard Rickett. Vienna: Georg Prachner, 1983. 7th ed. 166p. 2 maps.

Rickett came to Austria immediately after World War II as a member of the British Element of the Allied Commission, with previous personal knowledge of the First Republic. He gained further experience of both the Austrian viewpoint and that of the occupation forces as a British Council representative, later being responsible for English publications issued by the Austrian Government Press Service and other official Austrian bodies. This volume is an admirably condensed survey of the history of the country which displays not only the capacity to present a most readable account of the main historical trends but also a real understanding of their significance. The author's judgments are sound and illuminating and no better short introduction to Austrian history is available in English.

102 **The adventure of Austria.**
Christian Sapper. *Austria Today*, no. 1 (1985), p. 17-30. maps.

This is a popular narrative account of the whole history of the country from the earliest times to the present day, with some most helpful maps showing component areas at various stages of their development. It includes outline chronologies of each of the present nine provinces along with photographs of traditional costumes from each. A most readable introduction.

103 **Geschichte Österreichs von den Anfängen bis zur Gegenwart.** (A history of Austria from its earliest beginnings to the present day.)
Erich Zöllner. Vienna: Austrian Federal Publishing House, 1961. 2nd ed. 672p. 4 maps. bibliog.

The State Treaty of 1955 provided the impetus for the production of a number of definitive works for the general Austrian reading public on various aspects of Constitutional and State concern. A number of standard historical accounts of various government organizations has emerged. This publication is a history of Austria itself from its earliest beginnings to the present. There are four excellent maps, comprehensive notes and genealogical tables. A substantial, balanced work by a historian of note.

Celts, Romans and Babenbergs (279 BC-AD 1276)

104 **Noricum.**
E. Alföldy, translated from the Hungarian by Anthony Birley. London; Boston: Routledge & Kegan Paul, 1974. 413p.
maps. bibliog. (The Provinces of the Roman Empire).

Parts of Upper Austria, Salzburg, Tirol, Carinthia and Styria lie within the former Roman province of Noricum. Professor Alföldy offers a well-documented chronological account of the Roman occupation in a historical, social and epigraphic setting. The bibliography, which is specialized and extensive, contains 17 appendixes which deal with place-names, Roman administrators, fortresses, army units and their locations, and dated milestones. The work concludes with a critical survey of the current state of research on this province which includes a number of the author's own monographs.

105 **Die Kelten in Österreich.** (The Celts in Austria.)
Gerhard Dobesch. Vienna: Hermann Böhlau, 1980. 500p. 3 maps. bibliog.

Whereas Powell's study (q.v.) describes the characteristics of the Celtic people, this exhaustive and scholarly work is in effect a history of the documentation available on the period of their 250 year occupation of the Kingdom of Noricum, which includes parts of present-day Tirol, Salzburg, Upper Austria, Carinthia and Styria. The author focuses particularly on administrative aspects and the Celts relations with Rome. He makes extensive use of Roman classical historians such as Livy.

106 **Die Babenberger.** (The Babenbergs.)
Karl Lechner. Vienna: Hermann Böhlau, 1976. 478p. bibliog.

In the almost complete absence of works in English or English translation on the Babenberg dynasty, this definitive work may be of help to German readers at least. Although members of this family of feudal nobility from Franconia (north Bavaria) were active from the early 9th century, the dynasty as such stems from Luitpold I who was appointed Margrave of Austria in 976 when it was founded as the Ostmark or East March. This particular work was published to mark the dynasty's millennium and traces the Babenbergs' origin, rise and relations with the church together with their final extinction in 1246 through the death in battle of Duke Frederick II 'the Quarrelsome' who had no male heir. The author combines an account of the personalities involved with the territorial aggrandisements by which the small area on the fringe of the Holy Roman Empire became a sizeable dukedom comprising roughly the eastern half of present-day Austria. Under Babenberg rule, gold, silver and salt were mined extensively, while religious orders established monasteries further to the east and these soon became centres of cultural life. A strong literary tradition also flourished. It should also be noted that the Babenbergs were a race of administrators of above average ability and this work is essential to an understanding of the formative period of Austria before the Habsburgs.

107 **A history of mediaeval Austria.**

A. W. A. Leeper, edited by R. W. Seton-Watson and C. A. Macartney. Oxford: Oxford University Press, 1941. 420p.

Very few accounts of this period have been written in English and although this publication appeared over forty years ago, it still fills an important gap. Its literary standing is clearly reflected in the names of the two distinguished historians who edited the manuscript, which was incomplete at the time of the author's death in 1934. The editors revised the manuscript in the light of more recently published material, but failed to provide a bibliography. The period covered is from earliest times to the accession of Emperor Rudolph in 1273. The early chapters on Roman rule are particularly well-presented while the descriptions of archaeological sites and architectural features are vivid and impressive.

108 **Pannonia and Upper Moesia: a history of the Middle Danube provinces of the Roman Empire.**

András Mócsy, translated from the German by Sheppard Frere. London: Routledge & Kegan Paul, 1974. 453p. bibliog. (The Provinces of the Roman Empire).

Upper Moesia falls with minor exceptions outside the Austro-Hungarian boundaries but Pannonia corresponded roughly with present-day Lower Austria, Carinthia, Styria, Burgenland and Western Hungary. The key centres were Vindobona (Vienna), Carnuntum (east of Vienna), and Aquincum (Budapest). The archaeological research on which the book is based is clearly thorough and results in sound conclusions in the spheres of socioeconomic conditions, religion and politics. There is also an important emphasis on the tenuous nature of the connections with Rome and this is of some interest when considering the administrative problems of the Habsburgs. From time to time, however, the author tends to generalize on data which he admits to being incomplete. On balance a definitive standard work in an authoritative series, graced by a translation by the Professor of Roman Archaeology in the University of Oxford.

109 **The provinces of the Roman Empire: the European provinces.**
Theodor Mommsen, edited by Robert S. Boughton, translated from the German by William P. Dixon. Chicago, London: University of Chicago Press, 1968. 363p. vol. 5. book 8. bibliog. (Classic European Historians).

Theodor Mommsen, the distinguished German historian and archaeologist (1817-1903), has a personal and piquant parallel with the Austrian scene in that he supported the Saxon monarchy against the revolutionaries in Leipzig in 1848 and lost his Professorship by protesting against the subsequent repressive measures introduced after a coup-d'état by the diplomatist Friedrich von Beust who became Minister President. Mommsen then held Professorships at Zurich and Berlin where in 1885 he published in six volumes his *Provinces of the Roman Empire from Caesar to Diocletian* which was translated into English and was internationally acclaimed. The present publication is a reprint of extracts from this translation with minor corrections by the editor and covers the European provinces of the Empire only. Chapter 6 deals with the Danubian lands including of course parts of the territories of the Austro-Hungarian Empire and present day Austria. A long editorial introduction expounds and assesses the post-Mommsen research, but stresses that he is still a commanding authority with no real equal even today.

110 **The Celts.**
T. G. E. Powell. London: Thames & Hudson, 1958. 283p. 9 maps. bibliog. (Ancient Peoples and Places, no. 6).

A general study of the Celtic way of life. In about 279 BC the Celts established themselves in an area south of the Danube roughly corresponding to present day Carinthia and west Styria, displacing the Romans, who, however reconquered the region by 15 BC. Basing his studies on the testimony of ancient historians, native traditional literature and the results of modern philological research the author concentrates on the Celts' religious beliefs and practices, stressing their emphasis on the supernatural. The use of marginal notes is helpful to the reader wishing to trace the Austrian connection. This volume covers an important period in the early development of the country.

111 **Carnuntum: Rom an der Donau.** (Carnuntum: Rome on the Danube).
Eduard Vorbeck, Lothar Beckel. Salzburg, Austria: Otto Müller Verlag, 1973. 114p.

This is a product of four years excavation of the Roman and Celtic remains at Carnuntum, an important Roman fortress near present-day Hainburg in Lower Austria. The work contains some excellent aerial pictures of the site, a historical essay and some English accounts, with a German translation, of archaeological excavations of the 18th and 19th centuries.

House of Habsburg

General (1276-1918)

112 **History of the House of Austria.**

William Coxe. London: George Bell, 1882. 4th ed. 4 vols. maps.

Originally published in 1847, this was the first comprehensive history (1215-1840) of the Habsburgs to appear in any language and remained a standard work until superseded by weightier studies by German scholars towards the end of the 19th century. In the absence of any systematically arranged archival material, the author, Archdeacon of Wiltshire, relied heavily on published diplomatic correspondence and the private papers of statesmen, some of whom were his friends. The House of Habsburg is portrayed as the saviour of Christian Europe from Mohammedan barbarism, with the focus on the Court of Vienna as the nodal point around which 'the vast machine of European policy' had revolved through the centuries.

113 **The Holy Roman Empire.**

Friedrich Heer, translated from the German by Janet Sondheimer. London: Weidenfeld & Nicolson, 1968. 309p.

A fascinating, if eccentric, study of the whole history of the Empire, written in a conversatonal style which makes it all easy reading. It is extensively illustrated and there are particularly penetrating studies of the rise of the House of Habsburg, the reign of Charles V, the Thirty Years' War, and Maria Theresa. The author excels himself in his analysis of the art and architecture of the 17th and 18th centuries – the Imperial baroque style.

114 **A history of the Habsburg Empire, 1526-1918.**

Robert A. Kann. London: University of California Press, 1974. 646p. maps. bibliog.

Most historians when writing about the Habsburgs are apt to take a centralist view of the Empire and the nationality problems within its subject states. Professor Kann, however, adopts a different approach, and claims that equal attention must be given to all the different political groupings and ethnic communities of which the Empire was composed. He sees the essence of Habsburg history as being a correlation of supranational and national problems – but viewed from different angles. Thus, he looks at foreign and military affairs from the centre, but domestic, social and cultural issues are interpreted primarily from the viewpoint of the individual ethnic groups. This is a scholarly work with logical chapter divisions and sub-sections, which enables the reader either to study the work in narrative form or to use it as background reference to a particular subject or area of interest. The volume includes an extensive bibliographical essay on the literature in several languages as well as a chronology of important political dates, statistical charts and maps.

115 **A history of Austria-Hungary: from the earliest times to the year 1889.**

Louis Leger. London: Rivingtons, 1889. 672p. maps. bibliog.

When this history was published, Austria-Hungary covered an area of 261,000 square miles and had a population of 40 millions and was aptly described by the author as a multinational state with fourteen languages having no real historical or geographical entity and no natural frontiers. This is a chronological account, which of necessity moves from one geographical area to another and concentrates largely on 19th-century constitutional and political matters. There is an excellent preface together with tables providing genealogical information and showing the territorial losses and gains of the House of Habsburg through the centuries.

116 **The Habsburg Empire, 1790-1918.**

Carlile Aylmer Macartney. London: Weidenfeld & Nicolson, 1968. 837p. 6 maps. bibliog.

This massive tome has rightly been described by its publisher as an account of the '100 year struggle between dynastic empire and the new national, social and political forces within it'. It is a dedicated work by an acknowledged historian in his veteran years who knew the Empire at first hand as a young student before World War I and understandably, is written from the point of view of one who knew and appreciated the Establishment. It covers the broad spectrum – Viennese officials, Bohemian landowners, Hungarian Counts, the minutiae of constitutional law, the motivation behind Francis Joseph and his heir apparent, Francis Ferdinand and so on. It is at this level that the author's sympathies clearly lie, but he has nevertheless managed to give a clear, vivid and balanced picture of the political forces and social trends which sustained the whole of this remarkable complex. The bibliography is extensive.

117 **Rise of the Habsburg Empire, 1526-1815.**

Victor S. Mamatey. Atlanta, Georgia; New York: Holt, Rinehart & Winston, 1971. 182p. maps. bibliog. (Berkshire Studies in History).

Specifically intended for American history students, this book sets a stimulating intellectual exercise in that the reader is invited to co-operate in defining a number of loose terms such as 'Habsburg', 'Empire', 'Holy Roman', and 'Austria', and is given a bibliography of works in English to study. The whole treatment, too, is an attempt to judge history by the values prevalent at the time. As a clue to the answers the book opens with the defeat of the Hungarians by the Turks in 1526, which marked the end of the remarkable expansion through dynastic marriages which secured Habsburg hegemony over Spain, Bohemia and Hungary, in which latter area a foothold was retained despite the defeat. The co-existence of an Imperial and a Habsburg presence (the double-headed eagle on the Austrian flag even today stems from their personal emblem) was only legally regularized when Francis II, Holy Roman Emperor, proclaimed himself Francis I, Emperor of Austria in 1804 and the thousand-year-old Holy Roman Empire finally came to an end in 1806. The book ends with the Congress of Vienna in 1815 when Austria, having liberated itself from the Napoleonic connection, was free to go its own way.

118 **The army of Francis Joseph.**
Gunther Erich Rothenberg. West Lafayette, Indiana: Purdue University Press, 1976. 298p.

Mainly concerned with the army as an institution, this account examines its role in Francis Joseph's domestic and foreign policy, particularly the part it played in helping to prevent the disintegration of the Empire under the stress of growing nationalist divisions. The author introduces his work with a historical review of the Habsburg army's evolution through three distinct stages: from 1522 to 1625 by which time certain basic institutions had been established within the Empire; from 1625 to 1743 when a standing army was raised which placed the monarchy in the ranks of the great powers; and from 1743 to 1815 when important reforms were introduced making the army a powerful instrument in withstanding the impact of the Prussian and French wars. Even after the 1867 Compromise and the establishment of the Dual Monarchy the army remained loyal to the dynasty and continued to function in both parts of the Dual Monarchy as a powerful institution, free from the conflicts of nationality, language, politics and religion raging at the time.

119 **The Habsburg monarchy, 1809-1918: a history of the Austrian Empire and Austria-Hungary.**
A. J. P. Taylor. Harmondsworth, England: Penguin Books, 1981. 304p. maps. bibliog.

The author, who spent the last two years of the Habsburg monarchy in Vienna as a student, has produced a penetrating and readable account in his characteristically lucid, lively and personal style. He focuses particularly on foreign policy and the conflict between the supranational dynasty and the national principle and suggests that in the final days of the Empire there were no lost opportunities, but that the war had simply to be fought to a finish. A short appendix summarizes very concisely the ethnographical structure of the monarchy and could well be read as an introduction to the whole work.

120 **Memoirs of the Court, aristocracy and diplomacy of Austria.**
E. Vehse, translated from the German by Franz Demmler. London: Longman, Brown & Green, 1856. 2 vols.

'I draw characters: I preserve anecdotes' – from these introductory words the reader will appreciate that this is not a historical survey. Nor is it a portrayal of court life and manners as the title suggests. This work is much more of a social documentation covering a 300 year period from the reign of Maximilian I (1493-1519) to that of Francis II (1792-1806). A chapter is devoted to each emperor and, quoting liberally from contemporary sources, the author brings to life a number of different and fascinating personalities. He also includes in the appendixes examples of letter writing styles at the time of Maximilian I and diplomatic courtesy styles at the time of Charles V.

121 **The House of Habsburg.**
Adam Wandruszka, translated from the German by Cathleen and Hans Epstein. London: Sidgwick & Jackson, 1964. 196p. 3 maps. bibliog.

Professor Wandruszka has written a clear and very readable account of over 600 years of Habsburg dynastic rule which includes all the essentials and does justice to all the leading personalities. He shows himself to be a veritable master of compression and stylish economy in this publication of less than 200 pages, which also contains useful genealogical tables and a bibliography prepared for an English readership.

122 **Intellectual and social developments in the Habsburg Empire from Maria Theresa to World War I.**
Edited by Stanley B. Winters, Joseph Held, in collaboration with István Deák, Adam Wandruska. London, New York: East European Quarterly, 1975. 304p. bibliog. (East European Monographs, no. XI).

This collection of essays is dedicated to the distinguished historian Robert Kann. The theme running through the essays which have been written by ten experts, each a specialist in his particular field, is that the Habsburg Monarchy, the so-called 'sick man of Europe,' suffered from 'old age and stubbornness of old age rather than a congenital and terminal illness'. The subjects cover a wide spectrum, are well annotated and are directed at the scholar.

Middle Ages to Counter-Reformation (1276-1648)

123 **The military intellectual and battle: Raimondo Montecuccoli and the Thirty Years' War.**
Thomas M. Barker. Albany, New York: University of New York Press, 1975. 270p. maps. bibliog.

Montecuccoli was the son of an Italian nobleman who commanded brilliantly for the Holy Roman Empire both in the Thirty Years' War and later against the Swedes, Turks and French. He was also a major strategist and writer on the principles and practice of the profession of arms, which the present author considers to be generally neglected. Drawing on his own experience, both of command and administration (Montecuccoli had organized the Imperial Standing Army and paved the way for the later successes of Prince Eugene against the French), his writings had a profound effect, not only on his contemporaries but also on Frederick the Great and Napoleon. This important treatise studies these in detail and represents a major contribution to both military history and theory.

124 **Maximilian I (1459-1519).**

Gerhard Benecke. London, Boston, Melbourne: Routledge & Kegan Paul, 1982. 181p.

Maxmilian I is generally regarded as the founder of the modern Austrian State, consolidating his family's fortunes with skilful dynastic marriages and steering his way ably between conflicting feudal and commercial pressures. His own personality was a mixture of the shrewd and hard-headed political leader and a conscience deeply affected by the religious torments of the period leading up to the Reformation, which led him into the Italian invasion. Monographs on him are, however, few and far between, and this recent and definitive study supplements Christopher Hare's earlier classic published almost seventy years ago and entitled *Maximilian the dreamer: Holy Roman Emperor, 1459-1519* (London: Stanley, Paul 1913).

125 **The Emperor Charles V, 1500-1558.**

Karl Brandi, translated from the German by C. V. Wedgwood. London: Jonathan Cape, 1968. 655p.

This monumental work is the result of a lifetime of research by an internationally recognized authority on the subject, and has been excellently translated by a historian of considerable standing. It skilfully traces the rise of the Habsburg dynasty to the height of its greatness; with the Emperor adhering steadfastly to the principle of unity of faith against the stresses of the Reformation and the increasingly discredited principle of the Holy Roman Empire. The book refers to a wealth of surviving original documentation and comprehensive genealogical tables.

126 **Rudolf II and his world: a study in intellectual history, 1576-1612.**

R. J. W. Evans. London: Oxford University Press, 1973. 323p. map. bibliog.

This book traces with consummate insight the complex inter-relationships between the psychological makeup of a sensitive ruler, who eventually went mad, and the administrative demands of the Holy Roman Empire in a time of religious and territorial complexity – the Counter-Reformation and the lead-up to the Thirty Years' War. By inclination a patron of the arts with an obsession for the occult, magic, alchemy and astrology – he was beset by rival claims to power by other members of his family, yet held his own while he could. A scholarly, fascinating and original work by an eminent historian.

127 **The making of the Habsburg monarchy, 1550-1700.**

R. J. W. Evans. Oxford: Clarendon Press, 1984. 531p. bibliog.

Whereas many historians write about the decline of the House of Habsburg, this author investigates the causes of its rise. In this important, imaginative and scholarly study he concentrates on three main inter-locking themes: the Counter-Reformation with its associated social and economic changes; the balance between central and regional authority; the climate of ideas of the period, reflecting the development of an intellectual framework which sought to reconcile the magical and occult ideas inherited from the Renaissance with the sacramental ideas evolving in the course of the Counter-Reformation. This work is essential reading for the student of early Habsburg history.

128 **Renaissance in Österreich: Geschichte, Wissenschaft, Kunst.**
(Renaissance in Austria: history, science and art.)
Edited by Rupert Feuchtmüller. Vienna: Ferdinand Berger, 1974. 364p. bibliog.

This valuable reference work, for both the specialist and the amateur with a knowledge of German, contains thirty-eight essays dealing with history, science, technology and art, written by thirty-three specialists from Lower Austria. It is an impressive introduction to 16th-century Austria and deals with heraldry, arms manufacture, science, topography, manufacture of astronomical instruments, mechanical clocks and Renaissance architectural planning. The work was compiled in conjunction with the complete restoration between 1968 and 1974 of the late Renaissance castle of Schallaburg near Melk on the Danube, where a major exhibition was held in 1974.

129 **Ferdinand I of Austria: the politics of dynasticism in the age of the Reformation.**
Paula Suttner Fichtner. Boulder, New York: East European Monographs, 1982. 362p. bibliog.

Ferdinand I's struggle for the perpetuation of the House of Habsburg as a sovereign dynasty – which, like all Habsburg rulers, he regarded as a sacred duty – is the subject of this extensive study. What emerges is a clear picture of a man relentless and steadfast in his pursuit of family interests and a tenacious, open-handed and moderate ruler who nevetheless claimed a divine right to protect the Christian faithful against the Turks, against whom he waged endless wars. Style and ceremonial were also important to Ferdinand I and his patronage of the arts and architecture is a major theme of the book, which also focuses on the acquisition of Bohemia and parts of Hungary in 1526, which were to remain united within the Empire until its demise in 1918.

130 **Habsburg and Bourbon Europe, 1470-1720.**
Roger Lockyer. London: Longman, 1974. 594p. bibliog.

This work falls into six parts: a general introduction with a section on the economy of the 16th and 17th centuries; Reformation and Counter-Reformation; the Italian wars, and the Revolt of the Netherlands; the French Wars of Religion; Spain under Philip II; and the Turks in the 16th century. It is a well-documented account with supporting genealogical data and an excellent bibliography, mainly of books published in the last twenty-five years.

131 **Peasant classes: the bureaucratisation of property and family relations under early Habsburg absolutism, 1511-1636.**
Herman Rebel. Princeton, New Jersey: Princeton University Press, 1983. 354p. maps. bibliog.

The struggle for the emancipation of the peasant classes in the Habsburg dominions in the 16th and 17th centuries was long and bitter. This is a specialized study of the rural population of Upper Austria during the first half of this period, focusing on the social and economic relationships between members of families, households and communities. The author draws on much contemporary material for his account of the numerous peasant petitions, protests, strikes and armed uprisings of the time and for his detailed examination of the regulations covering such matters as property ownership, inheritance, credit, marketing and the use of labour. A survey of interest to the student of social and economic history of the middle Habsburg period.

132 **The Austrian military border in Croatia, 1522-1747.**
Gunther Erich Rothenberg. Urbana, Illinois: University of Illinois Press, 1960. 156p. 2 maps. bibliog. (Illinois Studies in the Social Services, vol. 48).

For 350 years (1522-1881) a zone on the southern frontier of Croatia, acting as a defensive screen against the Turks, was administered by a special Austrian military organization, composed almost exclusively of non-Croats, which controlled all the activities of the local inhabitants and supervised their economic life. This fascinating narrative account of its origins under Ferdinand I to its reorganization in Maria Theresa's reign deals mainly with administrative and military aspects and relates the organization's raison d'être to the wider historical issues of the Habsburg Empire and south-eastern Europe. The appraisal is detailed and extremely well-researched and, although clearly intended for the specialist, provides some absorbing general reading. A continuation work by the same author covering the second period entitled *The Military Border in Croatia, 1740-1881: a Study of an Imperial Institution* (Chicago, London: University of Chicago Press, 1966. 224p. map. bibliog.) focuses particularly on aspects of military life and descriptions of the various regiments involved, and concludes with an interesting comparison between the Austrian military border force and the development of the Russian frontier system of Cossack settlements.

133 **The Imperial Privy Council in the 17th century.**
Henry Frederick Schwarz, John I. Coddrington. London: Oxford University Press, 1943. 479p. bibliog. (Harvard Historical Series, vol. 53).

This subject may at first sight appear recherché and perhaps irrelevant to modern Austria. Anyone resident there for any time, however, will be well-aware of the awe in which the Civil Service stands for the general public and this is in direct descent from a radical alteration to the Imperial Constitution introduced by Ferdinand II in 1627. This established an autocratic and centralized system at the expense particularly of the Estates, the magnates, nobles and free towns of the fringe kingdoms of Bohemia and Hungary and it is fascinating to examine the early gradual transformation of the Privy Council, the hard core, from a primarily imperial to a more specifically Austrian form of bureacuracy. Not even the next major constitutional provision, which corresponded with the Compromise of 1867, failed to shake this, with the well-known results in terms of resurgent nationalism.

134 **Princes and artists: patronage and ideology at four Habsburg courts, 1517-1633.**
Hugh Trevor-Roper. London: Thames & Hudson, 1976. 174p. bibliog.

The four Habsburg courts in question were those of Charles V, Philip II of Spain, Rudolph II and Archduke Albert and Isabella who ruled the Southern Netherlands from 1598 to 1633. The author's theme is that during this period art was partly propagandist and partly sheer aesthetic pleasure and that the distinctive characteristics of patronage are explained by the 'world picture' of the age. In other words, art symbolized a whole view of life, of which politics were a part; and the court had a duty to propagate and sustain it. An interesting study for the art historian.

135 **The Emperor Charles the Fifth.**
Royall Tyler. London: George Allen & Unwin, 1956. 375p. maps. bibliog.

This is a substantial work by a noteable American historian. The influences which formed the Emperor's character and personality are well described as are his part in the rise of Burgundy, its subsequent eclipse and its re-emergence as a dominating factor in Europe. The religious, financial and foreign policy problems he faced are treated separately. The principal sources used are the Emperor's correspondence with his ministers and ambassadors, and other contemporary records. A synopsis of Charles' European travels (1500-58) is also included. A much earlier work *The Emperor Charles* (London: Macmillan, 1902) in two volumes by Edward Armstrong is recommended as a reliable character study of Charles V which stresses his defensive reaction to events and difficulties, often not of his own making, and the obstinacy and irresolution with which these were frequently confronted.

136 **The Thirty Years' War.**
C. V. Wedgwood. London: Methuen, 1981. 526p. maps. bibliog.

The Austrian role in the Thirty Years' War of 1618-48 figures prominently in this survey of a military and religious conflict involving the whole of Europe. The author was one of the most distinguished of latter-day English historians and she is particularly helpful over one of the less popular Emperors, Ferdinand II, and the only one not to be buried in the Habsburg vaults in the Capucine Monastery in Vienna. She has also compiled an important bibliography of the relevant works written in English, and incidentally, forty years earlier translated Karl Brandi's classic work on Charles V (q.v.). For a fascinating but much earlier study by a leading Victorian scholar, see Sir Adolphus Ward's *The House of Habsburg in the Thirty Years' War* which was the text of two lectures delivered at the Philosophical Institution, Edinburgh, in 1868.

Age of the Baroque (1648-1740)

137 **Double eagle and crescent.**
Thomas M. Barker. Albany, New York: State University of New York, 1967. 464p. 2 maps. bibliog.

This is a well-researched and scholarly study of the Turkish siege of Vienna and its relief in 1683. The siege was the subject of a masterful exhibition in Vienna for its tercentenary in 1983, for which this work was translated into German. This turning point in the Empire's history is analysed in three major sections: why the siege failed; the aftermath of failure; and what might have happened had it been successful. See also *The Turks at Vienna's Gates* (q.v.).

138 **The struggle for the Ottoman Empire, (1717-1740).**
Lavender Cassels. London: John Murray, 1964. 206p. bibliog.

In 1717 Prince Eugene of Savoy routed the Ottoman Grand Vizier's army and captured Belgrade against overwhelming odds. This account shows how, with the Turks demoralized and the French disconcerted, Austria and Russia, in alliance, tried for the next twenty-two years to exploit the situation and finally to dismember the Ottoman Empire; a policy which France tried to frustrate. There are good portrayals of the four main protagonists in this international diplomatic struggle: Czarina Anne of Russia; Emperor Charles VI of Austria; Cardinal Fleury of France; and the Turkish Sultans Ahmed III (1703-30) and Mahmoud I (1730-54).

139 **In quest and crisis: Emperor Joseph I and the Habsburg Monarchy.**
Charles W. Ingrao. West Lafayette, Indiana: Purdue University Press, 1979. 278p. maps.

This book is something of a landmark since the last full-length biography on this short-reigning Emperor (1705-11) appeared in 1798. One possible reason is the shortage of documentation on his personal life making it difficult to evaluate his character. Joseph I's own very considerable achievements however, in an important period of the Empire's history, are given an original and balanced treatment. His Commander-in-Chief, Prince Eugene of Savoy, scored decisive victories against Louis XIV of France in Italy, the Netherlands and Germany. In addition, Joseph introduced important measures of administrative and fiscal reform, including founding the Vienna Municipal Bank, and initiated the solution to Habsburg dynastic problems by introducing the Pragmatic Sanction, which enabled Maria Theresa to succeed in due course through the female line.

140 **A study in Austrian intellectual history.**
Robert A. Kann. London: Thames & Hudson, 1960. 367p. bibliog.

Combining a biographical with a social approach this penetrating and scholarly but very readable analysis of the major trends of Austrian intellectual history from late baroque to early romanticism is based largely on the lives and ideas of two remarkable men, both hardly known to English language readers of Austrian history. Abraham a Sancta Clara was a member of the Augustinian order, an imperial court preacher and a brilliant and witty writer of great originality in the early 18th century, while Joseph von Sonnenfels was a government official of Jewish descent who proposed many of Maria Theresa's judicial reforms. Both exercised a considerable influence on the Austria of their time and even beyond. The author has divided his study into six essays, each of which in its own way explains the typical elements and the cyclical pattern of Austrian intellectual development in which the more stable conservative periods appear far longer than the dynamic and relatively liberal ones.

141 **Spain under the Habsburgs.**
John Lynch. Oxford: Basil Blackwell, 1964-69. 2 vols. 6 maps. bibliog.

The work is titled as follows: vol. I, 'Empire and Absolutism (1516-1598)'; vol. 2 'Spain and America (1598-1700)'. The period covered is therefore from the accession of Charles I of Spain (the Emperor Charles V) to the death of Charles II. Without neglecting political issues the author expands on the social and economic forces at work and examines the conflict facing the Spanish Habsburgs of reconciling their mission as champions of Catholic Christendom with their determination to preserve their dynastic interests. As the book reveals, the brutal realities of power politics did in the end displace the idealistic and religious aims of the earlier years. For an account of the integration of the Spanish side into the general history of the House of Habsburg in this period see *The Habsburgs and Europe, 1516-1660* by H. G. Königsberger (Ithaca, New York: Cornell University Press, 1971).

142 **The Habsburg and Hohenzollern dynasties in the 17th and 18th centuries.**
Edited by C. A. Macartney. London: Macmillan, 1970. 379p. bibliog. (Documentary History of Western Civilisation Series).

Much of this substantial publication is taken up with reprints of documents of the period, in contemporary English translation. The documents illustrate various trends in political, social and religious life in the period under review. There is an extensive commentary on the Counter-Reformation in the first five chapters and a vivid contemporary account of the 1683 siege of Vienna. The section dealing with economic affairs explains how Phillip von Hörnigk, the mercantilist, exerted a profound influence on Austrian economic policy right up to the 19th century. Of particular interest to the research historian are certain papers on Maria Theresa's constitutional relationship with Hungary and Leopold II's political credo.

143 **Prince Eugene of Savoy.**
Derek McKay. London: Thames & Hudson, 1977. 271p. maps. (Men in Office Series).

This scholarly account pays tribute to Prince Eugene's status as one of the great generals of history, despite his rejection by Louis XIV as unfit for service in his army and his subsequent espousal of the Imperial cause. It highlights his political as well as his military achievements and describes the personal interests of this life-long bachelor prince. Particular attention is paid to his contribution to creating the multi-national Austrian state and his activities as a discriminating and influential patron of the arts. For an earlier work, with excellent illustrations, stressing the almost unlimited powers given him by his Emperors, see Nicholas Henderson's *Prince Eugene of Savoy* (New York: Praeger, 1964).

144 **Austria's Eastern question, 1700-1790.**
Karl A. Roider. Princeton, New Jersey: Princeton University Press, 1982. 256p. 2 maps. bibliog.

From 1720, with the departure of the imminent threat to Austrian territory by the Turks after their failure to take Vienna in 1683, the Habsburg Empire had to consider its attitude to the Ottoman Empire. It had to decide whether to: join Peter the Great's Russia and expel the Turks altogether from Europe; regain its lost territories by fighting the Turks directly; keep Russia out of the Balkans by bolstering up the Ottoman Empire – in other words, to preserve the *status quo*. This is a scholarly and readable exposition of how the problem was tackled, and it is set against the background of the historic religious confrontation between Christianity and Islam. For a more specialized and limited study, based almost exclusively on official archives, see the same author's *The reluctant ally: Austria's policy in the Austro-Turkish war, 1737-1739* (Baton Rouge, Louisiana: State University Press, 1972.).

145 **Leopold I of Austria.**
John P. Spielman. London: Thames & Hudson, 1977. 240p. 2 maps. bibliog. (Men in Office Series).

Power politics feature as much as biographical detail in this, the first exhaustive study of Leopold I (1657-1705) to have appeared in English since 1709. The author concentrates on the interplay between Leopold's preoccupation with the dynastic tie to Spain and the local interests of the Austrian Bohemian and Magyar nobility, and describes with clarity and authority the expansion of the Austrian monarchy in the face of Turkish onslaught in the East and French aggression in the West. The book also reveals how Leopold's diplomats and generals built the territorial base for the Empire which dominated Central Europe until its dissolution in 1918.

146 **The siege of Vienna.**
John Walter Stoye. London: Collins, 1964; New York: Holt, Rinehart & Winston, 1965. 349p. maps. bibliog.

This is a definitive account, probably the most comprehensive yet published in English, of the greatest threat to the Habsburg Empire before its final overthrow in 1918. The author presents a balanced picture of the motivation behind Mehmet IV, the Turkish Sultan, in undertaking what was intended as the culmination of the Ottoman advance into Europe after over 250 years. It also reveals the military and diplomatic dilemmas faced by Leopold I who had insufficient forces of his own and faced an attack on both fronts with the French enemy to the west. However, the defeat of the Turkish forces with the timely arrival of the Emperor's German and Polish allies, and the subsequent pursuit deep into Hungary, had far-reaching effects and opened up a new period in the military history of Europe. The narrative is self-assured, objective and exciting and this volume represents a major achievement on a major theme.

147 **Infanta of Spain.**

Gladys Taylor. London: Phoenix House, 1960. 150p. bibliog.

The Infanta Margareta Theresa (1651-73), daughter of Philip IV of Spain and married to the Emperor Leopold I, is probably best known to the general public through the famous Velasquez painting of her. Three of her children died in childbirth and she herself was only twenty-one when she succumbed to a tumour of the throat. This readable and sympathetically written biography of her short life provides a good picture of the rigid formality of the 17th-century Spanish Court and the almost morbid preoccupations of the Spanish Habsburgs with their religious devotions.

148 **Die Türken vor Wien: Europa und die Entscheidung an der Donau, 1683.** (The Turks at Vienna's gates: Europe and the outcome on the Danube, 1683.)

Vienna: History Museum, 1983. 422p. maps.

The 1983 tercentenary exhibition of the Relief of Vienna from the Turks in 1683, held in that capital, was one of the major cultural events of recent years. The exhibition befitted the historical significance of a victory in which half Europe contributed to the final halting of the gradual infiltration of the West by the Ottoman Empire which had been taking place since before the fall of Constantinople in 1453. Although written in German, the English-speaking reader can readily follow the historical charts and diagrams and appreciate the copious illustrations of Turkish artefacts, domestic and military, to which the various contributors from the Historical Museum of the City of Vienna pay full homage as the flowering of a defeated but highly significant culture. Another commemorative publication in German, containing thirty-two essays by international specialists, profusely illustrated and with full chronological tables and a register of names of the leading protagonists, was published in 1982 with the same title *Die Türken vor Wien* by Residenz Verlag Salzburg under the editorship of Robert Waissenberger. This again could not be more authoritative and even for non-German readers provides sufficient of the flavour to merit serious attention.

149 **The Siege of Vienna; a poem.**

W. C. London: Printed for H. Hills, 1685. 40p.

Dedicated to the Earl of Plymouth, Lord Lieutenant of Worcester, Governor of his Majesties Garrison of Hull, this stirring account by an anonymous poet of the 1683 Siege of Vienna in rhyming couplets includes brief marginal annotations noting the sequence of events, which are described with panache and their fair share of gory detail. The work concludes with a fervent *Te Deum* for the deliverance of the capital from the Turkish invader.

Reforms and First Revolution (1740-1848)

Maria Theresa (1740-80)

150 **Austrian culture, 1700-1800. Jesuits and Jacobins: enlightenment and enlightened despotism in Austria.**
Paul Peter Bernard. Chicago: University of Illinois Press, 1971. 198p. bibliog.

Some students of history have assumed that Austria remained relatively untouched by the Age of Enlightenment during the reigns of Maria Theresa and her successor Joseph II. However, this author finds there is a close relationship between the literary outpourings of the Austrian intelligentsia and the role and political theory of Joseph II, who tried to transform traditional depotism by introducing some controversial reforms. Accordingly, Josephinism, as the cult came to be known, was not just an abstract political theory: there were, the author contends, real 'flesh and blood' Josephinians who formed a coherent moderate body of opinion. This is a lively account of a period of considerable intellectual activity in the country's history.

151 **Gerard van Swieten and his world, 1700-1772.**
Frank T. Brechka. The Hague: Martinus Nijhoff, 1970. 171p. bibliog. (International Archives of the History of Ideas, no. 36).

Gerard van Swieten was chief physician to, and a trusted counsellor of, Maria Theresa who frequently looked to the Netherlands to find intellectuals, Catholic wherever possible, to serve her and the Habsburg dynasty. Van Swieten was a transmitter of ideas, an interpreter and mediator between the advanced Western European culture and the backward condition of Austria in the mid-18th century, and as such, exerted considerable influence. He was not an innovator, but his reforms of medical and scientific education and his reorganization of the Imperial library, of which he became Director, had far-reaching effects. This helpful study explains his invaluable contribution to the Austrian enlightenment and was published to commemorate the bicentenary of his death.

152 **Maria Theresa.**
Edward Crankshaw. London: Longmans, 1967. 366p. maps. bibliog.

This is the first full-length biography of Maria Theresa in English for sixty years. It depicts a fascinating, complex and often misunderstood personality, unprepared for the problems of a disaffected and bankrupt Empire and surrounded by senile advisers; but facing these with unbreakable will and nevertheless initiating far-reaching reforms. The volume includes extracts from Maria Theresa's voluminous correspondence with her many children, and provides an evocative picture of rococo Vienna in the days of Gluck and Mozart.

153 **The wild goose and the eagle: a life of Marshal von Browne (1705-57).**

Christopher Duffy. London: Chatto & Windus. 1964. 278p. maps. bibliog.

Von Browne is indeed an odd name for a soldier in the Imperial Armies in the Wars of the Austrian Succession and the Seven Years' War and who fought against the Turks, in Bosnia, Transylvania, Silesia, Moravia, and the Danube lands. He rose to the highest rank and was not an Austrian at all, but an Irishman and was typical of so many who served the Empire and were ennobled – often with even more improbable titles. Some even joined the opposition like Maréchal Macdonald who took the Styrian capital, Graz, for Napoleon – to the continued dismay and incredulity of the population. The author, however, is a distinguished lecturer at the Royal Military Academy, Sandhurst, and an expert on these intriguing sidelines of military history, and this work is an important contribution to our knowledge not only of the Irish intrusion into the larger European scene but of that scene itself.

154 **The army of Maria Theresa: the armed forces of Imperial Austria, 1740-1780.**

Christopher Duffy. London: David & Charles, 1977. 256p. maps. bibliog. (Historic Army and Navy Series).

Under Maria Theresa the Empire was involved in two major wars, the War of Austrian Succession (1740-48), and the Seven Years' War (1756-63). England, always against France after the experiences with Louis XIV and in pursuit of the balance of power theory, sided with Austria in the former but against Austria in the latter. Neither war gave Austria any substantial territorial gains. On balance, Dr. Duffy, of the Department of War Studies at the Royal Military Academy, Sandhurst, provides a most readable account of the heterogenous forces Maria Theresa assembled, in which the Czechs predominated, welded into a powerful military instrument despite their mixed successes in the field. The author supplies full details of the regiments engaged, including unexpected references to the emigré soldiers of fortune from Ireland (see the same author's *The Wild Goose and the Eagle q.v.*) and the whole military complex. He stresses Maria Theresa's personal interest in the fighting efficiency and welfare of her troops. Liberally illustrated and fully documented, this is an excellent introduction to a colourful and heroic period of the Empire's history, recalled incidentally by major exhibitions and celebrations in Austria in 1980, which was the 200th anniversary of Maria Theresa's death.

155 **Maria Theresa and other studies.**

George Peabody Gooch. London: Longmans, Green, 1951. 432p. bibliog.

This was one of the last works by a distinguished and long-lived historian who could deliver an hour-long lecture without notes of any kind. He based this volume on two sets of correspondence, published in the 19th century, between Maria Theresa and two of her eight children; Joseph II, and Maria Antonia, who as Marie Antoinette married Louis XVI of France. Neither gave her any domestic consolation in her personal travails over such worrying events as the Silesian wars:

Joseph was poles apart ideologically and Marie is exposed as a vapid personality with incorrigible frivolities, which she never grew out of. The author gamely puts this mass of documentation in its chronological setting. His touch is light, but the picture remains sad.

156 **The emancipation of the Austrian peasant, 1740-1798.**
Edith Murr Link. London: Oxford University Press; New York: Columbia University Press, 1949. 204p. bibliog.

The particular landowner-peasant relationship which had existed uninfluenced by the State for many years in the German Austrian lands was altered dramatically in the reign of Maria Theresa who introduced major agrarian reforms which eventually led to the full emancipation of the peasantry in 1848. This study outlines the position of the peasantry at the time of her accession and describes the reforms in some detail. These show that despite her natural sympathy for the peasants, Maria Theresa nevertheless had strong feelings about the fundamental rights of the nobility – a dichotomy of view which at times she found difficult to resolve.

157 **Maria Theresa and the House of Austria.**
C. A. Macartney. London: English Universities Press, 1969. 168p. bibliog. (Men and Their Times Series)

This brief biographical history of the Empress Maria Theresa is written in a lighter style than that normally adopted by this distinguished historian, yet it carries complete authority and conviction. The exposition of complicated administrative structures is very clear and the chapters on Maria Theresa's industrial and cultural reforms are excellent.

158 **Maria Theresa.**
Mary Maxwell Moffat. London: Methuen, 1911. 361p. maps. bibliog.

Although written over seventy years ago, this work has retained its interest because of the light it sheds on contemporary social conditions and the personal habits, likes and dislikes of Maria Theresa. Its main sources are despatches from ambassadors to the Court of Vienna and Maria Theresa's own correspondence, much of which has here been translated into English for the first time.

159 **The Austrian achievement, 1700-1800.**
Ernst Wangermann. London: Thames & Hudson, 1973. 201p. map. bibliog. (Library of European Civilisation Series).

This comprehensive and lavishly illustrated publication depicts the establishment of Habsburg Austria as a great power, not only in the military sphere, but also in the cultural sphere through the unique contribution it made during the 18th century to European civilisation in music, drama and architecture. The author shows how the religious, legal and educational reforms initiated by Maria Theresa and expanded by her successor, Joseph II, led to the gradual emergence of an informed public opinion on matters of artistic taste and achievement. Although social and cultural developments predominate due weight is also given to economic and religious influences.

160 **Serf, seigneur and sovereign: agrarian reform in 18th century Bohemia.**

William E. Wright. Minneapolis: University of Minnesota Press, 1966. 217p. bibliog.

The erosion and eventual loss of privileges enjoyed by the nobility in 18th-century Bohemia under pressure from Maria Theresa's and Joseph II's reforms was a far more gradual development than that in countries of Western Europe. This is a comparative study of the various systems of land reform then evolving with special focus on Bohemia. It is supported by a number of appendixes, illustrating different forms of contract, all in German.

Joseph II and the Napoleonic Wars (1780-1815)

161 **Joseph II.**

Paul Peter Bernard. Boston, Massachusetts: Twayne Publishers, 1968. 155p.

Joseph II, sole ruler (1780-90), after the death of Maria Theresa, is perhaps best known for his emancipation of the serfs, his dissolution of the monastic orders and his imposition of German as the official state language even in the fringe provinces. These were, however, only elements in a comprehensive extension of his predecessor's programme of creating a uniform, centralized but liberal state, inspired by the enlightenment of the age. Opposition to this 'Josephinism', as his theories were later described, led him inevitably into fierce repression and exposed the sharp conflict between enlightened principles and a desire to impose his will. This work is a well-documented analysis of this conflict over a wide range of subjects and its sequel, by the same author, studies one particular element in greater depth i.e., its impact on the workings of the criminal law. This is his *The Limits of Enlightenment: Joseph II and the Law*, (Urbana, Chicago; London: University of Illinois Press, 1979).

162 **Joseph II and enlightened despotism, 1780-1790.**

T. C. W. Blanning. London: Longmans, 1970. 184p. (Seminar Studies in History).

Basically designed for higher educational studies, this brief survey examines the main problems facing Joseph II in a historical and intellectual context. The work is based on eighteen original documents in English translation, contained in an appendix which can be studied independently of the main text. The author draws comparisons between Joseph II and two other 'enlightened despots', Frederick the Great and Catherine the Great, and concludes in desperate terms, as did the Emperor himself on his deathbed, that 'he was unfortunate in all his enterprises, sufferings and disasters'. A sad epitaph.

163 **Daily life in the Vienna of Mozart and Schubert.**
Marcel Brion, translated from the French by Jean Stewart. London: Weidenfeld & Nicolson, 1961. 288p. bibliog.

Drawing on a number of contemporary descriptions of Viennese life in the late 18th and early 19th centuries the author contrives to form a composite picture of society and its preoccupations. Music and theatre, both of which figure prominently, are seen as major unifying elements, while popular shows and entertainments, menageries and circuses, firework displays and even musical toys, which had a particular vogue at the time, all had their place in the life of the capital. The Biedermeier (ca. 1815-48) period is well-covered and the work concludes with a light-hearted view of the Congress of Vienna (September 1814-June 1815) seen through the eyes of a middle-class citizen bewildered at seeing his capital the scene of so much European activity.

164 **Joseph II: an imperial reformer for the Austrian Netherlands.**
Walter W. Davis. The Hague: Martinus Nijhoff, 1974. 338p. maps. bibliog.

Based on archival and monographic sources, this comprehensive study concentrates on the economically advanced, but constitutionally backward, Belgian provinces. It describes how Joseph II's well-meaning but frequently insensitive interventions into almost every aspect of public concern in this Habsburg dominion met only with increasingly stubborn resistance. The final, successful rebellion against the Habsburg Empire is fully described.

165 **The imperial loans: a study in financial and diplomatic history.**
Karl F. Helleiner. Oxford: Clarendon Press, 1965. 190p. bibliog.

The problems created by war-time lending to allied governments when borrowers fail to meet their financial obligations were successfully solved by mutual aid agreements after World War I. However, in 1795 and 1797 the Austrian Government, in pursuing the war against the French in which Britain sided with her, raised enormous sums in the London money market which were guaranteed by the British Government and which involved decisions of major monetary and military policy. In this study Professor Helleiner unravels the tangled web of these complicated negotiations and shows how subsequent demands by Britain for repayment during the next thirty years proved fruitless, due very largely to the evasion and bluff practised by the Austrian Government in pursuance of its national interests.

166 **Bohemia in the 18th century: a study in political, economic and social history with special reference to the reign of Leopold II, 1790-92.**
Robert Joseph Kerner. New York: Macmillan, 1932. bibliog.

This doctoral dissertation, fully revised in the light of later researches, is an important contribution to understanding why Bohemia presented such an intractable problem to the central Habsburg administration, particularly after the end of the Thirty Years' War in 1648. In concentrating on the reigns of Joseph II and Leopold II at the end of the 18th century, the author pinpoints a dilemma. Reforms by Joseph and their revision by Leopold II in the light of opposition may have temporarily affected the precise relationship between central government and the local administration. Notwithstanding this, they in no way satisfied the underlying desire in Bohemia for independence, religious tolerance and the official recognition of its Slav language.

167 **Napoleon's great adversaries: the Archduke Charles and the Austrian army, 1792-1814.**
Gunther Erich Rothenberg. *Journal of Modern History*, vol. 40 (1968), p. 155-65.

This is a skilfully written article by a distinguished military historian on the organization, leadership and achievements of the Austrian military machine in the Napoleonic wars. Most military studies of the Austrian rôle in the resistance to Napoleon have been written from a French point of view, and this is a most useful corrective. It concentrates less on the actual fighting than on the infrastructure of the army itself, which the author sees as a true reflection of all elements of Habsburg society.

168 **From Joseph II to the Jacobin trials: government policy and public opinion in the Habsburg dominions in the period of the French Revolution.**
Ernst Wangermann. London: Oxford University Press, 1969. 2nd ed. 218p. bibliog.

This study describes the impact of Joseph II's 'englightened despotism' on the life and political consciousness of his subjects and the discontent aroused by his reforms, especially among the non-privileged orders. Such discontent later turned to active opposition in the face of the repressive measures instituted by Francis II, who believed that only a conservative, and in many respects, reactionary, absolutism could prevent a régime of revolutionary terror in his Empire, as had happened in France after the French Revolution. This notable historian had earlier, in his essay 'The Habsburg Possessions and Germany' in the *New Cambridge Modern History, vol. 8, The American and French Revolutions, 1763-93*, edited by A. Goodwin (London: Cambridge University Press, 1965, p. 279-305) given a brief but clear and authoritative account of the repercussions of Joseph's foreign policy on the domestic difficulties studied more fully in the later work.

The age of Metternich and the Congress of Vienna (1815-48)

169 **A narrative of events in Vienna from Latour to Windischgrätz.**
Berthold Auerbach, translated from the German by John Edward Taylor. London: David Bogue, 1849, 252p.

The author, a German poet, presents a somewhat contemptuous but tragic account of the confusion, horror and public demoralization which marked the last days of the Revolution of 1848, portraying a profligate and utterly discredited aristocracy and a divided government administration. Latour was Austrian Minister of Defence at the time and was lynched by an angry mob of students and workers. Windischgrätz was the Commander-in-Chief of the imperial troops who captured Vienna from the revolutionaries in late October 1848.

170 **Stephan Széchenyi and the awakening of Hungarian nationalism, 1791-1841.**

György Barany. Princeton, New Jersey: Princeton University Press, 1968. 487p. map.

The Hungarian leader popularly associated with the Revolution of 1848 against Habsburg centralism and oppression was the radical nationalist, Ferenc Kossuth (1802-94), then a young and fiery provincial lawyer from the Slovak region. Nonetheless, the mastermind was his opposite counterpart in every way, the enlightened conservative reformer, Count Stephan Széchenyi (1791-1860), whom even Kossuth refers to as the greatest Hungarian. While in no way lagging behind Kossuth in attacking the Emperor, he widened the opposition case by rejecting a purely Magyar approach; all nationalities discriminated against were to be supported with help from other nations and in an atmosphere of liberty, progress and the emancipation of the under-privileged. Széchenyi's opposition to the Revolution of 1848 in no way made him ineffective as a constructive leader, for even after the defeat of the revolutionaries he continued to give Hungary inspiration in political and economic nationalistic terms and sowed the seeds for the 1867 Compromise, which was only achieved after his death. Although written primarily for university students in the United States and dealing only with events up to 1841, this compendious work places an individual nationalist movement in a wider European setting. It provides an important contribution to the understanding of this key period in the development of Austria which was progressively preoccupied with its nationality problems after the demise of the Holy Roman Empire in 1806.

171 **Metternich and the political police: security and subversion in the Habsburg Monarchy, 1815-1830.**

Donald E. Emerson. The Hague: Martinus Nijhoff, 1968. 197p.

This is a penetrating study of failure. Concentrating on the domestic policy of one who was a Minister for Foreign Affairs for forty years (1808-48), the author contrasts his aims and methods with those of the reformist Habsburg Emperor Joseph II (1780-90). Whereas Joseph upheld civil liberties and denounced domestic oppression, Metternich created a higher state police directed by the Foreign Office, which prophetically gave a foretaste of the Nazi régime. Operating through censorship, surveillance and controls on the movement of people and their residence, this attempt at ensuring the security of the state served instead only to subvert orderly government and public order. Moreover, Metternich, despite his own system, was taken by surprise by the Europe-wide revolutions of 1830 and 1848.

172 **Metternich.**

Andrew Milne. London: University of London Press, 1975. 181p. 9 maps.

This thoughtful book by a schoolmaster describes Metternich's rise, his role at the Congress of Vienna which presided over Napoleon's downfall, and his subsequent diplomatic achievements in the face of increasingly articulate opposition. It summarizes his two basic objectives as peace and stability in Europe, and the acquisition of a breathing-space for revitalizing the Habsburg Empire which he believed was fundamental to maintaining the European balance of power. The author concedes, however, that Metternich's conservatism in his domestic policies was sterile rather than dynamic in character.

173 **Vienna in the age of Metternich: from Napoleon to Metternich, 1805-1848.**

Stella Musulin. London: Faber & Faber, 1975. 328p. 3 maps. bibliog.

In this overall view of Viennese society in the Metternich era the author analyses the major figures of political influence and their relationships one with another. She describes in an engaging manner the lifestyle of each stratum of society and shows how, despite the outward glitter of the Congress of Vienna, it was still a world of insecurity, introspection and unease.

174 **The crimes of the House of Habsburg against its own liege subjects.**

Francis William Newman. London: John Chapman, 1853. 60p.

This tract by the free-thinking brother of Cardinal Newman is an abridged version of Elizabeth Peabody's book with the same title, published in New York in 1852 as a condemnation of Austria's oppression of the subject states. It is a powerful, vicious attack on the absolutist Austrian régime and deals in particularly scathing terms with the suppression of the Hungarian Revolution in 1848, in which England's failure to intervene is also deeply deplored.

175 **The Congress of Vienna.**

Harold Nicolson. London: Constable, 1946. 302p. 2 maps.

The author resigned from the British Diplomatic Service in mid-career to concentrate on writing. It is intriguing to find one who had served in the British delegation at Versailles after World War I writing in the period immediately following World War II about the negotiations which followed the Napolenic Wars. Despite difficulties in access to library sources in the confused situation after a major war, no one was better suited to draw conclusions and comparisons and his thumbnail sketches of the main protagonists at the Congress are a valuable addition to a masterly work.

176 **Metternich.**

Alan Palmer. London: Weidenfeld & Nicolson, 1972. 405p. maps. bibliog.

This biography illustrates well the extraordinarily wide range of Metternich's personal participation in the shaping of Europe during his long tenure of power as Foreign Minister from 1809 to 1848. The author claims that the vituperation to which he was so frequently subjected did less than justice to diplomatic skills second only to those of Talleyrand, and achievements that were often triumphs of expediency as much as rigid principle. The author was fortunate in that he was able to draw on Metternich's collected papers which re-appeared in 1972. These had been scrupulously sorted by his son at the time and published after his death, when they are understood not to have enhanced his reputation, but when taken fully into account in the present work contributed effectively to the assessment quoted above. It is not clear whether they were available to Arthur Herman in his *Metternich* (London: George Allen & Unwin, 1932. 370p. bibliog.) but this much earlier work, which presented a rewarding picture of Metternich's own personal predilections, habits and interests, made the running in countering contemporary and subsequent criticisms of his allegedly unwavering 'anti-revolutionary' political creed. Herman claimed that this was applied with more flexibility than had been recognized and was directed only towards achieving continued stability.

177 **Metternich's projects for reform in Austria.**

Egon Radvany. The Hague: Martinus Nijhoff, 1971. 184p. bibliog.

The aftermath of the French Revolution and the Napoleonic wars cried out for the rationalization and modernization of the political and administrative structure of the Habsburg Empire. Metternich's Emperor, Francis I, had, however, other ideas; and an internal rivalry developed between them. Metternich was first and foremost a foreign affairs specialist and this was his real portfolio; he never really gained control of the internal political scene for which he was also responsible. His successful reforms were outnumbered by the unsuccessful, on which this book concentrates, and he was equally at odds with his ministerial colleagues. The value of this book lies particularly in the study of Metternich's character.

178 **The Viennese Revolution of 1848.**

John R. Rath. Austin, Texas: University of Texas Press, 1957. 424p. 3 maps. bibliog.

This is undoubtedly the most comprehensive English work on this subject and the volume is written by a recognized authority on central European history. The reader is presented with a dramatic reconstruction of events and a vivid portrayal of the main personalities involved. The author analyses the revolution from a contemporary standpoint and offers a balanced and dispassionate all-round view. He is particularly concerned with public opinion in Vienna both before and after the event, as reflected in the extensive translations of contemporary writings which accompany his text.

179 **Austria and the Papacy in the age of Metternich: between conflicts and co-operation, 1809-1830.**

Alan J. Reinerman. Washington, DC: Catholic University of America Press, 1979. 254p. bibliog.

This is the first systematic study of this hitherto neglected aspect of the age of Metternich. It brings out the importance to Metternich of maintaining good relations with Rome in his lifelong struggle to preserve the Austrian Empire intact; and likewise the importance to Rome of Austria-Hungary as the sole protector and chief exponent of policy in Europe. The archives used are drawn from Vienna, the Vatican, Prague, Budapest and Madrid.

180 **Metternich: the 'coachman of Europe'.**
Edited by Henry F. Schwarz. Boston, Massachusetts: D. C. Heath, 1962. 107p. bibliog.

This collection of seven essays by a group of distinguished contemporary international historians reflects a wide spectrum of conflicting views on Metternich's achievements, ranging from Viktor Bibl's comment 'a narrow-minded reactionary who saw only the negative side of the French Revolution' to Henry Kissinger's description of him as 'the last champion of enlightenment and real conservatism'.

181 **Prince Felix zu Schwarzenberg, Prime Minister of Austria, 1848-1852.**
Adolph Schwarzenberg. New York: Columbia University Press, 1946. 244p. bibliog.

Despite other historians' criticisms of his lack of recognition of the emerging nationalities, the author shows how much Prince Schwarzenberg did both to transform chaos into order during these four important years and to create the Austrian unitary State. An interesting interpretative assessment which takes into account the lack of relevant archival material, for Schwarzenberg kept no personal memoirs. The author is a great grand-nephew of Prince Felix Schwarzenberg.

182 **The survival of the Habsburg Empire: Radetzky, the Imperial Army and the class war, 1848.**
Alan Sked. London, New York: Longman, 1979. 280p. map.

Field Marshal Radetzky is known throughout the world by the stirring march by Johann Strauss the elder, and certainly in Austria as the hero in the 1848-49 Revolutionary war of King Charles Albert of Piedmont and his Sardinians in the north Italian abortive struggle against imperial forces. This was an important feature in this turning point in Austrian history, which saw: the defeat of Hungarian resistance under Kossuth in an empire-wide revolutionary situation; the election of the Styrian Archduke John as president of the short lived Pan-German Parliament; and the resignation of the old régime figures Metternich and Ferdinand I, the latter in favour of the eighteen-year old Emperor, Francis Joseph I. This important study illuminates the basic paradox of a period of turmoil in which a widespread revolt, fostered in Italy principally by the patriotic nobility and elsewhere by the lower classes, was quashed in one vital theatre of war by a brilliantly-led and disciplined force equally manned by these 'lower classes'. It emphasizes the personal qualities of a remarkable commander and offers a penetrating analysis of the social problems involved.

183 **Austria in 1848-49: a history of the late political movements in Vienna, Milan, Venice and Prague.**
William H. Stiles. New York: Harper, 1852. 2 vols.

The author, the United States' Chargé d'Affaires at the Court of Vienna, by careful personal observation and recourse to a wide range of official documents, presents the reader with an honest, sober and impartial account of the revolutions of the mid-19th century in four major cities of the Habsburg Empire, a territory which was comparatively unknown outside Europe. He draws clear distinctions between the three parties which he claims made up the political spectrum of the period: the government party or monarchists; the radicals or 'reckless agitators; and the intelligent or moderate reformers. There are appendixes providing the texts of a number of treaties, protocols and ordinances.

184 **Metternich's Europe, 1813-1848.**
Edited by Mack Walker. London, Melbourne: Macmillan, 1968. 352p. (The Documentary History of Western Civilisation Series).

As can readily be surmized from the title of this series this is not so much a monograph on Metternich himself as a collection of material about this period inviting the reader to form his own judgment. The work contains contemporary personal recollections, official reports and even poems, pinpointing Metternich's contribution over a wide spectrum and placing it in an authentic documentary setting. It is invaluable as a portrayal of those elements with which he could so well have sympathized personally had he not been beaten to the ground by his reactionary Emperor, Francis I. The author catches the spirit of the age quite remarkably.

185 **The Congress of Vienna, 1814-1815.**
Sir Charles Webster. London: Thames & Hudson, 1963. 213p. bibliog.

This study by a distinguished political historian was originally prepared at the request of the British Foreign Office as a background for delegates attending the 1919 Peace Conference. It has been frequently reprinted since then. Written in eleven weeks, it gives a masterly and dramatic account of the interplay of personal rivalries and manoeuvres lying behind the Vienna negotiations. A historical monograph which is unlikely to be superseded.

Twilight of the Empire (1848-1918)

General

186 **The origins of the war of 1914.**
Luigi Albertini, edited and translated by Isabella M. Massey. London: Oxford University Press, 1952-1957. 3 vols.

This substantial work is by an Italian historian and editor of a leading daily newspaper. It is of particular importance in that it reports on the conclusions of an independent body of international historians determined to correct the bias shown by documents published by the protagonists in World War II in their own interest. It was only from 1937 onwards that scholars were given access to certain key diplomatic documents including: private, unpublished letters from ambassadors; records of special interviews; and the results of judicial enquiries. The full range of these documents totalled some 60,000 pages, and the author and his collaborators were able to compile a most comprehensive survey. Although naturally not the last word on this contentious theme, its breadth of documentation, and the rigorous and objective approach of its distinguished author, make it compulsive reading. For those requiring further detail on the life, career and plans of the luckless heir to the Austrian throne whose assassination at Sarajevo triggered off the whole tragedy, a good summary appears in the opening chapter of the slightly later work on the same subject by Sidney B. Fay entitled *Origins of World War I* (New York: Free Press, 1966. 2nd ed. rev.)

187 **The Austro-Marxists, 1890-1918; a psychobiographical study.**
Mark E. Blum. Lexington, Kentucky: University Press of Kentucky, 1985. 254p. bibliog.

In this original and strongly inspired analysis, the author traces the roots of the political philosophy of four leading exponents of Austro-Marxism in their various family and social backgrounds i.e., Karl Renner, Otto Bauer, Max Adler and Friedrich Adler. He devotes the major part of his study to a systematic examination of their thought and milieu, explaining that for them Austro-Marxism was not simply a description of objective political thought but a metaphor designed to help them deal with their personal problems and the needs of the day. However, the turmoil of World War I and the times in which they lived called for deeds not rhetoric and this was an imperative to which they were unable to respond.

188 **Political radicalism in late Imperial Vienna: origins of the Christian Social movement, 1848-1897.**
John Boyer. Chicago: University of Chicago Press, 1981. 577p. map. bibliog.

In this scholarly and thoroughly researched survey the author shows how the Christian Social Party, in a well-co-ordinated and systematic campaign, set out to destroy Viennese liberalism in the late 19th century. This was done in four separate and distinctive stages by directing attention first to the workers, then the clergy, then the civil service and finally, the property owners. Much of the work centres on the charismatic figure of Karl Lueger, the mayor of Vienna and a powerful and popular leader of his party.

189 **From Sadowa to Sarajevo: foreign policy of Austria-Hungary, 1866-1914.**
Francis Roy Bridge. London, Boston: Routledge & Kegan Paul, 1972. 457p. 4 maps. bibliog.

This is a lucid survey by a diplomatic historian of substance. The volume examines the intricacies of the Dual Monarchy's relations with the Great Powers of Europe and the smaller states surrounding it and analyses the diplomatic, military, political and economic factors involved. The work is based on Austrian and British state archives and a large number of private papers, with some original documents.

190 **Maximilian and Charlotte of Mexico.**
Egon Conte Corti, translated form the German by Catherine Alison Phillips. London, New York: Alfred Knopf, 1928. 2 vols.

Francis Joseph's eldest brother Maximilian renounced his imperial rights in 1864 to accept the emperorship of Mexico during the period of French Intervention under Napoleon III aimed at suppressing the Juárez revolution. His vision of recreating the glory of Charles V's Spanish Empire soon faded, however, and he was executed by the rebels in 1867; although his Belgian wife Charlotte survived, in poor mental health, for another 60 years. This is a thorough and fully-documented account, based on the author's researches into the Maximilian archives in Vienna. Complete texts of correspondence between Maximilian and Napoleon III, and between the two Empresses Charlotte and Eugénie are included. The Mexican venture is, however, depicted mainly from a European viewpoint.

191 **The battle of Königgrätz.**
Gordon Alexander Craig. London: Weidenfeld & Nicolson, 1965. 216p. maps. illus. bibliog. (Great Battles of History Series).

Königgrätz was the Austrian name for the small north Bohemian town on the River Elbe of Sádová, or Sadowa, as it is often more generally known. On 3 July 1866 the Austrians were decisively defeated by the Prussians in a battle which ended the so-called Seven Weeks' War and had immense political consequences. It enabled Prussia to impose a dictated armed peace on Europe and dented the supranational concept of the Habsburg monarchy. It also imposed a severe setback on parliamentary experiments in Austria under the Austria-Hungarian Compromise which followed. Furthermore, it marked the loss to Austria of the province of Venezia Giulia in north Italy which, after the earlier loss of Lombardy in 1859, restricted her possessions there to Venezia Friulana. This was the first battle in 19th-century Europe to make effective use of the technology of the Industrial Revolution, (for example, railways, telegraphy and the Prussian breech-loading rifle – the Austrians still used the muzzle loader). Such technology had, of course, been used in the American Civil War of 1861-65 which preceded the Battle of Königgrätz. Professor Craig traces the whole course of the war and provides full details of the battle.

192 **The fall of the House of Habsburg.**
Edward Crankshaw. London: Macmillan, 1981. 419p. rep. maps.

Any attempt to assess impartially the achievements and failures of the Habsburg Empire in its declining years must inevitably take full account of the nationalities problem. This distinguished writer is clearly sympathetic to the Habsburg dynasty in the face of Magyar opposition. He offers some vivid character studies of the main protagonists and paints an impressive portrait of the conflicting demands of all the national groups within the Empire, which, while clinging on the one hand to it for protection, sought to weaken it to further their own particular ends. Another work by the same author entitled *The Habsburgs* (London: Weidenfeld & Nicolson, 1971. 259p. map.) contains a shorter version of the argument but is handsomely illustrated with 38 colour plates and copious black-and-white illustrations; it is much more than the typical coffee-table book despite its format.

193 **Archduke Francis Ferdinand.**

Victor Eisenmenger. London: Selwyn & Blount, 1928. 285p.

Much of the content of this book, written by the archduke's personal physician, lies not unexpectedly in the wealth of medical details he offers regarding his subject's illnesses. Notwithstanding this, the author also provides some rare insights into court intrigues and the family life of the Archduke. Although, according to the introduction, the book is intended as an objective view by someone in Francis Ferdinand's confidence, there is a surprising streak of vindictiveness which emerges in some of the writing which tends to highlight the bad qualities as opposed to the good.

194 **Herzl.**

Amos Elon. London: Weidenfeld & Nicolson, 1975. 448p. bibliog.

Theodor Herzl (1860-1904) was born in Budapest and is generally regarded as the founder of Zionism. The author had the advantage of the full support from his older colleague, Alex Bean, the standard biographer of Herzl, in this up-to-date re-examination of Herzl's life and achievements. The volume is based on the Herzl archives in Jerusalem to which the author was given full access. Elon also discovered in Vienna various unpublished memoirs of Herzl's contemporaries, many of whom had had an important influence on him during his formative period there as a law student and later as a leading journalist and dramatist. This book is attractively written and well-illustrated with contemporary photographs; it strikes a pleasing balance between Herzl's ideological and emotional development.

195 **The Viennese enlightenment.**

Edited by Mark Francis. Beckenham, England: Croom Helm, 1985. 170p. bibliog.

The editor, a senior lecturer in political science at Canterbury University, New Zealand, has gathered in a single volume a collection of essays by a number of specialists illustrating the extraordinary wide range of Viennese intellectual and artistic achievement from the turn of the century to World War II. The six chapters are entitled: 'The genesis of the imperial mind' by S. A. M. Adshead; 'The Radetzky march, Roth and the Habsburg myth' by P. Manger; 'The Austrian mind in exile' by H. Kelsen, P. Schumpeter, W. Hayek, and M. Francis; 'Freud and the enlightenment' by M. Francis and B. Stacey; 'Arthur Schnitzler's literary diagnosis of the Viennese mind' by P. F. S. Falkenburg; and 'The challenge of the musical mind' by H. Lees.

196 **The Habsburg twilight.**

Sarah Gainham. London: Weidenfeld & Nicolson, 1979. 242p.

Here is an inductive approach to a key period. Rather than stating conclusions first and then giving illustrations, as many scholarly studies have done, the author deliberately examines a selection of leading figures of the period and invites the reader to put them into perspective. There are: Crown Prince Rudolph, the suicide of Mayerling; Karl Lueger, the socialist mayor of Vienna; Anna Sacher, founder of the famous hotel of that name in Vienna, and the chocolate cake (Sachertorte) that goes with it; Katharina Schratt, the actress who sustained the

Emperor Francis Joseph in his later years, both before and after his wife's assassination; Colonel Redl, the homosexual staff officer convicted of spying; Gustav Mahler, the misunderstood Opera Director and composer; Gustav Klimt, the breakaway painter of the Art Nouveau school; and Theodor Herzl, the founder of Zionism. Most of these came from the lower-middle classes, and the author's tentative conclusions – which the reader is invited to consider – on the nature of Viennese society at the turn of the century make excellent reading.

197 **An economic spurt that failed.**
Alexander Gerschenkron. Princeton, New Jersey: Princeton University Press, 1977. 172p. map.

A brief but significant period in the country's history at the turn of the century saw a bold attempt by the Austrian government, with heavy financial backing, to solve its economic problems and ease its nationalities' problems by building an international rail link between Vienna and the Balkans. The railway was designed to open up the Empire and improve inter-state communications. The scheme, which was imaginative and perfectly realizable, was at first successful but subsequently foundered because of the obstruction of the then Austrian Minister of Finance, himself an economist, for reasons of doctrinaire financial orthodoxy. This fascinating episode in Austria's industrial history is here recounted in clear and graphic terms.

198 **Francis Joseph and Napoleon III, 1852-1864.**
Charles William Hallberg. New York: Brookman Associates, 1955. 448p. bibliog.

This account of diplomatic history fills a much-needed gap in the study of Austro-French relations in the 19th century. The period covered was one in which France was on the offensive against her central and eastern European neighbours and had already championed the causes of the nationalities within the Habsburg boundaries. Austria, however, was on the defensive, forfeiting her claims against Turkey after her vacillation in the Crimean war and having to abandon all north Italy except Venice in the Sardinian war in which Napoleon was involved. Neither Napoleon III nor Francis Joseph could foresee that by 1870 Bismarck would have outmanoeuvred them both, with the Austrian Emperor remaining the more durable of the two. A clear account of the complexity of inter-state treaties and political groupings.

199 **The Habsburg Empire: the world of the Austro-Hungarian Empire in original photographs, 1840-1916.**
Franz Hubmann, edited by Andrew Wheatcroft. London: Routledge & Kegan Paul, 1971. 320p.

This well-presented scrapbook of superb photographs of everyday life in the Habsburg Empire during the reign of Francis Joseph comes from public and private archival collections from all over the monarchy. It ranges over the widest possible spectrum and includes family scenes, entertainers, travel, fashion, coffee houses, the peacetime activities of the army and navy and many more aspects of the social life of the middle and lower classes in different parts of the Empire.

200 **The Austrian mind: an intellectual and social history, 1848-1938.**
William M. Johnston. Berkeley, California; Los Angeles; London: University of California Press, 1972. 515p. bibliog.

This American writer offers a conspectus of the intellectual achievement of seventy major thinkers over nearly a century – a daunting task. Some key themes emerge: an Empire sustained by a bureaucracy but continually harassed by a background of pressures for reform; the stimulating creativity of Vienna – coffee houses and palaces as a background to the intellectual triumphs of the philosopher Wittgenstein and the psychiatrist, Freud; and the role of the provinces, especially Bohemia and Hungary, as reformist counterparts. This is basically a study of the educated middle class in Habsburg Austro-Hungary, with the emphasis on Vienna. It is important as an attempt at a synthesis by a non-Austrian scholar in the fortunate position of being able to distance himself from his subject – geographically, socially and philosophically. A deeply researched work which covers a great deal of ground. Nine years later the same author expanded on one of his main themes i.e., Viennese life, in his *Vienna: the Golden Age, 1815-1914* (New York: Clarkson N. Potter, 1981). Here he concentrated on the period from the end of the Napoleonic wars to the beginning of World War I, omitting the sequel but including the Biedermeier, with more illustrations and a most helpful chronological table of historical and cultural events, both within the Empire and beyond. The text is as perceptive as the earlier study and the whole 19th century in the capital is interpreted with the same capacity to get beneath the Austrian skin.

201 **The multinational Empire: nationalism and national reform in the Habsburg Monarchy 1848-1918.**
Robert A. Kann. New York: Columbia University Press, 1950. 2 vols. maps. bibliog.

The author, who has made a special study of the nationalities problem in the Habsburg monarchy, traces in volume 1 the growth of nationalism within the ethnic groups with an independent political history (Germans, Magyars, Czechs, Poles, Croats, Italians), and those without one (Slovaks, Serbs, Slovenes, Romanians and Ruthenians). The fact that Austria's political frontiers cut across the ethnic frontiers in most instances is well brought out. Volume 2 deals with the Empire's various attempts to introduce structural reforms, centred on the two different approaches of independent national states and political union, and analyses how and why these all failed.

202 **Suffragette for peace.**
Beatrix Kempf, translated from the German by R. W. Last. London: Oswald Wolff, 1972. 188p.

Originally published in German in 1964 to commemorate the 50th anniversary of her death, this is a brief descriptive and readable biography of Bertha von Suttner (1843-1914). It tells the story of a remarkable woman who gained international fame as an ardent propagandist and lifelong campaigner for the cause of world peace, and as a brilliant lecturer and distinguished writer. Suttner travelled widely in Europe, was at one time secretary to Alfred Nobel in Paris and later worked for the International Arbitration and Peace Organisation in London. Her major work *Die Waffen nieder* (Lay down your arms) written in 1890, made a world-wide impact. She was the first woman to win a Nobel Peace Prize and was one of the first women journalists of all time.

203 **The Habsburg Monarchy as a customs union: economic development in Austria-Hungary in the 19th century.**
John Komlos. Princeton, New Jersey: Princeton University Press, 1983. 347p. bibliog.

This expanded and revised version of a doctoral dissertation is a study of the interaction between the Austrian and Hungarian halves of the Dual Monarchy in the economic sphere. It describes the benefits of the existence of the Habsburg 'common market' to its two major constituents. Contrary to the accepted view of many historians, the author concludes that the enlarged market offered more advantages than drawbacks, and he provides copious statistical data in support of his argument.

204 **Habsburg Monarchy, 1867-1914.**
Arthur James May. Cambridge, Massachusetts: Harvard University Press, 1951. 532p. bibliog.

This is an accurate, clear, objective and comprehensive study of the Austro-Hungarian Monarchy from the Compromise of 1867 to the outbreak of World War I. It was written at a time when a detached historical view had become possible and while some other studies concentrate on the Establishment aspect and its contribution to the internal administration, this one, while maintaining an overall balanced view, is particularly strong on foreign policy and nationality problems. The volume ends with an interesting chapter on schemes for reforms which represented options which were always open to the Establishment but whose failure to come to fruition was as inevitable as the doom of the Empire itself.

205 **Last days of Imperial Vienna.**
Robert Pick. London: Weidenfeld & Nicolson, 1975. 259p. map. bibliog.

Based on press archival material and personal interviews and drawing on his own diaries and memory, this well-known essayist has recreated in vivid detail the atmosphere of tension and uncertainty in the capital in the last days of the Habsburg Empire. There are graphic accounts of the city workers being spurred on to revolution, Viennese politicians trying to hold the ring of a great Empire against the forces of disintegration and even of Viennese children being saved from starvation with food parcels from the Allies.

206 **Banking and industrialisation in Austria-Hungary: the role of the banks in the industrialisation of the Czech Crownlands, 1873-1914.**
Richard L. Rudolph. London; Cambridge, England: Cambridge University Press, 1976. 291p. bibliog.

Research into the economic history of the Austro-Hungarian monarchy is still largely undeveloped and this work is a useful contribution to a little-known but important subject. The author examines the relationship between the banks in the

Dual Monarchy and the primary industrial regions of Bohemia, Moravia and Silesia. After a brief survey of the overall development of the Austrian economy, the author discusses special features affecting economic developments in the Czech Crown lands, and examines the general financial structure of the major banks and sources of industrial credit during the period under review. A work for the economic historian.

207 **The Austrian court in the 19th century.**
Sir Horace Rumbold. London: Methuen, 1909. 383p.

Based partly on his experience as British ambassador in Vienna in the last quarter of the 19th century, this account is a combination of memoir and history. The approach and style of writing, though at times slightly pretentious, is clearly that of an observant diplomat and contains many passages of anecdotal relief which will delight the reader and give him a genuine flavour of Austrian court life and customs during this period.

208 **Austria, Great Britain and the Crimean War.**
Paul W. Schroeder. Ithaca, New York: Cornell University Press, 1972. 544p. 2 maps. bibliog.

This scholarly work is sub-titled 'The destruction of the European Concert' (Britain, Russia, Austria, France, Prussia), and examines the reasons for the breakdown of the existing international system in Europe and the spirit and style of European diplomacy which followed the Crimean War. The author argues that Austria's aim was not to exploit the situation but to achieve a European solution to the Eastern question through a consensus approach with the West. However, all her efforts were constantly frustrated by the Western Powers, with Britain in a spirit of confrontation, undermining the concert at Austria's expense.

209 **The end of Austria-Hungary.**
Leo Valiani, translated from the Italian by Eric Mosbreacher. London: Secker & Warburg, 1973. 474p. map. bibliog.

First published in 1966, this work has been extended to include a number of documents made available to the author since that date. The real strength of the Habsburg Empire has often been the subject of disagreement among historians. This writer takes the view that the Austria-Hungary connection was more of a stimulating than a retarding influence and that the reasons for the breakup were factors affecting nationalities and what he calls 'democracy demography'. He studies the question of federalism between the various nationalities of the monarchy but contends that, at least after the outbreak of World War I, it had very little chance of being implemented in the face of the explosive character of the antagonistic nationalism of its various peoples.

210 **Austrian national socialism before 1918.**
Andrew Gladding Whiteside. The Hague: Martinus Nijhoff, 1962. 143p. maps. bibliog.

Drawing on many archival sources and backed by an extensive bibliography, this survey serves as a useful introductory source for the reader wishing to study in depth the origins and development of the Austrian National Socialist movement. The author examines first how in the latter half of the 19th century, the Austro-Germans formed the movement to free themselves from Czech domination in the economic sphere and how their struggle to preserve their own language and culture became a national crusade. He then demonstrates that the lack of any clear-cut ideology and the ambiguity inherent in the movement led to its gradual fragmentation so that it later fell an easy prey to Hitler's aggressive actions.

211 **Happy retrospect: reminiscences of Count Wilczek, 1837-1922.**
Count Hans Wilczek, edited by his daughter, Elisabeth, Countess Kinsky-Wilczek, translated from the German by Arthur J. Ashton. London: G. Bell, 1934. 295p.

These reminiscences, which were written for the author's grandchildren, cover a life-span from the days of Metternich and Radetzky to the early years of the First Republic. In addition to holding the offices of privy counsellor and court chamberlain, Count Wilczek acquired a great reputation as a mathematician, geographer and explorer. His explorations in the Antarctic were largely responsible for setting up some of the earliest polar observation stations. He was also known for his support of many charitable organizations in Vienna, particularly those concerned with nursing and with housing the destitute. His many anecdotes are re-told with all the charm of a born raconteur.

212 **My adventures and misadventures.**
Prince Lajos Windischgraetz, translated from the German by Charles Kessler. London: Barrie & Rockcliff, 1966. 227p.

Charmingly written and modestly presented, these memoirs are based on three sets of the author's personal papers describing his activities as a soldier, politician and statesman. As a member of a distinguished family which had served the Habsburgs over many years, he was entrusted with diplomatic and military missions at an early age, during the course of which he became an ardent champion of the cause of Hungarian nationalism. With the connivance of the president and regent of Hungary, this led him to become involved in a scheme to finance revisionist propaganda by issuing forged French franc notes. During the subsequent public trial, he accepted full responsibility for his participation and was sentenced to four years' imprisonment. After World War II he went to Argentina as a geological prospector but ended up there as a dock labourer.

Francis Joseph and his family

213 **Francis Joseph, Emperor of Austria, King of Hungary.**
Eugen Bagger. New York: Putnam; London: Knickerbocker Press, 1927. 572p.

Written by a Hungarian American, this was the first standard biography to be published after the Emperor's death. It makes no startling disclosures, but develops its interpretation of the subject's character and personality from a wide spectrum of facts drawn largely from the traditional official sources.

214 **Clash of generations: a Habsburg family drama in the 19th century.**
Lavender Cassels. London: John Murray, 1973. 245p. map. bibliog.

The differences in temperament and outlook between the unbending and conformist Emperor Francis Joseph I and his worldly and frustrated son and heir Rudolph are set in strong relief in this story of a clash of personalities between age and youth. The work is based on what the respective protagonists wrote and did. The spotlight is also directed on Archduke Albert, the Emperor's older cousin and an ultra-conservative, who nevertheless questioned the Emperor's authority; and Archduke John Salvator, a relative of Rudolph's generation who was forward-looking and anxious for change in the suffocating atmosphere of the Habsburg Monarchy of the late-19th century.

215 **Elisabeth, Empress of Austria.**
Egon Conte Corti, translated from the German by Catherine Alison Phillips. London: Thornton, Butterworth, 1936. 393p. bibliog.

First published in 1934, this unsentimental work was immediately acclaimed as a masterly and convincing portrayal of this legendary and often misunderstood character. The author, using a number of unpublished documents in public and private collections, as well as correspondence between the Emperor Francis Joseph I and his Empress, and the diaries of Archduchess Valerie, their youngest daughter, throws fresh and interesting light on the conditions in which she spent her life.

216 **The lonely Empress: a biography of Elisabeth of Austria.**
Joan Haslip. London: Weidenfeld & Nicolson, 1965. 441p.

This is a popular, straightforward, chronological biography. It includes a short unevaluated bibliography, a list of manuscript sources and a good index. The portrayal of Emperor Francis Joseph is not flattering. There is some new material on Elisabeth's Irish and English connections, based partly on private papers made available in England.

217 **The Emperor and the actress: the love story of Emperor Franz Joseph and Katharina Schratt.**
Joan Haslip. London: Weidenfeld & Nicolson, 1972. 274p. bibliog.

The romantic friendship between the ageing Emperor Francis Joseph and the youthful Viennese actress, Katharina Schratt, which lasted for over thirty years, has caught the imagination of more than one writer. In this account the author uses some previously unpublished photos and correspondence between the two characters – some of which came on to the US market in the late 1950's – and shows how the Empress Elisabeth actively encouraged this relationship, which she hoped would bring the Emperor companionable solace and more into contact with the ordinary people of his capital.

218 **Mayerling: the facts behind the legend.**
Fritz Judtmann, translated from the German by Ewald Osers. London: George Harrap, 1968. 391p. bibliog.

The tragedy of Mayerling in January 1889, when the Emperor's son Crown Prince Rudolph committed suicide and shot his mistress, Mary Vetsera, at a hunting lodge, has probably given rise to more speculation, rumour and misinformation than any other single event in Habsburg history. Over the years the story has fascinated historians, novelists, journalists, scriptwriters, indeed writers of every description, and even film-makers. Their interpretation of the Crown Prince's motives and the sequence of events range from the purely romantic to the political and the psychological. Fritz Judtmann's painstaking and impartial analysis of both the official and other versions of the affair is a convincing attempt to separate fact and historically-unconfirmed hypotheses. He has even introduced some new material, partly based on evidence from descendants of some of the participants in the events surrounding the tragedy. He exposes the inconsistencies in the various accounts of these events and poses the questions which still need to be answered. For other treatments see Richard Barkeley's *The road to Mayerling* (q.v.); Judith Listowel's *A Habsburg tragedy* (q.v.); Carl Lonyay's *Rudolf: the tragedy of Mayerlng* (q.v.); Emil Franzel's *Crown Prince Rudolph and the Mayerling tragedy*(q.v.); and the offical police report *Das Mayerling Original* (q.v.).

219 **The Emperor Francis Joseph I: an intimate study.**
Eugen Ketterl, edited and related by Cissy Klastevsky, translated from the German by M. Ostheide. London: Skeffington, 1929. 253p.

The author of these reminiscences was Francis Joseph's valet-de-chambre for the last thirty years of the Emperor's life, with a staff of around a dozen under his control. He portrays his master with respect, but by no means sycophantically. The Emperor's servants, he tells us, were always treated with courtesy, his shouts being reserved for persons of rank. Discarded items from his modest wardrobe and personal effects were sold at public auctions, at which his used toothbrushes were much sought after. Ketterl accompanied the Emperor on military manoeuvres and foreign visits and gives his impressions of meeting Queen Victoria (who was accompanied by John Brown), Theodore Roosevelt and other rulers on these occasions. Despite the fact that after the Emperor's death he had to resort to legal action to ensure that he received his full pension, no trace of rancour colours his writing. The reader is offered a good deal more than 'below stairs' tittle-tattle.

220 **A Habsburg tragedy: Crown Prince Rudolf.**
Judith Listowel. London: Ascent Books, 1978. 316p. bibliog.

The author's grandfather was a member of the Hungarian Upper House and knew the entourage of Crown Prince Rudolph both in Austria and Hungary. Drawing on family records, discussions with descendants of Count Taafe (the Austrian premier at the time), as well as contemporary published material, Countess Listowel portrays Rudolph as highly intelligent, hard working but sadly misunderstood by his parents. Her rather surprising conclusion, based on an account given her by an unnamed descendant of the Crown Prince, was that although Rudolph contemplated suicide he was unable to take the final step, and that after shooting his mistress he himself was killed by a band of sharpshooters under the control of his elderly relative Archduke Albert, for reasons unexplained. Emil Franzel in his *Crown Prince Rudolph and the Mayerling tragedy* (Vienna: Herold Verlag, 1975, 86p.) does not attempt to get at the roots of the tragedy, but contrasts Rudolph's ambition for political power with his fear of the burden of responsibility: and the irreverence of the freethinker, which Rudolph undoubtedly was, with the respect he felt for his father and what he personified.

221 **Rudolf: the tragedy of Mayerling.**
Carl Lonyay. London: Hamish Hamilton, 1950. 219p. bibliog.

Two further accounts of the Mayerling tragedy offer the reader yet other perspectives. Count Lonyay, the nephew of the husband of Archduchess Stephanie (Rudolph's widow) by her second marriage, claims that the deliberate suppression of the facts by the Emperor and his court only served to heighten interest in the affair and give rise to continued conjecture and speculation. His book is a crushing indictment of the deception and duplicity practised at the court of Emperor Francis Joseph – 'a petty quill driver with whiskers attached and a sword dangling by his side.' Richard Barkeley, writing in defence of Rudolph in *The road to Mayerling: life and death of Crown Prince Rudolph of Austria* (London: Macmillan, 1958. 293p.) quotes from the royal archives at Windsor and regards his death as inevitably bound up with the fate of the Empire. He enumerates various motives for his suicide but reaches no conclusions, although he hints that dissatisfaction with the political conditions was the major contributing factor.

222 **The eagles die: Franz Joseph, Elisabeth and their Austria.**
George R. Marek. London: Hart-Davis, 1975. 505p. 2 maps. bibliog.

There is some excellent creative writing in this work by a well-known Viennese biographer. The author relates the lives of the Emperor and Empress to contemporary events, which themselves serve as the framework for the biography, impinging on Austria's fate at every turn. The characterization is skilful with the Emperor rigid and formal, Elisabeth capricious and restless, while the flavour, the tone and the turbulent creativity of Vienna in the midst of repression and rigidity at court are vividly captured. Only the main personalities are included, so as not to confuse the spectacle. A useful calendar of events in the political, historical, cultural and scientific fields is included as an appendix.

223 **The Emperor Francis Joseph and his times.**
Baron von Margutti. London: Hutchinson, 1921. 380p.

The author was the third generation of his family to serve the Habsburgs, and was an aide-de-camp in the imperial household from 1900 to 1917. He offers the reader attractively written first-hand impressions of life at the Vienna court, and others gathered 'from absolutely unimpeachable sources'. His highly observant and outspoken comments include some intriguing innuendos.

224 **Das Mayerling Original.** (The official Mayerling report.)
Vienna: Munich: Wilhelm Frick, 1955. 235p.

This is the text of the official file prepared by Baron Krauss, the president of the Imperial Police Presidium, on the Mayerling affair. It was discovered in 1955 in the Berlin State Archives and returned to Vienna. It is a facsimile of a collection of documents, police reports, observations, interview notes, and newspaper extracts, with a linking commentary – all heavily censored by the Emperor himself. Even so it is quite a dramatic presentation but hardly as authentic as it claims to be. A more recent, but surely not the final, twist to the whole tragic affair, is the claim made by Empress Zita, widow of the last Habsburg Emperor Charles I, and reported in *The Times* (20 December 1983) that Rudolph was in fact murdered by French agents sent by the future President Clémenceau, when angered by the Crown Prince's refusal to stage a coup d'état at his insistence to break the Empire's ties with Germany and form an alliance with France.

225 **The life of Crown Prince Rudolph of Habsburg.**
Oskar von Mitis, translated from the German by M. H. Jerome and Eileen O'Connor. London: Skeffington, 1930. 286p.

This was the first standard biography of Crown Prince Rudolph written without the assistance of official archives and other documentation not then available. It describes his travels and meetings with heads of state, his sympathies for Hungary and the southern Slavs, and his antipathy for the Hohenzollerns. A long appendix contains personal letters and documents found among Rudolph's effects, including letters to his cousin Ludwig of Bavaria, written during the last fifteen years of his life. The author presents a fairly dispassionate account of his subject's character as revealed by Crown Prince's actions and contemporary views.

226 **A nervous splendor, 1888-1889.**
Frederic Morton. Boston, Massachusetts: Little Brown, 1979; London: Weidenfeld & Nicolson, 1980. 329p. bibliog.

The author of this cameo is an American novelist who was born in Vienna and retains an interest in his roots. Taking as his peg the year in which Crown Prince Rudolph committed suicide at Mayerling because, in the author's view 'it seemed representative of a watershed when the Western dream started to go wrong', he weaves a story round the Prince which encompasses the full artistic flowering of the major practitioners of the day. Here are studies of: the psychiatrist Freud: the composers Brahms, Bruckner, Mahler, Strauss the younger and Hugo Wolf; the dramatist Schnitzler; and, surprisingly, Adolf Hitler, in the year of his birth.

227 **The secret of Sarajevo.**
Hertha Pauli. London: Collins, 1966. 320p. bibliog.

Archduke Francis Ferdinand, the victim of Sarajevo, has not always been well-served by historians. This book, written by the daughter of the court physician with the help of the archduke's grandson and with access to family papers, is mainly an attempt to rehabilitate him in a historical and personal context. The reader is confronted with a man, misunderstood and unpopular at court, ostracized by his brothers and sisters; with his morganatic wife, the Duchess of Hohenberg, excluded from all court functions. One's sympathies cannot fail to be aroused. The title of the book is somewhat misleading.

228 **Emperor Francis Joseph of Austria: a biography.**
Joseph Redlich. London, New York: Macmillan, 1929. 547p.

Written some ten years after the disintegration of the Habsburg Empire, this is one of the earliest English accounts of Francis Joseph to appear after his death. The author portrays him as a ruler who continued to regard his will as supreme over a long and critical period of European history, and whose main objective was to maintain his inherited Empire intact, rather than to be a great historical personality. The contradiction between these convictions and the political ideas and aspirations of his time is fully revealed. The source material includes much of the Emperor's correspondence.

229 **I was to be Empress.**
Princess Stephanie of Belgium. London: Ivor Nicholson & Watson, 1937. 270p.

Not written until the author was seventy-five, and censored by the Habsburgs because of her outspoken and critical descriptions of the stifling formalities of the Austrian court, these memoirs by the wife of Crown Prince Rudolph depict a simple, rather naïve and fanciful personality facing unwelcome pressures. Extracts from her correspondence with Crown Prince Rudolph throw a revealing light on his personality.

Nationalities problems

230 **The Eastern question, 1774-1923: a study in international relations.**
M. S. Anderson. London: Macmillan, 1966. 398p. 10 maps. bibliog.

This historically-accurate account of the complex series of events centred on the Ottoman Empire provides a good introduction for students of the subject. The rise of nationalism in the subject territories, the Balkan Wars and Austria's annexation of Bosnia in 1908 are well described.

231 **The nationality problems in the Habsburg Monarchy in the 19th century: a critical appraisal.**
Austrian History Yearbook. Houston, Texas: Rice University, 1967. vol. III.

The whole of the 1967 issue edited by John Rath of the *Austrian History Yearbook* (q.v.) was devoted to a reprint of a collection of papers presented at a conference held at Indiana in 1966 to discuss the nationality problem in the 19th century. A number of articles on related subjects were also included in this volume which runs to over 1,250 pages. Part I covers the dynasty and the imperial idea and examines the forces of consolidation, particularly the army, and views nationalism as applied to the Germans and Magyars as a disintegrating force. Part II deals with the other individual ethnic groupings, each of which is studied from the point of view of an integrating and disintegrating factor within the empire. In the final part social and economic subjects are discussed. One of the supplementary essays deals exhaustively with the current state of Habsburg studies in the United States. An invaluable compendium of knowledge on a most important subject.

232 **The whirlpool of Europe: Austria, Hungary and the Habsburgs.**
Archibald Ross Colquhoun, Ethel Colquhoun. London: Harper, 1907. 349p. maps.

The somewhat ambitious attempt in this work to interrelate the political, social and racial elements within the various countries of the Habsburg Empire only highlights the problems which the Dual Monarchy faced in the early years of this century, particularly in relation to the nationality problem. The authors' blend historical analysis with straightforward descriptive writing. The latter quality is shown to good effect in their accounts of social customs and the charming illustrations of peasant scenes and costumes which give this work a touch of immediacy.

233 **Shades of 1848: war, revolution and nationality conflicts in Austria-Hungary, 1914-1920.**
István Deák. In: *Revolutionary situations in Europe, 1917-1922*. Edited by C. L. Bertrand. Montreal: Concordia University, 1976. (Revolutionary Situations in Europe Series).

The author sets out to establish, with relevant examples, that the internal problems in the successor states of the Austrian Empire during World War I were caused mainly by nationality problems. He asserts, for example, that this was to a large extent the cause of the sudden rise of Bolshevism in Hungary and its subsequent setback in 1919; and that the support given to the successor states by the Entente (Russia, France, Great Britain) was accordingly the natural sequel.

234 **The nationality problem in Austria-Hungary: the reports of Alexander Vaida to Archduke Franz Ferdinand's chancellery.**
Edited by Keith Hitchins. Leiden, Netherlands: Brill, 1974. 188p. (Studies in East European History, no. 18).

Alexander Vaida was not only the Romanian National Party representative but was also the spokesman for all the non-Magyar nationalities during the coalition government in Hungary between 1906 and 1910. Archduke Francis Ferdinand favoured a federalized 'Great Austria' and was opposed to the Dual Monarchy and in pursuance of his aims needed the co-operation of the non-Magyar nationalities. He engaged Vaida as a member of his military chancellery and received regular reports from him on political conditions and public feeling in Hungary. The text of the letters and reports are in German, the excellent introduction, notes and index are in English.

235 **Francis Joseph and the Italians, 1848-1859.**
William A. Jenks. Charlottesville, Virginia: University Press of Virginia, 1978. 206p. bibliog.

This is the story of how Austria lost Italy in the mid-19th century. It is a penetrating analysis of Austrian policy over the whole spectrum, covering Lombardy and Venezia, Trieste, the central Italian Duchies, the Papal states and the two Sicilies. Some published sources have not been used but previously unpublished archives from Vienna, Rome, Turin and Paris have been utilized. The basic theme of the inherently uneasy relations between the Emperor of Austria and his satellites is presented with great clarity and the problem for Austria is shown to be primarily an internal one i.e., how the Empire was to be organized and governed; only secondarily was it regarded as having international implications.

236 **The social democrats and the conflict of nationalities in the Habsburg monarchy.**

Arthur G. Kogan. *Journal of Modern History*, vol. 21, no. 3 (Sept. 1949), p. 204-17.

The author starts from the premise that the international socialist movement in its early history had not concerned itself much with modern nationalism either in theory or practice. Notwithstanding this, socialists in the multinationalist states of the Habsburg Empire had had to face this problem long before 1914. The article shows how the Austrian social democrats were forced to meet this issue head on and evolve a nationalities programme in the final stages of the Empire. The writer concludes that its success could not be judged, however, since it was never tested in action and its structure in any case was swept away by subsequent events.

237 **The Habsburg Empire, 1804-1918.**

Hans Kohn. London; Princeton, New Jersey: Van Nostrand, 1961. 181p. bibliog. (Anvil Series).

Almost half of the text of this short history consists of selected readings from newspaper articles, political statements and official proclamations, thus providing a documented basis for judgments not always easily reached by other means. One of the views advanced is that the conservatism of the Habsburg dynasty and the nationalist intransigence of the Magyars and Germans prevented the establishment of a stable and democratic order in a multi-ethnic and multi-lingual state on the basis of democracy and federalism; unlike, for example, Switzerland where the German element also predominated.

238 **Nationalities problems in the Austro-Hungarian Empire.**

Ronald C. Monticone. *Polish Review*, vol. 13, no. 4 (autumn 1968), p. 110-25.

The author, an assistant professor of history at New York City University, traces the course of events in various parts of the Empire where resistance was active before and after the Compromise of 1867. He suggests that if only the Habsburgs had accepted federalization as a solution to the nationalities problem after the Revolution of 1848, the Empire might have assumed a different political outlook, perhaps looking towards England and France for its allies rather than Germany. However, even then, he concludes, federalization might not have enabled the monarchy to retain all its territories, especially the Italian Tirol, for which there was no solution.

239 **The lands between: a history of East Central Europe since the Congress of Vienna.**
Alan Palmer. London: Weidenfeld & Nicolson, 1970. 405p. maps. bibliog.

An initial analysis of the contradictions stemming from the Congress of Vienna (1815), and the effects of these in the area surveyed, is followed by well-presented summaries of the ensuing constitutional struggles and nationalist rivalries in the successor states. The story is continued through the 20th century, up to and including the Soviet invasion of Czechoslovakia in 1968. The treatment emphasizes how erroneous it is to blame the small states for the actions of the Great Powers.

240 **The 'sick heart' of modern Europe: the problem of the Danubian lands.**
Hugh Seton-Watson. Seattle, Washington: University of Washington Press, 1975. 76p.

These three lectures delivered at Washington University, though mainly concerned with Eastern Europe, include a clear and informative description of the Dual Monarchy established in 1867 and how the subsequent anti-Magyar ferment in surrounding countries stimulated Hungarian nationalism. The author's final conclusion is that despite changes in political systems, the underlying forces of nationalism persisted and 'sickened the heart' of the area.

241 **The making of a new Europe: R. W. Seton-Watson and the last years of Austria-Hungary.**
Hugh Seton-Watson, Christopher Seton-Watson. London: Methuen, 1981. 458p. map. bibliog.

Robert Seton-Watson was for many years Professor at the London University School of Slavonic and East European Studies. He was a distinguished academic and personal mentor of several British statesmen responsible for foreign policy after World War I. His two sons, both academics themselves, one occupying the Chair once held by his father, the other a lecturer at Oxford, have jointly undertaken a biographical study of their father, based on archival material and private papers of a number of individuals connected with him. They treat the subject under four periods: family history; 1905-1914; World War I; the Peace Settlements and creation of new States. Thus, the authors are not only recording history from the papers of a distinguished scholar, but are propounding the personal judgements of a practical and influential adviser with an intimate knowledge of the area and its events. One of the most significant of such judgements is that whereas the professor was not an uncompromising foe of the Habsburg Empire, as some would hold, he became convinced by the pre-1914 developments that the monarchy could no longer meet the needs of its peoples.

242 **The southern Slav question and the Habsburg monarchy.**
R. W. Seton-Watson. London: Constable, 1911. 463p. bibliog.

It is hardly an exaggeration to say that the southern Slav question was pivotal to the overall policy of the Habsburg monarchy and that the question of Croat-Serb unity lay at the very heart of the Empire's problems at the end of the last century.

Because of their geographical position the southern Slavs had the opportunity of upsetting the balance of power within the Dual Monarchy (Austria, Hungary) by allying themselves with Vienna rather than Budapest. Subsequent historical events, however, prevented this from occurring. This scholarly work by a historian of international standing is possibly the first summary in English of the history of the Croats and Serbs under Habsburg rule. Although written over seventy years ago, it can still be regarded as a standard work on the subject.

243 **The nationality question in Austrian education: the case of Ukrainians in Galicia, 1867-1914.**
Ann Sirka. Frankfurt, GFR; Cirencester, England: Peter D. Laing. 1980. 230p. bibliog. (European University Studies, Series 3, vol. 124).

At first sight this substantial monograph may seem to have little relevance to the mainstream of Austrian history. However, the problems of educational policy in this fringe area of the empire are typical of those which bedevilled the central administration in the period of the Dual Monarchy in an atmosphere of ever growing nationalist opposition. In annexing Galicia following Poland's first partition in 1772, Maria Theresa took over not only a Polish but a Ukrainian minority, with further complications in that although numerically equal, the Polish element, particularly the landed nobility and the urban middle classes, dominated the scene. Here, therefore, was a provincial administrative region with a different language and culture to that of either of the two centres of the Dual Monarchy and still further sub-divided within itself. It was a case with parallels in several other major areas, not only in the mainly German-speaking area (with an Italian minority in the Tirol and a Slovene one in Styria), but in Slav areas such as Bohemia and Moravia with sub-divisions of Slavonic languages as well. The problems so effectively set out here are thus a microcosm of the whole Habsburg scene in the concluding stages of its decline under the Dual Monarchy.

244 **Industrialisation of Bosnia-Herzegovina 1878-1918.**
Peter F. Sugar. Seattle, Washington: University of Washington Press, 1963. 275p. 3 maps. bibliog.

The former Turkish provinces of Bosnia and Herzegovina, the scene of the murder of Francis Ferdinand in 1914 which triggered off World War I, became Austro-Hungarian for all practical purposes in 1878. Initially, occupation was preferred for reasons of internal politics, but full annexation was decided on in 1908 to counter pressure from the Young Turk movement. The domestic history of this southernmost Habsburg province is a neglected subject and this important monograph does full justice to the way in which the central administration handled one of its gravest problems, the south Slav minorities. From public records in Sarajevo, Vienna, France and Britain, the author has pieced together the main strands of its progressive but slow industrialization, and considers the types of industry involved and its labour force.

245 **Serbia between east and west: the events of 1903-1908.**
Wayne S. Vucinich. Stanford, California: Stanford University Press; London: Oxford University Press, 1954. 304p. 3 maps. bibliog. (Stanford University History, Economics and Political Science Series, vol. 9).

A balanced and objective study based largely on Serbian and foreign diplomatic documents including hitherto-unpublished material. It traces the increasing antagonism between Serbia and Austria-Hungary during this period, and the check to Serbia's hopes of a rail link between Belgrade and the Adriatic that occurred with Austria's annexation of Bosnia in October 1908.

246 **The role of the Burgenland in the history of the Habsburg Monarchy.**
Fritz Zimmermann, Karl Stadler. In: the *Austrian History Yearbook*, vol. 8 (1972). Houston, Texas: Rice University.

These two surveys were written in connection with the 50th anniversary of Austria's acquisition of Burgenland from Hungary under the Treaty of St. Germain after World War I. The first, by Fritz Zimmermann, (p. 7-38), traces the close connections between Austria and Burgenland during the previous 900 years and shows how in many ways it had always had the characteristics of an Austrian province. Karl Stadler's contribution (p. 59-79) outlines the political intrigues, fraudulent plebiscite and Hungarian opposition which made the transfer of Burgenland one of the most protracted and difficult operations carried out by the peacemakers after World War I. It likewise describes how after the *Anschluss* in 1938, Burgenland was partitioned between Lower Austria and Styria, but the author does not explain how the Burgenland peasantry managed to maintain a provincial administration and preserve a provincial identity so successfully during the German occupation.

World War I

247 **Death of an Empire.**
Imre Balassa, translated from the Hungarian and edited by Harold Wimburg. London: Hutchinson, 1936. 280p.

Originally written in Hungarian and later adapted for an English readership, this intimate account of the tragic reign of Charles I of Austria, the last Habsburg Emperor, covers the period 1916 to 1922. The final stages of the drama with eleven different races pressing for autonomy after the death of the aged Francis Joseph and the powerlessness of the new and untrained Emperor, are vividly portrayed. A number of historical and family photos are included.

248 **Great Britain and Austria: a diplomatic history.**
Francis Roy Bridge. London: London School of Economics Research Monographs, 1972. 320p. bibliog.

In this well-researched and scholarly study, a leading diplomatic historian concentrates on Anglo-Austrian relationships in the prelude to World War I after nearly a century of mutual peace. He suggests that several accepted views should be challenged, notably that the media played a dominant part in creating the atmosphere for negotiations and that Count Aloys Lexa von Aerenthal, the Austrian foreign minister at the time of the Balkan wars, lacked skill and balance. Conversely he is not afraid to indulge in severe criticism of key British diplomats such as George Joachim Goschen, the ambassador at Vienna, and Nicholas Roderick O'Conor in Constantinople.

249 **The last Habsburg.**
Gordon Brook-Shepherd. London: Weidenfeld & Nicolson, 1968. 358p.

The reader is offered a sympathetic portrayal of Charles I, who withdrew from participation in the government of German-Austria in November 1918. He is portrayed as a man of courage, statesmanship and political acumen, surrounded by mediocre advisers. The author, while allowing that his rule was too short to form any evaluation in depth, stresses that Charles was well aware of Germany's expansionist aims and made valiant efforts to stem the course of events. The sources are unquoted, except for some interviews with the Empress Zita. This work provides a re-evaluation of Charles I's personality.

250 **Austria in dissolution.**
Stephen Burian, translated from the German by Brian Lunn. London: Ernest Benn, 1925. 455p.

Count Stephen Burian von Rajecz (1851-1922) was a Hungarian aristocrat who spent his working life in the Austro-Hungarian diplomatic service. In 1915, at the age of sixty-four, he was appointed foreign minister, succeeding Count von Berchtold who had negotiated the Empire into the war. Burian von Rajecz's plans for joint peace initiatives with Germany failed, however, and he resigned the following year; he also had the same lack of success on his recall in 1918. These memoirs, published posthumously, not only bring some fresh personal light into the Austrian World War I scene from an active, if relatively little-known participant, but contain analyses of some of the literature on the responsibility for that war which are of an important documentary value.

251 **Revolution in Central Europe, 1918-1919.**
F. L. Carsten. London: Temple Smith, 1972. 360p.

This volume is based on much unpublished material, including contemporary documents as well as archival sources. The author attempts to explain that the series of revolutions in central Europe, though outwardly successful, failed in their main objective – which was the democratization of state and society, because of overwhelming conservatism and social inertia.

252 **The road to Sarajevo.**
Vladimir Dedijer. London: MacGibbon & Kee, 1967. 550p. bibliog.

Controversy still persists among historians as to who, or what grouping, was the true instigator of the plot to assassinate Archduke Francis Ferdinand at Sarajevo. The author, who has had a lifelong interest in the subject, tries to unravel the complexities of the situation in Bosnia and Herzegovina in June 1914. He suggests that it was the Young Bosnians in their struggle for self-determination against their colonial status, rather than the Serbs, who played a major role. As a Bosnian and a distinguished partisan fighter in the Yugoslav resistance movement during World War II, Dedijer writes with great feeling and a strong sense of personal commitment. However, the corroborating evidence for some of his statements is not always to hand, and historical accuracy is at times obscured by personal prejudice. Nevertheless, this is a gripping story and an important contribution to the study of secret terrorist societies operating in the south-east Balkans in the early part of this century.

253 **Peace or partition: the Habsburg monarchy and British policy, 1914-1918.**

Wilfried Fest. London: George Prior, 1978. 269p. bibliog.

Based mainly on original archives, this survey describes how Britain had no real policy towards Austria at the beginning of World War I. It also indicates that as hostilities reached a deadlock Britain viewed with concern the growing dependence of Austria on Germany and in 1916 embarked on negotiations for a secret peace with Austria-Hungary after the accession of the last Emperor Charles I. The author reveals the contrasting influences of individual members of the British war cabinet, public opinion and the press at this time, and sets his analysis against the background of a general allied policy of favouring national self-determination for the peoples of central Europe.

254 **The desperate act – the assassination of Franz Ferdinand at Sarajevo.**

Roberta Strauss Feuerlicht. New York; Toronto; London; Sydney: McGraw-Hill. 1968. 168p. maps. bibliog.

This act, which triggered off World War I, was the sixth attempt to assassinate Francis Ferdinand in four years by the two gunmen who ultimately succeeded. They were young Bosnian left-wing extremists and were, remarkably, both still alive at the time of writing and gave extensive interviews. Cvetko Popovic described their motives, and Gavrilo Princip set the historical scene, claiming that it was an all-Bosnian affair with no involvement of the Serbian right-wing extremist Black Hand movement, as is normally implied. They made blunders in plenty, but this was part and parcel of their expressed view that it was all 'a local affair, our problem solved by us in our way'. A work of prime archival importance.

255 **Austro-Hungarian warships of World War I.**

René Greger. London: Ian Allan, 1976. 192p.

The author, whose father served in the Austrian navy, offers a 'Jane's fighting ships' treatment of every warship which served with the navy and even includes details of all aircraft designed and built for the Austro-Hungarian navy in World War I. The distribution of naval forces in the Mediterranean and the Danube flotilla in the Black Sea area are both considered, along with the specifications of ships laid down but not completed before the end of the war.

256 **Great Britain and Austria-Hungary during the first World War: a study in the formation of public opinion.**
Harry Hanak. London; New York: Oxford University Press, 1962. 312p. map. bibliog.

This is a valuable and well-annotated study of the attitudes of cultured and well-travelled Englishmen to the problems of Austria and its subject races in the 19th and early 20th centuries. The author shows how the sympathies of observers like the journalist, Wickham Steed, and the historian R. W. Seton-Watson, aroused by their contacts in the subject states, helped to advance the independence of Czechoslovakia and Yugoslavia and also gave English opinion a wider picture than that of a distant sprawling monarchy with which it was little-concerned.

257 **The Habsburg Empire in World War I: essays on the intellectual, military and economic aspects of the Habsburg war effort.**
Edited by Robert A. Kann, Béla Király, Paula Suttner Fichtner. Boulder, Colorado; New York: East European Quarterly, 1977. 247p. (East European Monographs, no. 23).

This is an important book on an insufficiently treated subject. It consists of papers by leading American and Austrian scholars presented to a conference held by the East European Section of the Centre for European Studies at the City University of New York. The Habsburg Empire in World War I is studied in three areas, domestic, military and intellectual. The somewhat surprising yet balanced conclusion is that the Empire was still an active, struggling and fighting reality right up to mid-1918 when the whole edifice collapsed under internal pressures and external reverses.

258 **Austro-Hungarian infantry, 1914-18.**
J. S. Lucas. London: Almark, 1973. 112p. bibliog.

The part played by the Austro-Hungarian armies in World War I may not be instantly recalled by contemporary readers, but their overall numbers and shattering losses paralleled those of their allies, the Germans. The author, who is on the staff of the London Imperial War Museum, is not only professionally well-placed to provide a detailed account of the organization, uniforms and equipment of these fated foot-sloggers, but has a personal and emotional interest in that his father-in-law was one of them. The appendixes on orders of battle and troop dispositions complete a well-documented study of material not previously available in a comprehensive format.

259 **Austria-Hungary and the war.**
Ernst Ludwig. New York: Ogilvie Publications, 1915. 220p.

On his return from an extended vacation trip to Europe at the height of World War I, the Consul for Austria-Hungary in Cleveland, Ohio, set to work on a book openly designed to influence American opinion in favour of the Austro-Hungarian cause. The result is a stirring propaganda effort, stressing the need to uphold the principles of international law and Christian civilization and vigorously denouncing Russia's expansionist aims and her policy of sowing disaffection among the subjects of the Dual Monarchy in the south Slav regions. With a rare degree of optimism, the author predicted a short war with an outcome favourable to, but not necessarily decisive for, Austria-Hungary's interests.

260 **The passing of the Habsburg monarchy, 1914-1918.**
Arthur James May. Philadelphia: University of Pennsylvania Press, 1966. maps. bibliog. 2 vols.

This two-volume work on a subject covered extensively, but seldom impartially, by historians is a sequel to the author's earlier work *The Habsburg Monarchy (1867-1914)* (q.v.). It is a solid appraisal of the various factors, both internal and external, which led to the final break-up of the Habsburg Empire. Although inevitably the work is largely concerned with diplomatic and military affairs, the author seeks to give due weight to relationships between Austria and Hungary and regards the Dual Monarchy as not entirely a failure in terms of the security, economic well-being and cultural betterment it brought to the two nations. The nationality question is not studied in great detail, although Czech resistance is rather played down while Magyar loyalty is somewhat overemphasized. There is an excellent chapter on American attitudes to the crumbling Empire – a subject often neglected by historians. The writing is fresh and clear throughout.

261 **The Emperor Karl.**
Count Arthur Polzer-Hoditz, translated from the German by D. F. Tait, F. S. Flint. London: Putnam, 1930. 470p.

As the last Habsburg Emperor's chief private secretary over a long period, the author was well-placed to compile these memoirs giving a pragmatic account of the final disruption of the Habsburg monarchy. He concludes that this process was primarily attributable to Hungarian chauvinism, and the book attempts to establish that Charles I's personal responsibility for it has been considerably exaggerated and misrepresented by historians.

262 **Austria-Hungary and Great Britain, 1908-1914.**
Alfred F. Pribram. London, New York, Toronto: Oxford University Press, 1951. 310p. bibliog.

The author is recognized as an outstanding historian and as such he had unique access to the documentation needed for this definitive study of a rather neglected subject. Moreover, he had already researched Austro-English relationships during the whole of the Napoleonic period; and the opening chapter of the present work, summarizing the whole field from 1200 to 1908, bears the fruit of this experience. He includes brief portraits of the monarchs, statesmen and ambassadors in the period under review and a detailed account of the diplomatic history, which encompassed the crisis in Bosnia-Herzegovina leading to its annexation in 1908 (after occupation since 1878), the two Balkan wars and the outbreak of World War I.

263 **The Imperial and Royal Austro-Hungarian Navy.**
Anthony Sokol. Annapolis, Maryland: US Naval Institute, 1968. 172p. bibliog. (Sea Power Monograph Series, no. 3).

Until its disbandment with the collapse of Austro-Hungary in 1918 and the creation of the modern state deprived of sea boundaries, the Imperial Navy had one of the longest histories of any in Europe and its full share of action in the Mediterranean and Black Sea areas. The author fought in its last and successful encounter, against the Italians, at Otranto in 1917 under the command of Admiral Horthy, later Regent of Hungary and a controversial figure in World War II. He has used his personal experience and enthusiasm in the preparation of this volume which summarizes the history of the navy from the Middle Ages onwards. One of the nine chapters is devoted to Admiral Tegetthoff's reorganization of the fleet between 1867 and 1897. The book is well-illustrated and documented and also stresses the navy's role in protecting trade, and the merchant navy, particularly in times of hostilities.

264 **The Habsburg Monarchy.**

Henry Wickham Steed. London: Constable. 4th ed. 1919. 304p.

This is a work of historical importance in that the author was a senior *Times* correspondent and an unrivalled observer of the European scene, writing originally just before the outbreak of World War I. His aim in this work was twofold: historical – to reveal the 'peculiar realities that lay behind the complicated phenomena of public and social life in the Habsburg dominions'; and reformist – to propose an evolution towards a form of internal organization better suited than the Dual Monarchy to the needs of its peoples. It was clearly too much to expect that this highly sympathetic piece of special pleading would have any influence on the course of events, and the distinguished author had to admit in later editions, including this final one, that the ultimatum to Serbia after Sarajevo was 'committing suicide'. This clear and penetrating exposition, however, has an immediacy in its writing that makes it transcend its period and renders it one of the most important studies of the whole tragedy.

265 **Eagles on the crescent: Germany, Austria and the diplomacy of the Turkish Alliance, 1914-1918.**

Frank G. Weber. Ithaca; London: Cornell University Press, 1970. 262p. map. bibliog.

The author considers Turkish entry into World War I as a liability resulting from Germany's earlier diplomacy and her commitments to Austria-Hungary, rather than as a successful outcome of German diplomatic manoeuvres. He expands on the conflicting attitudes between Germany and Austria in the formulation of Turkish war aims in the Near East and the extent to which these two countries were at times working at cross-purposes in Constantinople. The work also explores the war-time difficulties between the German diplomatic service and the Army High Command.

First Republic (1918-38)

266 **Austria: 1918 to 1972.**

Elisabeth Barker. London: Macmillan, 1973. 305p.maps. bibliog.

The author was at one time Reuter's correspondent in southeast Europe. She shows how the Austrians, despite their internal weaknesses, in their long and painful search for a national identity following the breakup of the Habsburg Empire, have somehow managed to manipulate to their advantage seemingly overpowering external forces, political, economic and social. The work also reveals how the Austrians have succeeded in creating a Western type democracy with its roots in past history but its objectives firmly directed towards the realities and demands of the contemporary scene. The work falls naturally into four periods: the First Austrian Republic and its fall, 1918-38; Austrians without a state, 1938-45; Austria under occupation, 1945-55; and independent Austria, 1955-72. The book is extremely well-researched and clearly presented and provides an invaluable account, well-suited to the general reader and the student, of this significant period of the nation's history.

267 **The Austrian Revolution.**

Otto Bauer, translated from the German by H. J. Stenning. London: Leonard Parsons, 1925. 287p.

Otto Bauer, a left-wing radical politician and theoretician, was Secretary of State for Foreign Affairs in the second government of the First Republic. However, he is better known as the founder of Austro-Marxism, an extreme form of socialism based on doctrinaire Marxist principles. This is an abridged version, in English translation, of his classic work *Die Österreichische Revolution* (Vienna, 1923), which presents his personal view of the turbulent political and economic scene of the early 1920's. Its main interest lies in his description of the emergence of the Social Democrats, which he supported, as a powerful and well-organized political force in opposition to authoritarian rule.

268 **Austrian democracy under fire.**

Otto Bauer. London: National Joint Council of the Labour Movement, Transport House, 1934. 52p.

The British labour movement issued this political pamphlet, written by the exiled leader of the Austrian Social Democrats following the abortive socialist uprising in 1934, in support of the 'Help the Workers of Austria' fund. It is a stirring defence of the Social Democratic Party interspersed with a graphic description of the fighting in Vienna.

269 **Austro-Marxism.**

Thomas Burton Bottomore, Patrick Goode. Oxford: Clarendon Press, 1978. 330p. bibliog.

The serious student of politics should find much of interest in this interpretative analysis of a school of political thought which exercised a considerable influence on European socialism in the early part of this century. Austro-Marxism is depicted here as a vigorous, undogmatic but scientific system, retaining a strong revolutionary character. The texts of addresses, lectures and essays contributed by prominent Austro-Marxist thinkers such as Max Adler, Otto Bauer and Karl Renner appear in English for the first time. The biographical notes are extensive.

270 **In search of the millennium.**

Julius Braunthal. London: Victor Gollancz, 1945. 338p.

This volume is written by a prominent Austrian socialist living in exile in Britain and is a personal testament, dedicated to Otto Bauer, the leader of the Austrian Social Democrats in the First Republic. It reviews the changes in socialist political perception which had occurred over the previous forty years and provides a strong expression of faith in socialism as an international creed. The book also contains intimate portraits of a number of leaders of the Austrian socialist movement with whom Braunthal had collaborated in earlier days.

271 **The tragedy of Austria.**

Julius Braunthal. London: Gollancz, 1948. 213p.

This is a stirring account of the course of events during the First and Second Republics, by an author who took a leading part in the events of the First and observed the start of the Second as an émigré. The work attempts to play down the responsibility of the Social Democrats for the political crisis which led to the 1934 uprising. The changes in Austria's international political outlook are explained as a pragmatic response to internal and external power relations, and are not considered to be founded on any firm ideological basis. The appendixes include correspondence between Engelbert Dollfuss and Benito Mussolini. The foreword is by Michael Foot, the former British Labour Party leader.

272 **In the twilight of socialism: a history of the revolutionary socialists of Austria.**

Josef Buttinger, translated from the German by E. B. Ashton. London: Weidenfeld & Nicolson, 1954. 577p.

An exciting description of the conspiratorial underground political organization which was formed by the militant Josef Buttinger after the abortive socialist uprising in 1934 as a breakaway movement from the Social Democrat party. It is uncompromising in its opposition to Schuschnigg the Chancellor. In the Revolutionary Socialists' view full-scale revolutionary action was the only possible hope for the future, though not through collaboration with the Communists. The author writes with fervour and a sense of mission and is remarkably candid in describing the internal wrangles within the Social Democratic movement which led to his disillusionment with Otto Bauer, the leader of the party, whose authority he still recognized, despite these disagreements.

273 **The rise of fascism.**

F. L. Carsten. London: Batsford, 1967. 256p. bibliog.

'Fascism' is an emotive word, often used today by political parties of all persuasions to vilify their opponents. Even when fascism was a ruling force between World War I and II it was subject to a variety of definitions. It is therefore salutary to examine this disciplined study by a distinguished historian and Professor of Central European History at London University. Carsten saw, at first hand, the build-up of Hitlerism in Germany in the 1930's. Covering fascism in Italy and Nazism in Germany and Austria, he traces two of the main constituent elements – nationalism and anti-semitism – back to before World War I. He also analyses the inter-war period and throws much-needed light both on the Austrian Pan-Germanism of Georg Schönerer and on the Heimwehr, the para-military organization led by Prince Starhemberg.

274 **Austrian catholics and the First Republic.**
Alfred Diamant. Princeton, New Jersey: Princeton University Press, 1960. 325p. bibliog.

This is essentially a disinterested non-partisan study of the Austrian Catholic Social movement between the wars. The author shows how Austrian Catholics, with their roots in the Habsburg dynastic past, were unable to distinguish between different social levels and viewed society as an organic whole, being motivated by a single purpose, the fulfilment of which they readily entrusted to a single agent – the State. Hence the establishment of the authoritarian régimes (1922-24, 1926-29) led by Chancellor Ignaz Seipel, himself a Catholic priest.

275 **Workers in arms: the Austrian Schutzbund and the civil war of 1934.**
Ilona Duczynska. New York, London: Monthly Review Press, 1978. 256p.

The author of this account of the February 1934 uprising in Vienna by the armed Left makes no attempt to conceal where her sympathies lie. To this extent this could be called a biased work, but nonetheless several incontestable conclusions emerge of clear importance to anyone seeking an understanding of the Austrian scene in the run-up to the *Anschluss*. Chief of these, perhaps, is that the coup failed even though the Socialist militia, the Schutzbund, was numerically stronger than the whole federal army. There is also a warm, and surely overdue, tribute to Theodor Körner, the World War I general whose advice could have been decisive had the political leaders not favoured direct confrontation rather than guerrilla tactics.

276 **The Heimwehr and Austrian politics, 1918-1936.**
C. Earl Edmondson. Athens, Georgia: University of Georgia Press, 1978. 352p. map. bibliog.

The Heimwehr (Home Army) was one of the most significant elements in the turbulent political atmosphere in post-World War I Austria. It had many affinities, both political and para-militarist, with the German Nazis, the British Union of Fascists and Mussolini's Fascists. However, the fascinating position so carefully studied here is its out-manoeuvring and eventual supplanting by the Nazis in the delicate build-up to Hitler's *Anschluss*. A serious and important historical account.

277 **An opposing man.**
Ernst Fischer, translated from the German by Peter and Betty Ross. London: Allen Lane, 1974. 418p.

These recollections and reflections by a leading Austrian politician, intellectual and writer terminate in 1945 when the Communists were routed in the first post-World War II elections. However, they give an absorbing description of how the author went into exile in Moscow after the 1934 rising as a Social Democrat and there became a convinced Communist. He recounts his reporting of the Trotskyist trials in 1937, and his unswerving loyalty, despite great personal risks, to his friends such as Georgi Dimitrov, the General Secretary of the Comintern. During World War II he regularly made broadcasts to Austria and Germany from Moscow. The impressive personality emerging is one of great strength of character and idealism.

278 **Facts and features of my life.**
Sir George Franckenstein. London: Cassell, 1939. 342p.

As Austrian ambassador in London from 1920 to 1938, and a great Anglophile, society figure and patron of music, the author established exceptional contacts for keeping his country informed of British hopes and fears during these eighteen critical years. The reader may feel that his easy, conversational style of writing perhaps understates his services in this respect.

279 **Code name 'Mary': memoirs of an American woman in the Austrian underground.**
Muriel Gardiner. London; New Haven, Connecticut: Yale University Press, 1983. 179p.

The author, wife of Josef Buttinger, the militant leader of the Revolutionary Socialists – the illegal underground organization formed after the abortive 1934 uprising – begins her story by describing her life as a medical student in Vienna in the late 1920's. She describes with instant recall her later daring activities including harbouring the persecuted, forging passports, and escorting refugees to the Austrian borders; she was decorated by the Austrian government for these services. Her conversion to socialism had begun in 1922, when she witnessed Mussolini's March on Rome, and later she forged contacts with the British Labour Party, Leon Blum, the French Popular Front leader, and, of course, her future husband.

280 **Dollfuss and his times.**
John Duncan Gregory. London: Hutchinson, 1935. 384p. maps.

Written shortly after the death of Engelbert Dollfuss, this book examines the problems inherent in the 1934 uprising, and the vision of the Christian corporate state which Dollfuss is portrayed as embodying. The sources include interviews with relatives and participants in the 1934 struggle.

281 **Austria from Habsburg to Hitler.**

Charles A. Gulick. Berkeley, California: University of California Press, 1948. 2 vols.

This avowedly partisan work, written from a strictly socialist angle, contains a mine of information and took over ten years to write. It supplies a stimulating corrective to more orthodox histories with its outspoken criticism of Austrian Right-wing leaders such as Ignaz Seipel, Engelbert Dollfuss and Kurt von Schuschnigg. The author also provides a strong defence of the Social Democrat politicians and their policies in their period of unsuccessful opposition, parliamentary as well as revolutionary, to the ruling régime after their initial post-World War I triumph under Chancellor Karl Renner from 1918 to 1920. A unique and unorthodox work.

282 **Austria still lives.**

Mitzi Hartmann. London: Michael Joseph, 1938. 295p.

This is the life-story of a young Austrian woman from a middle-class family with a cultured musical background, writing under a pseudonym; she died when only twenty-five. It provides a graphic account of the 1934 rising in Vienna and the disillusionment and despair of the following years, during which she spent some months in prison as a result of her strong anti-Nazi stand. It includes interesting comments on the *Anschluss*, the policies of the Social Democrats and the Austrian Youth Movement, and ends with a message of hope for the future of her country. A touching and sensitively-written account of a turbulent period in Austrian history.

283 **Europe and the Habsburg restoration in Austria, 1930-1938.**

Blair R. Holmes. *East European Quarterly*, vol. 9, no. 2 (1975), p. 174-84.

The writer describes how the ruling Christian Social Party under Chancellor Ignaz Seipel in the First Republic sought the support of the monarchists in order to provide a viable alternative to rule by the Social Democrats or the National Socialists. He then argues that, contrary to popular belief, most of the European powers favoured, or at least were not opposed to, a restoration of the Habsburg Empire right up to the mid-1930's.

284 **Disjointed partners.**

Peter J. Katzenstein. Berkeley, California; Los Angeles: University of California Press, 1976. 263p.

This liberally-annotated assessment of the political and historical relationships between Austria and Germany from 1815 to the end of World War II, examines six distinct patterns of such relationships in historical sequence. The author concludes that, in general, counter pressures and political autonomy were more in evidence than the pressures and support for political integration. He contends, however, that the 1938 *Anschluss* was a conquest by consent as well as by coercion, although subsequent events have confirmed Austria's resilience in maintaining a strong political independence.

285 **The coming of Austrian fascism.**
Martin Kitchen. London: Croom Helm; Montreal: McGill, Queens University Press, 1980. 299p. bibliog.

This book is not, as the title suggests, about national socialism in Austria but concentrates on the Austrian socialist movement. Drawing widely on archival sources, the writer examines with a critical eye the shortcomings and wrangles which beset the Right-wing elements of the movement and its lack of organized leadership in the early 1930s. He highlights the ambiguities in Engelbert Dollfuss's attitude towards the Nazis, scornfully dismissing his policies as both morally indefensible and inept. The account of the 1934 uprising is graphically presented and very clear.

286 **Ignaz Seipel (1876-1932): Christian statesman in a time of crisis.**
Klemens von Klemperer. Princeton, New Jersey: Princeton University Press, 1972. 468p. bibliog.

This biography of the remarkable priest, scholar and statesman who held office not only in the last Imperial cabinet but as chancellor and foreign minister under the First Republic, pays due tribute to Ignaz Seipel's immense services to Austria. He is portrayed as a controversial, impenetrable and ascetic figure of towering stature, whose unbreakable links with the Francis Joseph era did not prevent him from sponsoring imaginative plans for solving the nationality problems which the country faced. The disastrous effect on Austria of the decline of the ill-fated Weimar Republic is fully revealed. This important assessment reflects a clear, historical judgment and is based largely on archival material and contemporary literature.

287 **The Republic of Austria, 1918-1934: a study in the failure of democratic government.**
M. Macdonald. London: Oxford University Press, 1946. 165p.

This concise and objective account bears the imprimatur of the Royal Institute of International Affairs. The progressive collapse of parliamentary democracy after its optimistic enshrinement in the 1919-20 constitution (which is printed in full in the appendix) is traced to: counter-productive inter-party strife; the bad economic situation; and a foreign policy over which other powers, especially Italy, were allowed to dominate. There was also a decline in patriotism and a feeling of helplessness in a foreign world which was hastened latterly by the collapse of the parallel experiments in parliamentary democracy in the Germany of the Weimar Republic. An earlier work by Malcolm Bullock entitled *Austria 1918-1938: a study in failure* (London: Macmillan, 1939. 300p.) appeared immediately before World War II and covered similar ground though extending the period right up to the Nazi occupation. Although not graced by the same official patronage it provides more detail on the personalities concerned, particularly the first post-World War I Chancellor Karl Renner (to whom it pays a warm tribute), and his successors Ignaz Seipel and Engelbert Dollfuss. A useful chronology of events is also included.

288 **Hitler and the forgotten Nazis: a history of Austrian national socialism.**

Bruce F. Pauley. London: Macmillan, 1981. 292p. map. bibliog.

The Austrian expression of national socialism is something of a neglected field and this clear and well-argued study fills a useful gap. The author, with the aid of extensive source notes, produces evidence to show that despite their strong idealistic motivation the Austrian Nazis could not agree among themselves, were opposed to compromise and while fully committed to the idea of one German nation, wanted to retain autonomy for their own party.

289 **The rise of political anti-semitism in Germany and Austria.**

P. G. J. Pulzer. London, New York: John Wiley, 1964. 364p. bibliog. (New Dimensions in History Series).

This is a balanced and well-documented study of a field of personal emotion and prejudice on which Hitler was shrewd enough to capitalize from the early days of the rise of Nazism. It seemed impossible to the average citizen outside Germany in the 1930's that a blatant display of outright racist propaganda could dupe a material majority of citizens and that it could convince them that the Jewish people presented an effective threat to their economic and cultural existence. Moreover, to outsiders it seemed incredible that the party preaching this gospel would go to the lengths of implementing it in the subsequent holocaust. Of course both these propositions became facts and this work goes a long way towards explaining the historical reasons which operated both in Germany and in the Austro-Hungarian Empire after the latter's defeat by the former in 1866. A point of particular interest, and given full weight here as virtually a new revelation, is the general insistence by Austrian Jews from 1867 right up to World War II that they had certain inalienable historic minority rights as holders of Jewish nationality. A book which raises important questions and provides some heart-searching answers.

290 **The crisis of Austrian socialism; from red Vienna to civil war, 1927-1934.**

A. Rabinbach. Chicago, London: Chicago University Press, 1983. 296p. bibliog.

The real crisis of this turbulent period in Austria's history came when Otto Bauer, leader of the predominant Social Democrats, realized that his commitment to democracy was no longer justified. This was a tragedy for the Social Democrats: and this definitive work, which includes a useful summary of the background history from the 1867 Compromise onwards, is the latest and most comprehensive study of the whole process. The author is particularly discerning when discussing the reasons for the fortress mentality which imbued the Viennese socialists of the February 1934 uprising and held them apart from the rest of the country, with such disastrous results not only for the party, but for Austria as a whole.

291 **Ignaz Seipel, Mensch und Staatsmann: eine biographische Dokumentation.** (Ignaz Seipel, man and statesman: a biographical documentation.)
Friedrich Rennhofer. Vienna; Graz, Austria: Hermann Böhlau, 1978. 800p. bibliog.

This monumental and painstaking work draws on Seipel's previously unpublished notebooks, diaries and correspondence. It brings out his dual role as a statesman of great stature and as the uncontested leader of the Christian Social Party, whose opposition to socialism was unwavering and who believed it to be the most dangerous historical enemy of the Church. In assessing his achievements, the author records contemporary comments, but leaves these mainly unevaluated.

292 **Between Hitler and Mussolini.**
Ernst Rüdiger, Prince Starhemberg. London: Hodder & Stoughton, 1942. 290p.

These memoirs were begun in 1939 and rewritten in England when Ernst Starhemberg was serving in the Free French Air Force. His extrovert, exuberant personality emerges very clearly, and his contempt for the Nazis is never hidden. The book includes a vivid account of his refusal to accept the leadership of the Nazi movement in Austria. If his advocacy of martial law as the only effective basis for resistance to German infiltration had been adopted, it must be wondered whether this might not have deterred Hitler from imposing the *Anschluss* by force. Starhemberg's secret meetings with Mussolini are graphically described.

293 **Italy's Austrian heritage, 1919-1946.**
Dennison L. Rusinow. Oxford: Clarendon Press, 1969. 423p. 4 maps. bibliog.

This detailed and coherent study was developed from a dissertation written at St. Anthony's College, Oxford. It shows how the Austrian provinces of Venezia Tridentina and Venezia Giulia acquired by Italy after World War I brought problems for which the Italian government was never able to find a solution during the period surveyed. Attempts to integrate non-nationals into these two areas against their will merely strengthened the irredentist feelings of the Austrian and Slav minorities living in them. The military collapse of Italy in 1943 turned the clock back and postponed any final solution.

294 **Austrian requiem.**
Kurt von Schuschnigg, translated from the German by Franz von Hildebrand. London: Victor Gollancz, 1947. 270p.

This post-mortem study by Austria's Chancellor during the last four years before the *Anschluss* with Hitler's Germany was begun in 1938 and completed in 1945 – Schuschnigg having been kept in solitary confinement from 1939 to 1941 before being transferred in turn to the Sachsenhausen and Flossenburg concentration camps. Some of the author's initial account describing the inevitability of the gathering storm from 1933 onwards was in fact submitted to Gestapo censorship but other parts of it were kept hidden. Flashbacks depict Schuschnigg's meetings with Mussolini and his fateful personal encounter with Hitler. The second part of the book describing Austria as 'The Keystone of

Europe', provides the author's personal reflections on the political, economic and international issues which confronted him. Schuschnigg emigrated to the United States after the war and embarked on an academic career; he retired back to his native country in 1970 and published a considered further review of the period in his *Brutal Takeover: the Anschluss of Austria by Hitler*. (London: Weidenfeld & Nicolson, 1971. 383p. bibliog.) which was translated from the German by Richard Barry. His documentation by then was naturally more complete and he was able, after the passage of time, to go more fully into the attitude of the Western powers to the increasing domination of Hitler, and to set the whole period in a deeper perspective.

295 **Diplomatic twilight, 1930-1940.**
Sir Walford Selby. London: John Murray, 1953. 198p.

The author was British Minister in Vienna during the key period, 1933-37, which corresponded with the first stages of Nazi rule in Germany and the assassination of Dollfuss in Austria which formed the prelude to full takeover in 1938 with the *Anschluss*. His post gave him access to such leading politicians as Dollfuss and Schuschnigg, and to diplomats such as Franz von Papen. His vivid eye-witness account of the Austrian situation is written with authority and emotion and he presents measured criticism of British foreign policy of the day.

296 **Kurt von Schuschnigg.**
R. K. Sheridan. London: English Universities Press, 1942. 324p. bibliog.

In 1942, when this book was published, the last pre-World War II Austrian Chancellor was being held in solitary confinement in a Vienna hotel on his way to successive concentration camps before being liberated by the American armies. Schuschnigg was later exiled to Italy by the first Renner government in 1945 and then given a Chair at an American University. He returned to Austria in retirement and died there in 1977. The significance of this warm and generous tribute is that it is probably the first to appear in English after the *Anschluss* and its judgments, although well-documented at the time, were delivered before the post-World War II scene was even contemplated. The very dramatic account of Schuschnigg's last days in office, however, gains from its historical immediacy.

297 **The birth of the Austrian Republic, 1918-1921.**
Karl Rudolph Stadler. Leiden, Netherlands: A. W. Sifthoff, 1966. 207p. maps. bibliog.

Based largely on the 1919 Peace Conference papers, some of which had only recently been released, this extended and interpretative treatise considers the problems facing the emergent state of Austria between 1918 and 1921 and describes the steps leading to the establishment of the First Republic. The work is divided into three parts: the political issues; the territorial settlement; and economic problems. The author draws some interesting parallels with the situation at the end of World War II, with Karl Renner once more at the helm of the newly reconstituted Austria, with the revival of claims on South Tirol by the Austrians and on Slovene Carinthia by the Yugoslavs, and with the possible union between Austria and Bavaria once again being mooted. However, the two overriding considerations at the time of the 1919 Peace Conference, in the author's view, were the degree of surrender of privilege forced on the dominant race in a multi-national state in order to ensure its survival and the difficulties of fashioning a new existence when all its subject states had seceded.

298 **Native fascism in the successor states, 1918-1945**
Edited by Peter F. Sugar. Santa Barbara, California: ABC-Clio, 1971. 166p. (Twentieth Century Series, no. 4.)

This collection of papers, presented at an international conference in Seattle in 1966 on the history of the Habsburg Monarchy's successor states, deals with the theme of fascism used in its widest political sense, that is to say, movements that went beyond the extreme Right-wing philosophies. John Rath's contribution (p. 24-43), commenting on the First Republic, offers a penetrating analysis. He explains that although the corporative principle espoused by Dollfuss in 1934, and later by Schuschnigg was heralded as being the wish of the people, it was only reflected in legislation in a minor way, since the political autonomy of the provinces was severely reduced and all power remained vested in the federal government. The two main political parties, each supported by its own para-military organizations, are well portrayed. A clear and informative account.

299 **Continuity and change in Austrian socialism: the eternal quest for the third way.**
Melanie A. Sully. New York: Columbia University Press, 1982. 288p. bibliog. (East European Monographs, no. 64, (114)).

A detailed and well-documented study of the Social Democrat movement from its inception in 1889 to the present day. The author examines the various transformations which have affected the fortunes of the party and finds ambiguities in the ideological position of the movement in the First Republic, since the early social democrats were geared to a non-violent revolution though fully committed to the eradication of the capitalist system. There is an excellent chapter on the Revolutionary Socialists, the breakaway and illegal organization formed after the Social Democratic Party was banned in 1934 and which was severely critical of the latter's failures and yet maintained ties with the old party. The present social Democratic Party is seen as less heretical than its predecessor and more practically integrated in the country's political and economic system, seeking a middle way between idealism and realism. The chapter on organizational structure, membership and electoral performance should be of particular value to the student of politics. The style of writing is clear and stimulating throughout.

300 **Österreich: Zeitgeschichte in Bildern, 1918-1975.** (Austria: contemporary history in pictures, 1918-75.)
Erika Weinzierl, in collaboration with Peter Hofrichter. Vienna; Innsbruck, Austria: Tirolia Verlag, 1976. 290p. bibliog.

A minimum of commentary accompanies some 500 photographs depicting aspects of Austrian history from the beginnings of the First Republic (1918) to the 30th anniversary of the Second (1975). The work draws on government, archival and press material. An impressive coverage.

301 **The socialism of fools: Georg Ritter von Schönerer and Austrian Pan-Germanism.**
Andrew Gladding Whiteside. Berkeley, California: University of California Press, 1975. 404p. bibliog.

There can be no denial that Pan-Germanism, the call for close and effective links between Germany and those members of the Austro-Hungarian Dual Monarchy speaking German as their first language, was a historical force of some magnitude. In the last month before the departure of the last emperor, Charles I, in late 1918, the representatives of the Austrian Crown Lands followed his call for a federal state and set up a Provisional National Assembly for those lands as an independent state. This was set aside by the revolutionary movement which supported the declaration of a German-Austrian democratic republic as a component part of the German Republic and this subsequently evolved into the present republic as formerly constituted in 1919. Ritter von Schönerer, the subject of this study, was only a minor prophet supported by an uninfluential group of students, shopkeepers and artisans – the small folk of Vienna. He set himself up as the leader of the 'oppressed' Austrian Germans and was the first to preach racial anti-semitism. Compared with what followed his movement was relatively unimportant and was held by Hitler (an Austrian by birth who surely came into the category catered for) to be too bourgeois. Nonetheless the author is right in drawing our attention to Schönerer as a pioneer in anti-semitism which, of course, was one of the main planks of the German National Socialism which eventually engulfed Austria itself.

302 **Fascist movements in Austria.**
Robert S. Wittrich. *Wiener Library Bulletin*, vol. 30, nos. 43-44 (1977), p. 60-64.

In this brief article the author stresses the lack of strong Austrian nationalist feelings in the face of the powerful Pan-German movement in the 1920's and 1930's, which opposed with equal virulence both the liberal Jewish and Marxist intelligentsia. Hitler's rule, he claims, paradoxically seemed to revive Austrian patriotism, so that at the end of World War II the vast majority of Austrians really felt they were Austrians, not Germans.

German occupation (1938-45)

303 **Post-war German-Austrian relations: the Anschluss movement 1918-1936.**
Mary Margaret Ball. Stanford, California: Stanford University Press; London: Oxford University Press, 1937. 304p. bibliog.

Written just before the *Anschluss* this is largely a work of documentation with some evaluative comment. It is based on officially-published sources, particularly parliamentary debates and League of Nations' papers, as well as newspaper sources. Straightforward and skilfully presented, it covers very fully the latter part of this period, while the historical origins of the desire for *Anschluss* are less fully developed.

304 **Wien vom Anschluss zum Krieg: nationalsozialistische Machtübernahme und politisch-soziale Umgestaltung am Beispiel der Stadt Wien, 1938-39.** (Vienna from *Anschluss* to war: the National Socialist take-over and socio-political reorganization as evidenced in Vienna, 1938-39.)

Gerhard Botz. Vienna: Jugend und Volk, 1978. 646p. bibliog.

It is sometimes claimed that Austria's search for a national identity since World War II has tended to obscure past historical truths, and that in trying to prove the strength of her resistance to Nazi rule writers have too easily glossed over the better-documented evidence of her collaboration with the régime. This extremely well-researched and authoritative analysis lends some support to this view. The author, a leading authority on the subject, examines in considerable detail the various processes involved in the gradual take-over of Vienna by the National Socialists and illustrates his points with supporting statistics, tables and charts.

305 **Anschluss.**

Gordon Brook-Shepherd. London: Macmillan, 1963. 223p.

A dramatic account of the *Anschluss* based mainly on this journalist's personal reminiscences and his interviews with prominent personalities of the time, such as his discussion of Chancellor Schuschnigg's problems with the British Foreign Secretary, Anthony Eden. As this was one of the first accounts of these events to be written in English, the extensive source references are of particular interest to scholars and researchers.

306 **Thus died Austria.**

Oswald Dutch. London: Arnold, 1938. 270p. map.

A vivid account of events prior to the first month after Hitler's entry into Vienna based largely on personal experience. The author acknowledges grave misjudgments and mistakes made by Austria and her leaders. Moreover, he wonders whether the culture of a 'free, lovable, beautiful and serene land', with its multinational elements welded into a unique Austrian harmony, would readily exchange its easy-goingness and charm for the super-military, ruthlessly-organized and all too frugal life of the Third Reich.

307 **Fallen bastions.**

G. E. R. Gedye. London: Victor Gollancz, 1939. 507p. maps.

Hitler entered Vienna on 13 April 1938 after the collapse of the Schuschnigg régime under relentless political and military pressure. The author, who was later to report on the immediate post-World War II situation, represented the London *Daily Telegraph* before his expulsion by the Nazis. This exhaustive and detailed account of his personal experiences is based on his diary and is an important contribution to the documentation of the period.

308 **Austria, Germany and Anschluss, 1938-1939.**
Jürgen Gehl. London: Oxford University Press, 1963. 212p. maps.

This well-researched study is based on a doctoral thesis for St. Anthony's College, Oxford and includes a foreword by its Warden, Alan Bullock. The book illustrates the complex relationship between the Austrian Nazi Party and German foreign policy and their attempt to undermine the resistance of a sovereign state. Hitler is shown to be a master of improvization and opportunism combined with a consistency of ultimate objective.

309 **Austro-German relations in the Anschluss era.**
Radomir Luza. Princeton, New Jersey: Princeton University Press, 1975. 420p. map. bibliog.

In view of the extensive archival material now available it is not surprising that diplomatic historians should be particularly interested in this subject, even though their treatment of it has not always been free from political bias. Drawing on primary source material this clear and dispassionate survey begins with a sketch of the growth of the Greater-German concept from the days of the Habsburg monarchy to the depression in Germany in 1930. It goes on to show how Hitler's strategy was to unify Germany and Austria by a gradual process of assimilation. The author suggests that the *Anschluss* itself unwittingly hastened the modernization of Austria by promoting a sense of cohesion and identity among its people which found its ultimate expression in the Second Republic of 1945. What is certainly apparent to the reader is that the decision-making processes employed by Hitler were at times surprisingly haphazard and disjointed. Parts 1 and 2 of this definitive survey deal with the mechanics of the incorporation of Austria within the Third Reich and include tables of leading National Socialist personalities and the distribution of party membership in Germany and Austria. Part 3 covers the period 1940-45 when Austria was already a part of the German war effort.

310 **Country without a name: Austria under Nazi rule, 1938-1945.**
Walter B. Maas. New York: Frederick Ungar, 1979. 178p. maps. bibliog.

The scope of Austrian resistance to the Nazi régime in the early days of German occupation (1938-41) and later in World War II with some Allied support, is not widely known outside Austria. This work provides a straightforward, unvarnished and somewhat unemotional account, focusing on the major resistance groupings and their leaders. It is based almost exclusively on material already published in Austria.

311 **Exploding star: a young Austrian against Hitler.**
Fritz Molden, translated from the German. London: Weidenfeld & Nicolson, 1978. 280p.

This graphic narrative of the experiences of a son of the former editor of a liberal Viennese paper sheds an interesting light on the political and military aims of the Austrian resistance movement during World War II. It describes his hairbreadth escapes when finally operating in the Office of Strategic Services and acting as an underground liaison officer with the Allied Forces in Italy. Molden kept few notes or diaries and this account is based largely on memory and documentary evidence of the time; much of the latter has been preserved.

312 **Hermann Neubacher and the Austrian Anschluss movement, 1918-1940.**
Harry R. Ritter. *Central European History*, vol. 8, no. 4 (1975), p. 348-69.

Based on contemporary journals and archives the writer describes how this opportunist politician in the First Republic joined the Social Democratic movement but easily switched his allegiance to other political groupings depending on which one at any given moment seemed most likely to bring about the Austro-German *Anschluss*. In the end Neubacher was rewarded for his efforts by the Nazis who made him the first Mayor of Vienna after the German occupation in 1938.

313 **Ein Volk, ein Reich, ein Führer.** (One people, one state, one leader.)
Dieter Wagner, Gerhard Tomkowitz, translated from the German by Geoffrey Strachan. London: Longmans, 1968. 236p. maps.

Using journalistic sources and the personal testimonies of participants and witnesses, these authors provide a day-by-day account of the seven days following the night of 15 March 1938 during which the invasion and occupation of Austria by Hitler was begun and completed. The story concentrates on what happened at focal points of action, hour by hour, and on the accompanying background of treason and panic. The authors also show how the Nazis had perfected their aggression tactics beforehand and how they finally pre-empted Schuschnigg's plans for a referendum calling for a free, Christian Austria by marching in before it could be held.

314 **Delusions of grandeur: the Austrian National Socialists.**
Maurice Williams. *Canadian Journal of History* (University of Saskatchewan), vol. 14, no. 3 (Dec. 1979), p. 416-36.

The dilemma of Austrian Nazism between World War I and II was whether to stress its particular Austrian character, for its roots went back to 1904, or to opt openly for Pan-Germanism. The reference to 'delusions of grandeur' in the title indicates the folly of imagining that Hitler could ever have tolerated a Nazi Austria without incorporation within the Third Reich. The Austrian Nazis believed they had a particular development and identity and that their struggle was a domestic affair unaffected by the international problems of the day. They were, of course, to be brutally disillusioned. A factual and interpretative essay displaying North American detachment.

Second Republic (1945-.)

315 **The history of the South Tirol question.**

Anthony Evelyn Alcock. London: Michael Joseph, 1970. 535p. 3 maps. bibliog. (Graduate Institute of International Studies, Geneva).

Apart from two short and biased publications in the 1920's this is the first comprehensive study in English dealing with the complexities of the problems arising in the South Tirol after this region became part of Italy at the end of World War I. It deals extensively with the post-1945 period and draws on official documents from various sources, previously unpublished material and periodicals. The general theme of how national minorities inevitably tend to provoke international conflicts is developed with clarity. A definitive and monumental work.

316 **Russia and the Austrian State Treaty: a case for Soviet policy in Europe.**

Sven Allard. Pennsylvania; London: Pennsylvania State University Press, 1970. 248p.

As Swedish Ambassador in Vienna during the critical years of negotiations leading to the Austrian State Treaty of 1955, the author, writing from a neutral standpoint, provides a fascinating account of the diplomatic manoeuvering between East and West during this period. He highlights particularly the dualistic character of Soviet foreign policy, which, he argues, differs from that of the Western powers in that it is not only national but communist: political compromise is only acceptable if it furthers party interests at home and abroad. A rather less serious but thoroughly entertaining description of some of these events is offered by Masha Williams in *White among the Reds* (London: Shepheard Walwyn, 1980. 214p.). These memoirs of a White Russian interpreter serving with the Soviet occupation forces in Austria contain graphic details of the marathon conferences she attended and of her personal encounters with the four Allied Commanders involved. For an overall view of the whole subject from an American view see William B. Bader's study *Austria between East and West (q.v.)*.

317 **Austria between east and west, 1945-1955.**

William B. Bader. Palo Alto, California: Stanford University Press, 1966. 250p.

Meetings of the Allied Commission of the four occupying powers in post-World War II Austria were frequently marked by bitter wrangling and disagreement between the Western representatives and their Soviet counterpart. The tensions are well illustrated in this study which is based on official documents. The author examines the methods used by the Soviet Union, both in discussion and in practice, to influence events for their own political or strategic purposes. He also provides an interpretative examination of the motives which lay behind the delaying tactics of the Soviet Union during these ten years of negotiations about an Austrian State Treaty, and considers the various factors, both internal and external, which eventually induced the Soviet Union to reach an agreement. The part played by the Austrians, who showed themselves to be too tough and too politically astute to be easily dominated, and who performed a fairly convincing balancing act between West and East, is not overlooked.

318 **The Austrian solution: international conflict and co-operation.**
Edited by Robert A. Bauer. Charlottesville, Virginia: University Press of Virginia, 1982. 217p. bibliog.

A number of US and Austrian scholars and diplomats including two former ambassadors, all concerned in some way with the decision-making and negotiating processes which culminated in the State Treaty of 1955, have contributed to this volume. The book consists of essays which were prepared for a symposium held at the Johns Hopkins Foreign Policy Institute, Washington DC, in 1980 to mark the 25th anniversary of Austria's independence. Personal impressions and the part played by each writer is the theme, and a general feeling emerges that, at least in the early stages, neither the United States nor the Soviet Union had a really clear policy on the future development of the country they were occupying.

319 **Building an Austrian nation: the political integration of a western state.**
William T. Bluhm. London; New Haven: Yale University Press, 1973. 265p. map.

This is a study of the process by which the Austrian government and people developed a national consciousness after the experiences of the Nazi take-over, military defeat in World War II and four-power occupation. It was the first work to appear in English which made use of documentary tools such as electoral returns, demographic tables and attitude surveys, and it is based on an extensive research of post-war Austrian literature. The author asserts that political integration was achieved on the basis of economic development and not vice versa, and he presents stimulating conclusions on the inter-relationship between politics and culture.

320 **European recovery program: Austria, Country Study.**
Washington, DC: US Economic Co-operation Administration, 1949. 63p.

This report sets out the position of Austria in August 1948 after the nation became a member of the OEEC (Organization for European Economic Co-operation), which brought her into the West European economic system and entitled her to Marshall Aid. As the successor to UNRRA (q.v.), the Marshall Plan (named after the US World War II general), focused more on recovery than relief requirements in its programme of assistance to the Western countries after World War II. As far as Austria was concerned, technical aid was provided in the agricultural and forestry sectors, large quantities of fuel and other raw materials were imported, hydro-electric schemes were initiated and financial loans advanced to aid the economy. For a purely political assessment of this subject see Patricia Blythe Eggleston's *The Marshall Plan in Austria: a study in US containment of the Soviet Union in the cold war* (University of Alabama Press, 1980.)

321 **Between liberation and liberty.**
Karl Gruber, translated from the German by Lionel Kochan. London: André Deutsch, 1955. 240p.

This book was written while the author was still the Austrian Foreign Minister and before the signing of the Austrian State Treaty. It criticizes in outspoken terms the delaying tactics and inconsistencies of the Soviet authorities while they attempted to extract every possible concession from the West, and likewise accuses the three Western occupying powers of dragging their feet during the pre-Treaty negotiations and of failing to put Austria's case before the world in adequate terms. As a patriotic Tirolean, the author made tireless personal efforts to find a satisfactory solution to the problem of the South Tirol described here in some detail, a task specifically assigned to him by the Allied occupation powers as a test of Austria's emergent diplomatic capacity.

322 **The rebirth of Austria.**
Richard Hiscocks. London: Oxford University Press, 1953. 258p. bibliog. maps.

The author was the British Council representative in Austria and this book is based on his personal experiences and interviews with leading personalities of the period. The book was one of the first post-World War II accounts of Austria to be published in English. It portrays the gradual emergence of a national consciousness, the revival of the country's political, economic and cultural life and a desire for international co-operation. The description of the final days of the war is particularly dramatic.

323 **Four power control in Austria.**
John Mair. In: *Survey of International Affairs 1939-1946*. Edited by Arnold Toynbee. London: Oxford University Press, 1956. p. 269-390. maps.

The author, who served in the Political Division of the British Element of the Allied Commission in Vienna in 1945, was clearly well-placed to observe and comment on the deliberations of the Commission. Although working under the auspices of the Royal Institute of International Affairs he came to this task before the official papers were released and thus he offers a personal view of events during the first year of Allied occupation, particularly in the capital. This was a short but significant period as it culminated in the Control Agreement of 1946 which linked Austria to the maintenance of democratic principles in preparation for the subsequent State Treaty. In other words, it was a policy designed to establish an independent democratic state and not an imposed re-education policy as in Germany. Apart from the overall political view, a number of specific problems such as refugees, displaced persons, police and censorship are examined.

324 **Austria: problems and achievements, 1945-1963.**
Heinrich Siegler, translated from the German by Richard Rickett. Bonn: Siegler, 1967; New York: Heinemann, 1965. 167p. 3 maps.

Essentially a study in compromise and reconciliation, this annotated account of the main aspects of the country's political, economic and social development in the post-World War II period highlights Austria's own contribution to national unity and neutrality. The considerable factual detail is measured against the provisions of the State Treaty of 1955, parts of which are quoted verbatim in the appendixes. The 94 inter-governmental organizations of which Austria is a member are also listed.

325 **Tradition and innovation in contemporary Austria.**
Edited by Kurt Steiner. Palo Alto, California: Society for Promotion of Science and Scholarship (SPOSS), 1982. 222p.

On the occasion of the twenty-fifth anniversary of the 1955 State Treaty, which restored full sovereignty to the country after the four-power occupation, a conference on the title theme was held at Stanford University, California (May 1980), and was attended by Austrian and American scholars from various disciplines. This volume is based on the contributions made in the four sessions of that conference, which dealt with: the historical perspective; political and economic developments since 1945; public policy issues; education; health and welfare; and present-day Austrian cultural affairs. Extensive bibliographical references follow each section.

326 **Geschichte des Staatsvertrages.** (History of the State Treaty.)
Gerald Stourzh. Graz: Verlag Styria, 1980. 320p. map.

The long drawn-out and often acrimonious discussions between the four occupying powers during negotiations for a State Treaty in Austria after World War II, guaranteeing the country's independence and neutrality, are the subject of this revised and enlarged version of an earlier study. Almost half the book is taken up with official documents which reflect the passage of events and throw into stark relief the different and sometimes shifting political positions adopted by the Western Powers on the one hand, and the Soviet Union on the other. The documentation is very thorough and the accompanying commentaries are helpful in finding one's way through the many complicated issues involved. This book is a definitive official study which was published in connection with the 25th anniversary celebrations of the signing of the State Treaty.

327 **Alto Adige – South Tyrol: Italy's frontier with the German world.**
Mario Toscano, edited by George A. Carbone, and translated from the Italian. Baltimore, Maryland: Johns Hopkins University Press, 1976. 238p. maps.

This survey is based on a series of lectures for senior students at the Rome School of Political Science, and was originally published in Italy in 1960. It covers the period 1914 to 1967 and shows how the annexation conditions stipulated for Italy's entry into World War I made any subsequent settlement on lines unfavourable to Italy almost impossible. The author was a delegate at the United

Nations General Assembly in 1956 and attended the discussions on the South Tirol which took place there.

328 **Österreich: Die zweite Republik.** (Austria: the Second Republic.) Edited by Erika Weinzierl, Kurt Skalnik, with an introduction by Robert A. Kann. Graz, Austria: Verlag Styria, 1972. 2 vols. bibliog.

Commemorating the 25th anniversary of the State Treaty of 1955, this authoritative and well-documented publication records in factual and encouraging terms the country's achievements during the previous quarter-century. The work consists of a series of essays by a team of acknowledged Austrian experts in various fields. There are separate chapters on: wartime Austria; political development, 1945-72; defence; economy; the constitution and the law; decision-making organizations; social services; religion; education; arts and science; and the country's international position. The co-editors lend a mark of distinction to the work, as does Professor Kann, the eminent historian who writes the introduction.

329 **UNRRA – The history of the United Nations Relief and Rehabilitation Administration.**
Edited by George Woodbridge. New York: Columbia University Press, 1950. 3 vols.

Volume 2 of this history covers the field operations of this international relief agency which operated in Western Europe after the ravages of World War II. The section dealing with Austria (p. 295-320) describes the difficulties of negotiating with four separate occupying powers and the emergent Austrian government and the practical problems of distribution. The main requirement was for food, of which $82 million's worth was supplied in 1946, while agricultural machinery, medical supplies and clothing were other essential commodities which helped to ensure Austria's survival.

330 **Austria since 1945.**
Edited by William E. Wright. Minneapolis, Minnesota: Center for Austrian Studies, University of Minnesota, 1982. 150p. bibliog.

The Center for Austrian Studies in Minnesota was founded in 1977 with an endowment grant of $1,000,000 raised by public subscription in Austria and matched by an equivalent Government appropriation. It was established to commemorate the United States bi-centenary and as an expression of Austrian gratitude for American assistance in the immediate post-World War II period. A symposium on the theme 'Austria since 1945' was held by the centre in 1978, and this publication contains all the papers delivered on that occasion. Proceedings at subsequent annual symposia at the centre have been published in the *Austrian History Yearbook* (q.v.). At the inaugural conference three main aspects of Austrian life were discussed: Austrian national identity and political life, and economic as well as cultural achievements. The contributions are of an uniformly high order, and the chapter on 'the quest for an Austrian national character' by the editor offers a particularly perceptive view of this fundamental question.

Population

331 **The population of Austria.**

Peter Findl, Heimold Helczmanovski. Paris: United Nations, Population Division, 1974. 244p. (Committee for International Co-ordination of Nation Research in Demography Series).

More than fifty countries, including Austria, submitted monographs on national demographic issues to the United Nations in 1974 to mark World Population Year. The Austrian report, presented in a standard format and prepared by the Austrian Academy of Sciences, covered six main areas of interest in population growth from the 15th century to the present day: fertility; mortality; emigration; population composition, classified according to sex, age, marital status, families, households, religion, language and education – regional population development and distribution; manpower and employment; and legislation concerning the above.

332 **Beiträge zur Bevölkerungs- und Sozialgeschichte Österreichs; nebst einen Überblick über die Entwicklung der Bevölkerungs- und Sozialstatistik.** (Contributions to a study of Austria's population and social history together with a perspective of the development of population and social statistics.)

Edited by Heimold Helczmanovski. Munich: R. Oldenbourg, 1973. 448p. maps. bibliog.

Austria's leading demographer has collected in one substantial volume the contributions of a number of experts in the fields of social geography, economic and social history, and sociology which form the most authoritative statement on Austrian demography to date. The description of statistical methods and history is exhaustive. In chronological order the main subjects treated are: population development throughout Austria from the 16th century onwards; family structure in the rural areas in the 17th century; population and social statistics in the 18th and 19th centuries; and all the national censuses carried out since 1869. The work concludes with three treatises which consider as examples of modern socio-geographic methods: urban Vienna; the wine centre of Krems on the Danube in Lower Austria; and a mountain farming area in Carinthia.

333 **Bevölkerungsprobleme in Österreich.** (Population problems in Austria.)
Heimold Helczmanovski. Vienna: Federal Ministry for Education and Art, 1974. 31p. (Political Education Series, vol. 15).

This is a brief report in a series concerned with present-day sociological aspects of Austrian life. The author examines the continuing decline in the birth rate, increased regional population movement and the highest old age figures for any country in Europe barring Sweden. According to the 1981 census (q.v.) one fifth of the total population is over sixty years of age.

334 **Siedlungs- und Bevölkerungsgeschichte Österreichs.** (Austrian settlement and population history.)
Institut für Österreichkunde. (Institute for Austrian Ethnic Research.) Vienna: Ferdinand Hirt, 1974. 213p. bibliog.

This is a collection of ten papers presented at a conference held by the Institute for Austrian Ethnic Research at St. Pölten in 1972 which examined the various geographical, social, religious, political and economic factors which determined population settlement and movement in Austria from the earliest times to the present day. The volume contains much statistical data.

335 **Volkszählung, 1981.** (Census, 1981.)
Vienna: Central Statistical Office, 1982-84. 21 vols.

The most recent national census of 1981 (they are carried out every decade) showed a total population of 7,555,338, of which Vienna accounted for 1,515,666. The number of foreigners in the country as a whole was put at nearly 300,000, the majority of these being foreign migrant workers (Yugoslavs and Turks), the so-called 'Gastarbeiter'. In Vorarlberg, the most westerly province, every ninth person was non-Austrian.

Ethnic Minorities

336 **The Croatian minority of Burgenland.**

Thomas M. Barker. *Journal of Central European Affairs*, vol. 19 (April 1959), p. 32-56.

The province of Burgenland, the German-speaking part of Western Hungary which was ceded to Austria under the Treaty of St. Germain in 1919, also contains a Croat minority group. Croats had been settled in that area some 400 years before to offset the population losses during the Turkish wars or came as refugees after their expulsion from their homeland by the Turks. This brief article examines one particular frontier area and outlines the various legislative steps taken by the Austrian government to protect this ethnic minority and its education and culture. Paradoxically, however, the Croats themselves, living in declining numbers in small linguistic enclaves split up over three countries (Austria, Hungary and Yugoslavia, outside Croatia itself) are becoming less interested in their own survival as an ethnic group and are gradually moving towards total assimilation within the state.

337 **The Slovene minority in Carinthia.**

Thomas M. Barker. Boulder, Colorado: University of Colorado Press, 1984. 415p. bibliog. (East European Monographs, no. 169).

This is the most comprehensive and best documented account in English of the Slovene minority in Austria's southernmost border region to have appeared since World War II. The author, who had already contributed a valuable survey of the largest minority group in *The Croatian minority in Burgenland* (q.v.) traces here the history and development of Austria's second largest ethnic group, which numbers about 20,000. He explains that for the Slovenes, maintaining their language has historically been closely linked with their farming pursuits. As a result of the increasing use of automation in farming methods, however, many Slovenes have lost their jobs and have been forced to seek employment in other occupations or move to employment centres outside their own community and linguistic area. An additional problem, which affects other ethnic minorities to a much lesser degree, is that of tourism in Carinthia, which requires the exclusive use of the German language. The author discusses such issues in factual and realistic terms.

338 **Tourism in Austria: a case history of the influence of tourism on ethnic relations.**
J. A. Gamper. *Annals of Tourism Research*, vol. 8, no. 3. (1981), p. 433-46.

For many centuries the German- and Hungarian-speaking communities in the Oberwart area of Burgenland have co-existed, the former being based on trading and the latter on farming. The advent of tourism since World War II has invariably affected both groups and this has led to much closer co-operation and contact between them, thus breaking down ethnic boundaries which have existed virtually unchanged in that area for nearly 1,000 years.

339 **Handbuch der europäischen Volksgruppen.** (Handbook of European ethnic groups.)
Edited by M. Straka. Vienna: Braumüller, 1980. 658p. maps. bibliog. (Ethnos Series, vol. 8).

In this weighty publication about ethnic minorities in Europe, the general historical perspective is set out at some length in the introduction. This is followed by individual chapters on each ethnic group. As far as Austria is concerned the provisions of the 1976 Volksgruppengesetz (Law concerning ethnic minorities), guaranteeing full linguistic and educational, cultural and communication rights, are all outlined. The relevant sections are: 'Slovenes in Carinthia' (p. 484-93); 'Croats in Burgenland' (p. 495-99); and 'Magyars in Burgenland' (p. 602-07). The small Czech minority, largely in Vienna and numbering less than 8,000 is not included in this handbook.

340 **Minority groups in Austria: conflict or integration?**
Melanie M. Sully. *Journal of Area Studies* (Portsmouth Polytechnic), no. 1 (spring 1980), p. 33-36.

The author analyses the assimilation and independence of ethnic minorities in Austria – opposing forces both in the political and cultural spheres. She notes that, somewhat surprisingly, it is frequently the younger, rather than the older, generation which strives the hardest to preserve cultural ethnic traditions in the face of the continuing pressures for integration.

341 **Das Recht der Volksgruppen und Sprachminderheiten in Österreich.** (The Law concerning ethnic and linguistic minorities in Austria.)
Theodor Veiter. Vienna: Wilhelm Braumüller, 1970. 890p. bibliog.

This production is the culmination of a lifetime's work by a legal expert who has worked tirelessly on behalf of the ethnic minorities in Austria. It is a sober, penetrating and definitive study which examines the problem with sociological, ethnic and political considerations all being given their due weight. Part 1 is mainly theoretical and deals with constitutional aspects; part 2 is a historical survey of various ethnic groups, including Czechs in Vienna, Magyars and Croats in Burgenland, Slovenes in Styria and Carinthia, and Jews and Gypsies; part 3 outlines the various international agreements on ethnic minority groups; and part 4 studies a number of case histories of official complaints of ethnic injustices and how they have been handled. The work coincided with the 50th anniversary of the plebiscite in Carinthia in 1919 when the local population, including many Slovenes, voted to remain in Austria rather than become part of Yugoslavia.

Austrians Abroad

342 **Inside the Fourth Reich.**
Erich Erdstein, translated from the German by Barbara Bean. London: Robert Hale, 1977. 220p.

Bearing all the traces of a fast-moving spy thriller, this autobiography of an Austrian patriot, who fled to South America after the *Anschluss* in 1938, recounts in graphic style a series of espionage activities on behalf of the Allies. The author recalls: his imprisonment and how he shared a cell with the shipping magnate, Onassis; his subsequent escape; his near-capture of a Nazi leader, who claimed to be Martin Bormann; and his alarming confrontation with Dr. Josef Mengele, the Auschwitz concentration camp doctor. These are some of the highlights of the life story of a man who after World War II attempted to track down prominent Nazis who fled Europe with the cessation of hostilities.

343 **Die österreichische Emigration, 1938 bis 1945.** (Austrian emigration, 1938-45.)
Franz Goldner. Vienna; Munich: Verlag Herold, 1972. 348p. bibliog.

Based on official and some unpublished sources this is an account of the efforts made by refugees from Austria in different parts of the world to form a single representative body during World War II in their desire to re-establish their lost homeland. The activities of the three Habsburg Archdukes, Otto in France, Robert in London and Felix in the United States, who were working together to form such a body on the Allied side, and if possible establish a 'Free Austrian Battalion' to fight with the American forces, are fully documented. The curious alliance between the Habsburgs and their followers on one side and exiled Austrian communists on the other, linked by a common determination to restore an independent Austria, eventually led to disunity and all attempts to form a government-in-exile failed. Separate chapters are devoted to the activities of the various refugee organizations loosely associated with the Free Austrian

Movement in France, Britain, the United States, Sweden, the Soviet Union and Latin America.

344 **Prophets without honour.**

Frederic V. Grunfeld. New York: Holt, Rinehart & Winston, 1979. 347p. bibliog.

A fascinating study of the contributions made by 20th-century Austrian Jewish intellectuals in the fields of literature, philosophy, psychology, music, art and the sciences. The author not only discusses the major figures of the time but brings to the reader's notice a number of writers-in-exile who are only now being discovered and acclaimed as truly Austrian in tradition and style. The extensive bibliography of primary and secondary sources will be of special interest to the student of Austrian exile literature.

345 **The Austrian cockney.**

Martha Lang. London: Centerprise Trust, 1980. 67p.

In many ways this is a story typical of the thousands of Austrian emigrés who came to Britain after the *Anschluss* in 1938. Martha Lang, writing in a simple and unaffected style, tells of the initial difficulties which confront any refugee in a foreign country – language problems, strange customs and trying to find a job. A small success story which reveals something of the natural ability of the average Austrian to adjust and take the rough with the smooth.

346 **Austria and the Anglo-Saxon World: a survey of Austrian emigration to the United States.**

Wilhelm Schlag. In: *Österreich und die angelsächische Welt: Kulturbegegnungen und Vergleiche.* (Austria and the Anglo-Saxon world: cultural contacts and comparisons). Edited by Otto Hietsch. Vienna: Wilhelm Braumüller. vol. I. p. 139-96.

This is an extract from a two-volume work (1961-68) devoted to Austrian cross-currents in history, literature, art and society in Britain and the United States. It covers in broad outline the emigration to the United States of various religious and political groups and liberal-minded individuals of literary standing who fled from Austria as a result of repression and persecution from the early Protestant settlers in Georgia (following their expulsion from Salzburg in 1731 for refusing to accept Catholicism) to later arrivals after the Revolution of 1848.

347 **Guide to the archival materials of the German-speaking emigration to the United States after 1933.**

John Spalek, in collaboration with Adrienne Ash, Sandra H. Hawrylchak. Charlottesville, Virginia: University Press of Virginia, 1978. 1,133p. bibliog.

This is a remarkable work concerning a remarkable event. Between 1933, when Hitler came to power, and 1942, some 14,000 members of different professions, and not all Jewish, emigrated to the United States from Germany and Austria. This survey lists 700 of the more prominent figures in the world of science, art, music and literature, and provides details of their achievements, and where relevant, the document collections they managed to bring with them or which have been built up around them in the United States. There is no separation in the text between German and Austrian origins, but the reader should have little difficulty in identifying such well-known individuals as the musicians Bruno Walter, Robert Stolz and Kurt Weill; the authors Franz Werfel and Stefan Zweig; and many others of equal stature.

348 **The quiet invaders.**
E. Wilder Spaulding. Vienna: Austrian Federal Publishing House for Education, Science and Art, 1968. 310p.

The contribution to American life and culture made by the thousands of refugees who emigrated to the United States at the time of the *Anschluss* was immense and touched every sphere of human activity. The author, at one time US Cultural Attaché in Vienna, provides a detailed account of the Austrian contribution and devotes separate chapters to different professional groups such as musicians, playwrights, actors, lawyers, inventors, scientists, writers and architects. These were the 'quiet invaders', who, unlike some other European émigré communities, were content to be counted with the Germans at the start in their rush to obtain US citizenship 'without stopping to wave the flag of the often unpopular Habsburgs or the little-known Austrian Republic'. The work is well annotated and includes a useful index of personalities, many of whom are also featured in *The Guide to the Archival Materials of the German-speaking emigration to the United States after 1933*, compiled by John Spalek, (q.v.).

349 **Detailed reports on the Salzburger emigrants who settled in America.**
Edited by Samuel Urlsberger, translated from the German by Hermann J. Lachner. Athens, Georgia: University of Georgia Press, 1968-81. 6 vols.

The Archbishopric of Salzburg, an independent State within the Empire until its incorporation in Austro-Hungary in 1816, progressively became a stronghold of the Counter-Reformation. By the early 18th century the German Lutheran element in its population was being subjected to ever-increasing persecution and in 1731, the Archbishop expelled the Lutherans. Over 30,000 people left the countryside and 6,000 fled the capital; of these some reached America, settling particularly in Georgia. The diaries and letters of their pastors form the basis of this collection which was made at the time by one of the leaders, a pastor from Augsburg, Germany. The daily life of this early settlement in America makes fascinating reading.

350 **The return movement of Jews to Austria after the Second World War.**
F. Wilder-Okladek. The Hague: Martinus Nijhoff, 1969. 130p. bibliog. (Publications of the Research Group for European Migration Problems, no. 16).

The Jewish exodus from Austria after the *Anschluss* in 1938 and the holocaust which befell those who did not manage to escape are by now probably as well-documented as they ever will be. The statistics on the return journey after World

War II are, however, almost unknown even to scholars, and this carefully-researched and unique document on a most delicate subject not only provides accurate factual information but enters bravely into the psychological realm with an analysis of personal motives and reactions. Why did any Jews return at all? Was it for financial reasons to recoup personal losses? Was it pure nostalgia? Whatever the answer, we are left in no doubt over their personal unpopularity with the non-Jewish majority of the local population and of the depths of despair and pessimism which they encountered over what was after all, an absolutely legitimate and reasonable act of personal rehabilitation.

Language

351 **Österreichisches Wörterbuch.** (Austrian dictionary.)
Compiled by E. Benedikt, M. Hornung, E. Pacolt. Vienna: Federal Ministry for Education and Art, 1979. 35th ed. rev. 423p.

Although this is the standard dictionary for official use in Austrian higher and secondary schools, it is also widely used in offices and by researchers, journalists and radio and television writers. It is in fact much more of a general reference work than a dictionary, for it includes: grammatical and orthographic rules; an international pronunciation guide to the Greek, Latin and Cyrillic alphabets; verbs and declensions; scientific and technical phrases; grammatical expressions; chemical abbreviations; weights and measures; titles and forms of address; and even car registration codes!

352 **Wie sagt man in Österreich?** (How do you say that in Austria?)
Jakob Ebner. Vienna; Zürich, Switzerland: Dudenverlag, Bibliographisches Institut, 1980. 2nd ed. 252p. bibliog.

This dictionary contains over 4,000 entries of linguistic variants which are peculiar to Austria as opposed to other German-speaking countries. It includes dialect words and those used in Austria in a different sense from Germany, neologisms, and colloquialisms and provides details of their geographical origin. This work is suitable for anyone with a knowledge of German who reads or speaks it in its Austrian version.

353 **Language shift: social determinants of linguistic change in bi-lingual Austria.**
Susan Gal. San Francisco; London: Academic Press, 1979. 201p. bibliog. (Language, Thought & Culture Series).

For the past 400 years or so the small community of Oberwart in Burgenland has been a perfect example of German-Hungarian bilingualism. Over the centuries it has grown from a village inhabited by Hungarian peasants to an important trading centre between Austria and Hungary, visited regularly by German merchants, whose language now predominates in this area. The author explains the social motivations which have led to this language shift, a process which is invariably slow and deliberate.

354 **Englisch-Deutsches Glossarium finanzieller und wirtschaftlicher Fachausdrücke.** (English-German glossary of financial and business terms).

Edited by C. A. Gunston, G. M. Corner. Frankfurt-am-Main, GFR: Fritz Knapp, 1983. 8th ed. 646p.

The latest and enlarged edition in this well-established series of technical glossaries which contains over 3,000 entries of technical terms and expressions in common usage in the contemporary international financial and economic world.

355 **Langenscheidt's encyclopaedic dictionary of the English and German language.**

Edited by Otto Springer. London: Hodder & Stoughton, 1962-74. 4 vols.

This is a completely revised version of the classic dictionary by Eduard Muret and Daniel Sanders which was first published before World War I. In it American words are given equal prominence with English, while the entire work combines a blend of general and specialized vocabulary, offering a selection of technical terms, dialect, regional forms, proper names, idioms and slang. A most comprehensive and widely used bilingual dictionary which represents a further advance in lexicography.

356 **Some factors affecting the maintenance of bilingualism in Carinthia.**

David F. Stermole. *Papers in Slovene Studies*, (1977), p. 40-50.

The writer claims that although the gradual assimilation of the Slovene minority in Austria's southernmost province has hindered the continued spread of the Slovene language, several Slovene ethnic cultural organizations and farming co-operatives, particularly among the younger generation, are resisting this integration and remain proud of their cultural heritage, which they are trying to preserve.

357 **Sprechen Sie Wienerisch?** (Do you speak Viennese?)

Peter Wehle. Vienna: Überreuter, 1980. 298p.

The expansive but indispensable introduction to this scholarly work comprises nearly a third of the text. In the introduction the author explores the origins of a distinct Viennese dialect as far back as the Minnesinger (troubadour) of the 12th and 13th centuries and stresses the importance of French infills from the Napoleonic occupation ('fiacre', a cab, becomes 'Fiaker'). He also elaborates on the early 19th-century Viennese popular theatre of Ferdinand Raimund and Johann Nestroy (which still holds the boards) and comments that more Viennese speak Viennese than Londoners do Cockney and that quite apart from Hans Moser, an acknowledged popular entertainer, stars of the more formal State Opera have never felt it beneath their dignity to record Viennese ballads.

Religion

358 **Monasteries today.**

Joachim F. Angerer. *Austria Today*, no. 4. (1980), p. 8-17.

This illustrated article considers monasteries in contemporary Austrian life. It explains their importance to the tourist industry, and describes the various cultural activities, such as art and handicraft courses, which they organize and the different individual specializations of certain foundations, such as wine production, market gardening, forestry management and publishing.

359 **The spirit of Armenia.**

Elisabeth Bauer. *Austria Today*, no. 1 (1984), p. 34-36.

The Mekhitarist monastery in Vienna, which has been flourishing since 1811, when some Armenian priests first sought asylum there, is a thriving centre of Armenian culture. It houses the world's largest collection of Armenian newspapers and periodicals as well as an outstanding manuscript collection and a magnificent museum. Today it pays its way by running a very modern printing house and, in traditional monastic style, by distilling a rather bitter liqueur, which it is said, finds favour among the more discerning palates in the country. This short review outlines the history of the Mekhitarist Fathers and some of their other activities in Vienna.

360 **Buddhism in Austria.**

Austria Today, no. 4 (1983), p. 41-42.

In 1983 Austria became the first country in Europe to grant official approval to Buddhism as a recognized religion. This was an important development because State recognition brings with it many advantages, such as protection for the autonomy of religious observance and substantial tax concessions and financial privileges. This brief article explains how, despite the small number of adherents (about 5,000), there are flourishing schools of Buddhist teaching and meditation in Vienna, Salzburg, Graz and in the western alps of Vorarlberg, as well as a

Department of Tibetan and Buddhist Studies at Vienna University. It should also be added that a Buddhist peace pagoda in traditional style has recently been erected on the banks of the Danube near the UN headquarters.

361 **The Catholic Church today: Western Europe.**
Edited by M.A. Fitzsimons, translated from the German by Emily Schlossberger. London: University of Notre Dame Press, 1969. 350p. bibliog.

Professor Erika Weinzierl, Director of the Institute for Contemporary History at the University of Vienna, has contributed a chapter (p. 61-85) on the Catholic Church in Austria in this general survey. She opens with a brief outline of the church's organizational structure, the distribution of clergy and church membership (which since 1975 has been falling at an average annual rate of 20,000). The author then turns to theological training colleges, Catholic schools and various Catholic lay organizations. In a section on relations between church, state and the political parties she is able to show that the tensions and antagonisms between the major political parties vis-à-vis the church, which were so destructive in the inter-war period, no longer exist; and that this fundamental change in attitudes has contributed substantially to the stabilization of Austrian domestic politics today. A final section deals with Catholic representation in the mass media and scientific and cultural life.

362 **The Jews of Austria: essays on their life, history and destruction.**
Edited by Josef Fraenkel. London: Vallentine, Mitchell, 1967. 585p. bibliog.

In the words of the editor, the purpose of this collection of thirty-five essays is 'to record the great deeds of nearly seventy generations and to preserve the memory of Austria's Jewish martyrs'. It is in fact a well-documented and inspiring tribute to the contribution made by Austria's Jews, from the 12th century to the end of World War II, to the intellectual, scientific and economic life of the country. The sweep is impressive and the writing powerful, particularly in the final section which deals with the holocaust. The introductory chapter offers an extremely clear and well-balanced historical outline and there are individual chapters on certain leading Jewish figures such as Theodor Herzl, the founder of modern Zionism; the authors Arthur Schnitzler and Stefan Zweig; and the composers Gustav Mahler and Arnold Schoenberg. A valuable compendium.

363 **Die Kartäuser in Österreich.** (The charterhouses of Austria.)
Edited by James Hogg. Salzburg, Austria: Institute for English and American Studies, 1980-81. 2 vols. (Analecta Cartusiana Series).

Embellished by 120 superbly produced plates these two volumes contain a series of papers written for the Second International Congress on Carthusian History and Spirituality in 1980. They include essays on a number of individual charterhouses in north-eastern Austria and the writings of certain Carthusian authors as well as general articles, one of which describes in some detail the magnificent collection of paintings in the abbey of Klosterneuburg, near Vienna.

364 **The Mormons in the Habsburg lands, 1841-1914.**
Stanley B. Kimball. Houston, Texas: Rice University, 1974. (Austrian History Year Book), vol. 9-10 (1973-74), p. 123-68.

When the Mormons established their first Austrian mission with two priests in 1865 it was to be expected that they would make little headway in the conversion of Catholic souls. Indeed, at that time the practice of any religious faith other than Catholicism was forbidden, except in one or two provinces where Lutherans and Calvinists were tolerated. This brief account opens up a little-known chapter in Austrian religious history and tells of the Mormons' persistent and gallant struggle in the face of countless rebuffs, severe harassment, trials and imprisonment. Today the Mormon community, which is legally recognized, numbers about 3,000. The sources quoted in this review originate mainly from Utah and, to a lesser extent Vienna.

365 **Nazi control of the Austrian Catholic Church, 1939-1941.**
Radomir V. Luza. *Catholic Historical Review*, vol. 63, no. 4 (Oct. 1977), p. 537-72.

At the time of the *Anschluss* the Austrian bishops somewhat naïvely hoped to reach an accommodation with Hitler without their dominant position in society being affected. However, their hopes were quickly dashed when Hitler introduced a series of systematic and savage measures designed to completely eliminate the influence of the Catholic Church in private and public life throughout the country. These involved a direct assault on the structure of the Catholic Church, the confiscation of church property, the enforcement of obligatory civil marriage and the restriction of educational and social activities. All of these measures were backed up by a campaign of moral and political vilification against leading churchmen. The sequence of events is clearly outlined in this well-documented but brief survey which also reveals that there were nevertheless differences of view among the Nazi leaders appointed to deal with church affairs which were often cleverly exploited by the Catholic Church hierarchy.

366 **Protestanten in Österreich.** (Protestants in Austria.)
Gustav Reingrabner. Vienna: Hermann Böhlau, 1981. 312p. maps. bibliog.

This is a definitive and well-documented history of Protestantism in Austria, published to commemorate the 200th anniversary of the Edict of Tolerance of 1781 which virtually abolished discrimination against Protestants. In a chronological account, liberally supported by annotations and illustrations, the author shows how in the 17th and 18th centuries the Protestants in the successor states suffered severe hardships and repression, whereas in Germany the evangelical confession had been accepted and freely practised since Luther's time in the early 1500's. The long and bitter struggles, the massive emigrations to Germany and overseas in Maria Theresa's reign (when over 30,000 Protestants were expelled from the Salzburg area) and the contact continuously maintained with their brethren in Germany are all described in detail. Reviewing more recent history the author, the Superintendent of Burgenland, stresses the dangers of outmoded attitudes rooted too much in the past and deplores the decline in the numbers and the influence of Protestants in contemporary Austrian public life.

Society, Welfare and Medicine

367 **The surgeon's surgeon: Theodor Billroth, 1829-1894.**
Karel B. Absolon. Lawrence, Kansas: Coronado Press, 1979. 282p. illus.

Theodor Billroth is generally regarded as the father of gastro-intestinal surgery and was the first person to perform a successful resection of the cervical esophagus in 1877. This book, the product of ten years' research, is an evaluation of Billroth's surgical activity, his artistic inclinations and his humanist ideas. It is the first comprehensive biography of this remarkably gifted man and places him in the economic, political and cultural setting of his day. The work contains a number of facsimile reproductions of contemporary documents and many extracts from Billroth's correspondence with the composer, Johannes Brahms, who was a very close personal friend.

368 **Österreichischer Gesundheitsführer.** (Austrian guide to health.)
Hademar Bankhofer. Vienna; Königstein, GFR: Athenäum, 1982. 196p. maps.

The author, a freelance journalist and broadcaster with a special interest in all forms of nature healing, has compiled a valuable guide to natural health establishments throughout the country. These include spas, thermal baths, homeopathic centres, nature reserves, health farms, sports and fitness centres and specialist clinics. The arrangement is by province, each selection being preceded by a map indicating the various centres, followed by a short description of the facilities they offer and, in many cases, a photograph of the establishment concerned.

369 **Psychiatry in Vienna – an illustrated documentation.**
Contributions by Peter Berner, Walter Spiel, Hans Strolzka, Helmut Wyklick. Vienna: Christian Brandstätter, 1983. 144p. illus.

Sigmund Freud and Alfred Adler, who were pre-eminent in founding the Vienna school of psychoanalysis at the turn of the last century, based much of their research on earlier studies by such people as Josef Breuer (1842-1925), Constantin von Economo (1876-1931) and Baron Richard von Krafft-Ebing (1840-1902), who are also featured in this handsomely produced publication. The text is in German with a full English translation and the book's particular merit lies in its wealth of illustrations, mostly historic photographs with detailed captions. The four expository articles by the professional staff at the Vienna School of Medicine are not over-technical and the publication should be of great interest to all students of Austrian social and medical history as well as the informed reader. For an up-to-date view of the current state of Austrian research and teaching in the fields of psychiatry and neurology – invariably considered by the Viennese School to be parts of the same speciality – see J. T. Salvendy's article entitled 'Psychiatry in Vienna to-day' published in the *Canadian Psychiatric Association Journal* (vol. 16, no. 2, April 1971, p. 171-80).

370 **Handbuch der Sicherheit.** (Safety handbook.)
Günther Bögl. Vienna: Peter Müller Verlag, 1981. 360p.

Compiled by the General Inspector of the Federal Security Service in the Ministry for Internal Affairs, this volume is intended to be both a reference work and an aid to general knowledge about safety. Its aim is to encourage a greater awareness among the public of safety measures in the home and industry. The author provides details of the executive organs concerned with the legal and constitutional aspects of health and safety, and other associated bodies such as the fire service, the Red Cross and the Samaritans. The appendix contains a list of officials.

371 **Freud and his early circle.**
Vincent Brome. London: Heinemann, 1967. 275p. bibliog.

This volume examines the personal struggles of the early pioneers of psychoanalysis who worked with Freud as members of his circle, the so-called 'Committee'. The author has drawn on some of Freud's correspondence and unpublished letters which were not available to his standard biographer, Ernest Jones, when he wrote his 3-volume, *Life and work of Sigmund Freud* (London: Hogarth Press, 1955-67). The bitter feuds and quarrels between the leading protagonists of the 'Committee' are vividly depicted.

372 **Freud: the man and the cause.**
Ronald W. Clark. London, Toronto: Granada, 1982. 652p. bibliog. (A Paladin Book).

This is a masterly achievement in that the author, who already has a number of widely-praised biographies of eminent scientists and philosophers to his credit, shows a remarkable ability to describe complex scientific thought and work in an exciting but accurate way. In this thoroughly researched volume he makes use of much previously unknown material which he has skilfully woven around the known facts about Freud and his work. It is an admirably balanced and compelling book, portraying not only Freud as a private person and public figure but clearly defining the cause for which he stood and the controversies which he generated. There are copious reference notes and an extensive bibliography. This is likely to remain a definitive biography for many years to come.

373 **Mid-decade 1980: review and evaluation of progress.**
Edited by Rosemarie Dorrer, Irmtraut Leirer, translated from the German by Angelika Loskot. Vienna: Federal Press Service, 1980. 72p.

The United Nations proclaimed 1975 as International Women's Year focusing on the objectives of 'equality, development and peace'. It adopted a ten-year plan of action to implement these objectives and declared it the 'Women's Decade'. This is the half-term report for Austria, based on expert evidence and data provided by various federal ministries. The report sets out the progress achieved to date and highlights those measures still to be taken during the second half of the decade. There are individual sections on: women in the household and family; women and education; women at work; the health situation of women; women in politics; women and crime. The report summarizes a number of laws passed during the period concerned incorporating the principle of women's equality within Austrian legislation, such as the Family Law, the reform of the Abortion Law and a number of educational measures designed to eliminate discrimination of underprivileged children. The concluding chapter lists priorities and targets for the 1981-85 period, affecting family care, education, the labour market, health, the media and political participation by women.

374 **Integrated social policy: a review of the Austrian experience.**
Paris: Organization for Economic Co-operation and Development, 1981. 257p. bibliog.

This very wide-ranging examination of the country's 'interlocking' social policy was part of a broader study designed to help other OECD countries to learn from Austria's unique experience in this field. The report describes how socio-political measures, in their broadest sense, are co-ordinated in an overall policy covering employment, health, housing, transport, education and finance, aimed at providing equality of opportunity and ensuring the success of the social partnership scheme. This is peculiar to Austria and under it the senior participants are all members of Parliament as well as political party functionaries. In this dual capacity they play a positive co-ordinating role.

375 **Ferdinand von Arlt and Ernst Fuchs: two representatives of the Vienna School of Ophthalmology.**
Alexander Jokl. *International Record of Medicine*, vol. 170 (1957), p. 702-07.

Von Arlt and Fuchs were two outstanding ophthalmologists of the 19th century. Both came from Bohemia and both were some time professors of ophthalmology in Vienna. Von Arlt published his major work on ophthalmic surgery in 1874 and it became a textbook throughout Europe during his lifetime. His student, Fuchs, already a professor at the age of thirty, assumed von Arlt's mantle as a great teacher, holding courses for foreign doctors in their own language and maintaining an extensive practice in Vienna. This short article describes their achievements in the context of European medical advances during this period.

376 **Family policy: government and families in 14 countries.**
Edited by Sheila B. Kamerman, Alfred J. Kahn. New York: Columbia University Press, 1978. 522p.

This volume consists of a series of papers presented at an international conference sponsored by the Carnegie Corporation and the Austrian Ministry of Health, Education and Welfare in New York at Columbia University in 1977. Chapter 16, dealing with Austria and written by Edith Krebs and Margarete Schwarz from the Austrian Chamber of Labour (p. 185-216), shows that the concept of a family policy enshrined in government legislation is relatively new in Austria and is not mentioned in the Federal Constitution, although all political parties support a policy of protecting and sustaining the family. There are however, differences of approach: the conservative and Catholic groups make the distinction between families and non-families, while the socialists stress the class differences in a capitalist society.

377 **Wien und die Weltmedizin.** (Vienna and world medicine.)
Compiled by Erna Lesky. Vienna: Hermann Böhlau, 1973. 242p.

Experts from ten European countries representing a wide-range of medical specialization have contributed to this collection of twenty papers presented at the 4th Symposium of the International Academy for the History of Medicine (Vienna) held in London in September, 1973. The papers are published in German, English and French.

378 **The Vienna medical school of the 19th century.**
Erna Lesky, translated from the German by L. Williams and I. S. Levij. London, Baltimore: Johns Hopkins University Press, 1976. 599p. bibliog.

Commissioned by the US National Library of Medicine, this well-researched and definitive work presents a historical account of Viennese medicine in its heyday. Based on archival sources and liberally illustrated, it describes the state of medical research in the 19th century and the establishment of the First Medical School under Joseph Andrew von Stifft, followed by the reforms in medical training and research carried out by Carl von Rokitansky who founded the Second Medical School in 1836. The early energetic development of specialized medical subjects and the wide interchange of discussion between Vienna and other major medical centres in the world soon established Vienna as a great international centre of medical learning and practice. Separate chapters deal with individual medical discoveries and disciplines, including dentistry. The concluding chapter reviews the literature on the history of Viennese medicine from its early beginnings to the present day. The book contains a number of rare and hitherto unpublished photos.

379 **Carl Rokitansky: 19th century pathologist and leader of the new Vienna School.**

Robert Joseph Miciotto. Ann Arbor, Michigan: University Microfilms International, 1981. 301p.

In the history and development of Austrian medicine in the 19th century Carl Rokitansky's (1804-78) contribution was of paramount importance. He is generally acknowledged as the founder of modern anatomical pathology and he played a leading role in the pioneering work of the Second Medical School of Vienna in the 1830s. This doctoral dissertation, submitted to the Johns Hopkins University, is the first extensive assessment of Rokitansky's professional life and work to appear in English. The author begins with a general overview of his subject's achievement in the re-orientation of medicine in Vienna, quoting liberally from his own medical treatises. He continues with a study of Rokitanksy in relation to the history of pathology, noting that in his forty-eight years in medical practice the doctor was involved in no less than 90,000 autopsies and faced violent criticism from a certain Dr. Virchow in his attempt to formulate a unitary concept of disease. The author follows with an account of Vienna as an international medical centre in the mid-19th century. Two interesting appendixes complete the work: a copy of Rokitansky's medical school curriculum; and a short autobiographical sketch, written in retirement in a modest unaffected style – a self-portrait of considerable appeal.

380 **Freud, the man, his world, his influence.**

Edited by Jonathan Miller. London: Weidenfeld & Nicolson, 1972. 180p. bibliog.

The titles and authors of the ten essays in this collection dealing with different aspects of Freud's social, scientific and philosophical make-up are as follows: 'Freud, Viennese Jew' by Friedrich Heer; 'Freud and medicine' by George Rosen; 'Freud's Vienna' by Martin Esslin; 'Freud and Marx' by George Lichtenstein; 'Freud and Philosophy' by Anthony Quinton; 'Psychoanalysis' by Octave Mannonil; 'The concept of parental guilt' by Catherine Storr; 'Freud and art' by Michael Podro; 'Freud and surrealist painting' by Dawn Ades; and 'Morality, responsibility' by Jonathan Miller.

381 **Social Security in Austria.**

Othmar Rodler, Hermann Urbanetz. Vienna: Federal Press Service and the Austrian Federation of Social Insurance Institutions, 1980. 68p.

Austria can boast of being one of the most advanced countries in Europe as far as social security is concerned. This situation relates back to the important social legislation passed during the life of the First Republic. However, any historical survey will certainly go back further in time and mention the General Mining Act of 1854 and the Workers' Compensation and Health Insurance Act of 1887. This brief survey outlines the history of social security in Austria, while separate sections deal with present-day organization and benefits, unemployment insurance, welfare services, and bi-lateral agreements with a number of foreign countries.

382 **Pioneers of Austrian aviation medicine.**
Gustav Schubert. *Clio Medica*, no. 2 (1967), p. 135-36.

The contribution made by Austrian medical science in the international field during the 19th and 20th centuries is well-known and has been clearly documented. This short article describes the pioneering work of two Austrians, less well-known, but who played an important part in the early days of aeronautics. Ritter von Wenusch was the first person to construct a human centrifuge, while Hermann Schrötter, the son of the famous Viennese laryngologist, designed an airtight gondola for use in balloon ascent.

383 **The development of hygiene in Austria.**
Manfred Skopec. In: *Proceedings of 5th International Symposium on the Comparative History of Medicine – East and West, Susono-shi, Shizuoka, October 1980*. Edited by Teizo Ogawa. Tokyo: Juntendo University, School of Medicine, 1980, p. 129-44. bibliog.

Traces the development of public hygiene in Austria from 1805, when an important lecture was given in Vienna on 'medical police' by Professor Peter Frank, Director General of Public Health in Austrian Lombardy, to the establishment of the first chair of hygiene at Vienna University in 1885. The author illustrates how Frank led the way not only in pioneering public health regulations but also in making a particular study of the social environment on the individual. His four volume work on public health, dealing especially with the social aspects of disease including poverty, prostitution, child welfare and pregnancy, led to considerable advances being made in the field of public health and sanitation. Contributions made by other prominent medical figures in the 19th century, such as Theodor Billroth (1829-94), Johann Joseph Berndt (1770-1842) and Josef Skoda (1804-81), are also briefly outlined in this paper.

384 **The history of dermatology in Austria.**
A. Wiedmann. *Excerpta Medica*, vol. 11, no. 13 (1957), p. 418-19.

This brief survey by the Professor of Dermatology at the University of Vienna opens with the founding of the Austrian Dermatological Clinic in Vienna in 1849 by Ferdinand von Hebra (1816-80), who gave the accepted 'efflorescence theory' the pathological basis on which dermatological diagnosis still rests today. Hebra also developed a new therapy of skin diseases, one of his most beneficial therapeutic innovations being the water bed treatment. The author then outlines the contributions made to the development of dermatological and syphilitic research and treatment by Hebra's successors, including Moritz Kaposi (1837-1902), Gustav Riehl (1885-1940), Leopold Arzt (1885-1955) and Wilhelm Kerl (1880-1945). The concluding paragraph briefly describes the two other Austrian dermatological clinics in Graz and Innsbruck, which were founded in 1874 and 1887 respectively.

385 **Austria: its literary, scientific and medical institutions.**
W. R. Wilde. Dublin: William Curry; London: Longman Brown, 1843. 325p.

Sub-titled 'Notes upon the present state of science and a guide to the hospitals and sanitary establishments of Vienna' this volume contains a wealth of interesting information on medical conditions in the Empire's capital in the mid-19th century. The author was a distinguished Irish surgeon, and despite the weight of censorship and a reluctance on the part of the authorities to impart official information to a foreigner, he nevertheless managed to find out a great deal about a number of different medical institutions from personal visits and conversations with professionals in various fields of medicine. He regards the absence of an Austrian Academy of Sciences in Vienna, when both Prague and Budapest could boast of one, as an insult to the German race, but is warm in his praise for Viennese medical training in opthalmology and certain children's diseases. He was also particularly impressed by the internationally-known deaf and dumb institute in Vienna which had been founded as far back as 1779.

Politics and Government

386 **Political action: mass participation in five western democracies.**
S. H. Barnes, M. Kaase. London: Sage Publications, 1979. 607p. bibliog.

These are the findings of an international study of the social basis for political actions, compiled from national sample surveys undertaken by eight teams but with carefully controlled questionnaires and common techniques. The Austrian element is interpreted in the text and needs a little delving to identify the national conclusions, but its authority is well-established, since the Austrian team was led by Dr. Leopold Rosenmayr, the professor of sociology at Vienna University.

387 **The changing face of western Communism.**
Edited by D. Childs. London: Croom Helm, 1980. 286p. bibliog.

Professor Karl Stadler, who contributes the chapter on Austria (p. 260-275) reviews post-war developments in the Austrian Communist Party. He shows how in 1945, despite the backing of the occupying Soviet forces, the communists were decisively beaten in the elections. He also indicates that they continued to lose ground as a result of pressure from the powerful coalition subsequently formed by the two major political parties, the Socialists and the People's Party. The Party's fortunes further declined after 1955, when Austria gained her sovereignty and today it is neither politically significant nor influential.

388 **Political oppositions in Western democracies: Austria, the pooling of opposition.**
Frederick C. Engelmann. In: *Political oppositions in Western democracies*. Edited by Robert A. Dahl. Newhaven, Connecticut: Yale University Press, 1966, p. 260-83.

This short but close-packed chapter from a history of organized political opposition in the western democracies, deals with post-World War II Austria. It is prefaced by an account of political conditions under the Dual Monarchy and refers to the formation of the Social Democratic and Christian Social Parties in 1889 which marked the start of a legalized opposition. In the First Republic the three major groupings – clerical-Catholic, Marxist-socialist, and liberal-national – all set up para-military organizations in a situation where agreement could not be reached on a ruling coalition. The significant development after World War II was the practice of 'Proporz' by which the overall percentages of votes cast affected not only the allocation of cabinet portfolios but the staffing of government corporations and nationalized industries as well. The poor electoral showing of the Communist Party in 1945 elections resulted two years later in their withdrawal, not only from the coalition government but from any attempt at forming an effective opposition, including participation in the 'Proporz' system, which is the peculiarly Austrian variant of the US 'spoils system'.

389 **Das politische System.** (The political system.)
Edited by H. Fischer. Vienna: Europaverlag, 1977. 2nd ed. 655p.

In this collection of essays by a team of specialists the most important components of the political system as it operates in Austria today are subjected to detailed analysis. The book clearly reveals how much of public, economic and cultural life is still permeated by politics and how this constitutes a particularly Austrian tradition.

390 **The political system in Austria.**
Franz Grössl. Vienna: Federal Press Service, 1984. 23p. (Austria Documentation).

This short pamphlet provides a brief outline of: the Austrian constitution and its history dating back to the constitution of the Austro-Hungarian monarchy in 1867; the State structure, including legislature and public administration; the judiciary; constitutional and administrative courts; the media; political parties; labour legislation; and industrial democracy.

391 **The public service.**
Viktor Hackl. *International Review of Administrative Sciences* (Brussels), vol. 28, no. 2 (1962), p. 168-81.

The organization and structure of Austrian government administration, with illustrative diagrams, is described in clear terms in this paper which was presented at the 12th International Congress of Administrative Sciences held in Vienna in the summer of 1972.

392 **Austria: an administrative state – the role of Austrian bureacuracy.**
Raoul F. Kneucker. Österreichische Zeitschrift für Politikwissenschaft vol. 2 (1973), p. 95-127. (Austrian Contemporary Journal for Political Science).

This was a foretaste, based on interviews with leading civil servants, of a planned larger work surveying the gradual development of a civil service and tracing its emergence from an executive élite to an 'open' public service. It covered the main central ministries and the provincial governments, concentrating on: recruitment and promotion; relationships with the politicians; reforms and innovations; style and traditions; and co-operation with parliament.

393 **The 'third camp'.**
Wilhelm F. Kroupa. *Austria Today*, no. 1 (1984), p. 10-12.

Since 1983 the Austrian Freedom Party (Freiheitliche Partei Österreichs) has been participating in government in coalition with the Socialist Party. This is a brief account of the origins and growth of the Austrian Freedom Party in its different guises throughout its history, but always acknowledging its adherence to the principles of liberalism. Its present leader is Norbert Steger, Vice-Chancellor and Federal Minister of Trade. See also Max E. Riedlsperger's *The lingering shadow of Nazism* (q.v.).

394 **The lingering shadow of Nazism: the Austrian independent movement since 1945.**
Max E. Riedlsperger. New York: Columbia University Press, 1978. 214p. (East European Monographs, no. 42).

This is a well-documented analysis of the formation, with initial setbacks, of the Austrian Freedom Party, the only potentially significant representation of a third force in Austrian politics since 1945, after the collapse of the Communist Party. It derives its main impetus from former Nazis who had been disenfranchized as a result of the application of the de-Nazification decrees after World War II. However, as this account makes clear, the party was unable to exert any direct political influence largely due to its heterogenous composition, the imprecision of its aims and the suspicions entertained by the other two major parties that it was simply a means to infiltrate Nazis into the political arena. It is perhaps relevant to note that by 1985 the third force, i.e., the Austrian Freedom Party, had not only established itself as a political party of recognized status but had also achieved manifest success in elections, both local and national. This culminated in its invitation by the Socialist Party which found itself without an overall majority, after the 1983 election, to join it in forming a coalition government, in which the party leader Norbert Steger became Vice-Chancellor.

395 **The transformation of Austrian socialism.**
Kurt L. Shell. New York: State University of New York, 1962. 305p. bibliog.

While still retaining traditional labels, the author shows that present-day socialists in Austria are as far removed from a policy of the dictatorship of the proletariat as in the 1930's and that they are well-attuned to the actual political and economic setting in which the party now finds itself. The main reasons for this greater flexibility and decrease in radicalism, the author contends, are the lessons learnt from a repressive Soviet occupation in the post-World War II period and the establishment of a welfare state with a mixed economy, which has forced the party to adapt itself to an entirely new situation.

396 **Government policy declaration.**

Fred Sinowatz. Vienna: Federal Press Service, 1983. 48p.

This is the text of the acceptance speech of the present Federal Chancellor on taking office in May 1983. The speech sets out, at considerable length, the policies of the new coalition government of the Socialist and Freedom Parties.

397 **Political parties and elections in Austria.**

Melanie A. Sully. London: Hurst, 1981. 194p. 4 maps. bibliog.

For the English reader seeking a comprehensive survey of the first two decades of post-World War II Austrian politics, both from a general and party political viewpoint, this clear and competent exposition should amply satisfy his needs. The author, an acknowledged expert on her subject, stresses in her introduction the role of the political parties in providing an important element of continuity and in helping to create a stable State structure since 1945. She then devotes a separate chapter to each of the four main political parties, (Socialist, People's, Freedom, and Communist) outlining their history, organization, ideology and degree of electoral support. There is much statistical data with tables of election results. The main bibliography, listing principally works in German, is conveniently divided into the following sections: pre-World War II Austrian history; post-War Austrian politics; and parties and elections; while there are also specialized bibliographies for each of the political parties. An invaluable well-researched study.

The Law, Police and Constitution

398 **The general civil code of Austria.**

Edited by Paul L. Baeck, translated from the German by R. Winiwarter. Dobbs Ferry, New York: Oceana Publications, 1972. 293p.

The Austrian general civil code was first enacted by imperial edict in 1811. This work provides the full text with subsequent amendments and commentary and was prepared for the Parker School of Foreign and Comparative Law at Columbia University, New York.

399 **The international legal status of Austria, 1938-1955.**

Robert Eugene Clute. The Hague: Martinus Nijhoff, 1962. 157p.

The author examines the legal consequences of the *Anschluss* of 1938 and the subsequent Allied occupation of Austria after World War II in the light of the traditional international law of State succession. He indicates that in the field of international relations, there is a slow but persistent movement, still to be ratified by legislation, to outlaw all illegal acquisitions of territory.

400 **Planning law in Western Europe.**

Edited by J. F. Garner. Amsterdam, The Netherlands: North-Holland Publishing, 1975. 350p.

Town and country planning laws in thirteen West European countries are quoted with full texts and explanatory notes and the chapter on Austria (p.9-40) is by Siegbert Morscher and has been translated from the German by Dorothée Schaeubinger. The constitution and legal background in each country is explained, and a description is provided of the legal processes for drawing up national and regional plans for land control, the forms of authority required for land development and how to obtain them.

401 **The Austrian law of companies with limited liability.**
Translated from the German by Julie Goldberg. Vienna: Manz Verlag, 1984. 122p. bibliog. (Recht-Wirtschaft-Aussenhandel, Bd. 7).

The full text of this law, summarized in Peter Meinhardts *Company Law in Europe* (q.v.)· is given in the original German with the English translation alongside.

402 **The Austrian penal act.**
Introduced by Roland Grassberger, Helga Nowoty, translated from the German by Norbert D. West, Samuel I. Shuman. South Hackensack, New York: Fred B. Rothman; London: Sweet & Maxwell, 1966. 170p. (The American Series of Foreign Penal Codes, vol. 12).

The Austrian penal code, together with the French code, is the oldest one operating in Europe today. It dates back to the time of Maria Theresa and Joseph II, with the major reforms being enacted almost a century later in 1852. A number of important supplementary statutes have been passed since 1945 with further amendments following the State Treaty of 1955.

403 **Administrative Court procedure.**
E. C. Hellbling. *International Review of Administrative Sciences* (Brussels), no. 2, vol. 28 (1962), p. 119-32.

A paper delivered at the 12th International Congress of Administrative Sciences held in Vienna in July 1962. The Administrative Court is part of the central legal set-up in Austria under the Second Republic and acts as a watchdog on the proceedings of the whole processes of government.

404 **Austrian business law.**
Edited by Kurt Heller, with the collaboration of Heinz Löber, George Bahn, Werner Hube, Günther Horväth. Deventer, Netherlands: Kluwer; Vienna: Manz, 1984.

An up-to-date outline of the legal, accounting and tax aspects of Austrian law. The particular value of this work for Anglo-American readers lies in the emphasis placed on the divergent approach to doing business exercised in Austria compared with that in other Western countries, on which the authors, as international consultants, are expert.

405 **Die Gendarmerie in Österreich, 1849-1974. 125 Jahre Pflichterfüllung.** (The gendarmerie in Austria. 125 years of devotion to duty).
Edited by Leopold Kepler. Graz, Austria: Leykam, 1974. 362p. bibliog.

Well-documented and lavishly illustrated, this publication, issued to commemorate 125 years of the history of the Austrian gendarmerie, is intended for a popular readership. The short review of its earlier history is followed by a more extended survey describing its various activities today including traffic control, criminal investigation, mountain rescue, frontier control and drug searches.

406 **The Austrian federal constitution.**
Translated from the German on behalf of the Austrian Federal Ministry for Foreign Affairs by Charles Kessler. Vienna: Verlag Manz, 1984. 138p.

This is the text of the Austrian Federal Constitution as revised in 1929. The volume also contains subsequent additions and amendments and other important constitutional provisions, including, most importantly, the Constitutional Law on the Neutrality of Austria, enacted by an independent Austria in October 1955 following the State Treaty and the withdrawal of the allied occupying forces.

407 **Company law in Europe.**
Peter Meinhardt. Farnborough, England: Gower, 1981. 3rd. ed. 523p. bibliog.

This publication sets out the basic features of company law in twelve European countries, including Austria. It concentrates on public and private limited companies and provides details of special types of companies. The text reflects the law as at 1 January 1980 and each country is divided into sections and follows a sequence of standard headings. The chapter on Austria covers: basic law; the formation of a limited company; the registering of companies; the name, objects and capital of a limited company; shares and their allotment; general meetings; management boards; contracts; accounts; audits; and private companies. The entry covers forty-four pages and is compiled by Dr. Schönherr, a professor of commercial and company law at Vienna University.

408 **The Austrian law on extradiction and mutual assistance in criminal matters.**
Edith Palmer. Washington, DC: Library of Congress, Law Library 1983. 166p. bibliog.

The text of the law, which has an added significance for Austria in relation to suspected Nazi war criminals living abroad, is quoted in full with brief explanatory notes.

409 **State absolutism and the rule of law; the struggle for the codification of civil law in Austria.**
Henry E. Strakosch. Sydney, Australia: University Press; London: Methuen, 1967. 267p. bibliog.

In this scholarly analysis of a neglected subject the author explains that codification of Austrian civil law was a lengthy and hard fought process. It was part of a great political contest between the State, aspiring to a monopoly of government, and various groups combining in pursuance of a common aim, namely, the defence of the primary elements of the social order. The book elaborates this theme in a historical context.

410 **Hungary and Austria: a new look at crime.**
Keith Wardrop. Croydon, England: Institute for the Study and Treatment of Delinquency, 1977. 30p.

A British forensic psychiatrist's report on a study tour to Budapest and Vienna made in September 1977. It summarizes current Austrian legislation affecting juvenile offenders, and describes the Austrian probation service, institutions and children's homes, and a visit to a local establishment housing mentally-abnormal offenders, considered to be of criminal responsibility.

Foreign Relations, Defence and Military Affairs

411 **Austria's defence in transit.**
Dennis Chaplin. *Military Review* (Fort Levenworth, Kansas, USA) vol. 57, no. 1 (Jan. 1977), p. 57-64.

Although not a member of NATO, Austria plays a particular role in NATO security planning because the country's geographical position, like that of Switzerland, separates Italy from the other European NATO States. A territorial wedge is thus formed between the northern and southern NATO zones. The author offers a scenario of possible Soviet encroachments and outlines the system of defended areas along transit routes most likely to be used by any invader. He concludes that the restructuring of the Austrian army, with a new emphasis on the army as a mobile alert force rather than its role in the context of static military groupings, is having to face severe recruitment problems and financial cutbacks. Notwithstanding this, it is asserted that a change in the top command forecast at the time of writing, and since effected, could reverse this situation.

412 **Close up Austria.**
Military Technology (Special Supplement), vol. 7, no. 7 (1983). 47p.

This special issue is devoted to an in-depth report covering all aspects of the country's defence efforts which are based on the 'hedgehog' principle i.e., 'peace-loving, yet ready for self-defence'. It includes an interview with the outgoing Minister of Defence, Otto Rösch, and a substantial section on the nation's defence industry with details of weapon and equipment specifications and potential.

413 **Unser Heer.** (Our Army.)

Edited by Herbert Fürlinger, Ludwig Jedlicka. Vienna: H. Fürlinger, 1963. 547p. 4 maps.

The difficult task of popularizing the army in a neutral state and lending respectability to it as a profession is freely admitted in the introduction to this compendious work, sponsored by the Federal Ministry for Home Defence and surveying 300 years of Austrian soldiering. The earlier account follows a straightforward historical course, while the post-World War II material introduces a note of recruiting fervour and shows signs of some emotional bravura. There are some excellent illustrations and extensive source notes.

414 **The Austrian officer at work and at play.**

Dorothea Gerard. London: Smith, Elder, 1913. 343p.

During the First World War the imperial and royal armies of Austro-Hungary were unleashed in a struggle which, by all accounts, they sustained without a substantial break in morale until late in 1918. It was their heyday, and playwrights of the Schnitzler generation and film producers ever since have brought it unforgettably to our attention. This is a further offering, a lighthearted book by the wife of a cavalry officer intent on 'showing the English that Austrians are good at play but equally skilled in war'. The deeds of valour which she describes are not all backed up by historical evidence and the reader is asked to accept their 'intrinsic probability as episodes which are typically Austrian'.

415 **Das Steiermärkische Landeszeughaus in Graz: eine Übersicht über seine Geschichte und seine Waffen.** (The Styrian arsenal in Graz: a survey of its history and weaponry.)

Peter Krenn. Graz, Austria: Styria Verlag, 1978. 2nd rev. ed. 92p.

Among the armouries of Europe the provincial arsenal in the Styrian capital of Graz is unique in retaining its original arrangement unchanged since 1642 and the major part of its collection in working order. It contains some 29,000 pieces of armour, weapons and other military equipment, mostly from the 16th and 17th centuries comprising the actual weapons borne by Styrian soldiers and last used in the siege of Vienna against the Turks in 1683; they have never left the armoury since that date. This brief history of the arsenal with a guide to its contents contains sixteen full page photographs and a summary in English translation.

416 **Land of encounter.**

Vienna: Federal Press Service, 1984. 64p. (Austria Documentation).

Active neutrality and an enduring commitment to international co-operation, serving both the interests of the country's independence and world peace, are the corner-stones of Austria's present day foreign policy. This brochure aims to demonstrate how this is being pursued in different spheres of public life. There is a brief section on the workings of democracy, explaining how economic stability has been achieved through the uniquely Austrian instrument of 'social partnership'. This is followed by an article on the country's role in the international arena, with special emphasis on its United Nations peacekeeping and humanitarian activities and the part played by Vienna in providing an important international centre for the UN and a number of intergovernmental organizations such as the Organization of the Petroleum Exporting Countries (OPEC) and the International Atomic Energy Agency. Other examples of Austria's contribution in the international fields of culture, education and sport are described with well-chosen black-and-white illustrations.

417 **Medal ribbons and orders of imperial Germany and Austria.**
D. G. Neville. Huntingdon, England: Balfour Publications, 1974. 94p.

In this well-illustrated textbook the author presents a selection of orders, decorations and medals, some rare and much sought after, from his extensive private collection. He prefaces his work with a brief historical outline and a note on the origins of the various orders and their classification. The section on imperial Austria is attractively annotated and the coloured photography is of a high order. There are few modern books on this subject, certainly none in English, and this publication fills a useful gap. It is of interest not only to the experienced collector but also to the novice venturing into this field for the first time. For a comprehensive standard work on this entire subject the reader with a knowledge of German is directed to Roman von Prochaska's work (q.v.).

418 **Asylum in Europe: a handbook for agencies assisting refugees.**
Edited by Anne Paludan. Geneva, Switzerland: International University Exchange Fund, 1979. 2nd. ed. 152p.

Austria's humanitarian role and activities in the international field since World War II have been quite out of proportion to her small geographical size and her population of only 7.5 million. During the past four decades she has offered shelter to no less than 1.75 million refugees, either in transit, by helping them to travel to other destinations, or by granting them permanent asylum. This has involved considerable sacrifices on the part of the Austrian people. The Traiskirchen Reception Centre near the country's eastern border has played a significant part in these activities, and this was particularly the case during the Hungarian Uprising in 1956 and the Soviet intervention in Czechoslovakia in 1968. The Centre's continuing role is outlined in the section on Austria in this publication (p. 26-34), which also summarizes the country's principal laws on asylum, passport control and naturalization. In addition, the volume lists a number of non-governmental organizations assisting refugees in Austria and quotes some useful addresses and relevant publications.

419 **Ordenshandbuch.** (Handbook of orders and decorations.)
Roman von Prochaska. Munich, GFR: Graf, Kleinau, 1979. 4 vols.

A superbly-illustrated and well-researched handbook depicting armorial bearings, decorations, orders and medals of every possible description from the earliest days of the Habsburg dynasty to the present. A definitive, standard work.

420 **Austrian neutrality in post-war Europe: the domestic roots of a foreign policy.**

Thomas O. Schlesinger, translated from the German by the author. Vienna: Wilhelm Braumüller, 1972. 158p. bibliog. (University Book Publications Series.)

The author, who was an interpreter for the US occupation forces after World War II, has produced an exceptionally well-researched study of an important problem affecting not only the internal psychology of a newly-restored nation, but the whole complex of international relationships on a world-wide scale. He asks whether the policy of neutrality truly reflects the Austrian political culture and the people's image of their national mission. Neutrality, he points out, is for the small state; major powers are by definition non-neutral, and as evidence in his enquiries, he provides a careful analysis of Austrian political reactions to some highly relevant cases: the Hungarian Uprising of 1956; Soviet intervention in Czechoslovakia in 1968; and border problems with the Italians over South Tirol and Yugoslavs over Carinthia.

421 **Austria and its permanent neutrality: background, reality and defence.**

Gerald Stourzh, Karl Zemanek. *Austria Today*, no. 3 (1983), p. 17-32.

In the first part of this article Professor Stourzh summarizes briefly the course of the negotiations which led to the State Treaty of 1955, while his co-author Professor Zemanek explains the meaning of permanent neutrality, as opposed to neutralism – a concept which Austria has rejected. The final section considers the three main factors which determine the country's security policy: internal stability; an internationally-orientated foreign policy; and a comprehensive defence system. This latter, the basic principles of which are no state secret, are set out clearly with explanatory diagrams.

422 **Austria – permanently neutral.**

Karl Stuhlpfarrer. Vienna: Federal Press Service, 1983. 35p. bibliog. (Austria Documentation).

A brief survey of Austria's foreign policy since the end of World War II. The author traces the passage of events which affected the country's international position prior to the State Treaty of 1955 and its subsequent constructive collaboration in various fields through membership of such bodies as the United Nations, the Council of Europe, the European Free Trade Association and the Organization for Economic Co-operation and Development. The author also lays stress on Austria's participation in the UN peace-keeping operations in the Middle East and Africa and her aid to development programs in the Third World, and particularly her valuable contribution in the area of humanitarian aid to the 1,750,000 refugees who have found either temporary, or permanent, asylum in the country since 1945.

423 **The permanent neutrality of Austria.**
Alfred Verdross, translated from the German by Charles Kessler. Vienna: Verlag für Geschichte und Politik, 1978. 71p.

Commentators have often overlooked the fact that Austrian post-world War II neutrality, which emerged from the 1955 State Treaty and ended the four-power occupation, was not imposed but volunteered. The Allies guaranteed independence only and were not unanimous over the question of neutrality, which was then enshrined in the Constitution by the Austrians themselves. This authoritative study was sponsored by the Austrian Ministry of Foreign Affairs and examines the purely legal side of the concept of neutrality, both domestic and international, and considers the parallel patterns in Switzerland and Sweden.

424 **Soziale Verteidigung: Zivil Widerstand: Immerwährende Neutralität.** (Communal defence: civil resistance: permanent neutrality).
Heinz Vetschera. Vienna: Braumüller, 1978. 175p. bibliog. (Austrian Studies in Legal and Political Science, vol. 2).

This is part of a series on legal and political studies by an author who faces up fairly and squarely to the essence of neutrality – what would happen if a neutral state were attacked? He quotes the constitution and describes the likely effects – the breakdown of public utilities and the weakening of morale under pressure from foreign propaganda. As for the military, he rather assumes that self-defence is an anachronism and quotes appositely from the case histories of Norway in World War II and Czechoslovakia in 1968. For him, the answer lies in positive neutrality: Austria as 'pig in the middle' between East and West has it in its power to make its own case history.

425 **The Austrian example.**
Kurt Waldheim, translated from the German by Ewald Osers. London: Weidenfeld & Nicolson, 1973. 230p. 4 maps. bibliog.

Originally published in 1971, and written while the author was Secretary General of the United Nations, these reflections on Austria's policy of 'active neutrality' and fulfilment of its obligations to the international community reveal a strong patriotic feeling underlying the balanced and perceptive view of a distinguished statesman. The book describes the transformation of Austria in Europe's crisis region of the immediate post-World War II period into a zone of peace and economic and political advance. The author underlines the close relationship between Austria's domestic and foreign policy and concludes with a generally optimistic forecast of the country's future. For a consideration of Waldheim's career see Sri Chinmoy's *A soulful tribute to the Secretary General: the pilot supreme of the United Nations* (Aum Publications, 1978).

Economy

426 **Handbuch der österreichischen Wirtschaftspolitik.** (Handbook of Austrian political economy.)
Compiled by H. Abele, S. Schleicher, E. Nowotny, G. W. Winckler. Vienna: Manzsche Verlag und Universitätsbuchhandlung, 1982. 480p. bibliog.

No less than thirty economic specialists have contributed to this exhaustive survey of Austria's post-World War II economic policy and achievements. The four main parts comprise: economic theory; institutions and decision-making processes; different aspects of the economy such as banking and finance, industry, technology, energy needs, agrarian developments, transport and housing; and specific case studies. The bibliography cites a number of articles and monographs published in English in the United States and Britain.

427 **The political economy of Austria.**
Edited by Sven. W. Arndt. Washington, DC; London: American Enterprise Institute, 1982. 224p.

This volume presents the edited proceedings of a conference sponsored jointly by the American Enterprise Institute for Public Policy Research and the Austrian Institute, New York, which was held in Washington in October 1981. The conference examined Austria's post-World War II economic achievements with particular reference to the institutional arrangements which made them possible. The participants included leading economists, industrialists, bankers, civil servants and academics from the United States and Austria. The nine papers included here were all presented by Austrian economic policy makers, or their advisers, and are followed by commentaries by selected American participants.

428 **Austria: Economic Report.**
London: Lloyds Bank, 1984. 26p. occasional.

The Economics Department of the Lloyds Bank Group produces this report for the use of its clients and businessmen trading with Austria. It includes a number of up-to-date fact sheets and statistics on the domestic economy of Austria, the structure of production, the country's external trading position and its general trading policy.

429 **Survey of the Austrian economy, 1984.**
Compiled and annotated by Joseph Docekal. Vienna: Institute for Economic and Social Affairs, 1984. 71p. annual.

Published every September with a minimum of commentary, the aim of this survey is to present, in a popularized form, an up-to-date picture of the country's economy and its international standing in all important sectors. It includes statistical data, diagrams and tables.

430 **Economic Surveys: Austria.**
Paris: Organization for Economic Co-operation and Development, 1961-. annual.

These detailed surveys, produced by OECD committees for each of its member countries, are valued not only for their critical evaluation of economic trends but also for their consideration of economic and financial prospects and potentialities in the coming year. The accompanying statistical appendixes include a wide-range of economic indicators. The 1984 report for Austria has seventy pages.

431 **Prosperity amidst crisis: Austria's economic policy and the energy crunch.**
Wilhelm Hankel, translated from the German by Jean Steinberg. Boulder, Colorado: Westview Press, 1981. 234p.

Austria's former Vice-Chancellor Hannes Androsch, himself a distinguished economist, has written a foreword to this publication expressing the hope that it will help economic policy making in Austria. The author presents a comprehensive up-to-date survey of the development, condition and potential of the Austrian economy against the background of increased unemployment in the Western world, the oil crisis and the growing political ascendancy of the third world. He outlines the difficulties of maintaining a stable economy in a small country, where inflation and employment policies can so easily be blown off course by outside factors. However, he pays tribute to Austria's economic growth, the expansion of her export capacity and her advance in the technological field. With almost full-employment and a negligible inflation rate her recent performance has, proportionately speaking, outstripped that of West Germany even though the Austrian Schilling is tied to the German Deutschmark. The author asks how long an economic and financial policy of 'prosperity on credit' can be sustained but he suggests no answers. A book to provoke discussion among economists.

432 **Carl Menger and the Austrian School of Economics.**
Edited by J. R. Hicks, Wilhelm Weber. Oxford: Oxford University Press, 1973. 235p.

Carl Menger was the father of Austrian economics and this is a collection of papers presented to a symposium held in Vienna in 1971 to mark the centenary of the publication of his major work *Principles of Economics*. The main themes of his pioneering achievements are set in their historical context and reference is made to such distinguished names as Friedrich von Wieser (1851-1926), Ludwig von Mises (1881-1973), and Friedrich August von Hayek (b.1899).

433 **Österreich über alles, wenn es nur will.** (Austria abaove all, if it really wanted to be.)
Philipp Wilhelm von Hörnigk. Vaduz, Liechtenstein: Topos Verlag, 1978. 420p.

First published anonymously in 1684, this classic is a reprint of the 1753 Frankfurt and Leipzig editions which had a tremendous success and considerable influence. The author, a great patriot and extensive traveller, spent most of his life in Austrian public service and strongly supported the mercantilist doctrines of his day. Here he is clearly and forcefully propounding that theory and although he paints a rather too favourable picture of Austria's economic resources, this work is remarkable in its overall geographical conception. The volume represents a landmark in patriotic Austro-German economic literature.

434 **Austria, Europe and the world in the 1980s.**
Herman Kahn, Ernest Schneider, John Trammell. Vienna: Central Savings Bank and Commercial Bank, 1983. 73p. (Perspectives Series).

Three American economists from the Hudson Strategy Group, New York, have contributed to this appraisal of Austria's economic position in the 1980's in a world and European political context, as seen from an American point of view. A second part of this study discusses possible long-term development options and the future outlook for Austria. The general conclusion is that European, as opposed to world, economic prospects in the next decade will not be as favourable to Austria as in the past, but that the present political and social stability of the country will be sustained and that any fundamental changes in social values or political thinking will be gradual. Indeed, the group wonders whether the country's structure might not become too rigid for it to find the innovative solutions to future problems, since the phenomenon of low unemployment, low inflation and high production will not continue for long and is in fact already coming to an end.

435 **Method, process and Austrian economics: essays in honour of Ludwig Mises.**
Edited by Israel M. Kirzner. Lexington, Massachusetts: Gower Publishing, 1983. 262p. bibliog.

A selection of eighteen papers presented to a conference on Austrian economics organized by the author in New York in 1982 to mark the centenary of the birth of Ludwig von Mises, the disciple of the founder of the Austrian School of Economics, Carl Menger. It examines aspects of Menger's theories and perspectives and the editor contributes a valuable introduction. A scholarly presentation, aimed at the professional economist.

436 **Quarterly Economic Review: Austria.**
London: Economic Intelligence Unit, 1952-. quarterly.

Austria is one of 160 countries regularly covered in this world-wide series of reports by an international economic research organization. It aims to include in each issue: an analysis of recent political developments in the country concerned; government economic policies; investment and consumer spending trends; and an evaluation of foreign trade data. Statistical tables are also attached. The average length of each report is twenty pages. A much respected source of current economic information.

437 **The capitalist alternative; an introduction to neo-Austrian economics.**
Alexander H. Shand. Brighton, England: Harvester, 1984. 242p. bibliog.

The author, a senior lecturer in economics at Manchester Polytechnic, has made an important and up-to-date contribution to economic thinking. Despite the civic honours bestowed on the current doyen of the economist world, Professor Friedrich Hayek, his influence on practical politics in Britain, the author contends, is arguably less than its potential. This serious study enables the reader to form his own views on why this should be. It covers methodology, micro- and macro-economics as well as general social topics. The author also contributes short biographical notes on the leading Austrian exponents, Carl Menger, Ludwig von Mises, Friedrich Hayek and Israel Kirzner. The work is aimed at the general reader and is not over-loaded with technical terminology or mathematical models.

438 **Prices and incomes policy: the Austrian experience.**
Hannes Suppanz, Derek Robinson. Paris: Organization for Economic Co-operation and Development, 1972. 72p.

This report was prepared by an international study group of trade unionists and employers from five OECD countries, which met to examine and comment on Austria's remarkably successful economic record since she gained independence in 1955. Hannes Suppanz of the Institute for Industrial Research in Vienna contributes the first part, which describes the institutional framework and the establishment of the Prices and Wages Commission in 1957. This is followed by a brief survey of the Austrian economy, with special reference to income distribution and wages structure. Derek Robinson, a British statistician and economist, acting as rapporteur, summarizes the group's discussions and concludes that Austria, taking a pragmatic approach, has only been marginally interested in proving the success, or otherwise, of her economic system with quantifiable statistics and has been much more concerned with the general economic climate.

439 **The fundamentals of Austrian economics.**

Thomas C. Taylor. London: Adam Smith Institute, 1981. 68p.

Carl Menger founded the Austrian School of Economics at the turn of the century and this work is a straightforward but comprehensive introduction to the schools philosophy. The Austrian School differs fundamentally from the Keynesian approach and argues that the economy cannot be reduced to a set of averages and aggregates and therefore cannot be quantified or predicted in the way favoured by macro-economists. In other words, it operates on a free market which is not to be manipulated by economists and policy makers. The author outlines this and other key Austrian concepts such as the theory of capital, inflation and the business cycle.

Finance and Banking

440 **Austria's monetary situation.**
Vienna: Austrian National Bank. monthly.

This brief survey appears in German, English and French. It outlines the current monetary situation in Austria and includes summaries of reports on fiscal matters as well as economic indicators.

441 **The Austrian banking system.**
Fritz Diwok, translated and revised from the German edition of *Struktur ausländischer Banksysteme: Österreich.* (Structure of foreign banking systems: Austria). Vienna: Creditanstalt-Bankverein, 1983. 162p. bibliog.

In this useful guide to the country's banking system the author, the general secretary of the Austrian Banker's Association, has updated much important information contained in the original German edition of 1981. Particular emphasis has been placed on the increasing internationalization of Austrian banking activities and moves towards establishing an all-purpose banking system. The publication is in six parts, covering: the general economic background, with an outline of the banking system and the main provisions of the 1979 Banking Act; the activities of the central banking sector as a whole; a survey of commercial, mortgage and foreign banks; savings banks and credit institutions; building societies; and post office savings banks. Statistical tables are also included.

442 **Neuere geldpolitische Konzepte und die Politik der österreichischen Nationalbank, 1959-1978.** (Recent politico-financial concepts and the policy of the Austrian National Bank, 1959-78.)
Peter Höller. Vienna: Association of Scientific Societies of Austria, 1981. 180p. bibliog. vol. 26.

This is one of a series of dissertations produced at the Johannes Kepler Institute, University of Linz, in 1980 on monetary theory and the policies of the National Bank of Austria, with a critical analysis of the latest developments in monetary supply and demand. There is much statistical data and an extensive bibliography of books, periodicals, essays and dissertations.

Trade, Industry and Investment

443 **Austria: glass industry review.**
Glass International, (Mar. 1984). 19p.

This survey, compiled with the assistance and co-operation of the Glass Industry Association in Vienna, reviews the location, composition and production activities of the Austrian glass manufacturing industry. It includes a list of the Associations' members and provides details of certain selected firms specializing in decorative glass manufacture.

444 **Austrian Trade News.**
London: Austrian Trade Commission, 1947-. monthly.

Designed for businessmen and investors in Austrian industry, both potential and actual, this promotional publication provides details of new Austrian products, inventions and technical developments, lists forthcoming trade fairs and economic congresses in Austria and presents information about business language courses in Britain and Austria.

445 **Austria's largest metallurgical complex.**
Steel Times International, vol. 7, no. 3. (Sept. 1983), p. 14-23.

The Voest-Alpine metallurgical group accounts for most of the Austrian steel industry's producing capacity. This article describes the activities of both the Linz works in Upper Austria, the largest metallurgical plant in the country, and the blast furnace plant at Leoben-Donawitz in Styria. The combine is known world-wide.

446 **Austrian regional development policy: the impact of policy on the achievement of planning goals.**

W.H. Berentsen. *Economic Geography*, vol. 54 (April 1978), p. 115-34.

Two of the problems facing industrialized countries today, in relation to regional development, are the movement of the population away from rural areas and regional income differentials. This analysis, covering a fifteen year period (1957-71), shows that Austrian government efforts to solve these questions were only partially successful. This was due to a number of economic factors, and particularly the overriding effect of free market forces. The expansion of tourism in western Austria raised income levels in these predominantly rural areas. However, improved social services, better commuting facilities and more secure employment opportunities were all factors which promoted greater urbanization and attracted migration from the rural areas. The author contends that decentralization of labour-intensive industry away from Vienna should be more actively encouraged since this would mean more jobs in the rest of the country.

447 **Doing business in Austria.**

London: Price Waterhouse, 1984. 91p.

Austria can offer a number of attractions to the foreign investor such as a stable and vigorous economy, a skilled workforce, a strike-free industrial climate and a soundly-based currency. This useful guide, issued by a well-known firm of accountants in London, provides an outline of the general investment situation in the country and describes the actual technical processes connected with foreign business, such as exchange controls, restrictions on foreign investment and regulation agencies. Other aspects covered are labour relations and social security. A somewhat similar guide is *Hints to Exporters – Austria*, (London: British Overseas Trade Board, 1979, 40p.) which contains some practical details about business transactions with Austria and includes a list of useful business addresses, which is updated from time to time.

448 **500 Jahre Druck in Österreich.** (Five hundred years of printing in Austria.)

Anton Durstmüller. Vienna: Association of Printing Trade Bodies, 1982. 392p. bibliog.

The earliest known printed work to appear within the boundaries of present-day Austria was an Italian-German dictionary dated 1482 and printed in Innsbruck. This quincentennial commemorative presentation traces with some superb reproductions the history and development of the printing trade in Austria from this early beginning to 1848; a second volume covering the final period up to 1982 is in preparation. The documentation is exhaustive and clearly and attractively set out, while the tables in loose-leaf folders, showing in diagrammatic form the leading printers and associated craftsmen, with their period of activity and location, and (where applicable) their present successors, is a handy reference guide even for the non-German speaker. The bibliography is extensive and covers all aspects of the printing and allied crafts such as typography, lithography, illustration and cartography.

449 **Economic and financial aspects of East-West co-operation.**
Vienna: Central Savings Bank and Commercial Bank, 1979. 252p. (Perspectives Series, Sept. 1979).

A symposium held in Vienna in 1979 under the auspices of the Central Savings Bank and the Commercial Bank of Austria was attended by delegates from thirty Eastern and Western countries including Britain. This is a selection of papers presented on that occasion which deal almost exclusively with various aspects of Austria's trade with Eastern Europe through the medium of the Council for Mutual Economic Assistance (Comecon). They show that Austria's exports to this area account on average for just under 14% of her total exports; imports from the same source being about 10%. The Central Savings Bank at that time claimed to have as much as 70% of its foreign business tied up in East-West transactions.

450 **Goods and know-how from Vienna.**
Vienna: Information Centre for the Vienna Economy, 1983. 141p.

The purpose of this brochure, published in German and English, is to provide businessmen and traders, particularly from abroad, with factual information about the small- and medium-sized firms in the metropolitan area of Vienna, so as to encourage investment. The work emphasizes that Vienna, apart from being an international tourist attraction, is also a thriving centre of industry and commerce. It is proposed to update the information at irregular intervals.

451 **Experience gained in establishing new industries in developing areas of Austria.**
Joseph Gründler. In: *Transfer of technology for small industries*. Paris: Organization for Economic Co-operation and Development, 1971, p. 201-03.

An international seminar on 'The role of small-scale industry in the transfer of technology' was held in Austria in July 1973 and was attended by delegates from 15 countries. Among the speakers was Joseph Gründler, of the Austrian Ministry for Social Administration, who outlined the difficulties in trying to attract new industries to the less developed areas of Austria. Among the problems are the high training costs involved and the lack of leisure amenities for employees. It should be noted that small- and medium-sized industrial firms make a major contribution to Austria's GNP.

452 **History in blue smoke.**
Austria Today, no. 2 (1984), p. 41-43.

The growing and import of tobacco, as well as the manufacture of tobacco products in Austria, was established as a State monopoly by the Emperor Joseph II in 1784. This report outlines the history of the Austrian 'Tabakregie' and changes in smoking habits among the population during the past 200 years. It also describes the 'Tabak-Trafik', a uniquely Austrian institution which allows certain shops, generally run by war victims and the disabled, to have the sole monopoly of the sale of tobacco.

453 **The industrial policy of Austria.**

Paris: Organization for Economic Co-operation and Development, 1971. 168p.

Compiled at the beginning of the European industrial boom in the early 1970's, this report presents a relatively encouraging and reassuring picture of the Austrian economy at that time. A short introduction to the post-war geographic and economic background is followed by an analysis of developments since 1950, which underlines the predominance of small- and medium-sized firms in the country's economy. A separate section examines the nationalized industries with special reference to quality control, manpower, research and export promotion.

454 **Embargoes in East-West trade and the European neutrals: the case of Austria.**

Paul Luif. *Current Research on Peace and Violence*, no. 4 (1984), p. 221-28.

Austria's policy of active neutrality in the international arena and independence at home has exposed the country to various economic pressures from the United States, particularly on the question of the transfer of advanced technology to the Eastern European countries with whom Austria has established good trading relations. The author, a member of the Austrian Institute for International Affairs at Laxenburg, near Vienna, examines this question and shows how such pressures have affected the operation of a number of US firms in the country. He then explains that Austria is trying hard to reduce her vulnerability to major power coercion as well as her technological dependence on the United States.

455 **Trade between East and West: the case of Austria.**

Egon Matzner. Stockholm: Almqvist & Wiksell, 1970. 169p. (University of Stockholm, Stockholm Economic Studies, New Series, no. 12).

Partly because of historical and traditional reasons Austria has a special relationship with the Eastern bloc. This survey examines the factors which have influenced Austria's trade with the East since 1945 as part of the country's gradual integration within the European and world economy. The author outlines the problems facing Austria in dealing with states with centrally-planned economies and a large public sector, and suggests that the trade and payment agreements reached with the Comecon countries have helped to reduce the rigidities of bilateralism in trade and are an important ingredient in Austria's policy of maintaining stable trade relations as part of her overall economic strategy. The survey is supported by a number of statistical tables. This subject is not one which attracts much attention from economists and this survey therefore fills a useful gap.

456 **Participation in Austrian business.**

Vienna: Creditanstalt-Bankverein, 1977. 6th ed. 82p.

The Austrian Association of Banking and Credit Institutions publishes on an irregular basis this practical guide intended to assist foreign companies, or individuals, seeking to establish branch activities in Austria. Each guide contains up-to-date information on the economy, and the labour and tax laws and regulations governing business partnerships and companies. It is a multi-lingual production.

457 **The timber industry.**
Wilfried Puwein. *Austria Today*, vol. 6, no. 4 (winter 1980), p. 25-29.

Since Austria is the most heavily wooded country in central Europe with 44% of its land area under afforestation, the timber industry inevitably plays an important part in the country's economy. The author sets out the current situation with supporting statistics on the sawmill, pulp and paper, and wood manufacturing industries.

458 **The book trade of the world.**
Edited by Siegfried Tambert. Hamburg, GFR; London: Andre Deutsch, Bowker, 1972. 3 vols.

The Austrian section (p. 87-103) is in volume 1 (Europe and International). It provides a brief outline of the history of printing and publishing in the country followed by separate sections on: organization; trade press; copyright; book production; publishing; the wholesale and retail trade; imports and exports; book reviews; literary prizes; the antiquarian book trade and auctions. Each section has brief bibliographical references. Although published over a decade ago much of the information is still valid.

459 **State controlled enterprise in Austria.**
Wilhelm Weber. *International Review of Administrative Sciences* (Brussels) vol. 28, no. 2 (1962), p. 192-205.

In this paper presented at the 12th International Congress of Administrative Sciences, held in Vienna in July 1962, the author traces government controlled economic development from the beginnings of the State railway system in the late 1850's to the establishment of the country's public utilities before World War II. As re-constituted in 1945 Austria was the country with the largest public economic sector in the Western world. The effects of the more recent Nationalization Acts and the different forms of control in various enterprises are also discussed. A second and complementary paper presented at the same symposium by Karl Wenger entitled 'Government control of the economy in Austria' deals with: the various organs of economic administration; restrictions on private property; freedom of enterprise and settlement; currency, credit, and prices; and quality control.

460 **Update on the electronics industry in Austria.**
Monique B. Yvart. *Electronics*, vol. 29, no. 2 (Feb. 1984), p. 68-69.

Various aspects of the Austrian electronics industry are discussed, including foreign investment, component production, imports and exports, videotape recorders and future prospects for the industry.

Agriculture and Forestry

461 **Agricultural policy in Austria.**
Paris: Organisation for Economic Co-operation and Development, 1976. 45p.

One of the series of reviews of agricultural policy in OECD member countries carried out in the mid-1970s. This report outlines the position of Austrian agriculture at the national and regional level in the year 1975. It covers production, employment, investment, prices and incomes and the second part of the report sets out future policy objectives and measures with the aid of diagrams.

462 **Rural problems in the Alpine region: an international study.**
Michel Cépède, E. S. Abensour, in collaboration with Paul and Germaine Veyret. Rome: Food and Agricultural Organization of the United Nations, 1961. 201p. map.

The remit of an international symposium held under the auspices of the UN Food and Agriculture Organization in the Austrian Alps in 1959 was 'to inform respective governments of the nature of the essential economic and social problems affecting their rural populations', with special reference to the eastern alpine regions. This report is based on the conclusions reached. As far as Austria is concerned, over 100 communities were studied in a three-fold altitude classification. The participating countries, apart from Austria, were France, Germany, Italy and Switzerland.

463 **Facts about Austrian agriculture.**
Vienna: Organization of Chambers of Agriculture, 1985. 8p.

This leaflet offers brief up-to-date statistics on various aspects of agriculture and forestry including production, marketing and consumption. It lists the main exporting and importing organizations in the country and provides membership figures for, and addresses of, the provincial chambers of agriculture.

464 **Silvicultural planning in avalanching forests.**
G. Fiebiger. Davos, Switzerland: Swiss Federal Institute for Snow and Avalanche Research, 1979.

The dangers of avalanches in steep mountain afforested areas are always present in Austria but can be minimized by careful silvicultural planning, as this report of three tree-planting schemes in Upper Austria indicates (p. 331-348).

465 **The Eastern Alps.**
Elisabeth Lichtenberger. London: Oxford University Press, 1975. 48p. maps. bibliog. (Problem Regions of Europe Series).

Although the series is designed for educational purposes, this particular volume deserves a wider general readership because it highlights a serious and continuing problem which faces all the Alpine countries today, particularly Austria. This problem is how to find a use for land in the highlands which is no longer farmed, and how to maintain services to an ever-decreasing rural population. The author, an acknowledged international expert on physical and economic geography, suggests that in addition to increasing the tax concessions already being paid to mountain farmers by the Austrian government, encouragement should be given to allow the formation of rural co-operatives, more afforestation, and additional valley industries.

466 **Österreichs Land-und Forstwirtschaft.** (Austrian agriculture and forestry.)
Erwin Walter. *Österreich in Geschichte und Literatur*, vol. 15, (autumn 1971), p. 163-84.

Although only one-fifth of the total land area of Austria is covered by arable land, agricultural production supplies about 85% of the country's food requirements. Forests cover about two-fifths of the country and are mainly in the hands of large-scale enterprises and are to a great extent the property of the State or province, local communities, co-operatives or the church. This article analyses structural changes and developments in Austrian forestry and agriculture since the end of World War II.

Transport and Communications

General

467 **Narrow gauge railways of Europe.**

Peter Allen, P. B. Whitehouse. London: Ian Allan, 1960. 172p.

This comprehensive picture of a basically dying genre, which is nevertheless being systematically restored wherever possible for the modern enthusiast, includes as a highlight a description of the last journey on the celebrated Salzkammergutbahn from Salzburg to Bad Ischl. It is aptly described by the authors as 'an illustrated scrapbook of the European scene'. The Austrian section is on p. 61-67 and the journey mentioned above is on p. 149-153.

468 **Are the waterways leading into dry dock?**

Austria Today, no. 2 (1982), p. 25-37.

The Rhine-Main-Danube Canal was scheduled for completion in 1982 but a heated debate still continues as to whether, with a cutback in the budget, the last 90 kilometers stretch should be built at all. This report tells the story of one of the great building projects of the century, dating back to the early 1920's and designed to create a 3,500-mile shipping link between the North Sea and the Black Sea. Both Germany and Austria have invested large sums of money but political and economic considerations still bedevil the whole question. The writer also provides a brief survey of the history of the First Danube Steamship Company, one of the oldest in the world, and includes an account of the two Austrian shipbuilding yards on the Danube, at Linz and Korneuburg, which build not only river passenger vessels but ocean-going ships, floating cranes and racing yachts.

469 **Steamships, statesmen and bureaucrats: Austrian policy towards the steam navigation company of the Austrian Lloyds, 1836-1848.**
Ronald E. Coons. Wiesbaden, GFR: Franz Steiner Verlag, 1975. 209p. bibliog. (Mainz Institute of European History, vol. 74).

Lloyd Triestino, an Italian company, took over from the Austrian owners after World War I when Trieste was handed over to Italy. The company had first been established in 1838, operating a shipyard in the chief Austrian naval base in the Mediterranean and developed strong navigation links with the Levant. The central theme of this book is that of subsidies, and the relationship between a bureaucratic state, run on orthodox lines, and an active private enterprise – set principles versus economic necessity.

470 **Domenig dry dock.**
Peter Davey. *Architectural Review*, vol. 172, no. 1025 (1982), p. 48-51.

Describes the construction of a dry dock, designed by the architects Domenig and Giencke, for steamship travel on the Wörthersee, a lake in Carinthia much visited by tourists. The author explains that particular care has been taken to ensure that the construction blends in with the picturesque scenery and allows for an uninterrupted public promenade along the east bay of the lake. An artificial island has been built and much of the complex has been sunk below a platform so as not to obscure views across the lake, the depth of which was sufficient to allow for the construction to be completed without dredging or excavation.

471 **Austrian travel wonderland.**
William James Keith Davies. London: Ian Allan, 1974. 125p. maps. bibliog.

This is a travel book with a difference in that it not only tells the reader what to see on arrival but how he can reach his destination. The descriptions of landscape and life in all the nine provinces are fully illustrated and well-documented with the right kind of map and plan. Different modes of transport are covered including railways of all periods, narrow-gauge railways and reserve-track tramways, the postbus network (where the local commuter travels with the mail), steamers on lakes and rivers, and modern motorways. A much more factual and useful book than the title suggests.

472 **Report on Danube navigation. Submitted to the Advisory and Technical Committee for Communications and Transit of the League of Nations.**
Walker D. Hines, with the aid of Major Brehon Somervell. Lausanne, Switzerland: League of Nations, 1925. 187p. map.

An exhaustive report covering the technical, commercial and administrative problems affecting the river. Individual sections cover: the utilization of the river; the river fleets; general characteristics of Danube traffic; economic conditions resulting from World War I policies; physical problems; frontier formalities; port facilities; the International Danube Commission; traffic statistics; shipyards; customs; police; and a summary.

473 **The Danube.**

Emil Lengyel. London: Victor Gollancz, 1940. 573p. maps. bibliog.

Although the Danube is world famous, the origins of its name are still hotly disputed. That part of it which flows through Austria, and of course Vienna, is known, somewhat surprisingly, as the brown Danube. In this well-indexed and attractively written account, the author links the Danube with the Habsburg Empire in a blend of nostalgia and romanticism, but in no way neglects either the natural landscape or the commercial aspects of river shipping.

474 **Railway holiday in Austria.**

Oswald Stevens Nock. Dawlish, England: David & Charles; London: Macdonald, 1965. 158p. maps. bibliog. (Railway Holiday Series, no. 3).

This racy book is just what the title says – a railway holiday; no matter that it was undertaken in the summer, and that the extra edge which the snow adds to the excitement of those alpine passes can only be hinted at. The author, one of the most prolific of railway writers, is sufficiently competent professionally to lean on the archives of the Austrian Federal Railways for all the technical details needed to turn this into a useful compendium for the railway 'buff' as well as the tourist. The significance of the Austrian network is that it transcends a purely domestic situation such as that in Britain, because its main lines are integral parts of so many through routes covering the whole of Europe.

475 **Satellite communications earth station.**

Gustav Peichl. *Domus*, vol. 611 (Nov. 1980), p. 12-15.

This brief, illustrated article, by the architect concerned, describes in layman's terms the earth station (telecommunications by satellite) at Aflenz, Upper Styria. This underground complex has been ingeniously designed and constructed in a sloping wooded hillside, which has necessitated a careful remodelling of the landscape. Since its inception the station has been expanded and is now handling traffic on an increasing scale.

476 **Bradshaw's August 1914 Continental guide.**

Introduced by J. H. Price. Newton Abbot, England: David & Charles, 1977. Rep. 584p.

This is an off-shoot of what became Britain's national railway timetable from 1838-1961. The Continental version, serving as timetable, guidebook and hotel directory, appeared as a separate volume from 1847 until the outbreak of World War I and after the inevitable break until its final demise in 1939. The text provides a fascinating picture of communications in the whole of the Austro-Hungarian Empire at its geographical peak. Interestingly enough, the countries of the Dual Monarchy are separated out and appear on p.221-255, while the extensive travel guide to individual cities and locations shows Austria on p. 494-507 and Hungary on p. 508-515. The detailed European railway map is of real historical value, particularly for the contemporary spelling of the place-names recorded before so many were to change with the creation of new nations.

477 **Austrian steam locomotives: an introductory survey 1937-1980.**
R. A. Whitehead. Tonbridge, England: R. A. Whitehead, 1982. 160p.

This is basically a technical work – a detailed catalogue of types of locomotive, combined with a history of the system and its operating practices. It represents the most comprehensive work on this subject in English. As such it has earned the recommendation of the doyen of Austrian locomotive designers in the last days of steam, Professor Giesl-Gieslingen. It also earns a bonus for the general reader in that there is a full indication of the political and economic motives for each major expansion of the network. For those seeking an approach in which text is subservient to the fascination of picture, V. C. K. Allen's informative work entitled *Austrian Steam from Lineside* (D. Bradford Barton, 1975) is recommended.

Postage stamps

478 **The people on Austrian stamps: a concise biographical dictionary.**
J. F. Giblin. Manchester, England: published under the auspices of the Austrian Philatelic Society of Great Britain, 1961. 103p.

Commemorative stamp issues of prominent Austrian personalities have figured largely in the country's postal history and have generally been of a high quality. This monograph contains 128 biographies of such people, who have appeared on stamps from 1850, the date of the first issue, up to 1960. The author has referred to standard Austrian and German national biographies and where relevant has included a bibliography. The variety of people depicted on Austrian stamps presents a wide spectrum of Austrian national life, which should be of interest not only to the Austrian philatelist but to anyone concerned with the history and culture of the country especially from the mid-19th century onwards.

479 **Handbook of the pre-stamp postmarks of Austria.**
Edwin Müller. New York: Collectors Club, 1981. reprint ed. 199p.

This is the first illustrated handbook of Austrian pre-stamp postmarks to have appeared in English. It is prefaced by a fascinating account of the horse-drawn postal communication service operating in the 16th and 17th centuries within the Austrian territories under the concession traditionally granted to the family of the Counts of Thurn and Taxis by the Bavarian court. In 1722 this postal service became a government institution and continued up to 1850, when Austrian stamps were first issued. This volume lists, describes and evaluates all the postmarks used throughout the Empire, with the exception of Lombardy Venetia, which up to 1855 operated an entirely separate system. The range and variety is enormous and covers occupation postmarks, military and field posts, sea-borne correspondence and even disinfection post-marks when letters were opened, fumigated and resealed. A work not just for the specialist, but also for the reader with an interest in historico-geographical aspects of the middle-Habsburg period.

480 **The cancellations of Hungarian post offices on the stamps of Austria, 1850-67.**
G. S. Ryan. London: Royal Philatelic Society, 1980. 641p. 35 maps. bibliog.

The literature on Austria's postal history and philatelic development, mainly in German or Hungarian, is extensive but specialized and abstruse. This work, in English and German, while covering a specialized field, presents a very important period in Austria's philatelic history with clarity, both in pictorial and literary terms. It is the first comprehensive and consolidated history of all recorded Hungarian cancellations used on Austrian stamps from 1850 – the date of the first issue – to 1867, when an independent Hungarian postal authority was set up and started issuing its own stamps. Prior to this, all Austrian stamps used throughout the Empire were printed and issued in Vienna. The author, an international collector and authority on this subject, has not only illustrated these cancellations in facsimile photogravure, frequently in colour, with annotations, but has also included thirty-nine grid maps of Hungary indicating German locations of each post office cancellation, with the Hungarian name in brackets. His simplified classification makes for easy identification, while the points system he has introduced – and which is now universally accepted by the philatelic world – helps one to establish the relative rarity and value of each cancellation. The philatelist, concerned with the classic issues of Austria, will see this as an indispensable reference work, while the general reader will find the author's account of the Empire's early postal history particularly interesting.

481 **Stanley Gibbons stamp catalogue. Part 2, Austria and Hungary.**
London: Stanley Gibbons, 1982. 206p.

There are few countries in the world which, relative to their population, have contributed more to philately over the years, in both design and practice, than Austria. In 1851 the first newspaper stamps in the world were issued in Vienna; in 1869 the first postcards (correspondence cards) appeared in Austria; in 1918 the first stamps for a regular airmail service were issued in Austria, and moreover, it is almost certain that the 1906 issue of Bosnia was the first landscape series to be issued anywhere in the world. Austria is featured on p. 1-90 in this composite catalogue, and her entire philatelic range is presented, from the classic 1850 issue, with its many variants, up to the present day. Also included are the Military Post administrations in Romania, Bosnia, Serbia and Montenegro, and the Austrian post offices in Crete and the Ottoman Empire. The classic issues of Lombardy-Venetia, which was part of the Austrian Empire up to 1866, are also well-represented. This is history in pictorial miniature and two useful features of this specialized catalogue are the index of stamp designs, which have invariably been of a high quality, and an explanation of the various inscriptions on Austrian stamps, particularly in the early issues.

Employment and Training

482 **The scars of unemployment: a comparative study, 1933-1983.**
Compiled by Michael Freund, Birgit Flos, Janos Marton. *Austria Today*, no. 4 (1982), p. 49-54.

In 1932 a group of Viennese social scientists carried out the first in-depth study of the effects of large-scale unemployment on an industrial community. Their findings were published in *The unemployed of Marienthal* (1933), which was translated into many languages and is still a standard teaching aid in social science schools around the world. A half-century later another team of social scientists visited the same area and their findings are summarized in this brief report. Unemployment was said to be still above an acceptable level, though many inhabitants had found work in Vienna by daily commuting the 18 mile journey. The presence of a large force of Yugoslav migrant workers was causing some cultural clashes and friction, while industrial activity, in the local glass and chemical plants, was said to be picking up slowly.

483 **Gastarbeiter in der städtischen Gesellschaft.** (Foreign migrant workers in urban society.)
Helga Leitner. New York; Frankfurt-am-Main, GFR: Campus, 1983. 328p. bibliog. (Campus Research, vol. 307).

This survey deals exclusively with the large group of Yugoslav migrant workers in Vienna during the mid-1970's when they numbered over 74,000. It describes their living conditions, social characteristics, occupations and the problems of assimilation, which were very acute, mainly for cultural and linguistic reasons. The work contains a mass of statistical data and many charts and tables. A book which will be of interest to any demographer or student of the manpower and labour situation in Vienna during this important period of reconstruction and improvement of public services in the capital.

484 **The new labour code: worker participation in industry.**
Vienna: Austrian Federal Press Service, 1974. 23p.

One of the most significant measures in the field of Austrian social policy to be enacted in the Second Republic was the new labour code which came into force in July 1974. It was the product of more than ten years' hard bargaining between the political parties, trade unions and industry. The code covers five main areas: agreements between employers and employees at a national level; workers' organizations within individual firms; the role of the unions; agreements between employers and employees in individual firms; and workers' rights to management participation, training and arbitration councils. The overriding body is the Parity Commission for Wages and Prices, an entirely new concept, which meets under the chairmanship of the Chancellor himself and includes representatives from Government, employers and employee organizations. This brief summary outlines the main provisions of the code. A short pamphlet, issued by the Federal Press Service entitled *The national approach to labour and industry* (Austria Documentation, 1984. 17p.) summarizing and updating the above, makes the additional point that the system of economic and social partnership is not merely confined to the Parity Commission, but plays a vital role in all fields of public administration as well.

485 **Underdeveloped areas in industrialised countries; the Austrian report to the European Co-ordination Centre for Research and Documentation in Social Services (Vienna.)**
Edited by Max Streit. Graz, Austria: Institute for Sociology, 1967. 44p. maps. bibliog.

The region chosen for the Austrian part of this project dealing with underdeveloped areas in industrial countries, both in Western and Eastern Europe, lies in the south-eastern part of the country, covering areas of Burgenland and Styria, where seven administrative units were the subject of a regional development study. The report stresses the fact that although Austria was only able to frame a regional development policy after she had gained her independence in 1955, federal recognition of the problems involved and financial help towards their solution were making their impact by the 1960s.

486 **Vocational training in Austria's business enterprises.**
Vienna: Federal Chamber of Commerce, 1977. 30p.

Legislation, finance, equipment, in-service training, refresher courses and apprentice examinations are the main aspects of industrial vocational training outlined in this slim brochure, which also lists schools and Chambers of Commerce throughout the country.

487 **Youth organisations and youth work in Austria.**
Vienna: Federal Press Service, 1984. 32p. (Austria Documentation).

Although this pamphlet cannot claim to be a complete survey, it describes the activities of the main organizations affiliated to the Austrian Federal Youth Union, which is responsible for promoting the interests of young Austrians and for providing services beyond the scope of the individual and independent organizations. There are also a number of other youth unions, of a political, religious and social character, which are not affiliated to the Federal Youth Union, as well as sports associations and institutions for youth work run by adults, which are listed and briefly described.

Trade Unions

488 **Trade unions and national economic policy.**
Jack Barbash. London; Baltimore: Johns Hopkins Press, 1972. 206p.

This is essentially a study in the structure of union responsibility which emphasizes the need for it to be rooted in viable policies and institutions to ensure a suitable environment for the successful execution of national economic policies. The period under examination is the 1960's and each West European country is reviewed separately with special attention being paid to incomes policy, manpower planning and industrial relations. In the chapter on Austria (p. 43-59) emphasis is placed on the trade union movement as a major source of political authority, marked by certain peculiarities which distinguish Austria from other Western industrialized nations as well as those in the Eastern bloc.

489 **Die österreichischen Gewerkschaften.** (The Austrian trade unions.)
Fritz Klenner. Vienna: Association of Austrian Trade Unions. 3 vols. 1951-79. bibliog.

This definitive history of the Austrian trade union movement by one of its leading members is an exhaustive and detailed study, and although the author's interpretation is clearly that of a committed trade unionist, his commentary on present-day structures and the social partnership is at times strongly critical. Volume 1 covers the period from the early guilds up to the first quarter of the 20th century; and volume 2 deals with the First Republic and the illegal organizations which operated in the corporative state set up by Chancellor Engelbert Dollfuss. The final volume discusses the movement in the Second Republic up to 1966, when the coalition between the two major parties, the Socialists and People's Party, ended, and explains how the movement is now coping with the demands and challenges of modern technology. The foreword to the entire work, by the General Secretary of the Trade Unions Federation, is addressed to the youth of Austria. An abridgement to the first two volumes of this study, in English and entitled *The Austrian Trade Union Movement* (Brussels: International Confederation of Free Trade Unions, 1966. ICFTU Monographs, no. 3) has also been published.

490 **White collar trade unions: contemporary developments in industrialised societies.**

Adolf Sturmthal. London; Urbana: University of Illinois Press, 1966. 412p.

In this general review, one chapter (p. 37-89) is devoted to Austria in which the contributor, Ernst Lackenbach, analyses the implications of the continuing increase in the number of white collar workers, particularly in the public services, for the country's industrial relations system. Whereas employees in private industry are organized in one of the sixteen unions representing their particular trade, public servants have only a single union. The writer points out that differences in legal representation and collective bargaining practices between these two groupings have been gradually reduced despite the distinction being very clearly set out in employment legislation.

Statistics

491 **Demographic yearbook.**
New York: United Nations, 1948-. annual.

Official demographic statistics from 225 countries, including Austria, are featured in this yearbook which covers: distribution and trends in population; birth and mortality rates; marriage and divorce; and international migration. A definitive basic source of statistics on population.

492 **European historical statistics, 1750-1970.**
Edited by B. R. Mitchell. London, Basingstoke: Macmillan, 1975. 827p.

The usefulness of this reference work lies in its provision of a wide range of statistical data for economists and historians in such a way as to avoid both the difficulty of identifying sources (all of which are mentioned in the introduction) and the labour of extracting data from a variety of places. A consolidated list of boundary and currency changes which have occurred in each of the countries featured (which includes Austria) during the period under review precedes the various tables covering: climate; population; labour force; agriculture; industry; external trade; transport and communications; finance; prices; education; and national accounts. The starting date of 1750, which naturally does not apply to all tables, has been chosen as representing the beginning of the Industrial Revolution.

493 **The statesman's yearbook.**
Edited by John Paxton. London: Macmillan, 1864-. annual.

In compressed form this valuable reference source provides essential statistics on: area and population; climate; constitution and government; defence; the economy; industry and trade; communications; the judiciary; and education and the social services for the countries of the world. It also lists a number of books of reference for more extensive consultation. In the 1985-86 issue (122nd ed. Austria is featured on p. 171-175.

494 **Republic of Austria, 1945-1975.**
Vienna: Central Statistical Office, 1976. 206p.

The first three decades in the life of the Second Republic saw the materia reconstruction of the country after the devastation of World War II, a majo economic recovery, a cultural rebirth and, most importantly, the re-establishmen of Austria as an independent sovereign state. These statistical tables reflect th development of the country's population, economy, social system and cultur during this period. Each of the four sections dealing with these different aspects i preceded by a brief summary of the most significant data.

495 **Statistics on radio and television, 1960-1976.**
Paris: UNESCO, 1979, 124p. (Statistical Reports and Studies, no. 23).

Contains international statistics on broadcasting and receiving facilities, includin those for Austria, for the period 1960 to 1976. It also covers aspects o programme contents as they have evolved during this period. There are a numbe of explanatory charts and graphs.

496 **Statistisches Handbuch für die Republik Österreich.** (Statistical Handbook for the Republic of Austria.)
Vienna: Central Statistical Office, 1950-. annual.

The Austrian Central Statistical Office was founded in 1863 and has regularl published statistical information since that date. The present series of its *Statistica Handbook* dates from 1950 and provides data on: geography; population education; cultural affairs; employment; social security; incomes; wages; prices housing; environment; the balance of payments; agriculture; trade; energy mining; building; commerce; foreign trade; transport; industry; taxes; an election results. It also includes comparative tables for other countries. The 198 edition contained 681p.

497 **UN Statistical Yearbook.**
New York: United Nations, 1948-. annual.

This yearbook contains up-to-date economic, financial, social and cultura statistics from all member countries, including Austria. It provides data on: al forms of production; energy; trade; transport and communications; and th consumption of agricultural products and fertilizers. It also includes summar statistics on: the balance of payments; prices and wages; national accounts; publi debt; and development assistance. The final section deals with health, housing education, science and technology and the social services.

498 **UNESCO Statistical Yearbook.**
Paris: UNESCO, 1963-. annual.

A basic work of reference which provides up-to-date statistics on: education science and technology; libraries; book production; newspapers; the cinema radio and television in member countries, including Austria.

Environment and Conservation

499 **Living cultural heritage: Austrian contributions to the maintenance of historical monuments.**

Fritz Braun. Vienna: Federal Press Service, 1975. 127p. map.

Austria has been particularly active in the Council of Europe in helping to establish consistent international standards for the protection and conservation of historical buildings and successive governments have accepted that many architectural monuments can only justify their survival by actively serving some contemporary function. This account of Austria's problems and achievements in the field of conservation was published in connection with European Architectural Heritage Year. Apart from monuments, the report also covers: general housing; roads; urban renewal schemes; pedestrian precincts; and organization and financial support at governmental level for special projects in the provinces. Under the Hague Convention on the Protection of Cultural Property in the Event of Armed Conflict, no less than 34,200 individual monuments in Austria are classified in varying degrees of priority to qualify for such protection.

500 **The high Tauern.**

Anton Draxl. *Austria Today*, vol. 6, no. 4 (winter 1980), p. 49-53.

This article is an illustrated description of Austria's first National Park in the Grossglockner and Grossvenediger regions spanning the borders of Tirol, Salzburg and Carinthia. The total area is roughly the size of the province of Vorarlberg (approximately 1,000 square miles) and is a region with an extremely ancient culture. This article explains the measures being taken to protect the environment while still providing adequate tourist facilities and activities.

501 **European environmental law.**

Edited by S. Ercman. Bern: Bubenberg Verlag, 1977. 420p.

This is a legal and economic appraisal of various aspects of environmental protection carried out in a number of European countries, including Austria. The sections relating to Austria cover, for example: control of water pollution (p. 31-32); control of air pollution (p. 127-38); noise abatement (p. 181); and nature conservation (p. 221). Although there is no environmental law as such in Austria, there are a number of statutes and provisions of both a federal and regional nature which specify the controls mentioned above. See also *Protection of the environment in Austria* (Vienna: Federal Press Service, 1985. 46p.).

502 **Vienna: sounding the tocsin.**
Sarah Gainham. *Interplay*, vol. 1, no. 7 (1968), p. 20-23.

Writing from bitter personal experience the author discusses some of the mounting problems facing Vienna, such as over-crowding in the central residential districts, traffic jams, the spread of industrialization, the impact of tourism and the difficulties resulting from the existence of a large foreign element working in the capital.

503 **Über Veränderungen der alpinen Gebirgsnatur durch den Einfluss der Menschen.** (Changes in alpine ecology due to the influence of man.)
Günther Pass. *Montfort*, vol. 30, no. 1. (1978), p. 79-87.

The writer examines the impact of alpine agriculture, forestry, hunting, tourism and hydro-electric schemes on the biological balance in the Austrian Alps since the beginning of the century.

504 **Atemgift und seine Messung: Die Wiener Luft und Wiener Parks im Urteil der Wiener.** (Respiratory toxins and their measurement: Vienna and its parks as judged by the Viennese.)
Lore Scheer. Institut für Wohlstandanalysen (Institute for Welfare Research), August 1975. 29p.

From the findings of this limited survey of air pollution in Vienna and its parks, including the Vienna woods which lie within the city limits, it appears that in relation to other European capitals, Vienna compares quite favourably. Notwithstanding this, the level of sulphur oxides content is high due to nearby coal deposits and heavy oil extraction plants. However, according to another opinion poll conducted by the same institute, 42% of the sample considered that the air was badly polluted; while on the question of accessibility to public parks and other recreation areas, 20% of those interviewed regarded the route too dangerous to attempt due to heavy traffic! The survey is accompanied by a brief summary in English.

505 **For example, Emmersdorf.**
Helmut Voitl. *Austria Today*, no. 1 (1984), p. 8-9.

An experiment said to be unique in Europe is taking place in the ancient settlement of Emmersdorf in the province of Carinthia. It is in fact the establishment of a commercially-run undertaking for ecology, enivironmental protection and information, covering an area of 175 hectares. The complex includes organic farming, solar generators, and a chemical workshop for the production of non-toxic cosmetics. The research will be carefully documented and will be available for environmentalists on film and video.

506 **Urban renewal in Austria.**
Peter Weber. Vienna: Austrian Regional Planning Studies (ÖROK), no. 25. 1981. 57p. maps. bibliog.

A number of OECD member states, including Austria, are participating in the European Campaign for Urban Renaissance which was launched in 1974. This report outlines the particular problems Austria faces, such as the uneven distribution of population, increased demands for improvements in the quality of life, environmental conditions, the growth of suburban areas and financial stringency. It continues with a report mid-way through the ten-year programme, and describes some of the redevelopment and restoration schemes undertaken by the government. The text is accompanied by a number of photographs, diagrams, charts and maps.

507 **Bauten von gestern – heute erlebt.** (Buildings of the past discovered for the present.)
Edited by Christine Wessely. Vienna: Verband der Wissenschaftlichen Gesellschaften Österreichs, 1979-80. 2 vols.

Few European countries are proportionately richer in building styles than Austria, with its gradual transition from the plaster-faced brick of the Burgenland plains in the east to the distinctive timber constructions of the Tirolean and Vorarlberg Alps in the west. This publication contains contributions from thirty-nine experts describing a wide spectrum of maintenance and renovation projects throughout Austria, ranging from the most modest village houses to monasteries and palaces. The text is in German but each chapter is followed by a slightly condensed English translation. The work is not only intended for architects, or the reader with a personal or professional interest in Austria, but is also suitable for the interested layman. Both volumes are profusely illustrated in monochrome with many 'before and after' representations.

Science and Technology

508 **A mecca for U-bahn builders.**
Peter Blake. *Austria Today*, no. 2 (1984), p. 46-48.

One of the outstanding Austrian technological innovations in the 1970's was the New Austrian Tunnelling Method, which is now in world-wide use. It was first applied to the reconstruction of the Vienna Underground, so as to retain the essential features of the Jugendstil (Art Nouveau) architecture of the stations designed by Otto Wagner at the turn of the century. The author describes the method and its particular advantages over more traditional tunnelling techniques.

509 **Current from the current: power stations on the conveyor belt.**
Austria Today, no. 2 (1982), p. 34-36.

A brief account of the series of hydro-electric power stations on the Danube, which already provide nearly 30 per cent of the country's electrical needs. The entire programme, which has attracted considerable international interest, is scheduled for completion in 1995. Flood danger has been virtually eliminated and sewage purification plants have been constructed for all settlements on both banks of the river, thus considerably improving the quality of the Danube waters.

510 **Austria's technological dependence: basic dimensions and current trends.**
Otmar Höll. Vienna: Austrian Institute for International Affairs, Nov. 1980. 63p. bibliog. (Laxenburg Paper, no. 2).

This is one of a number of surveys in an English-language series published by the Austrian Institute for International Affairs, a body which commands wide respect. The series presents the results of research projects commissioned by the Institute and this review, which is set within the context of United States world-wide supremacy in technological development and Austria's economic dependence on Germany, is less favourable than the OECD report (q.v.) published some ten years previously. The author notes that Austria's overall trade performance had deteriorated during this period, that she had suffered a sharp drop in the export of raw materials while her foreign trade deficits were still increasing. Furthermore, the advantages of her joining EFTA (European Free Trade Association) had been partially counterbalanced by the activities of the European Economic Community (EEC) in the domestic markets. Criticism is levelled by the author at the Austrian business community for its hesitant attitude to research and innovation in public and private enterprises, which still remain underfunded. The author also claims that foreign investment, especially in the export-orientated growth sectors such as the electrical and pharmaceutical industries, was top-heavy. A useful but somewhat discouraging report.

511 **Innovations and developments: a selection of projects from the fields of technology and medical technology.**
Vienna: Federal Press Service, 1981. 40p. (Austria Documentation).

There are over 700 research establishments in the industrial sector in Austria and almost twice as many non-industrial research institutes. This review of only twenty-two technological projects is therefore highly selective, but it does give an impression of the multiplicity and scope of Austrian technological innovation. The projects featured represent three fields: improvements and advances in automation in industrial manufacture and production; invention and innovation in environmental conservation; and developments in the field of medical research.

512 **Reviews of national science policy: Austria.**
Paris: Organization for Economic Co-operation and Development, 1971. 246p.

This volume is the twelfth in a series of country reviews by the OECD, of which Austria was a founder member. Despite its long history of scientific achievement it was not until 1953, when negotiations on the State Treaty were in their final stages, that Austria was in a position to frame an independent national science policy, with a formal programme of research and development, as an instrument of government. Since Austria is a small country with limited financial resources, the need for an effective co-ordinated science policy with the right priorities is vital. This report indicates that, generally speaking, during the period 1955-71 national research had been underfunded and that changes in organization were necessary. There are four parts to the review: a general survey of research and development activities; relationships between the country's economic structure and research; main trends in training; and science policy institutions – their aims and achievements. The OECD examiner's report concludes the survey with recommendations for future action. Statistical tables accompany the text.

Education

513 **The Austrian educational system.**
Oskar Achs. Vienna: Federal Press Service, 1984. 42p. (Austria Documentation).

This pamphlet serves the needs of anyone seeking a brief outline of the country's educational system. It includes a short history, a survey of the present school system and a summary of the major legislative measures in the educational field taken by governments since the end of World War II. Moreover, since this booklet is intended for a non-Austrian readership, mention is made of the education of foreign children in Austria, particularly in Vienna, where over fifty international organizations have their headquarters with some 30,000 foreign officials working in them.

514 **Austria: organization of education in 1978-1980.**
Vienna: Federal Ministry of Education and Arts in co-operation with the Federal Ministry of Science and Research, 1981. 157p. bibliog.

A report, presented at the 38th International Conference on Education in Geneva in November, 1981, and based on the Austrian 1962 Education Act and subsequent amending legislation. Part I deals with the organization and structure of the educational system at all levels as well as curricula, pilot projects and teacher training; part 2 covers recent legislation, finance, innovation, and research; supporting statistical data is given in part 3, and the documentary evidence for the report is contained in the final section.

515 **Reviews of national policies for education: Austrian school policy.** Paris: Organization for Economic Co-operation and Development, 1979. 106p.

In 1977 a review of the country's entire educational system, excluding higher and adult education, was undertaken in connection with the series of surveys regularly conducted by the OECD of the national educational policies of its member states. The report on Austria is a reassuring one, reflecting stable and fruitful relationships between federal and provincial authorities and, since major educational reforms require a two thirds parliamentary majority, a wide consensus of views among the political parties. The various levels of education within the Austrian system – nursery, primary, secondary, post-secondary, specialist, technical and teacher-training schools, are all covered. Considerable stress is laid on the system's traditional basis, for in Austria educational innovation is cautious and deliberate, not over-adventurous and ideological.

Literature

General, literary history and criticism

516 **Austrian life and literature, 1780-1938.**
Edited by Peter Branscombe. Edinburgh, Scotland: Scottish Academic Press, 1978. 93p.

A collection of eight essays on Austrian life and literature from the time of Joseph II to the end of the First Republic. They cover relatively unfamiliar and neglected territory, but have as their theme subjects typical of the recurring preoccupations of Austrian writers and audiences alike throughout history.

517 **I saw the world: poems from Walther von der Vogelweide.**
Set into English verse after the mediaeval German by Ian Colvin. London: Edward Arnold, 1938. 128p. bibliog.

The title line is taken from a poem by the greatest German lyric writer of the Middle Ages, Walther von der Vogelweide (1170-1230), who served at the Court of Leopold V in Vienna and later espoused the cause of the Hohenstaufen family in their struggle for succession against the Welfs, who were supported by the Pope. He later switched his allegiance to the Welfs but throughout his life he remained strongly anti-papal, as his poems well illustrate. In his lyrical works he praised the virtues of charity, faithfulness and loyalty and the spiritual value of Christian crusade and pilgrimage. He wrote in a free, uninhibited style and many of his poems were moral and political in content, and often couched in satirical terms. The translator has selected a number of his lyrical love poems, as well as some of his political ones and some epigrams, and has succeeded in both language and style in capturing the 'bare beauty of early Gothic' in masterly fashion.

518 **The Oxford companion to German literature.**
Henry Garland, Mary Garland. Oxford: Clarendon Press, 1976. 977p.

This well-arranged reference work is the result of a project lasting ten years. The book is an exhaustive fund of factual information, in a very accessible form, covering the literature of the German-speaking countries, including Austria, from the 8th century to the 1970s. The work is not aimed solely at the academic user researching a specific topic, for it meets, equally skilfully, the needs of the general reader seeking a friendly introduction to the German literary achievement. The arrangement is alphabetical, on similar lines to the other Oxford Companions to Literature, while a special feature is the extensive system of cross-references, which helps to draw the reader's attention to the close interaction between literature and all aspects of history, as well as aiding him in his search for a particular item of information. The range is impressive, since the volume includes not only biographies of writers and men of letters, but entries on literary movements and styles, accounts of historical figures and events, literary journals and similar publications and even first lines of well-known poems. A considerable achievement and an enjoyable, companionable guide.

519 **The woman question and politics in Austrian interwar literature.**
Lynda J. King. *German Studies Review*, vol. 6, no. 1 (Feb. 1983), p. 75-100.

A specialist on Austrian feminist literature, Professor King of the University of Texas at Austin, has contributed a valuable article on Austrian womens' movements from the latter part of the 19th century to the days of the First Republic, by which time Austrian women had gained both suffrage and equality under the constitution. The author then studies five works written by Austrian women novelists during the 1920s and analyses their portrayal of womens' emancipation, spotlighting the particular aspect of women working outside the home. A wide spectrum of viewpoints is revealed in these writings, from an overcommitment to a political dogma at one end of the scale to a feeling of passivity and a negative attitude to the social problems of the day at the other end.

520 **Modern Austrian literature.**
Riverside, California: University of California, 1961-. quarterly.

This authoritative and scholarly journal edited by Donald G. Daviau contains literary essays and critiques, translations, book reviews and notes on Austrian authors of the 19th and 20th centuries and their writings. From time to time special issues appear devoted to a single writer or topic, for example: Schnitzler (vol. 10, nos. 3-4, 1977); Kafka (vol. 11, nos. 3-4, 1978); Zweig (vol. 14, nos. 3-4, 1981); Rilke (vol. 15, nos. 3-4, 1982); and Austrian women writers (vol. 12, nos. 3-4, 1979).

521 **Literaturgeschichte Österreichs.** (A history of Austrian literature).
Josef Nadler. Salzburg, Austria: Otto Müller Verlag, 1951. 2nd ed. 568p. bibliog.

This was the first comprehensive survey of Austrian literature, from its earliest manifestations to the dawn of the Second Republic, to appear after World War II; and as yet it has not been superseded by any subsequent study. It is straightforward in its treatment and is extremely well-annotated. The five parts comprise: Gothic and Romanesque sagas, court and religious writings (996-1450); Renaissance and baroque (1450-1740); the age of transition – the Austrian imprint (1740-1866); the modern period (1866-1918); and new developments (1918-45). A definitive work.

522 **German men of letters.**
Edited by Alex Nathan. London: Oswald Wolff, 1965. 2nd ed. 5 vols.

This series is intended for educational purposes but it is also suitable for the general reader with some background knowledge of German literature. Each volume contains twelve essays of literary criticism by different leading Germanists. Five specifically Austrian writers are featured as follows: Franz Grillparzer (vol. 1, p. 101-20) by E. E. Pabst; Arthur Schnitzler (vol. 2, p. 57-75) by H. B. Garland; Oskar Kokoschka (vol. 3, p. 37-55) by W. I. Lucas; Robert Musil (vol. 3, p. 237-66) by Yvonne Csilt; and Johann Nestroy (vol. 3, p. 275-99) by Gertrud Seidmann. Each volume contains a bibliography.

523 **Österreichisches Literaturhandbuch.** (Austrian literature handbook.)
Hans F. Prokop. Vienna: Jugend und Volk, 1974. 254p.

Over 1,200 Austrian writers are listed in this reference book with brief details on their careers and output. However, the main value of the work lies in the fuller information provided about organizations and their awards promoting contemporary Austrian literature. Information about literary periodicals is also included.

524 **An anthology of Austrian drama.**
Douglas A. Russell. London; Toronto: Associated University Presses, 1982. 442p.

Professor Russell of Stanford University provides an introductory preface to this anthology. He places six Austrian plays in English translation, each illustrating some distinctive element peculiar to the country's dramatic output, in their historical and sociological perspective. In doing so, he provides the reader with some interesting background political and cultural information, particularly regarding the long-standing strict censorship laws which operated in the Habsburg Empire. The plays featured (with author and date of publication in parenthesis) are: *The Talisman* (Johann Nestroy, 1840); *King Ottokar, his Rise and Fall* (Franz Grillparzer, 1823); *La Ronde* (Arthur Schnitzler, 1896); *Electra* (Hugo von Hofmannsthal, 1909); *Goat Song* (Franz Werfel, 1921); and *The Raspberry Picker* (Fritz Hochwälder, 1965).

525 **Österreichische Lyrik aus neun Jahrhunderten.** (Nine centuries of Austrian lyrical poetry.)
Edited and selected by Wulf Stratowa. Vienna: Paul Neff Verlag, 1948. 408p.

Published shortly after World War II this was the first major anthology of Austrian lyrical poetry to have appeared since 1919. It spans almost a thousand years and special care has been given to the selection of lyrics by the early mediaeval Minnesänger poets, such as Walther von der Vogelweide (c.1170-1230) whose poems are accompanied by translations in modern German. A number of lesser known, but promising poets, who may not have reached their full maturity in their lifetime, are also included. A selective and impressive collection.

526 **Handbook of Austrian literature.**
Edited and introduced by Frederick Ungar. New York: Frederick Ungar, 1973. 296p.

This useful reference work, the first of its kind in English, lists the names of seventy-nine authors living within the boundaries of the Austro-Hungarian monarchy between the 1830's (when it is generally considered that the foundations of Austrian – as opposed to German – literature were first laid) and the present, and who wrote or still write in German. Each entry includes a short appraisal of the literary style and output of the author concerned, an inventory of published works, including those translated into English, and a bibliography. The editor's note explains that the majority of entries have been translated from Hermann Kunisch's *Handbuch der deutschen Gegenwartsliteratur* (Handbook of present-day German literature) (Munich: Nymphenburger Verlagshandlung, 3 vols. 1969-70). A special sign indicates that the article concerned, about a quarter of the total, has been specially prepared for this American edition.

527 **Viennese popular theatre: a symposium.**
Edited by W. E. Yates, John R. P. McKenzie. Exeter, England: University of Exeter, Department of German, 1985. 168p.

The major popular theatres of Vienna, specializing in dialect comedy and spectacular drama, interacting closely with the court theatres and producing some superb actor-dramatists, enjoyed a considerable reputation throughout Europe in the first half of the 19th century. This collection of essays, by seven English and four Austrian specialists, is based on papers presented at a colloquium held at Bedford College, London, in May 1984, which examined a number of issues central to a full appreciation of this dramatic art form, such as: language and style; theatrical conventions and popular taste; and the treatment of political material in popular comedy.

19th-century classical writers

528 **Ferdinand Raimund.**
John Michalski. New York: Twayne, 1968. 142p. bibliog. (Twayne's World Author Series, no. 39).

This is an excellent general introduction to Raimund (1790-1836), the greatest actor-dramatist of his day. The author examines each of Raimund's eight plays – his total output and all written within a space of ten years – and shows how each of them was set against a background of spirits, humans and demons in which the life of man is governed by supernatural powers, and where character and compassion are more important than rank and station. Deeply rooted in the baroque tradition, particularly the tradition of the Viennese popular theatre, Raimund raised the comic type to the level of character and exercised considerable influence on the development of theatrical presentation and characterization. The extensive bibliography includes a number of unpublished dissertations.

529 **Raimund and Vienna: a critical study of Raimund's plays in their Viennese setting.**
Dorothy Prohaska. Cambridge, England: Cambridge University Press, 1970. 210p. map. bibliog. (Anglica Germanica Series, no. 2).

Much that has been written about the playwright and actor, Ferdinand Raimund, one of the founders of what is now regarded as Austrian literature, tends to be anecdotal and often unreliable. This scholarly and readable study focuses on Raimund as a dramatist, with Vienna as the scene of his activity, and illustrates his originality and close affinity with the spirit of his age. Separate chapters examine his dialogue, the setting and action of his plays, his characters and his themes. A convincing and definitive appraisal.

530 **Nestroy, satire and parody in Viennese popular comedy.**
W. E. Yates. Cambridge, England: Cambridge University Press, 1972. 207p. bibliog.

This work is probably the first monograph in English to be published on this prolific and popular comedy writer of the 19th century. The author portrays Johann Nestroy (1801-62) as a satirist of distinction and a master of language, both expressive and carrying social and political implications. He illustrates his points by examining five of Nestroy's eighty-three plays in depth. An appendix analyses Nestroy's use of wordplay and puns which has established him as the innovator of a special type of satirical writing which became popular later in German and Austrian cabarets. The bibliography is comprehensive and there is a useful glossary of unfamiliar German words explaining how they are used in Nestroy's texts.

531 **Bruderzwist in Habsburg.** (Fraternal Habsburg strife.)
Franz Grillparzer, edited by Bruce Thompson. Glasgow, Scotland: Scottish Papers in Germanic Studies, 1982. 111p.

Generally considered to be his most significant historical drama, Franz Grillparzer presents here a dramatization of the events preceding the Thirty Years' War (1610-48) in the form of a political testament, written in the years just before the Revolution of 1848 and portraying the interplay of obsolete authority and overweening ambition to change the world by violent means. The plot concerns Archduke Matthias who succeeds in deposing his brother Rudolf II and finds himself in a position of power and responsibility which he cannot handle. The German text and English translation are printed on facing pages.

532 **King Ottokar, his rise and fall.**
Franz Grillparzer, translated from the German by Arthur Burkhard. Yarmouth, Massachusetts: Register Press, 1962. 160p.

Franz Grillparzer (1791-1872), in his historical plays, of which this is a good example, tends to present his characters in mythological and psychological terms. Here he elevates Rudolph I, the founder of the Habsburg dynasty, to the level of a secular saint, while his antagonist King Ottokar is shown in contrasting terms in complex, psychological detail. However, the real inspiration for this work was the figure of Napoleon, whose successes and ultimate failure had long fascinated Grillparzer. This is a patriotic play illustrating the futility of the pursuit of fame and greatness in the character of King Ottokar, shown as a weak and ordinary mortal beneath the mask of bravado. The play was published in 1825.

533 **The poor fiddler.**
Franz Grillparzer, translated from the German by Alexander Henderson, Elizabeth Henderson. New York: Frederick Ungar, 1967. 108p.

Franz Grillparzer's fame rests firmly on his dramatic output, but this, one of only two short stories he wrote, is still considered a brilliant piece of characterization with a wealth of psychological insight. First published in 1847 it is a story in a Viennese setting of a man totally out of step with the practical world, a social misfit and failure in life who nevertheless arouses the reader's sympathy because of his gentleness and honesty. A prototype of the 'anti-hero', he is a character who figured so frequently in the works of later Austrian writers such as Schnitzler, Rilke and Doderer. This is an extremely readable translation of a seminal work, with a helpful introduction by Ivar Ivask and some charming line illustrations by Lily Kehlmann.

534 **Essays on Grillparzer.**
Bruce Thompson, Mark Ward. Hull, England: Hull University German Department. 1978. 91p. (New German Studies Monographs, vol. 5).

This brief review of studies on the dramatist Franz Grillparzer, undertaken by British scholars between 1945 and 1975, contains interesting essays on his historical dramas by Edward McInnes and on his political views by one of the coauthors, Bruce Thompson. The latter presents Grillparzer as being attached to liberalism and combining an essential and inbuilt loyalty to the Habsburg monarchy with an antagonism to the oppressions of Metternich's police state; in other words, desirous of reforms but within the existing system of government. The same author has also contributed an interesting monograph on Grillparzer's use of irony as a device in both the arrangements of his plots and the presentation of dramatic episodes and individual characters, i.e., *A sense of irony: an examination of the tragedies of Grillparzer*. (Bern: Herbert Lang, 1976. Literaturwissenschaftliche Texte: Theorie und Kritik. Band 4).

535 **The plays of Grillparzer.**
George Wells. London, Oxford: Pergamon Press, 1969. 166p. (Pergamon Oxford German Series).

The plays of Franz Grillparzer, Austria's leading classical dramatist, are not widely-known in the English-speaking world and have received little attention from Germanists. This work is an exposition of the playwright's dramatic techniques and the principles guiding his historical treatment of the wide range of subjects which made up his output, divided here into three main categories: plays of action; Greek tragedies; and historical dramas. The writer has deliberately adopted a somewhat controversial approach in order to provoke discussion of a neglected field. Another recognized authority, W. E. Yates, in a critique commemorating the centenary of the dramatist's death, *Grillparzer – a critical introduction* (Cambridge, England: Cambridge University Press, 1972) places the genesis of Grillparzer's dramas in the context of his life and then charts the progress of their composition. The grouping here is not by categories, but by themes such as ambition, duty and love, politics and culture. The writer brings out very clearly the dramatist's subtlety of characterization, his concern for moral values and the ideals underlying his views of history and the human condition.

536 **Poems and letters of Nikolaus Lenau.**
Edited and translated from the German by Winthrop H. Root. New York: Frederick Ungar, 1964. 182p.

Nikolaus Lenau was born in 1802, the son of a middle-class German family which had settled in Hungary. His home life was disrupted and unhappy and he suffered a basic instability of temperament and approach to life which expressed itself in the feeling of pessimism and resignation which pervades so much of his writings. A visit to America in the 1830's, in an attempt to restore his equilibrium and his fortunes, which were at a very low ebb, was a financial disaster and badly affected his health. In 1845 he suffered a nervous breakdown and five years later died in a mental asylum. His poetic reputation was established with his first collection of poems in 1838, *Neuere Gedichte* (Later poems), which are intensely lyrical in character and marked by striking images and metaphors in his portrayal of nature. His epics and dramas, though less successful, are important for tracing his psychological development and his lifelong struggle with the ultimate issues of spiritual and moral freedom. He is still acknowledged as one of Austria's greatest lyrical poets, as this collection of poems indicates.

537 **Adalbert Stifter.**

Margaret Gump. New York: Twayne, 1974. 172p. bibliog. (Twayne's World Authors Series – Austria.)

Adalbert Stifter (1805-68) is not well-known in either the United States or Britain, even though his works have been translated into seventeen languages. His entire life was spent in the region of Vienna, apart from his early schooling at a Benedictine Monastery in Upper Austria, and he never achieved financial independence, having to earn his living as a poorly-paid school inspector, which he much resented. Stifter's private life was unhappy and there was much friction in his childless marriage. He wrote two major novels *Der Nachsommer* (q.v.) and *Witiko* which was part of a lengthy trilogy about mediaeval Bohemia. In addition he produced thirty or more short stories, all simple in their construction and setting, and drawn from modest anecdote, folk-tale or ancient chronicle. His characters are placed in a family, village or utopian country estate milieu, and exemplify the triumph of moral law. This is a perceptive analysis of his life and work, well-balanced and revealing. The bibliography is extensive and helpful to any student of this somewhat neglected writer.

538 **Der Nachsommer.** (Indian summer.)

Adalbert Stifter. Pesth: Gustav Heckenast Verlag, 1857. 3 vols.

This 19th-century classic of Austrian prose fiction written in 1857 has yet to appear in full in English translation. It is a long story, in which an old man's wisdom is gently conveyed to a young man of great receptivity who has a tremendous eagerness to learn. There is no conflict, no tension in the model country estate which Freiherr von Risach planned and built in his later years, with its harmonious and highly-ordered life sealed off from the world of passion and strife. The pursuit of the perfect life ends with the young man's marriage to the daughter Natalie and his eventual management of the estate. This remarkable novel, with its lack of dramatic effects and its single-minded idyllic approach, has a quality and distinction of its own, in strong contrast to the drab wretchedness of the author's own life, which ended in suicide.

Late 19th- and early 20th-century writers

539 **An annotated Arthur Schnitzler bibliography, 1965-1977.**

Jeffrey B. Berlin. Munich: Wilhelm Fink, 1978. 72p.

The wealth of bibliographical material on Arthur Schnitzler (1862-1931) in German and English which appeared during these twelve years is clear evidence of the revival of interest in his writings. This bibliography covers Schnitzler's narrative and dramatic works, his essays, sketches and philosophical writings, correspondence, poetry and translations. A useful index lists titles, themes and personal names.

540 **Studies in Arthur Schnitzler.**
Edited by Herbert W. Reichert, Herman Salinger. Chapel Hill, North Carolina: University of North Carolina Press, 1963. 116p. (University of North Carolina Studies in the Germanic Language and Literature, no. 42).

As one of the most representative writers of pre-World War I Arthur Schnitzler, dramatist and novelist, had a far-reaching influence as an exponent of Austrian letters. His popularity, however, receded with the rise of expressionism in literature in the 1920's. Notwithstanding this, interest in his writings was revived with the founding of the International Arthur Schnitzler Research Association in the United States in 1961, marking the centenary of his birth. The association now has over 150 members in thirteen different countries. This is a notable commemorative volume of eight essays on different aspects of Schnitzler's work by a team of scholars, three of whom were not Germanists. The essays were originally presented as papers at the University of Kentucky and were previously published in the form of a *Festschrift* in 1963.

541 **My youth in Vienna.**
Arthur Schnitzler, translated from the German by Catherine Hutter, with an introduction by A. J. P. Taylor. London: Weidenfeld & Nicolson, 1971. 304p. bibliog.

The lively introduction to this work by A. J. P. Taylor provides a fascinating backcloth to the intellectual life of Vienna at the turn of the century, with which Schnitzler was so closely associated. The text of the autobiography had been carefully authenticated by him, but his will stipulated that it should only be published after his death. Although it only spans the first thirty years of his life it is particularly revealing about his early medical training, as before becoming a writer he had been a specialist for nervous disorders. As a contemporary of Freud he anticipated many findings of psychoanalysis, and as early as 1890 he had used the term 'the unconscious' in his cycle of plays, *Anatol*. Many translations of Schnitzler's works have appeared in English collections. A selective list, together with a bibliography, can be found in Frederick Ungar's *Handbook of Austrian Literature* (q.v.) on p. 239-240.

542 **The Round Dance and other plays.**
Arthur Schnitzler, introduced and translated from the German by Charles Kessler. Manchester, England: Carcanet New Press, 1981. 221p.

The title play in this collection is well-known to international audiences through Max Ophuls' film *La Ronde* made in 1950. Schnitzler himself considered the play too immoral for a Viennese viewing and it was first performed in Berlin in 1920 amidst riots and demonstrations. It describes the search for sexual satisfaction in a vanished world where people have little real communication but play games with a language almost devoid of authenticity. Underneath the casual dialogue, however, there lies a carefully worked out technique with nuance and intonation being more expressive than actual content. Many of his plays revolve around the 'Süsses Mädel' (sweet girl), an amoral working-class prototype invented by the author, expressing a blend of sentimentality and realism, touched by melancholy and despair. *The Round Dance* as well as *Reigen* and *Anatol*, which are also in this collection, are good examples. A further selection of Schnitzler's plays, compiled by a team of five translators, edited by Egon Schwarz, is entitled *Arthur Schnitzler: Plays and Stories* (New York, Continuum, 1982. German Library Series, vol. 55).

543 **Undiscovered country.**

Arthur Schnitzler, in an English version by Tom Stoppard. London: Faber & Faber, 1980. 94p.

The adaptation of European plays for English speaking audiences has been one of the particular achievements of the British playwright Tom Stoppard. *Das weite Land,* (The vast domain) was written in 1911 and was produced in this version at the National Theatre in London in 1979, based on a literal transcript and adapted with the help of a German linguist and Stoppard's own theatrical skills. The play is set in turn-of-the-century Viennese society, suggesting a world of 'golden leisure and civilised deceit'. In true Schnitzler style it cleverly pinpoints decadence with wit and irony. The hero is vain and rather ridiculous, but tormented by his twisted sense of honour.

544 **Vienna 1900. Games with love and death.**

Arthur Schnitzler. Harmondsworth, England: Penguin Books, 1974. 365p.

These four stories, which formed the basis of a BBC TV serial devised and dramatised by Robert Müller, offer the reader a glimpse of life in Vienna during the sultry summers of 1900 and portray different situations of sexual motivation. *Mother and son*, translated by Agnes Jacques, depicts a claustrophobic relationship between a widow and her teenage son. *The man of honour*, translated by Eric Sutton is the story of a young man having to choose between his wife and mistress. *A confirmed bachelor*, translated by E. C. Slade, describes the disruption of a bachelor's life after the suicide of his sister, while the *Spring Sonata*, translated by J. H. Wisdom and Marr Murray, is a charming vignette of a young widow trying to recapture her first love. These are deceptively languid sketches of sexual turmoil only disguised by manners and convention.

545 **Arthur Schnitzler: a critical study.**

Martin Swales. Oxford: Clarendon Press, 1971. 288p.

This attempt at a balanced evaluation of Schnitzler's limitations, as well as his moments of real achievement, focuses mainly on those works which the author himself considered worthy of publication. Various themes emerge, such as the ambiguities in Schnitzler's style and narration, his preoccupation with language and morals and his interest in psychoanalysis. In sum, his writings are judged to reveal a vision of great human insight and artistic control and the author asserts that the modernity of his major works is still not being fully recognized by critics today.

546 **Selbstbildnis.** (Self-portrait.)
Hermann Bahr. West Berlin: S. Fischer Verlag, 1923. 310p.

The importance of Hermann Bahr (1863-1934) in the literary world at the turn of the century lay in his discovery and promotion of young talented writers and artists in the fulfilment of his self-appointed artistic mission in life, namely to raise the general cultural level of Austria by acting as a mediator between the public and the arts. He was a prolific writer of dramas, essays and narrative prose, but his exact literary merit has been hard to establish due to his frequent changes of direction (Marxist, impressionist, Catholic, monarchist). Furthermore, the subjects he treated were often of a temporary nature, so that many of his writings have not survived their time. His autobiography is arguably his most important work and brings out very clearly the dynamic forcefulness of his personality and the considerable influence he exercised as 'the midwife of modern Austrian literature.'

547 **Poems of thirty years.**
Franz Werfel, translated from the German by Edith Abercrombie Snow. Princeton, New Jersey: Princeton University Press,1945. 119p.

It was as a lyric poet that Werfel (1890-1945) first gained recognition and his early volumes, particularly those of poems up to 1925, were among the most important products of expressionism. This anthology of 50 poems, covering the period 1908-38 and first published in 1939 (Stockholm: Behrmann – Fischer Verlag) expresses his sympathy with men and all living creatures in a form of proclamation, often punctuated with ecstatic hymnlike outbursts, placing all the emphasis on a few words. Many of these poems almost defy translation and are not even easily accessible in German. However, this particular rendering is masterly in its grasp of the poet's intention and form of expression. The original text and its English translation appear on facing pages.

548 **The song of Bernadette.**
Franz Werfel, translated from the German by Ludwig Lewisohn. St. Albans, England: Mayflower Books, 1970. 446p.

Franz Werfel (1890-1945), a close friend of Franz Kafka, married the widow of the composer Gustav Mahler after World War I and emigrated to the United States at the time of the *Anschluss*. His literary output was voluminous, comprising novellas, sketches, poems, essays, lectures and plays. All of his works were closely bound up with the countries and locations where he lived, such as Vienna and Prague and various places in Italy, Turkey and France. It was to Lourdes in this last country that Werfel fled in 1940 to escape from the advancing Germans. He wrote this evocative story after reaching the United States as an offering of thanks to divine providence for his eventual safety. This epic poem about Bernadette Soubirous, who developed such remarkable healing powers, is written in the form of a novel of gripping intensity, designed to 'magnify the divine mystery and holiness of man' a thread that runs through many of his works. For a selective list of English translations of Werfel's works in collection, see Anneliese Kuchinke-Bach's article (p. 277-78) in the *Handbook of Austrian Literature*, edited by Frederick Ungar (New York: Frederick Ungar, 1973).

549 **Star of the unborn.**

Franz Werfel, translated by Gustave O. Arlt. New York: Viking, 1946. 645p.

Sacrifice and self-abandonment in the service of others were two humanistic values which had a particular attraction for Werfel (1890-1945), who linked them to a religious orientation. He regarded man's destiny as being fixed and he viewed the development of the universe from the same standpoint. Although interested in the forces of contemporary change, for example in technology, psychology and social problems, he remained profoundly suspicious of progress all his life. In this last novel, set in an 'astro-mental' world, he shows that civilization cannot solve man's problems, for even the most advanced of civilizations contain seeds of decline, revolution and destruction, both internal and external. For an overall view of Werfel's philosophy and output W. H. Fox's article 'Franz Werfel' in *German Men of Letters*, vol. 3 (1964), p. 109-25 can be recommended.

550 **The correspondence between Richard Strauss and Hugo von Hofmannsthal.**

Translated from the German by Hanns Hammelmann, Ewald Osers. New York; Cambridge, England: Cambridge University Press, 1980. 558p.

In his foreword to this revealing work Edward Sackville-West, the music and art critic, describes the relationship between Richard Strauss, the rough and robust composer, and Hugo von Hofmannsthal, the stylish elaborate librettist, as that of 'a Siamese cat working out a modus vivendi with a Labrador'. This temperamental incompatibility between the two artists, their difference in background and outlook finding a compromise in a common purpose and mutual respect, is well-reflected in this correspondence, which provides a running commentary of their collaboration in bringing to fruition, step by step, over a period of twenty-five years, six operas which have now become classics ('Electra', 'The Knight of the Rose', 'Ariadne in Naxos', 'The Woman without a Shadow', 'The Egyptian Helen', and 'Arabella'). The problems of fusion between word and music are discussed here with a searching and quite unique intensity. The two translators, each handling the letters of one of the protagonists and then exchanging their translations for editing by the other, have achieved a remarkable unity and impeccable results.

551 **Everyman.**

Hugo von Hofmannsthal, edited and translated by Margaret Jacobs. London, Edinburgh: Thomas Nelson, 1957. 78p. bibliog.

Visitors to the annual Salzburg Festival will surely be familiar with the traditional open-air performance of 'Jedermann' in the Residenzplatz, associated with Max Reinhardt, who first produced it in 1911. Based on a late 15th-century English morality play, the central figure is suddenly visited by Death and commanded to give an account of his life before the throne of God. The play progresses without formal acts or scenes. The editor of this work, in an excellent introduction, discusses the psychological action, the motives and feelings of the central character, particularly his attitude to wealth and riches. She also discusses the treatment of the religious significance of the play, which does not follow the conventional Church teaching of the age.

552 **Hugo von Hofmannsthal, 1874-1929.**
Edited by W. E. Yuill, Patricia Howe. London: University of London, 1979. 144p.

This is a collection of thirteen papers delivered at a symposium held in March 1979 at Bedford College, London University, in commemoration of the 50th anniversary of Hugo von Hofmannsthal's death, and illustrating the author's place in a general European context and tradition. The subjects discussed included: the literary influences of John Keats, Oscar Wilde and Alfred de Musset, the French poet, on Hofmannsthal; his social and political attitudes; and his theatrical views.

553 **The last days of mankind: Karl Kraus and his Vienna.**
Frank Field. London: Macmillan; New York: St. Martin's Press, 1967. 280p. bibliog.

An historical enquiry into the society which provoked an extraordinary cultural efflorescence at the turn of the century as seen through the life and work of Karl Kraus, the celebrated Viennese polemicist and satirist (1874-1936). His play. *The last days of Mankind* (1922) a masterpiece of World War I, was a dire prophecy of gloom with the sense of impending tragedy further heightened by the fact that its author was Jewish. In it is a brilliant portrayal of coffee-house life in Vienna with its gossip and intrigue, wit and sophistication contrasting in stark terms with the grim reality of the social and economic problems of the time. The author's commentary is discreet and Kraus is liberally quoted throughout the work.

554 **Die letzten Tage der Menschheit.** (The last days of mankind.)
Karl Kraus. Munich: Kösel Verlag, 1957. 770p. (Heinrich Fischer Edition of Collected Works, vol. 5).

This truly remarkable work is a drama about World War I which, with its 100 scenes, would take ten nights to perform on the stage, with no hero and no unity of space, time or action. A satirical tragedy, in powerful language and with prophetic vision, it was an apocalyptic warning of the impending disaster which was to engulf the world. It must rank as one of the most vigorous denunciations of war ever to have been written. The play, which cannot easily be followed by today's reader without some explanatory notes, covers a vast fresco of events – at the front with its 'iron rule' of war and conquest and at home, with the goodnaturedness of ordinary people, caught up helplessly in a doom-laden tragedy from which there is no escape. Kraus was one of the very few writers who never for one moment succumbed to the chauvinistic venom which filled the air in those years and he was totally uncompromising in his condemnation of the corruption and treachery of his age. There is perhaps still a message in this play for the world to-day as he shows how man in his time achieved a technical superiority over himself which only served to threaten him with terrible and unavoidable disasters. Finally, there is Kraus' extraordinary personalized use of language – 'I do not command words, I am at their command' – which presents a real challenge to any would-be translator of this highly unconventional work.

555 **R. M. Rilke: a verse concordance to his complete lyrical poetry.**
Edited by Ulrich K. Goldsmith, Thomas Schneider. Leeds, England: W. S. Maney, 1980. 1,593p.

This massive tome, the product of careful and laborious research, provides a valuable reference tool for the student specializing in the works of Rilke (1875-1926), the greatest poet of his age. The work is divided into two parts, the first covering his German poems, and the second his French and Russian poetry. There is an alphabetical list of first lines coupled with an index and a ranking frequency list of German forms of expression.

556 **An unofficial Rilke: poems 1912-1926.**
Selected, introduced and translated by Michael Hamburger. London: Anvil Press Poetry, 1981. 115p.

Michael Hamburger has purposely chosen a number of Rilke's (1875-1926) unfamiliar and uncharacteristic poems to form this collection. Many of them were disavowed by the poet himself, while the merit of others has not always been recognized; but whatever their standing, they can in Hamburger's view only be interpreted in terms of Rilke's loss of faith and his sense of disorientation. The introduction to this work is both penetrating and sympathetic and describes with particular sensitivity the nature of Rilke's personal and artistic crisis and argues for a complete revaluation of his miscellaneous poems, too often considered to be second-rate. Another selection of his poems, from his middle period (1902-07), many of them appearing in English for the first time, has been published under the title *The unknown Rilke; selected poems* (Oberlin College, 1983. 141p. Field Translation Series B.) The poems were translated by Franz Wright and introduced by Egon Schwarz. They reflect the impact of French culture on Rilke, particularly the work of the sculptor François Rodin, whose secretary he became and whose influence on his writing was considerable, raising it from an imprecise lyricism to an exact and graphic presentation. In both works the translation is of a high quality.

557 **Duino elegies.**
Rainer Maria Rilke, introduced by Stephen Spender and translated by J. B. Leishman. London: Chatto & Windus, 1977. reprint. 161p.

Once described as 'the Austrian who has achieved the highest form of sublimation' Rainer Maria Rilke (1875-1926) was the uncrowned king of poetry of his age. Through the effect of his nature upon his associates, his friends and his extensive correspondence he exerted his personality in a remarkable way, not only as a creative artist but as an individual; in fact, he created something of a legend about himself. The ten poems comprising this work were begun in 1912, when he was enjoying the hospitality of Princess Marie von Thurn und Taxis, both an inspiration and influence on his work, but they were not completed until ten years later when he was in Switzerland. Rilke was for ever driven by a sense of vocation, what he called 'earth's mandate', not only to interpret the world but to safeguard its permanency and stability. These elegies reflect his mystical experiences and are concerned with the relationship between love, life and death – the summation of all his struggles expressed in complicated verse. The sensitive introduction by a leading English poet is matched by the adroit and perceptive translation of this challenging work. A list of Rilke's works and English translations, together with a selective bibliography, can be found in Ungar's *Handbook of Austrian literature* (q.v.).

558 **The notebooks of Malte Laurids Brigge.**
Rainer Maria Rilke, translated from the German by Stephen Mitchell, with an introduction by William Gass. New York: Vintage Books, 1983, 277p.

Written between 1904 and 1910 this work represents a kind of autobiographical and factual commentary on the *Neue Gedichte* (New poems) which were written during the same period, when Rilke was much influenced by the French sculptor Rodin with whom he had worked in Paris. This is generally referred to as his middle or classical period, imposing a certain measure of restraint on him, which was contrary to his inmost nature but felt to be a necessary step in his literary development.

559 **The other side.**
Alfred Kubin, translated from the German by Denver Lindley. London: Victor Gollancz, 1969. 349p.

Alfred Kubin (1877-1959), a Bohemian by birth, was a brilliant artist and illustrator of great originality, who became a narrative writer under the impact of ideas and visions which came to him whilst studying Eastern mysticism. This is his only novel, written in the space of three months in 1909, and later illustrated with 52 pen and ink drawings. It describes a 'dream state' somewhere in Asia, gradually moving towards its disintegration – a foretaste perhaps of the political and cultural collapse of the old Europe which was to follow World War I. Kubin wrote an autobiography to accompany the second edition and added to it as further editions were published. The reader is offered some rare insights into his character and method of working, while this posthumous publication contains a supplementary essay by him on his life and work written in his declining years and published here for the first time.

560 **Robert Musil and the culture of Vienna.**
Hannah Hickman. London, Sydney: Croom Helm, 1984. 203p. bibliog.

The recent publication of Musil's (1880-1942) notebooks and essays in full has provided the author with unique and exclusive material, which she has examined assiduously and used extensively in her evaluation of Musil's thinking and intellectual standing. She particularly stresses his multi-disciplinary accomplishments, for he was an engineer, philosopher, mathematician and physicist and was almost equally brilliant in all of these fields. In her exposition of Musil's complex and enigmatic character she throws into strong relief his astounding originality, his powers of analytical observation and his superb use of language. For a largely philosophical interpretation of Musil's works the reader could well consult F. G. Peters' *Robert Musil: master of the hovering life* (q.v.).

561 **Musil in focus.**
Lothar Huber, John J. White. London: London University, Institute of Germanic Studies, 1982. 147p.

This is a series of new analyses and interpretations of certain aspects of Robert Musil's (1880-1942) monumental but uncompleted work *The man without qualities* (q.v.) and his shorter fiction, plays and other writings by a group of British and Austrian academics in commemoration of the centenary of the author's birth. It is the first full-length all-round study of Musil to have appeared in the United Kingdom. A scholarly and valuable appraisal of a very important writer.

562 **The man without qualities.**
Robert Musil, translated from the German and with a foreword by Eithne Wilkins, Ernst Kaiser. London: Secker & Warburg, 1979. reprint. 3 vols. (1953-60).

One of the longest novels in literary history, this work was originally planned in two volumes and four parts. The first two parts were published in 1930 and 1932 respectively, the third part was published posthumously and privately, and the fourth part contains some unfinished chapters which have not yet appeared in English translation. Musil (1880-1942) was determined to give his message to the world and his constant pre-occupation with this mammoth work made it impossible for him to finish it. It is in fact an analysis of life and thought in the dying days of the Habsburg Empire all projected in an unhurried sweep of many aspects of life, all bursting with ideas and with the action, such as it is, taking place within the space of one year. There is no proper plot and the real action lies not in what the characters do but within their states of mind, their emotions, ideas and interrelationships. Ulrich, the main figure, is a neutral character who never takes sides and reduces everything to its essentials. This was one of Musil's methods of exposing false values in a disintegrating society. A work of remarkable originality and of major importance in Austrian literature of the first half of this century.

563 **Young Törless.**
Robert Musil, translated from the German by Eithne Wilkins, Ernst Kaiser. London: Secker & Warburg, 1955. 217p.

The author was only twenty-two when he began to write this strange and compelling exposure of conditions in a military boarding school, where young Törless undergoes terrifying and weird experiences at the hands of his fellow students. However, this is not just a robustly written school story, for Musil, with a sure touch of genius, has broadened his theme into a wider perspective and the work becomes a study of power and its misuse – a foretaste of events which were to engulf his country a generation later.

564 **Robert Musil: master of the hovering life.**
Frederick G. Peters. New York: Columbia University Press, 1978. 281p. bibliog.

This perceptive and convincing study of one of Austria's most significant and influential writers of the first half of this century is a blend of literary criticism and philosophical interpretation. Inevitably, it is much concerned with Musil's (1880-

1942) greatest work *The Man without qualities*. The latter, the author sums up as a philosophical and intellectual tour de force, not just a presentation of the decline of a great culture in the closing years of the Habsburg Empire, but an attempt to analyse the degeneration of values which were at the very root of western civilized morality. The book's title is an expression of the author's view that Musil's whole search in life was to find a living balance between religion and knowledge, between reason and mysticism and that it was only through his writing that he could seek to achieve a fusion of these two elements.

565 **Robert Musil, an introduction to his work.**
Burton Pike. Ithaca, New York: Cornell University Press, 1961. 214p. bibliog.

This work represents a critical guide for the general reader and an outline for the scholar. The first part of the study discusses Musil's philosophy and the second part is devoted to individual criticism of his writings. The author contends that Musil's influence can be detected in the work of such writers as Bertolt Brecht, Thomas Mann and James Joyce and examples of this are provided. A more recent assessment, *Robert Musil and the crisis of European culture, 1880-1942*, by David Luft (Berkeley, California: University of California Press, 1980) focuses on the relationship between metaphysics and the novel in the early part of the 20th century with particular reference to Musil. Luft claims that Musil still remains an enigmatic figure in Austrian, and indeed, European literature and that his works present particular problems for translators.

566 **A confidential matter: the letters of Richard Strauss and Stefan Zweig, 1931-1935.**
Translated from the German by Max Knight. London: Berkeley, California: University of California Press, 1977. 121p. bibliog.

After Hugo von Hofmannsthal's death in 1929 Richard Strauss the composer, after searching for some time for a worthy successor as his librettist, eventually agreed to collaborate with the writer Stefan Zweig (1881-1942) on an operatic adaptation of Ben Johnson's comedy *The Silent Woman*. The uneasy correspondence exchanged between the two over the following four years illustrates the difficulties which the librettist, a Jew, encountered with the Third Reich in collaborating with an Aryan composer who was sponsored by the Nazis but thought he could bend the régime to his own way of thinking.

567 **European of yesterday.**
D. A. Prater. Oxford: Clarendon Press, 1972. 390p. bibliog.

Stefan Zweig, poet, dramatist, essayist, novelist, biographer, librettist, translator and autobiographer, enjoyed an enormous literary success in his lifetime, particularly in the 1920's and 1930's. For several years he was the most translated author in Europe, with works available in nearly forty languages. However, today his writings have fallen into relative obscurity. Donald Prater's sympathetic account of the life-story of this sensitive, unusually interesting and complicated personality is an attempt to redress the balance. The author contends that the very ideals for which Zweig fought, not always successfully, including peace, liberty of the individual and the moral unity of Europe are still relevant today. Zweig's message therefore has a convincing significance for us. In addition to the already considerable volume of material available, the author also has had access to a large proportion of Zweig's unpublished letters and has made use of a number of other sources drawn from personal experience. The bibliography included in this volume is extensive, although not intended to be comprehensive. For this the reader is directed to *Stefan Zweig's bibliography* by Randolph J. Klawiter (Chapel Hill, North Carolina: University of North Carolina, 1965, University of North Carolina Studies in The Germanic Languages and Literature, no. 50).

568 **The royal game and other stories.**

Stefan Zweig, translated from the German by Jill Sutcliffe, with an introduction by John Fowles. London: Cape, 1981. 250p.

It is hard to imagine, when reading these five stories, how such a gifted and remarkable writer as Stefan Zweig should have suffered such literary obscurity since his death in 1942. Indeed, there is a compelling magneticism about these stories, which all explore in some way or other different manifestations of singlemindedness – obsessional love, revenge, honour – almost to a point of madness as in the title story (*Schachnovelle*), which was written in the last four months of his life. 'The royal game' is the story of a man who outwits the Gestapo and manages to find the courage to go on living. He is a man who, though scarred, neither runs away from life nor gives way to despair. The other English titles in this collection are: 'Amok'; 'The burning secret'; 'Fear'; and 'Letter from an unknown woman'. This is a most welcome publication commemorating the centenary of Zweig's birth and it contains an excellent introduction.

569 **The diaries of Franz Kafka, 1910-1923.**

Edited by Max Brod, translated from the German by Joseph Kresh, Martin Greenberg. Harmondsworth, England: Penguin Books, 1972. reprint. 519p. (Penguin Modern Classics).

Franz Kafka (1883-1924) was one of the most important and influential prose writers of the first half of this century. Born in Prague, the son of a rich Jewish merchant, he studied literature, medicine and the law but later moved to Berlin to write. His unsatisfactory love affairs, his difficult relationship with his father and his psychopathic sensitivity eventually broke down his health and he died of tuberculosis in a sanitorium near Vienna in 1924. In these diaries, prepared for publication by his life-long friend Max Brod, he noted down literary ideas, dreams, daily occurrences and comments on his reading, but little of historical or biographical value. They reveal very clearly the inner world in which he lived and describe his fears, and his feelings of isolation, frustration and guilt. They also contain some stringent criticisms of living persons, all identified by initials only. The diaries were first published by Shocken Books, New York in 1949. A complete and unabridged collection of his works, nine in all, was published to commemorate the centenary of Kafka's birth i.e. *Franz Kafka* (London: Secker & Warburg, 1983. 914p.).

570 **In the penal settlement: tales and short prose works.**
Franz Kafka, translated from the German by Ernst Kaiser, Eithne Wilkins. London: Secker & Warburg, 1973. reprint. 298p.

This collection of Kafka's short stories represents all those he actually had published in newspapers, journal or book form. The title story, written at the outbreak of World War I was first published in 1919 and the first English translation appeared in 1949. The other stories, with their English titles, are; *Two dialogues*; *Meditation*; *The Judgement*; *The Transformation*; *A Country Doctor*; *A Hunger Artist*.

571 **The trial.**
Franz Kafka, translated from the German by Willa Muir, Edwin Muir. Harmondsworth, England: Penguin Books, 1974. reprint. 255p.

This remarkable novel first appeared in 1925 after the author's death and was first published in England by Victor Gollancz in 1935. A film of it was made in 1962. This novel established Kafka with a unique reputation in modern European literature and there have been, and there are still, many attempts at its interpretation. The work describes the experiences of a man arrested on a charge which is never specified and against which he tries to defend himself, but this only involves himself all the more in his existentialist guilt. In the narrative Kafka tries to unravel some of the fundamental dilemmas of human life and reveals a highly sensitive mind, oppressed and bewildered by the burden of living.

572 **Kafka centenary exhibition catalogue.**
Oxford: Bodleian Library, 1983. 55p.

The 1983 Kafka Centenary Exhibition in Oxford opened fifty years to the day after the public burning of his books by the Nazis in 1933. This catalogue of the exhibition is liberally illustrated and contains in the first part ('From Pen to Print') some of his original manuscripts and early editions of his works, many of which have been housed in the Bodleian Library since 1961. The second part ('Paths out of Prague') includes material from other collections, private and public, illustrating his work and influence on literary and philosophical thought after his death in 1924.

573 **The nightmare of reason.**
Ernst Pawel. London: Harrill, 1984. 466p. bibliog.

Max Brod, Kafka's associate and literary executor, refused to carry out the latter's instructions to burn all his papers after his death in 1924 and these were of material assistance to him in compiling his biography of Kafka, published in 1937. However, Brod was too close a friend to provide a really discriminating assessment of this remarkable writer and thinker. This study, based partly on new material now available, is attractively written, closely argued and supported by some excellent photographs. Kafka appears as a loner and recluse, but also as a man of 'great courage and prophetic vision, condemned to see the world with such blinding clarity that he found it unbearable'. It is estimated that the literature on Kafka and his work currently comprises some 15,000 titles in most of the world's major languages. The bibliography contained in this study includes only publications in book form and in English, covering his life and background, literary criticism and interpretation.

574 **Flight without end.**

Joseph Roth, translated from the German by David Le Vay in collaboration with Beatrice Musgrave. London: Peter Owen, 1977. 144p.

Written in Paris in 1927 this work is perhaps the most personal of Joseph Roth's (1894-1939) novels. It tells the story of a young ex-officer of the Austro-Hungarian Army in World War I, who makes his way back from captivity in Siberia and service with the Bolshevik army, only to find that the old order had changed and there was no place for him in the new 'European' culture which had replaced it. Roth's own spiritual experiences as an exile, unable to accept new values and ideologies are mirrored with sensitivity and anguish in this moving work.

575 **The Radetzky march.**

Joseph Roth, translated from the German by Eva Tucker. London: Allen Lane, 1974. 319p.

Joseph Roth, son of Jewish parents and later converted to Catholicism, worked as a journalist in Berlin and Vienna and travelled widely in Europe. He was an important novelist, essayist and critic who chronicled his country's past with a sense of nostalgia and genuine attachment. The action in his work develops from individual situations, anecdotes and traits of character – a mixture of theatrical and descriptive representation. His characters seem to be completely enmeshed in their own particular time as this novel, one of his best and published originally in 1932, admirably illustrates. The setting here is bleak and isolated, that of the old Austro-Russian border; the main protagonists, though predictable in their actions are presented in a variety of forms and brilliantly portrayed. An important contribution to the mythologization of imperial Austria.

576 **Jugend ohne Gott.** (Youth without God.)

Ödön von Horváth. London: Harrap, 1974. 140p. bibliog. (Modern World Literature Series).

Ödön von Horváth's (1901-38) writings have attracted a good deal of attention in recent years and his plays or *Volkstücke* (popular pieces), representing a continuation of Austria's long tradition of popular comedy are among the most frequently staged productions in the German-language theatre of to-day. Born in Fiume, the son of a diplomat he travelled extensively in his youth and although his first language was Hungarian he wrote exclusively in German. His first major drama. *Geschichten aus dem Wiener Wald* (Tales from the Vienna Woods), with its attack on 'stupidity, deceit and exploitation', won him immediate fame. This later work (1938), a short story, written in the space of a few months and translated into eight languages, is, however, set in a political context. It is a damning indictment of the National Socialist movement and particularly its brainwashing of German youth and its premilitary training in preparation for war. The story, taut and concise in style, is written in the first person and deals with the moral conflict of a teacher torn between his professional pride, his responsibility as a servant of the State and his personal search for the truth. The composition is unusual in that Horváth makes use of letters, diaries and newspaper reports in the story, which adds to its immediacy and authenticity. Thomas Mann, the celebrated German novelist, considered this to be the finest literary work of his time. Ian Huish has provided an excellent commentary; he has also written a more extended assessment of Horváth's literary merits entitled *Horvath, a study* (London: Heinemann, 1980), which can be warmly recommended.

Modern writers

577 **Modern Austrian writing: literature and society after 1945.**
Alan Best, Hans Wolfschütz. London: Oswald Wolff; Totowa, New Jersey: Barnes & Noble, 1980. 307p.

In this serious appraisal of Austrian intellectual development and activity since World War II the joint authors have discerned three distinct literary trends which they discuss in depth, explaining the background and particular context of each. Firstly, they instance writers in the Austrian tradition with roots in the pre-*Anschluss* era but who have made their mark in the literary world since 1945. Secondly they identify a group of writers who grew up in the Nazi era and whose works display an intense scepticism. Thirdly, they consider the more avant-garde writers who react strongly to established Austrian literary traditions. The combination of these three different elements, in the authors' view, contributes powerfully to the contemporary literary scene.

578 **Austrian poetry, 1945-1980.**
Edited by Martin Green. *Literary Review*, vol. 25, no. 2 (winter 1982). (Fairlegh Dickinson University, New Jersey).

The whole of this issue of this international journal of contemporary writing was devoted to a selection of modern Austrian poetry in English translation. The introductory essay by Beth Bjornklund, assistant professor of German at the University of Virginia, who was also responsible for the translation, sets today's Austrian literary scene. This is followed by a series of recorded interviews, all in English, with six representative poets featured in the anthology. The scope of both theme and treatment in this selection of forty-seven pages is impressive.

579 **Austrian poetry today.**
Edited and translated by Milne Holton, Herbert Kuhner. New York: Schocken, 1985. 275p. bibliog.

Selections from the works of forty contemporary Austrian poets, some less well-known and unusual ones among them, are featured in this anthology. The poems illustrate various aspects of the themes, tendencies and pre-occupations of Austria's current literary tradition. The work includes extensive biographical notes.

580 **Studies in modern Austrian literature.**
Edited by Brian Murdoch, M. G. Ward. Glasgow: Scottish Papers in Germanic Studies, 1981. 122p.

This is a set of eight papers presented at a conference on modern Austrian literature, held at St. Andrews University, Scotland in March 1980, by Austrian, English and Scottish specialists. Three of the essays are in German. The subjects cover various aspects of literary style and treatment, the Viennese theatre and language.

581 **Anthology of modern Austrian literature.**
Edited and introduced by Adolf Opel. London: Oswald Wolff, 1981. 279p. bibliog. (International PEN Books Series).

Austrian literature has often been regarded as simply an offshoot of German literature because of the common language and the close political and cultural ties between the two countries. In his introductory essay the author aims to show that there are in fact two distinct and independent literatures which have evolved side by side. He claims that the roots of a specific Austrian literature are to be found in the 'supranational style and time-transcending tradition of the baroque which is still alive today'. The actual selection of works by the fifty-nine modern Austrian writers featured in the anthology is not just a survey of representative Austrian post-1945 literature, but is intended to convey a general picture of Austria in modern times. The contributions therefore largely relate to a particular Austrian situation, be it historical, political, social or psychological. The author suggests that one of the most significant characteristics of modern Austrian writing is not so much the subject but the unique way in which it is approached and handled so that what is well-known and familiar almost to the point of banality is often projected in an entirely new light. There are biographies of authors and translators and a useful bibliography of English translations of the authors represented.

582 **The Vienna group: six major Austrian poets.**
Edited and translated by Rosmarie Wardrop, Harriett Watts. New York: Station Hill, 1985. 92p.

The so-called Vienna Group was a small collection of avant-garde Austrian writers, who during the 1950s and 1960s experimented with everything from black humour verse in Viennese dialect to concrete poetry. This short anthology of poems by six of its principal members, H. C. A. Artmann, the leading spirit, E. Jandl, Friederike Mayröcker, Gerhard Bluhm, Friedrich Achleitner and Konrad Bayer, appears in an English translation which captures the mood of its high spirited and comic language in a remarkable way. It can be warmly recommended as an example of an unusual but extremely successful and widely acclaimed form of modern Austrian poetic expression.

583 **The broken eagle.**
C. E. Williams. London: Paul Elek, 1974. 281p. bibliog.

Nine major authors, spanning the period from the late Habsburg era of the 1890's to the *Anschluss* in 1938, all born within the boundaries of the Austro-Hungarian Empire and with German as their language, are the subject of this fascinating study designed to show how far politics impinged on the literature of the period. The author presents and discusses a number of political themes and problems as mirrored in the published, and (where available) the private, writings of this representative selection of writers, from the traditional political standpoint of the librettist Hugo von Hofmannsthal to the fiercely radical views on political issues expressed by the satirist and polemicist Karl Kraus. However, these attitudes changed as new political, social and racial tensions came to the fore and their whole image of the Habsburg Monarchy after its collapse in 1918 was badly shaken by the rise of fascism. The work is well annotated and there is a useful appendix giving a chronological account of the main historical events during this period.

584 **Bambi: a life in the woods.**

Felix Salten, translated from the German by Whittaker Chambers. London: Jonathan Cape, 1950, rev. ed. 223p.

English readers will probably best remember this story of a deer and its adventures in an Austrian forest from the Walt Disney film, for which an abridged verse script was prepared and charmingly translated by Henry Louis Spink in 1944. The book first appeared in 1928 and the English translation contained an inspiring foreword by John Galsworthy. It was widely acclaimed as a minor masterpiece of simple lyrical writing, with a gentleness of touch and delicacy of perception rare in the literature of the day.

585 **Die Schlafwandler.** (The sleepwalkers.)

Hermann Broch. Zürich, Switzerland: Rhein-Verlag, 1931. 369p.

Hermann Broch (1886-1951) started life as a manager of a family textile firm but at the age of forty-two turned to intellectual pursuits and started the study of mathematics, philosophy and psychology. It was during this period that he produced his first great novel *The Sleepwalkers*, a trilogy focusing on the total disintegration of the world and its values by a gradual process, in three phases (1888, 1903, 1918). Broch felt that the novel of his time could no longer tell a story, and he considered that his work had to move into the 'ultra-scientific' and operate on many levels, from the instinctive ones to the magic and metaphysical ones. A useful bibliography on Broch accompanies Walter Weiss's discerning essay (p. 36-40) in the *Handbook of Austrian literature* (q.v.).

586 **The death of Virgil.**

Hermann Broch, translated from the German by Jean Starr, with an introduction by Bernard Levin. London: Oxford University Press, 1983. 416p.

First published in 1946, this evocative lyrical novel, described by Thomas Mann as 'one of the most representative and advanced works of our time' makes great demands on the reader's imagination, but is extremely well-translated in this edition, while the reader is considerably helped by Bernard Levin's sensitive introduction. In 1936 Broch (1886-1951) wrote a radio play (*Die Heimkehr des Vergil*), which he revised as this novel ten years later and which established his international reputation. The story tells of the dying poet, Virgil, suspended between life and death just as his age was suspended between the pagan and the Christian eras. With history at a turning point Virgil realizes that what in his writing he had considered was beauty may well have been only falsified history. The death agony of a dissolving world, 'literature at the end of a culture', is mirrored with particular intensity in the monologue of the dying poet. A review of this work by H. J. Weigand, 'Broch's *Death of Virgil*: program notes' appeared in the *Publications of the Modern Language Association of America*, no. 62 (1947).

587 **Auf dem Floss.** (On the raft.)
George Saiko. Zürich, Switzerland; Cologne, GFR: Benziger Verlag, 1970. 573p.

This novel was written in the immediate post-World War II period when the author (1892-1962) was acting Director of the Albertina, the famous museum of graphic arts in Vienna. He had previously been a regular contributor to a number of art journals, including *The Studio* (London), in the early 1930's. On the surface this work appears to be simply a portrayal of Austrian life during the latter years of the First Republic, but in fact it introduces an entirely new element in Austrian literary interpretation, namely, that of 'magical realism'. In Saiko's view the discursive novel was in danger of being out-paced and even displaced by documentaries and factual reports. It therefore needed a new dimension if it was to retain its social function in interpreting the world. His aim was to 'make irrational rational through literary interpretation'. A critique of this work by F. T. Csokor appeared in *German Life and Letters*, (1954-55), p. 85-88.

588 **The strong are lonely.**
Fritz Hochwälder, adapted and translated by Eva Le Gallienne from the French version by J. Mercure, R. Thiebergen. London: Heinemann Educational Books, 1968. 89p. (Hereford Plays Series).

Fritz Hochwälder was born in 1911 in Vienna of Jewish parents who perished during deportation to Poland in 1938; he himself escaped to Switzerland, where he still lives. This play, originally published in 1947, was first performed in London in 1955 with Donald Wolfit in the leading role and was an immediate international success. It is colourful, concentrated and theatrically extremely effective. The play portrays the crisis of the Jesuits in the 18th century in Paraguay, where their attempts to teach the Indians European values and introduce law and justice conflicted with the interests and colonization policies of the Spanish Empire and eventually led to their forcible dissolution. The author chose this theme to illustrate 'the eternal problems of mankind, the questions of social justice and the realm of God on earth'.

589 **The demons.**
Heimito von Doderer, translated from the German by Richard Winston, Clara Winston.
New York: Alfred Knopf, 1961. 2 vols.

Undoubtedly one of the most important Austrian novels to have appeared this century and with the same title, in German translation, as Dostoevsky's famous work *The Possessed*. The author (1896-1966) worked on it for thirty years and it was published on his 60th birthday. It is a vast fresco of life in Vienna in the 1920's, tracing links between the lowest classes, the intellectuals and aristocrats.

A novel of great psychological depth, powerful and macabre. For a considered appraisal of this work see H. M. Waidson's article in *German Life and Letters*, no. 11 (April 1958), p. 214-40.

590 **The Strudlhof steps.**
Heimito von Doderer. Munich, New York: Alfred Knopf, 1962. 908p.

The publication of this novel, written in 1951 when the author was fifty-five, established Doderer (1896-1966) as a narrative writer of the first rank. Like his other novels it is a broad panoramic view of Vienna in the 1920's. The character of René Stangeler is semi-autobiographical and the work takes its title from a flight of steps in a district of Vienna. Brief extracts of this novel have so far only appeared in English in anthologies.

591 **Auto-da-Fé.**
Elias Canetti, translated from the German by C. V. Wedgwood. Harmondsworth, England: Penguin Books, 1973. 522p. reprint.

This is a savage, grotesque story of the inevitable self-destruction of an isolated individual, slipping into madness; a view of the dark side of mankind. It was hailed as a masterpiece, and won a Nobel Prize for literature.

592 **Crowds and Power.**
Elias Canetti, translated from the German by Carol Stewart. Harmondsworth, England: Penguin, 1973. 560p. bibliog.

Written in 1960, a quarter of a century after the publication of his much acclaimed *Auto-da-fé*, this work studies the interplay between crowds and human behaviour. The author (1905-) analyses different types of crowds, from Pueblo Indians to Shi'ite Moslem festivals. The extensive bibliography lists a number of books which had some influence on the author when writing this extraordinary and evocative book.

593 **Sprechgrille and selected poems.**
Paul Celan, translated from the German by Joachim Neugroschel. New York: E. P. Dutton, 1971. 255p.

Paul Anczel (1920-70), whose pseudonym was Paul Celan, was born in Bukovina in northern Romania in 1920, and after the country's occupation by German troops in World War II was sent to a forced labour camp, which he survived, though both his parents were killed. Later, he studied French and German linguistics and worked as a translator. He published his first poems in a Romanian anthology *Agora*, describing them as 'messages in a bottle' which could either be picked up or lost; the essential need was to communicate. His poems are full of images and gestures, held together by a language as disciplined as it is associative. The German text and English translation in this collection are on facing pages. A poet of considerable promise, Celan committed suicide at the age of forty-nine.

594 **Herod's children.**

Ilse Aichinger, translated from the German by Cornelia Schaeffer. New York: Atheneum, 1965. 395p.

Ilse Aichinger (1921-) was one of the first important Austrian writers to appear after World War II and emulated Franz Kafka in developing the modern narrative form, the parable, to convey truth. In *Die grössere Hoffnung* (The greater hope) the title of the German original of *Herod's children*, published in 1948, as in so many of her writings, her surrealist approach brings together the past and the present, the possible and the actual, as the story unfolds of a Jewish girl watching reality being transformed before her horrified eyes. Home and homeland become a prison, adults become phantoms and childhood the end of life. The 'greater hope' lies in the future, but anyone who hopes will have their lives shattered by a shell blast. A brief review of this work appeared in *Book Week*, no. 17 (Nov. 1963), p. 6. Another major work, in English translation, entitled *The bound man (Der Gefesselte)* (London: Secker & Warburg, 1955) develops Sartre's idea of man being constantly bound to the human condition, which in his view was that of the individual 'condemned to be free'.

595 **Hundred poems without a country.**

Erich Fried, translated from the German by Stuart Hood. London: John Calder, 1978. 147p.

Although an exile living in London for over forty years, Erich Fried (1921-) has never lost touch with his native tongue and language. He is well-known for his translations of such authors as Dylan Thomas, T. S. Eliot and Graham Greene, but his poetry, which is largely political in thought and expression, is his most essential work. This selection also shows his immense command of language and his use of wordplay, as well as his passionate commitment to contemporary affairs and the unsolved problems of our day. This volume has been published in seven languages and won the International Publishers' Prize in 1977. The translator and English internationalist Professor Hood was at one time a leading member of the BBC's External Broadcasting Services, where Fried himself worked for sixteen years. Two of Fried's other works have appeared in English translation by George Rapp, *Last honours* (London: Turrett, 1968) and *On pain of seeing* (London: Rapp & Whiting, 1969).

596 **The last sortie.**

Herbert Zand, translated from the German by C. M. Woodhouse. London: Rupert Hart-Davis, 1955.

Herbert Zand (1923-70) was one of the authors emerging in the post-World War II period who, from a traditional standpoint of realism, tackled the problems of his time critically and developed the novel of 'the encircled', of which this work is a good example. It is a record of his personal war experience, he had been severely wounded on the Eastern Front in World War II, and recounts the events of a major battle which threatens to trap the inhabitants and defending troops of an east German town. The whole mood and environment, people, things, conversations, all spell out this theme of encirclement. The translator, as a leading member of the war-time Greek resistance movement, is particularly well-qualified for his task, which he fulfils admirably. The feeling that there is no way out is also powerfully expressed in *The well of hope* (London: Collins, 1957.

159p.), translated by Norman Denny. This is a story of a pilot who crashes in the north African desert, but by a superhuman effort and great strength of will manages to survive against all odds.

597 **The thirtieth year – and other stories.**
Ingeborg Bachmann, translated from the German by Michael Bullock. London: Andre Deutsch, 1964. 187p.

A strong streak of lyricism runs through all Ingeborg Bachmann's (1926-) prose works which describe experiences of pain and joy and powerful temptations. She looks to the impossible and unattainable. In the title story the man, panic-stricken on waking one morning to find he is thirty, fails to follow the call for freedom and commits himself to the everyday and thus effects 'a renunciation of all truth'. This unconventional work caused a sensation when first published in 1961 and quickly became a best-seller. Ingeborg Bachmann is also an opera librettist of considerable talent.

598 **Concrete.**
Thomas Bernhard, translated from the German by David McLintock. London: Dent, 1984. 147p.

When first published in 1982 with the title *Beton* (Suhrkamp, Frankfurt-am-Main) this short novel caused a sensation and soon became a quality best-seller. It is a story of a middle-aged man, living an isolated life in the country, who wants to write a work on the composer Felix Mendelssohn but is unable to start it because of his sister's domineering attitude. As a result he escapes to Majorca, but becomes so obsessed by the memory of a widow he had met there some two years back that he tries to find out what has happened to her. The result of his search leads him to a cemetery – hence the significance of the title. The author (1931-) has written an autobiography, several short stories and a number of stage plays.

599 **The ride across Lake Constance.**
Peter Handke, translated from the German by Millicent Roloff. London: Eyre Methuen, 1973. 75p.

Peter Handke (1942-) who has achieved a considerable impact as a playwright, writes in an antitheatrical setting. This play is based on the legend of a horseman who rode over the frozen Lake Constance in a snowstorm and dropped dead with fright on discovering what he had done. In the play the characters talk and play games together, skating over the 'thin ice' that separates them from unspoken danger. What starts as clear in the beginning of the play gradually becomes more obscure with each sentence and gesture by the actors. A curious but powerful portrayal of different forms of human behaviour.

600 **Wittgenstein's Vienna.**
Allan Janik, Stephen Toulmin. New York: Simon & Schuster, 1973. 315p. bibliog.

This is an extraordinarily successful book, equally illuminating on both aspects of its crisp title. Wittgenstein (1889-1951) was one of eight gifted children of a Viennese industrialist with three other brothers who all committed suicide. He was a mathematician and an engineer who took to philosophy and published his magnum opus *Tractatus Logico-Philosophicus* in 1919 on his return from the trenches in World War I. He emigrated to England in 1937 and became a highly unorthodox Cambridge professor. His second major work, *Philosophical Investigations* (1953) was published posthumously. His Vienna is that of the twilight of the empire, in which the determination of Francis Joseph and his machine to hang on to power, however uncomprehendingly, fostered a culture 'erecting insuperable barriers to the meaningful discussion of real and urgent problems', to quote from the joint authors, an Anglo-American team of philosophers, one of whom had studied under Wittgenstein. Here is the whole of the Habsburg scene, art, music, thinking, life: a hundred years of philosophy made comprehensible to the layman. This rich mix demands intensive reading, but the results are rewarding to a quite unusual degree. For specialists in Wittgenstein as a philosopher his colleague Freidrich Waismann, a member of the 1920's Vienna Circle, recorded a series of interviews with him from 1929-32. The interviews dealt with Wittgenstein's ideas on the philosophy of mathematics. However, Waismann subsequently destroyed the recordings fearing a distortion of Wittgenstein's beliefs on publication. See *Wittgenstein and the Vienna Circle*, translated from the German by Joachim Schulte and Brian McGuiness (Oxford: Basil Blackwell, 1979).

601 **Fairy tales and children's stories.**
Renate Kolvin. London: Richard Harden, 1980. 98p.

The author, a Viennese living in London, wrote these charming stories for her son during his childhood. Most of them have been broadcast in a German translation by Radio Vienna in Children's Hour programmes. The attractive black-and-white drawings which embellish the text are by Mary Ransford, a successful book and poster illustrator still in her teens.

602 **The cucumber king.**
Christine Nöstlinger, translated from the German by Anthea Bell. London: Beaver Books, 1984. 126p.

First published in 1972, this original and very amusing children's story was awarded the German Federal State Children's Book prize, and along with two other works by the same author, *Conrad* and *Lilliput* (equally well translated into English) has remained a firm favourite among juvenile readers. This is the story of a king who has been overthrown by his subjects and who seeks asylum with an ordinary Austrian family. His sly habits and overbearing manner make him unpopular except with Dad, who sympathizes with him and hatches a plot to get him reinstated among his former subjects.

603 **Hawks and nightingales.**
Edited by Peter Tyran, translated from the Croat by Herbert Kuhner, Peter Tyran. Vienna: Braumüller, 1983. 171p.

This anthology of Croatian lyric poetry from Burgenland was published to commemorate the 450th anniversary of the first Croatian settlement in that area after the expulsion of Croats from their southern homeland by the Turks. It is perhaps surprising, but rather gratifying, that despite the growing forces of assimilation, Croat youth in Burgenland should be making a determined effort to assert its ethnic individuality in such a publication.

The Arts

General

604 **Crossroads of European art: a concise history of art and architecture in Austria.**
Edzard Baumann. Salzburg, Austria: Festungsverlag, 1964. 203p. bibliog.

This is neither a guidebook nor a reference work, but a book to whet one's appetite. The author, a US art historian specializing in mediaeval art, has revised and expanded a series of lectures given at Salzburg seminars over a period of years into a survey designed to depict the distinctive Austrian character of a number of monuments within the wider scope of European historical and intellectual development. It is a straightforward but selective account, showing a marked predeliction for the baroque. In general, the author concentrates more on architecture than sculpture and painting, although all branches of 20th-century art are well-covered. The bibliography is comprehensive but contains exclusively works in German.

605 **Baroque art and architecture in central Europe.**
Eberhard Hempel, translated from the German by Elisabeth Hempel, Marguerite Kay. Harmondsworth, England: Penguin Books, 1965. 343p. maps. bibliog. (Pelican History of Art Series, edited by Nikolaus Pevsner.)

The short account of the Austrian baroque movement by Eberhard Hempel (p. 87-121) in this classic series reveals sensitivity, balance and a not over-scholarly approach and should satisfy the reader seeking a brief, but accurate, outline of the subject. The special characteristics of Baroque architecture, sculpture and painting are sketched in the opening pages, while the following four sections deal with: the 'Heroic age' (1600-39); 'The post-Thirty Years War period' (1640-82); 'The main Baroque period' (1683-1739); and 'Rococo' (1740-80).

606 **Heritage of beauty; architecture and sculpture in Austria.**
S. Kruckenhauser. London: C. A. Watts, 1965. 272p.

Kruckenhauser first became famous in the 1920's for his skilled photographic technique when making films of Austrian skiing. Here he offers some remarkable pictures, many taken from unconventional and unusual angles and revealing many hidden treasures. All of the subjects of his photographs are pre-19th century, and the close-ups are particularly noteworthy. The collection is grouped as follows: buildings in landscape settings; towers and cupolas; roofs; doorways; courtyards and facades; light and shadow in the interior; ceilings; carvings; and expression in sculpture. The introductory essay by the distinguished art historian Professor E. H. Gombrich sets the scene for this superb presentation of 256 black-and-white photographs of Austrian sculpture and architecture in masterly fashion, and, like the illustrations themselves, cannot fail to delight the reader.

607 **Focus on Vienna, 1900: change and continuity in literature, music, art and intellectual history.**
Edited by Erika Nielsen. Munich: Wilhelm Fink, 1982. 149p. (Houston German Studies, vol. 4).

This prestigious collection of fourteen papers is selected from those presented at the 1979 symposium on 'Finale and Prelude, Turn of the Century, Vienna', sponsored by the University of Houston, Texas. It studies inter-relationships in the intellectual peak of the avant-garde Secession period when Vienna flowered while the Empire decayed. The leading protagonists included the writers Hugo von Hofmannsthal and Rainer Maria Rilke, artists like Gustav Klimt, and composers like Gustav Mahler and Anton von Webern, but one of the fascinating themes to emerge was a parallel upsurge of provincial talent outside the capital, intent on positive reaction against social and intellectual change – such as the Styrian romantic poet, Peter Rosegger (1843-1918). The whole complex was highlighted by the 1902 Beethoven Exhibition in Vienna (as at the 1983 Edinburgh Festival) when all cultural trends were fused in an oustanding manifestation of Austrian exhuberance at its peak.

608 **Fin-de-siècle Vienna: politics and culture.**
Carl Emil Schorske. London: Weidenfeld & Nicolson, 1980; Cambridge University Press, 1981. 366p.

Scholarship and originality are the hallmarks of this penetrating study by an American Professor of History, who, in a collection of seven essays, sets out to illustrate how modern art and thinking grew out of the political and social distintegration of turn-of-the-century Vienna. Each essay deals with a different cultural phenomenon such as the theatre, architecture and the birth of urban modernism, politics and psychology, art, literature and music. Surprisingly, in a work of this nature, there is no bibliography, although there are numerous source annotations, sixty-three black-and-white photos and sixteen colour plates.

609 **England und Österreich: Kulturbegegnungen im Spiegelbild des Buches.** (England and Austria; cultural contacts mirrored in books.)
Compiled by Laurenz Strehl. Vienna: Austrian National Library, 1969. 85p. bibliog.

This catalogue, published regrettably only in German, commemorates the British Week in Vienna held in October 1969. At that time 255 exhibits were on display illustrating the cultural links maintained between England and Austria over the centuries through the medium of illuminated texts, manuscripts, incunabula, books and paintings, mainly portraits. A comprehensive range of subjects, with explanatory text was offered, including history, travel, music and the theatre.

610 **Vienna 1900: Vienna, Scotland and the European avant-garde.**
Peter Vergo, with contributions by George Dalgleish, Jane Kidd, Hugh Cheape, Elizabeth Wright. Edinburgh: HM Stationery Office for the National Museum of Antiquities of Scotland, 1983. 80p.

This is the catalogue of a most prestigious exhibition, specially mounted for the Edinburgh International Festival of 1983, whose director, John Drummond, contributes a foreword paying tribute in particular to the major Austrian sources in Vienna and London and two leading American foundations. The period concerned is that of the Vienna Secession, led by Gustav Klimt, from the classical mould of the Vienna School of Applied Arts, which in turn was influenced by the simplified style of the architect Adolf Loos. The whole gamut of art, architecture, design, and music was affected deeply by the Secession movement and features in the magnificent illustrations (thirty colour, eighty-six black-and-white). The main text is by the leading European expert Peter Vergo and the Scottish element, selected by Andrew McIntosh Patrick of the Fine Art Society, comes into due prominence with the work of the Scottish designer Charles Rennie Mackintosh and the watercolourist Margaret Macdonald, both of whom had strong Viennese connections. The whole catalogue is a worthy record of a major historical movement whose influence is still emphatically with us.

611 **Vienna Secession.**
Robert Waissenberger. London: Academy Editions, 1977. 144p. bibliog.

The Vienna Secession movement was only intended to last for about ten years, but so great was its influence, not only on art but also on music and literature, that its traditions were carried on well into the 1930's and even beyond. This brief introduction to the subject includes separate chapters on three of the leading artists of the movement, Gustav Klimt, Egon Schiele and Oskar Kokoschka. It also describes the Jugendstil (Art Nouveau) of the period in general terms and touches on the influence of such important contemporary English artists as Aubrey Beardsley and Walter Crane on book illustration design. The bibliography is extensive and the index contains brief biographical notes about the members of the movement.

Visual

Art

612 **The art of the Danube school.**
Austria Today, no. 2 (1982), p. 38-40.

The so-called Danube school was a transitional form of art which flourished between the late Middle Ages and the dawn of the Renaissance. It was never formally taught in any school or centre and developed, quite suddenly, a completely indigenous style, entirely due to local factors. It reached new heights in painting, sculpture and achitecture but just as suddenly as it had emerged it vanished, under pressure from the Counter-Reformation. This brief sketch discusses three examples with illustrations of church pictorial art in the early 16th century.

613 **Master drawings in the Albertina: European drawings from the 15th to the 18th century.**
Otto Benesch, with the collaboration of Eva Benesch, translated from the German by Richard Rickett, M. Schön. London: Evelyn Adams & Mackay, 1976. 377p.

The Albertina in Vienna, named after its founder Duke Albert of Saxe-Teschen, son-in-law of Maria Theresa, is one of the greatest collections of graphic art in the world. It contains well over a million items dating back to the 14th century, including 30,000 catalogued drawings by the German artist Albrecht Dürer. This publication, with its 236 illustrations, its extended commentaries by two prestigious art historians, its catalogue lists and index of artists, provides a most comprehensive and attractively presented guide to the European drawings from 1400-1800, all of superb quality. A detailed account of the Dürer collection, with an inventory and bibliography, by Walter Koschatzky and Alice Strobl, translated from the German by Heide and Alastair Grieve can be found in *Dürer drawings in the Albertina* (London: Secker & Warburg, 1972. 364p.).

614 **Kunst in Österreich vom frühen Mittelalter bis zur Gegenwart.**
(Art in Austria from the early Middle Ages to the present.)
Rupert Feuchtmüller. Vienna: Forum Verlag, 1972. 2 vols. bibliog.

A well-illustrated art book by a distinguished art historian, which is directed at the general reader and contains a minimum of technical terms. The layout is easy to follow as all paragraphs have side-headings. The work tends to concentrate on architecture and the visual arts with less emphasis placed on handicrafts. The first volume covers the Romanesque, Gothic and Renaissance eras and the second the Baroque period and the 19th and 20th centuries.

615 **Die österreichischen Maler des 19ten. Jahrhunderts.** (Austrian artists of the 19th century.)·
Heinrich Fuchs. Vienna: Heinrich Fuchs Selbstverlag, 1972-74. 4 vols.

This definitive encyclopaedia of Austrian artists of the 19th century contains brief biographical details, facsimile autographs and representative black-and-white reproductions of their art. An enlarged supplementary two-volume edition with some additional names was published by the same author in 1978. The last quarter of the 19th century was a period of intensive activity in Austrian pictorial arts and Fuchs has also produced a two-volume work with over 1,800 entries and entitled *Die österreichischen Maler, 1881-1890* (Vienna: Heinrich Fuchs Selbstverlag, 1976) which is on similar lines. This latter work illustrates the output of artists born within the borders of Austria-Hungary during this period, some of whom were still active well into the 20th century.

616 **The old Vienna school of painting.**
Bruno Grimschitz. Vienna: Kunstverlag Wolfrum, 1961. 165p.

Described as essentially middle-class, the 'old Vienna School of Painting' aimed to portray 'the enormous variety of everything that is to be seen on earth'. Within these wide terms of reference, the reader is offered an extraordinarily broad range of pictorial representation, executed between 1815 and 1860, including, for example, landscapes by Ferdinand Waldmüller, portraits by Friedrich von Amerling, miniatures by Moritz Michael Daffinger, and works of considerable quality by many other artists. Two-thirds of the 121 plates are in colour. The introduction is clear and straightforward.

617 **Ars Austriae.** (The art of Austria.)
Bruno Grimschitz. Vienna: Kunstverlag Wolfrum, 1962. 331p.

This distinguished art historian surveys and interprets a representative selection of Austrian art, ranging from the artefacts of the Hallstatt period (750-450 BC) to the modernist works of the Vienna Secession at the turn of the century. The introductory text, though compressed, is clear and marks all the essential milestones in the country's artistic development during its long history. The illustrations are in black-and-white.

618 **Oskar Kokoschka: the artist and his time.**
J. P. Hodin. London: Cory, Adams & Mackay, 1966. 251p. bibliog.

Much of this work is taken up with an assessment of Kokoschka's life and work from 1944 onwards when the artist was living in London. It is largely based on meetings and conversations, and throws light on Kokoschka's contradictory character and his attitude to contemporary political and economic thought, scientific and technical problems, philosophy and the arts. There is a stimulating comment on Kokoschka's interest in psychology and graphology.

619 **Moderne Malerei in Österreich.** (Modern painting in Austria.)
Werner Hofmann. Vienna: Kunstverlag Wolfrum, 1965. 208p. (Austrian Painting Series, vol. 3).

In this presentation the 100 colour reproductions of Austrian painting, from the Congress of Vienna of 1815 to 1960, are of works drawn from museums, galleries and private collections in the United States, Germany and the Netherlands, as well as Austria itself. They are fully representative of the period and include works by such well-known artists as Gustav Klimt, Egon Schiele, Koloman Moser, Alfred Kubin, Oskar Kokoschka, Paris von Gütersloh and Fritz Hundertwasser. Each painting is depicted on a full page in colour, with a commentary by Hofmann on the facing page. The non-German speaker, even if unable to follow the narrative, will nevertheless get a good pictorial impression of the different genres and styles of this productive period of Austrian art.

620 **The art revival in Austria.**
Edited by Charles Holme. London: Studio, 1906. 225p.

This special issue of *Studio* art magazine is devoted to the great art explosion of Vienna at the turn of the century, which was centred mainly on the Wiener Werkstätte (Vienna Workshops) movement, of which it contains representative examples in 181 pages of plates. There are short critiques of all the artists represented. The section on painting is by Ludwig Hevesi and there are other short essays on the plastic arts by Hugo Haberfeld and architecture by Otto Wagner. Of particular interest are the plates showing examples of the decorative arts which include ceramics, jewellery, book-binding, book illustrations, woodwork, glass and textiles.

621 **Dionysian art and populist politics in Austria.**
William J. McGrath. New Haven, Connecticut: Yale University Press, 1974. 269p. bibliog.

The somewhat formidable title of this scholarly work should not discourage the general reader, who will find in it a fascinating account of the remarkable influence exerted by a small intellectual circle on the general political and cultural life of Vienna at the turn of the last century. The so-called 'Pernerstorfer' circle, named after its founder, was essentially a collective of ideas, drawing its inspiration from the philosophers Friedrich Nietzsche and Arthur Schopenhauer and Richard Wagner the composer. It was strongly opposed to Austrian doctrinaire liberalism, striking out to cross the fixed frontiers of academic disciplines and set up an alternative culture in a wide variety of fields. The group included a number of writers, philosophers, artists and musicians, of whom Gustav Mahler the composer and Alfred Adler the political thinker are probably the best known.

622 **Gottfried Helnwein.**
L. Mazakarini. *Graphis* (Switzerland), no. 221, vol. 38 (Sept./Oct. 1983), p. 76-85.

In introducing the reader to the work of this controversial contemporary graphic designer the writer reviews the wide range of his output, which includes magazine and book covers, posters, water colours and etchings. The author explains that

Helnwein regards his original work as less important than its reproduction, because 'all art is communication'.

623 **The art of Egon Schiele, 1890-1918.**
Erwin Mitsch, translated from the German by W. Keith Haughan. London: Phaidon Press, 1975. 268p. bibliog.

Briefly describes the development of Schiele's art and provides a critique of the works the artist exhibited from his late teens up to the end of the Vienna Secession. Includes some 80 plates, many in colour, and 70 black-and-white illustrations.

624 **Art and Society: the new art movement in Vienna, 1897-1914.**
James Shedel. Palo Alto, California: Society for the Promotion of Science and Scholarship (SPOSS), 1982. 232p. bibliog.

In this persuasive and well-documented presentation the author, an assistant professor of history at Georgetown University, examines the achievements and experiences of the Viennese Secession as an art movement, very much aware of its European context and reacting to circumstances as a force for social and cultural influence. Thus it is a study of the movement's impact upon the popular, official and cultural environment of which it was a part. The author offers fresh insights into the movement, using some unpublished sources. The extensive bibliography includes a number of dissertations and newspaper articles.

625 **Modern Austrian art: a concise history.**
Kristian Sotriffer, translated from the German by Alisa Jaffa. London: Thames & Hudson, 1965. 140p. bibliog.

There is sometimes a tendency to regard Austrian 20th-century art as provincial and derivative and to under-estimate the distinctive Austrian element in painting, the graphic arts and sculpture. The author sets out to correct this impression in this short introductory survey of the development of art from the turn of the century to the present day. Much of the work is taken up with brief biographies of some fifty modern artists.

626 **Art in Vienna, 1898-1918.**
Peter Vergo. London: Phaidon Press, 1975. 256p. bibliog.

The author is less subjective in his interpretation of the Secession movement than Robert Waissenberger (q.v.). By making extensive use of the artists' own writings and eye-witness accounts of exhibitions and work on various Viennese buildings, he offers the reader an attractive documentary study. While giving due weight to such prominent figures as Gustav Klimt, Egon Schiele and Oskar Kokoschka, he also expands on the work of Otto Wagner in architecture and Josef Maria Olbrich in the applied arts. A fascinating and lively presentation.

Architecture

627 **J. B. Fischer von Erlach.**

Hans Aurenhammer. London: Allen Lane, 1973. 193p. bibliog.

Although the literature in German on this outstanding Austrian architect is fairly extensive, the English-speaking world has not always appreciated his greatness and his rightful claim to be the virtual creator of Austrian baroque. This is the fullest study yet published in English and sets Fischer von Erlach in the context of his time, artistically, socially and philosophically. It brings out his originality and extraordinary inventiveness and explains in clear terms the symbolism of the decorative elements in his more elaborate buildings, particularly palaces and churches. This book, by a leading expert on baroque architecture, is beautifully illustrated and includes a chronological list of all Fischer von Erlach's works, including architectural drawings. It can safely be recommended to the general reader with an intelligent, but not necessarily an informed, interest in the subject.

628 **Baroque churches of Central Europe.**

John William Patrick Bourke. London: Faber & Faber, 1978. rev. ed. 309p. bibliog.

This comprehensive treatise is aimed at the 'interested, educated, but perhaps somewhat bewildered traveller'. It stresses (p. 185-230) the different historical influences in each of the three main areas covered (Southern Germany, Switzerland and the Habsburg Empire) which have affected a common architectural currency, and offers a penetrating analysis of what is meant by the spirit of baroque (1650-1780). Every church worth recording in each country is then described for its noteworthy exterior and interior features, grouped by architect, and rounded off by a chapter on stucco ornaments and statuary and fresco painting. There is a useful glossary of terms for those not familiar with German architectural language. A most helpful compendium, amply meeting its declared target.

629 **Britain and Vienna, Fin de Siecle.**

9H (London), no. 6 (1983), 96p.

This collection of papers presented at a colloquium organized jointly by the Warburg and Austrian Institutes in London in June 1982, and published by the former in a special issue of its biennial magazine edited by Wilfried Wang, examines the cultural links between Britain and Austria at the turn of the century. Special attention is paid to architecture and, in particular, to Adolf Loos, one of the leading figures in the Austrian Fin de Siècle movement and a strong Anglophile. The contributions are by eminent art historians, British and Austrian, with a contemporary essay by Loos himself and an extended extract from Otto Wagner's *Modern Architecture* (1884). This latter work, sets out the author's theories and views on architectural design, and was a masterpiece of compression and clarity which exerted a considerable influence on architectural thinking and construction of the time. This special issue contains many photographs and diagrams, plans and elevations, with copious annotations and presents an extremely useful survey of this significant period.

630 **Dehio-Handbuch die Kunstdenkmäler Österreichs.** (Dehio Handbooks to the art monuments of Austria.)
Originally edited by Dagobert Frey, continued by Karl Ginhart. Vienna, Munich: Anton Schroll, 1963-76, 9 vols.

The Dehio series, covering the whole of the religious and secular buildings of Germany and Austria in a format devised by the German art historian Georg Dehio, is the continental equivalent of *The buildings of England* by the late Sir Nikolaus Pevsner which was extended to Scotland and Wales after his death. Each location is arranged alphabetically and the key buildings are subjected to similar pressurized detailed examination although with no illustrations. The non-German reader should be able to find his way around with the help of a dictionary, and this is infinitely worthwhile, since the scholarship and presentation of the contributions are almost beyond praise. The author of the Styria volume, for example, was Eberhard Hempel, who wrote *Baroque art and architecture in Central Europe* (q.v.) for the Pelican History of Art series, edited by Pevsner.

631 **Austria: her landscape and her art.**
Viktor Griessmaier, translated from the German by Marguerite Kay. Vienna: Anton Schroll, 1954. 361p. map. bibliog.

The author invites the reader to forget people, and their dress and customs, as well as flora and fauna and to concentrate on what is typically Austrian in the landscape and buildings. This picture he presents in over 300 black-and-white illustrations. The text is discreet and the photographs speak for themselves.

632 **Building in Austria.**
Johann Kräftner. Vienna: Christian Brandstätter, 1984. 208p.

This description of a century of Austrian architecture, from 1890 to the present day, is accompanied by over 380 photographs, plans and sketches, all handsomely presented; the text is in German, English and French. The author shows that although it has been a century of violent upheavals and change, there has been a continuity of traditions in Austrian architectural planning and development, with fresh impulses now combining in the direction of a new breakthrough in imaginative conception and execution. Whereas Vienna, as the capital of a great Empire, was at one time the model for all architectural development, this is no longer the case. A pluralism, drawing on local traditions as well as the international scene, now plays the determining role in shaping the country's architectural landscape.

633 **Joseph Maria Olbrich, 1867-1908.**
Ian Latham. London: Academy Editions, 1980. 156p. bibliog.

'To each age its art and to art its freedom' proclaims the inscription over the main door to Olbrich's masterpiece, the Secession Building of 1898 in the Vienna Ringstrasse. This Secession developed as a reaction against the classical historicism of the 19th century and found its way to architecture in the Art Nouveau style based on 'functional concepts'. Olbrich, a lively, exuberant character, also designed cutlery, costume, tapestry and posters. Contemporary quotations from a wide circle of colleagues and critics enliven this study, the first one to be published by a young English architect whose interest was kindled in the 1970's. The author's professional knowledge has helped him to produce an authoritative and sympathetic appraisal of a major architect.

634 **From baroque to rococo: an introduction to Austrian and German architecture from 1580 to 1790.**
Nicholas Caryll Powell. London: Faber & Faber, 1959. 184p. map. bibliog.

A substantial work providing an in-depth analysis of baroque and rococo architecture in the German-speaking countries of Austria, including the former Austrian provinces of Bohemia, Moravia and Silesia, and southern Germany. The coverage extends beyond the most celebrated landmarks and stresses the role of southern Germany as a source for the Austrian schools. The first eleven chapters set out the material by building type, and the final three summarize the achievement under the headings 'frescoes', 'sculpture' and 'colour'.

635 **Monks, nuns and monasteries.**
Sacheverell Sitwell. London: Weidenfeld & Nicolson, 1965. 205p.

This comprehensive study of the environment for the monastic life covers the whole period from the Middle Ages to the 18th century in Western Europe and the areas of the Eastern Church. Chapter 2 (p. 66-94) deals with the Holy Roman Empire, Austria and Bavaria in the 18th century. Sitwell's erudition is stylishly expressed as always and no excuse is offered for his personal judgments, for example, that: Italian architects and painters in the early 18th century, the chief influence on this area, were not first rate; Prague is more interesting than Vienna, and that of the Austrian monasteries only St. Florian, Wilhering and Seitenstetten are superlative. Mediaeval German monasteries are not to his taste. A fascinating work, by probably the foremost English writer on English architecture.

636 **Rethinking Josef Hoffmann.**
M. E. Vertrocq. *Art in America*, vol. 71, no. 4 (April 1983), p. 170-75. bibliog.

Examines the work and reputation of the Secession architect Josef Hoffmann, with special reference to an exhibition of seventy of his classic designs at Fort Worth Art Museum in Texas. The exhibition itself is reviewed, and the criticism is voiced that Hoffmann's functionalism has in the past tended to be under-valued.

637 **Die Wiener Ringstrasse.** (The Vienna Boulevard.)
Edited by Renate Wagner-Rieger. Wiesbaden, GFR: Franz Steiner Verlag, 1969-80. 11 vols.

A wealth of scholarship and detail informs this entire series which covers Viennese architecture from 1850 to the outbreak of World War I. Although the overall coverage is comprehensive, there are individual volumes dealing with different areas of interest, such as public buildings, monuments, fountains, sculpture and ornamentation. The text is in German, but Volume I contains an extended and clear introduction to the entire field by the editor, with translations in English and French. The series is liberally illustrated with black-and-white photographs, prints, sketches, plans and specifications.

Applied arts

638 **Needlework: an illustrated history.**
Harriet Bridgeman, Elizabeth Drury. New York, London: Paddington Press, 1978. 368p. bibliog.

Dora Heinz, curator of the Textile Department of the Austrian Museum of Applied Art in Vienna, has contributed the chapter on Austria (p. 218-26) in this comprehensive historical survey of needlework in the western world. The book is handsomely illustrated and contains a useful glossary of technical terms. Starting with the mediaeval embroidery of the 13th century, principally on religious vestments and altar frontals, the author then traces, for example: developments in the Renaissance period, with its rare examples of gold embroidered coats of arms and superb ecclesiastical wall hangings; the professional embroidery commissions by the Church and court in the 18th century; amateur work by embroiderers in Maria Theresa's reign; the highly productive creations of the Viennese Workshop movement at the turn of the century; and its derivative offerings of more modern times.

639 **Vienna in the age of Schubert: the Biedermeier interior.**
Gerhart Egger (et al.), translated from the German by Rita Moore. London: Elvon Press, 1979. 111p. bibliog.

This was the catalogue of the 1979 exhibition at the London Victoria and Albert Museum, a highly representative collection of the applied arts of this important period in Austrian life (ca. 1815-48). The Bierdermeier (age of the 'nice little man') was the extension of the Napoleonic Empire style into domestic furnishing at a time when the Austrian middle class looked inwards under the repressive régime of Metternich; it had a lasting influence on the Austrian way of life, particularly in Vienna. The catalogue is beautifully illustrated throughout and the literary contributions, all by Austrian experts, are of the highest quality. After an introduction by Wilhelm Mrazek there are essays on: furniture by Franz Windischgraetz; silver by Gerhart Egger; porcelain by Waltraud Neuwirth; glass by Willhelm Mrazek and Waltraud Neuwirth; textiles by Angela Volker; clocks by Erika Hellich; and painting by Gerbert Frodl. This is emphatically the best introduction to the period in English.

640 **Biedermeier furniture.**
Georg Himmelheber, translated and edited by Simon Jervis. London: Faber & Faber, 1974. 115p. map. bibliog. (Faber Monographs on Furniture).

'Biedermeier' was a German term for an off-beat figure something like the English Mr. Punch. It came to be applied in the Metternich period, between the end of the Napoleonic wars and the Revolution of 1848, to a style of furniture which, although derived from the Empire style, used simple geometric forms in a fresh and charming way – simple and not flamboyant. This met the needs of the age when political oppression drove a very wide spectrum of the population to concentrate on an inward-looking domesticity, and although 'Biedermeier' was initially a term of abuse, its qualities were reappraised in the Vienna Exhibition of 1896 and successfully revealed to a largely unfamiliar audience at the London

Victoria and Albert Exhibition of 1979 (see above). This study not only illumines the period but provides the technical detail.

641 **Schmiedehandwerk im Barock.** (Baroque wrought ironwork.)
Otfried Kastner. Linz, Austria: Wimmer, 1971. 308p. map.

A leading authority on the subject provides over 170 illustrations, many in colour and with accompanying text, of various examples of Austrian wrought ironwork forged between the 16th and the 18th centuries. The examples range from simple drainpipe gutterings and locks to elaborate grilles in churches and palaces.

642 **Wiener Werkstätte Keramik.** (Vienna Workshops ceramics).
Waltraud Neuwirth. Vienna: Selbstverlag Waltraud Neuwirth, 1984. 240p.

Neuwirth, head of the ceramics and glass departments of the Vienna Workshops (Werkstätte) at the Museum of Applied Arts in Vienna, has published the first of a projected three-volume complete register of 'one-off' ceramics produced in the workshops. It covers the Secession period (1903-17), and subsequent volumes will cover the period 1917-20 and 1920-31. Along with an explanatory text there are sketches, supplemented by contemporary photographs and reproductions from art journals. Very few pieces of this period have so far been catalogued and published, as many of them are in private hands and access is difficult. It is intended that in time other applied arts, such as jewellery, glass, metal, and textiles should be similarly catalogued. The text is in German and English.

643 **Meissener Marken und Wiener Bindenschild; Original, Imitation, Verfälschung, Fälschung.** (Meissen Marks and Viennese inscriptions: genuine, imitation, falsification and forgery.)
Waltraud Neuwirth. Vienna: Selbstverlag Waltraud Neuwirth, 1977. 128p. bibliog.

It is known that imitations and forgeries of period porcelain works are plentiful, especially in Britain and although a great deal of literature has been published on the subject, doubts still exist about dating. In this work, which contains 129 illustrations, Neuwirth surveys the current state of research.

644 **Vienna workshops – avant-garde, art deco, industrial design.**
Waltraud Neuwirth. Vienna: Selbstverlag Waltraud Neuwirth, 1984. 240p.

In 1984 the Austrian Museum of Applied Art mounted an exhibition in Vienna of artifacts of the Vienna Workshops (Werkstätte) produced at the turn of the century, and now held either in museums or private collections. The accompanying catalogue, with 80 colour plates and 110 black-and-white illustrations, is fully representative, and includes some photos which have not been published before. It is chronologically arranged, describes the artistic trends of the Art Deco movement and the similarities and differences in the work of the artists concerned. The author also highlights the importance of the workshops in the development of industrial design and factory production, not only in Austria but in Europe as well. Neuwirth's commentary bears all the marks of her internationally-recognized scholarship. The text is in German and English.

645 **Porcellane e vetre antichi e moderni d'Austria.** (Old and modern porcelain and glass from Austria.)
Lugano, Switzerland: Comune di Lago, 1978. 83p.

This is the attractively-illustrated catalogue of an exhibition held in Lugano, Switzerland in April 1978. It displayed porcelain and glass, mainly from the Vienna Secession period at the turn of the century, and included exhibits from Austrian museums and the private collection of the Austrian Consul-General in the Ticino, who is a well-known art-lover and collector. The descriptions of objects and the artists concerned are in Italian, German and English.

646 **German and Austrian ceramics.**
Selection and text by Günter Reinheckel, translated from the German by R. J. Charleston, Eileen Martin. Tokyo: Kodansha, 1978. 330p. map. bibliog. (Masterpieces of Western Ceramic Art, vol. VII).

Beautifully printed, in English and Japanese, and handsomely presented, this substantial tome contains 127 colour and 114 black-and-white plates, illustrating representative examples of German and Austrian ceramics from about 750 AD to the beginning of this century. The volume contains detailed descriptions and extended notes on the colour plates. Although German pieces predominate, Austria is featured in some very fine examples, particularly of Viennese porcelain in its middle period. A prestigious publication.

647 **Marks on German, Bohemian and Austrian porcelain, 1710 to the present day.**
Robert E. Röntgen. Exton, Pennsylvania: Schiffer, 1981. 636p.

Almost half of all European porcelain in museums, private collections and antique shops today will have been produced in either Germany, Bohemia or Austria. This is the first comprehensive survey of the porcelain producers in this area and the marks they used, numbering over 3,300 in this work. There is an extensive list of manufacturers, according to location, while an important and interesting feature of this definitive reference work is the recording of porcelain marks that could be mistaken for those of other manufacturers. The period covered is from the time of the opening of the renowned du Paquier porcelain factory in Vienna to the present day.

648 **The undervalued Biedermeier style.**
S. Sacharow. *Antique Collector*, vol. 54, part 4 (April 1983), p. 54-59.

In recent years there has been a resurgence of interest in Biedermeier (c. 1815-48) furniture, particularly among art specialists and collectors. This short article explains how, in shaping the finished product, Biedermeier artists exploited the wood to maximum visual effect, subordinating decoration to the characteristic flatness of the furniture's surface. Some popular pieces and motifs are described and illustrated.

649 **Wiener Werkstätte (Viennese Workshops); Design in Vienna, 1903-1932.**
Werner J. Schweiger, translated from the German by Alexander Lieven. London: Thames & Hudson, 1984. 272p. bibliog.

This valuable reference work is one of the most comprehensive illustrated accounts in English of the development of the designs of the Vienna Workshop movement yet published. Almost a third of the 700 illustrations are in colour and cover not only the history of the movement but exhibitions and their accompanying catalogues, examples of graphic design, and special creations relating to the applied arts, particularly jewellery, glass and costume.

650 **Austrian textiles.**
Fritz Stellwag-Carion. Leigh-on-Sea, England: F. Lewis, 1960. 72p. (Survey of World Textiles, vol. 15).

Since over a quarter of Austrian textile output is exported, this article provides a useful summary for non-Austrians. The latter may feel that sometimes the Austrian costumes are a little dated, but the waterproof 'Loden' cloth holds its own uniquely and the Vorarlberg has an important embroidery industry. Silk fabrics woven on the Jacquard system are another speciality, while the staple production of coloured woven or printed cotton and worsteds continues as a strong line.

651 **Old Vienna porcelain, 1718-1864.**
W. Strohmer-Novak. Vienna: Kunstverlag Wolfrum, 1950. 70p.

The forty plates in this collection of exquisite porcelain figures illustrate some fine representative examples of Vienna porcelain, from the Baroque to Rococo, and neo-classical to late Biedermeier – a span of some 150 years. The text provides a short history of the manufacturing processes, styles and motifs.

652 **Viennese porcelain.**
Klára Tasnádi-Marik, translated from the Hungarian by Elizabeth Hoch, Elizabeth West. Budapest: Corvina, 1971. 103p.

The fortunes of the famous du Paquier porcelain factory in Vienna are followed in three periods: the early years from its founding in 1718 up to 1784, described as its 'golden age'; the middle period from 1784-1805 under the energetic businessman, Baron Konrad von Sorgenthal; and its final period of decline until its closure in 1864. This was due to rising production costs, greater competition and the lack of any State subsidy. Other European countries, notably France and Germany, considered a subsidy to be essential to the maintenance of their own industries.

653 **Vienna handwork of petit point.**
Austria Today, no. 4 (1982), p. 57-58.

Viennese petit point embroidery has a long history dating back to Maria Theresa's reign in the mid-18th century, when it was prized among the middle classes for its association with the imperial court. Today it is still a thriving industry, as this brief sketch, which describes the methods and motifs used, indicates.

654 **German and Austrian porcelain.**
George W. Ware. Frankfurt, GFR: Lothar Woeller, 1952. 244p. bibliog.

The reader is offered an unsophisticated and refreshing approach to a subject which has been a life-long interest of the author, an American amateur collector. The chapters on the history of ceramics and techniques of production are particularly informative and the work contains lists of major porcelain factories and their markets, a glossary of terms and an inventory of auction and collection catalogues.

Performing

Music, opera and ballet

655 **The music guide to Austria and Germany.**
Elaine Brody, Clarie Brook. London: Macmillan, 1979. 271p. maps.

Originally published by Dodd, Mead (New York, 1975) this handbook provides a mass of useful information for the 'musical traveller' of whatever standard, from the dilettante to the specialist. It lists opera houses, concert halls – giving brief descriptions of each – musical libraries and museums, schools and conservatories. A section is devoted to musical landmarks, including commemorative plaques, and establishments other than museums but open to the public. Details of festivals, competitions, ticket agencies, music publishers and periodicals are also included. The authors are both professional musicians who travel frequently throughout Europe. See also *Music Handbook for Austria* edited by H. Goertz (q.v.).

656 **Musikhandbuch für Österreich.** (Music Handbook for Austria.)
Edited by Harald Goertz for the Austrian Music Council. Vienna: Doblinger, 1971. annual.

An invaluable reference work for the student of music or interested amateur. The 1984 edition contained over 2,500 entries covering: the general administration of representative bodies; educational and research institutions; theatre and concert administration; orchestras; ensembles; bands; church music; audio-visual aids; television and the record industry; musical associations; libraries; festivals; music publications; instrument makers; musical monuments; and a general survey of the country's musical life, province by province. See also *The music guide to Austria and Germany* (q.v.).

657 **The golden age of Vienna.**

Hans Gal. London, New York: Max Parrish, 1948. 71p. (The World of Music Series).

This slim volume by a distinguished Austrian émigré, pianist, composer and musicologist makes good reading of a discursive and evocative kind and is punctuated by shafts of acute observation. The leading Austrian composers from Mozart to Schubert are surveyed in the context of the city they chose to live in and the illustrations are particularly apt. A timely initial tribute is paid to the composer Christoph Gluck, who is usually counted as writing Italian opera in, and for, the French, but is shown here as exerting a decisive influence during his Vienna period.

658 **Austria – land of music.**

Harald Goertz. Vienna: Federal Press Service, 1984. 88p. (Austria Documentation).

In the course of a short summary of Austria's musical heritage the author, a well-known musicologist, shows how musical tradition and form have evolved as a continuing thread throughout the centuries and are still prominent in present day Austria. For example, the Vienna Boys' Choir, founded in 1498 by Emperor Maximilian I, has gained international acclaim as the two-page introduction to its November 1985 British tour prospectus indicates (Anglo-Austrian Musical Society, London). See also 'Austria's singing ambassadors' (*Austria Today* 2 (1983), p. 59-61). Goertz's brochure, intended as a publicity handout, is particularly informative about recent developments and the current musical situation in Austria.

659 **Music and Musicians in Vienna.**

Richard Rickett. Vienna: Georg Prachner, 1981. 2nd ed. 158p.

The main thread running through this brief survey of the Austrian musical scene from the mid-18th century to the Second Viennese School at the turn of the last century, is the continuity of musical heritage and tradition which linked such composers as Haydn and Mozart, Beethoven and Schubert, Mahler and Bruckner. The author devotes separate chapters to the main composers of the time, focusing mainly on biographical detail rather than musical evaluation.

660 **Vienna's great conductors.**

B. H. Haggin (interviewer). *Encounter*, vol. 49, no. 1 (1977), p. 19-40.

Hugo Burghauser, former bassoonist and chairman of the Vienna Philharmonic Orchestra, reminisces about the great conductors under whom he performed and who dominated the musical scene in Vienna between the wars. These included Arthur Nikisch, Richard Strauss, Bruno Walter, Otto Klemperer and Arturo Toscanini. He also describes how they dealt with often conflicting ideological pressures from the Nazis and the demands of their art.

661 **O ye millions, I embrace ye: the New Year's concerts of the Vienna Philharmonic.**
Kurt Dieman, translated from the German by Edwin Kowanda. Vienna: Federal Publishing Office, 1983. 208p.

The English title is taken from Natalia Macfarren's translation of Schiller's *Ode to Joy* which is featured in the final movement of Beethoven's Choral Symphony and refers to the many millions of viewers around the world who regularly watch the television transmission of the New Year's concert performed annually by the Vienna Philharmonic. This publication commemorates the 25th anniversary of the first television showing of the concert and includes articles on the orchestra, its conductors, and the programmes performed since the outbreak of World War II to the present day. The excellent colour photography of behind-the-scenes activities adds considerable embellishment to the text. The commentary on, and pictures of, the Viennese Ballet, which regularly forms part of the television transmission, are particularly rewarding. A lighthearted but authentic background exposé of what has become a memorable international event in the Viennese social and musical calendar.

662 **The Vienna Philharmonic.**
Erwin Mittag, translated from the German by J. R. L. Orange, G. Morice. Vienna: Gerlach u. Wiedling, 1975. 125p.

Austria's premier orchestra, the Vienna Philharmonic, was founded in 1842, a few years after the deaths of Beethoven and Schubert. This brief history has been compiled from the orchestra's archives, statistical records, programme notes and correspondence spanning nearly a century and a half. Individual chapters are devoted to each of the orchestra's permanent conductors during this period which include such illustrious names as Richter, Mahler, Weingartner, Richard Strauss, Fürtwängler, Toscanini, Krauss, Bruno Walter and von Karajan. There are accounts of some of the more memorable concerts and a dramatic description of the closing stages of World War II, when the entire orchestra and their families, numbering almost 200, were recruited to form an ambulance unit in Vienna, thus enabling the orchestra to remain together in the most critical days of its history.

663 **The Vienna opera.**
Heinrich Kralik, translated from the German by Richard Rickett. London: Methuen, 1963. 189p.

A comprehensive study by an influential Austrian critic of a key institution in Austrian artistic, intellectual and social life. The book is generously illustrated, especially in the chapter on singers, conductors and ballet. It is particularly revealing on the influence of the post of General Music Director, whose powers and position in the State hierarchy are conspicuously more important here than in most state or royal opera houses. The organizational turmoils of the 1960's, so graphically described, are by no means only of historical interest, since they are manifestly endemic in the whole Viennese situation. For an expansion of the musical aspects from one who at one time actually worked on the staff of the Vienna Opera, the reader should consult Marcel Prawy's *The Vienna Opera* (q.v.).

664 **The Vienna opera.**

Marcel Prawy, translated from the German, photographs by Cartier Bresson, Erich Lessing (et al.). London: Weidenfeld & Nicolson, 1970. 224p.

Prawy, an opera-goer for forty-five years, handles this fascinating subject with the detachment of an art critic and the involvement of an administrator, for he was at one time executive director of the second of the Vienna State Opera Houses – the People's Opera (Volksoper), which concentrates mainly on operetta. The result is a charming highly readable book, written in a conversational style, despite its wealth of documented detail. The work includes an objective account of the opera house under the Nazi régime from 1938 to 1945.

665 **Gluck and the birth of modern opera.**

Patricia Howard. London: Barrie & Rockliff, 1963. 111p.

Different aspects of the composer, Christoph Gluck's (1714-87) musical development are examined, particularly in relation to his treatment of the aria, recitative, chorus and ensemble, the overture and operatic texts.

666 **The collected correspondence and papers of Christoph Willibald Gluck.**

Edited by Hedwig Müller, E. H. Müller von Asow, translated from the German by Stewart Thomson. London: Barrie & Rockliff, 1962. 239p.

Most books written in English about this innovative operatic composer who spent much of his life in Vienna, examine his musical development but tend to neglect his personality. Work on this comprehensive collection of letters and documents started in the mid-1920's, was held up by World War II and eventually appeared in 1962; it was thus nearly forty years in preparation. The book is revealing in the picture it paints of Gluck's character and habits and it contains a number of letters addressed to the composer, not all of them on musical topics. The period covered is from 1750 to Gluck's death in 1787.

667 **Haydn: a creative life in music.**

Karl Geiringer, in collaboration with Irene Geiringer. London: George Allen & Unwin, 1964. 2nd ed. rev. 430p. bibliog.

The fruits of thirty years of scholarly research have culminated in this solid and exhaustive appraisal of Haydn (1732-1809), the man and his music. The work draws in large measure on the vast Esterházy collection of music and documents which was opened to the public by the Hungarian National Library in the 1950's. The two chapters on Haydn's visits to London and Oxford in 1791 and 1794, respectively, are very well documented.

668 **Haydn: chronicle and works.**
H.C. Robbins Landon. London: Thames & Hudson, 1976-80. 5 vols. bibliog.

This definitive work by the leading Haydn scholar of our age covers five periods as follows: the early years (1732-65); Haydn at Esterháza (1766-90); Haydn in England (1791-95); years of the 'Creation' (1796-1800); and the late years (1801-09). The dates of publication are however, not sequential and the author reserved his summing-up for the last volume to appear, which covered Haydn's early years.

669 **Joseph Haydn: his life in contemporary pictures.**
Lázló Somfai, translated from the Hungarian by Mari Kuttna, Károly Ravasz. London: Faber & Faber, 1969. 244p.

This extremely well-presented collection of reproductions of documents, portraits, prints, busts, paintings, programmes and other material, arranged in chronological order and with linking commentaries is, in effect, a scrapbook of Haydn's life. It includes extracts from his letters and those of his contemporaries, and views and descriptions of the places he visited. One of its special features is the reproduction of all known portraits of the composer, with details of their provenance and present location, where known.

670 **Joseph Haydn of Eisenstadt.**
Christina Stadtlaender, translated from the German by Percy M. Young. London: Dennis Dobson, 1968. 127p.

These extracts from the archives of Eisenstadt and other places which Hadyn visited during his long life reveal him in his many guises – as composer, relative, ratepayer, lover, countryman and servant to the Esterházy family. This is essentially an anecdotal, bedside book, which throws interesting light on the composer's daily life and habits during the thirty years he lived and worked at Eisenstadt.

671 **The magnificence of Esterháza.**
Mátyas Horányi, translated from the Hungarian by András Deak. London: Barrie & Rockliff, 1962. 280p. map.

A consideration of the palace of Esterháza in western Hungary provides the essential background to any study of Haydn, who performed his music there for almost thirty years. Based largely on the Esterháza archives which are now lodged in the National Library in Budapest, this work is concerned mainly with Haydn's dramatic and operatic performances and includes illustrations and sketches of scenery and costumes designed for his operas. There is an interesting list of singers showing when each was employed there and in what role.

672 **The letters of Mozart and his family.**
Emily Anderson, revised by Alec Hyatt King, Monica Carolan. London: Macmillan, 1966. 2nd ed. 2 vols.

'Wolfgang is extraordinarily jolly, but a bit of a scamp as well' wrote Father Leopold of his precocious son in 1763. This frank observation is typical of the letters between the whole Mozart family (father to son; father to daughter; and son to all and sundry – often finished by father or mother, perhaps to eliminate any scatalogical elements which tended to creep in). Leopold also pruned some of his own letters in order to exclude irrelevant matter. This important collection, consisting of 616 letters written between the years 1762 and 1791, was intended as a primary source for a biographical study of Mozart but the author died in 1962.

673 **Mozart: his character and his work.**

Alfred Einstein, translated from the German by Arthur Mendel, Nathan Broden. London: Panther Books, 1971. 510p.

Subsequent works on Mozart (1756-91) may have discovered new points of detail but none has achieved the epic sweep of this masterly and monumental work, which was first published in 1946 (Cassell). Opening with an illuminating study of the man and his age, Einstein proceeds to analyse each work, grouped by categories, quoting contemporary documentation and providing his own penetrating musical appreciation. The writing is scholarly and encyclopaedic but the wonder of the work is its infectious vitality which brings Mozart to life on every page.

674 **Mozart.**

Wolfgang Hildesheimer, translated from the German by Marion Faber. London: Dent, 1982. 408p. bibliog.

This work, an expanded version of a public lecture given in 1956 in commemoration of the bicentenary of Mozart's birth, attempts 'to restore and cleanse a fresco which has been painted over for years'. In other words a re-evaluation and re-interpretation of some of the traditionally-held views about Mozart. The author refuses to indulge in either eulogy or apologia, finding that as more facts come to light, the more puzzling do their circumstances and explanations appear. For example, he claims that Mozart's own reactions to the external and internal conditions of his life were seldom illuminated in his output, and very often deliberately obscured by him. There are thus no easy answers to the elusive Mozart, who corresponds to no ideal, fits no pattern and remains withdrawn from us behind his music. An original but inconclusive appraisal.

675 **Mozart: the man – the musician.**

Arthur Hutchings. London: Thames & Hudson, 1976. 131p.

Generously illustrated and with a foreword by Kingsley Amis, this publication contains a number of fascinating pictorial essays providing much useful information about Mozart's journeys, his contemporaries and the world and society in which he worked and lived. The accompanying text is lucid, graceful and compelling, and the author shows a real mastery of his subject and his intentions. An effective and absorbing introduction for the general reader; and much more than its coffee-table format might initially suggest.

676 **Mozart: a biography with a survey of books, editions and recordings.**

Alec Hyatt King. London: Clive Bingley, 1970. 114p. bibliog.

The biographical element in this short work is, of necessity, much compressed to facilitate the provision of the extensive bibliographical section which includes books, essays and critiques in English, accompanied by short annotations. The bibliography is divided into the following categories: biographies; general criticisms; church music; operas; chamber music; symphonies and concertos. The various editions of Mozart's published music are also included. The list of selected recordings is by Brian Redfern.

677 **Mozart.**

Hugh Ottaway. London: Orbis, 1979. 208p. bibliog.

The author, in this lavishly-illustrated work, has tried to present the much-romanticized life story of Mozart in a basically 'unromantic' way, with a sense of realism but without detracting from the phenomenon of the composer's unique creativity. Mozart's life and works are considered together in chronological order, musical examples are kept to a minimum and musical terminology is carefully explained for the general reader. The final chapter, in the form of an epilogue, summarizes the changing attitudes to Mozart which have emerged in successive generations since his death. An attractively-written account.

678 **Mozart and the Masons: new light on the lodge 'Crowned Hope'.**

H. C. Robbins Landon. London: Thames & Hudson, 1982. 72p. bibliog.

The 1980 Walter Neurath Memorial Lecture, sponsored by Birkbeck College, London University was delivered by Professor Robbins Landon, the leading expert on the composer Haydn. In it he revealed that recent documentary research had shown Prince Esterházy, Haydn's patron, to have been the Grand Master of the Masonic lodge 'Crowned Hope', which Mozart is now known to have joined in 1781, not as a 'visiting brother', as had hitherto been supposed, but as a full member. Furthermore, from a contemporary painting on display at the exhibition in Vienna in 1980 commemorating the 200th anniversary of Maria Theresa's death, the members of this lodge, including Mozart, have now been positively identified. It is remarkable that in view of the proscription of the practice of Masonry in Austria from 1795 to 1918 so many membership lists before that time should have survived. Landon's unexpected revelations are of considerable historic importance. See also Katharine Thomson's *The Masonic thread in Mozart* (q.v.).

679 **The Masonic thread in Mozart.**

Katharine Thomson. London: Lawrence & Wishart, 1977. 207p. bibliog.

The complex history of European Freemasonry in the latter half of the 18th century is described here as a basis for assessing its influence on the life and music of Mozart who, as a practising Roman Catholic, as well as a Mason, felt able to compose both his Requiem and the 'Magic Flute' opera in the year of his death. A glossary of musical terms enables the reader to follow the argument which is sustained by detailed examination of the so-called 'Masonic' works, both instrumental and vocal. See also H. C. Robbins Landon's *Mozart and The Masons* (q.v.).

680 **Schubert: a documentary biography.**

Otto Erich Deutsch, translated from the German by Eric Blom. New York: Da Capo, 1977. Reprint of 1946 ed. 1,040p. (Music Reprint Series).

This is the remarkable product of researches initiated by an international authority on Schubert (1797-1828) as far back as 1914. Work was halted by both world wars but was resumed after the hostilities had finished. Over 1,200 documents, covering the composer's life, output, first performances and the major personalities in his circle, are set out chronologically, each annotated in an entirely factual way with no subjective interpretation. The author personally visited every location concerned. The translation, by an eminent British musicologist, matches the quality of the original text.

681 **Schubert.**

Arthur Hutchings. London: Dent, 1973. rev. ed. 233p. (Master Musicians Series).

In this publication, part of a well-known series, the author paints a fascinating picture of Viennese social life in the early years of the 19th century. In this setting, Schubert is portrayed as an impulsive, spontaneous composer whose life was his art. The thumb-nail sketches of some of his contemporaries make excellent reading.

682 **Johann Strauss, father and son and their era.**

Hans Fantel. Newton Abbot, England: David & Charles, 1971. 246p. bibliog.

This is much more of a social commentary than a straightforward historical account. The author manages, in rather a light and fanciful way, to catch a glimpse of a moment in time when music in Vienna, with its sixty piano factories, was not just entertainment but 'a personal necessity' and did so much to break down class barriers. A number of contemporary documents are quoted and all compositions of both father I (1804-49) and son II (1825-99) are listed. In the final chapter the author tells how after the *Anschluss* the Germans tried to obliterate evidence of the family's Jewish ancestry by destroying the birth registry documents, which were miraculously 'returned' in 1945 after World War II.

683 **Prince of Vienna: the life, the times and the melodies of Oscar Straus.**

Bernard Grun. London: W. H. Allen, 1955. 224p. bibliog.

At first glance this work appears somewhat trivial – a typical discursive journalistic write-up of the life story of a celebrity. However, this is not a true assessment of this accurate and carefully compiled book. The author is a Viennese himself and is an authority on his period. He is also a prolific arranger of music for theatre and film with a central European flavour. The subject of the present volume is a Viennese operetta composer who had a plaque erected in his honour in his native town of Bad Ischl with the name 'Oscar Strauss' although he had nothing to do with the two Johanns of waltz fame. Notwithstanding this he does deserve permanent recognition for his pre-World War I composition 'The chocolate soldier', which was based on Bernard Shaw's *Arms and the man* and the ever-haunting theme-song for the film *La Ronde* which he wrote when he was eighty years old.

684 **Bruckner.**
Derek Watson. London: Dent, 1977. 174p. bibliog. (Master Musicians Series).

Part of the interest of this book lies in the calendar of contemporary events in the musical world and the thumbnail sketches of Bruckner's (1824-96) contemporaries. This is a vivid account of the struggles and achievements of Bruckner, a composer of substantial symphonic and choral works who was also a brilliant organist. The work includes a description and analysis of his music.

685 **Hugo Wolf.**
Frank Walker. London: Dent, 1968. 2nd ed. rev. 522p. bibliog.

Hugo Wolf (1860-1903), one of Austria's greatest songwriters, was a prolific correspondent and has provided much documentation for musicological treatment. The author has produced a source book of substantial proportion based on Wolf's own writings and published articles, as well as interviews with his contemporaries, associates and members of the family. The bibliography is extensive and the catalogue of Wolf's compositions, published and unpublished, is exhaustive and probably complete. This book is not simply a book for the expert or scholar but is also suitable for the informed and enquiring reader. A very readable account.

686 **Recollections of Gustav Mahler.**
Natalie Bauer-Lechner, edited by Peter Franklin, translated from the German by Dika Newlin. London: Faber Music, 1980. 250p. 2 maps. bibliog.

Natalie Bauer-Lechner, who maintained a close friendship with Mahler for ten years after the break-up of his marriage in 1890, had an extraordinary perception of the composer's creative ideas, and wanted to convey to others the spiritual and intellectual values she had gained through her association with him. In these extracts from her personal diary, written with great sensitivity and in worshipping terms about the composer, she shows a remarkable ability to recall conversations almost verbatim. Her accounts of Mahler's views on his own, and other people's, performances make absorbing reading.

687 **Mahler: a documentary study.**
Edited by Kurt Blaukopf, with contributions from Zoltan Ronan, translated from the German by Paul Baker (et al.). London: Thames & Hudson, 1976. 280p. maps.

Of the 316 illustrations in this handsome presentation nearly a quarter are in colour, while the text contains a number of documents from world-wide sources, including some of Mahler's private correspondence which is published here for the first time. The towns and cities where he lived, the people he met and the concert halls in which he conducted, are all portrayed; and the whole collection is set against the background of the political, social and cultural environment of the Habsburg Empire at the turn of the century.

688 **Gustav Mahler: an introduction to his music.**
Deryck Cooke. London: Faber Music, 1980. 127p.

A useful guide for the general listener. The book contains a brief introduction to Mahler (1860-1911) by an acknowledged authority who reconstituted a number of his unfinished works and provides a short biographical sketch showing the very human side of this complex character. This is followed by an assessment of Mahler's musical output, his symphonies being covered in three sections dealing with: the dates of composition and performance; their orchestration; and a general description. The texts of all Mahler's vocal works with English translations by the author are included.

689 **Mahler.**
Michael Kennedy. London: Dent, 1977. 196p. bibliog. (Master Musicians Series).

Gustav Mahler, a key figure in the musical life of Vienna from the turn of the 19th century, was a conductor and composer of eminence whose reputation suffered more than most from misunderstanding. This misunderstanding stemmed largely from his widow, Alma, who was twenty years his junior. The progressive popularity of his works from the 1960's onwards, in which the conductor Bruno Walter and the contralto Kathleen Ferrier played a decisive part, is one of the most important recent developments in Viennese music. The author provides the full background to Mahler's personality as a corrective to these misunderstandings. An important study.

690 **The second Vienna school: expressionism and dodecaphony.**
Luigi Rognoni, translated from the Italian by Robert W. Mann. London: John Calder, 1977. rev. ed. 417p. bibliog.

An enthusiastic and scholarly work, which analyses the musical and literary style of Schoenberg (1874-1951), Berg (1885-1935) and Webern (1883-1945) – the three leading exponents of the dodecaphonic musical school. The author also examines their relationships with other art forms and draws comparisons with the orchestral and stage works of composers of other musical schools with reference, for example, to Mahler and Stravinsky.

691 **Schoenberg.**
Charles Rosen. London, Glasgow: Fontana, 1976. 124p. bibliog.

Together with Alban Berg and Anton Webern, Arnold Schoenberg (1874-1951) represents the quintessence of the 20th-century Austrian contribution to world 'modern' music. This critical assessment by a practising British musicologist of some stature provides both background and technical analysis.

692 **Arnold Schoenberg: his life, world and work.**
H. H. Stuckenschmidt, translated from the German by Humphrey Searle. London: J. Calder, 1977. 581p.

A notable contribution to the growing list of works on Schoenberg. By sheer volume, at least, this is the largest and most comprehensive work available, well translated and documented. It has added piquancy in that the author was one of his last pupils.

693 **Arnold Schoenberg.**
Egon Wellesz. New York: Galaxy Music; London: Galliard, 1971. 156p.

The author is an eminent musicologist and composer, and a one-time student of Schoenberg. He sets out to make the technique of this avant-garde early 20th century composer intelligible both to the musician and layman. Wellesz writes with warmth and feeling and describes graphically the rowdy scenes which accompanied the early performances of Schoenberg's compositions before hostile audiences in pre-World War I Vienna.

694 **Alban Berg, 1885-1935.**
Rosemary Hilman. Vienna: Federal Press Service, 1984. 61p. (Austrian Documentation).

Alban Berg's life and musical output are placed in the general cultural context of the Vienna of his time in this booklet which commemorates the centenary of his birth. The work includes a useful comparative chronology of musical and political events during his lifetime and there are many prints and photographs.

695 **Alban Berg.**
Karen Monson. London: Macdonald & James, 1980. 396p. bibliog.

The background for this illuminating analysis was based on research for a series of broadcast talks in 1977. Berg is portrayed both as one of the few 20th-century musicians of the Schoenberg school who enjoyed success in his lifetime and as a modernist in terms of inspiration, combining 'sincerely-inspired nostalgia with the contemporary idiom'. He played a very important role in the continuity of the Viennese music tradition.

696 **Alban Berg: the man and his music.**
H. F. Redlich. London: John Calder, 1957. 316p. bibliog.

This transcription of an earlier tribute in German is largely concerned with an analysis of the second Viennese School of music at the turn of the century, the problems of tonality and Berg's (1885-1935) musical contribution to its development. A later section is purely biographical and includes Berg's lecture on *Wozzeck*, his controversial opera produced in 1929, which is written in the form of a personal testament and published here for the first time. A scholarly work.

Theatre and film

697 **International Film Guide.**
Edited by Peter Cowie. 1964-. annual.

This film year book contains a critical review of the past year's activities in the film industry of each country covered. It contains details concerning production, film festivals and technical developments. In the 1984 issue, Austria (p. 68-70) is described as being in a rather stagnant situation as regards the cinema, with retrenchment in production and dwindling cinema audiences.

698 **Filmkunst.** (The art of film.)
Vienna: Austrian Association for Film Documentation and Research. 1949-. quarterly.

The Austrian film industrty staged a dramatic revival after World War II. However, in recent years, as in other countries, it has shifted to production for television rather than for the cinema. This professional periodical of the industry contains reviews of films, technical articles, and sketches of artists and technicians as well as information about the Austrian Film Museum in Vienna which, since 1964, has held one of Europe's best-stocked film archives of both classical and avant-garde productions.

699 **Le cinéma autrichien.** (The Austrian cinema.)
Bernard Frankfurter, with the collaboration of Janine Euvrard. *La revue du cinéma: l'image et son écran*, no. 365 (Oct. 1981), p. 117-23.

The Austrian cinema and film industry is not widely known outside its country of origin. This brief, all round critical view of its history and present activities by a journalist and film critic of some standing is therefore welcome. Compared with its brilliant past, both before and after World War I, with such famous names as Alexander Girardi and Helene Odilon and later the stars who came from the theatre such as Paul Hörbiger and Paula Wessely, the Austrian cinema of today is said to be in a somewhat parlous state. The author contends that contemporary Austrian films contain no social or political message, concentrate too much on actuality at the expense of continuity, and are generally more concerned with technique than with content. He proceeds to highlight the acute financial stringency which affects the industry as a whole, as state aid is only offered for production, and then on an inadequate scale, and not for distribution where so much of the financial outlay is involved. The increasing use of films on television, about 200 a year, is also seen as harmful to the cinema, because 'live' audiences are diminishing.

700 **Kino in Österreich, 1896-1930. Der Stummfilm.** (Cinema in Austria, 1896-1930; the silent film.)
Walter Fritz. Vienna: Austrian Federal Publishing House, 1981. 166p. bibliog.

The author, a well-known film historian and Director of the Austrian Film Archives, reviews the development of the silent film in Austria from its earliest beginnings. He shows how the cinema was closely associated with the theatre, literature and politics of the time. There is an interesting chapter on Austrian film propaganda in World War I, and some fascinating facts emerge. For example, it transpired that Alexander Girardi (1850-1918), a character comedian in opera, was also a cinema star – and that Robert Stolz, the composer, was already writing music for the cinema in 1913. It is also interesting to note that such famous producers as Alexander Korda, Paul Czinner and Michael Curtis all started their careers in Vienna.

701 **Kino in Österreich, 1945-1983. Film zwischen Kommerz und Avantgarde.** (Cinema in Austria, 1945-1983; from commercial to avant-garde film.)
Walter Fritz. Vienna: Austrian Federal Publishing House, 1984. 244p. bibliog.

During the 1930's many Austrian film artists saw better chances of making a career in Hollywood than Vienna, while others were forced to leave the country for political reasons. It was not until after 1945 that the Austrian film industry was revived, with the emergence of such names as Romy Schneider, Senta Berger, Oskar Werner and others. This account of the Austrian cinema in the post-war period shows how in recent times the emphasis has shifted to television, and cinema audiences have been dwindling. The bibliography is extensive and includes a complete list of producers and titles of full length films produced since World War II. This is a sequel volume to the author's *Der Stummfilm* (Silent film) (q.v.).

702 **The third man.**
Graham Greene. London: Lorrimer, 1968. 134p. (Modern Film Scripts).

One of the first post-World War II films to be shot on location, in 1949, *The Third Man*, directed by Alexander Korda, produced by Carol Reed and featuring Orson Welles and the Viennese zither player Anton Karas brilliantly captured the 'wet, brooding, defeated presence of post-war Vienna', its devastation and corruption. This is the full film script.

703 **Masks of the prophet: the theatrical world of Karl Kraus.**
Kari Grimstad. Toronto: University of Toronto Press, 1982. 297p. bibliog.

This account of the stated views of Karl Kraus, the celebrated Viennese satirist and polemicist, on drama, the theatre, actors and critics, contains much direct quotation from *Die Fackel* (The Torch), the satirical paper which he edited from 1899 to 1936. In particular, the author examines Kraus' own theatricality, which she describes as his 'management of illusion', identifying three types of illusion in the process – the illusion of childhood, that of maturity and that of fraud and deception. At various times, the author claims, Kraus employs such illusions, which, although sometimes conflicting, are all part of his theatrical approach. For the reader curious about the theatre of Kraus' time this well-documented account contains much of factual interest and original comment.

704 **The Trapp family singers.**
Maria Augusta Trapp. London: Collins, 1966. 255p.

The enormous success of the film *The Sound of Music*, with its stunning views of Austrian mountain scenery in glorious technicolour, undoubtedly provided an extra fillip to the tourist industry in the Salzburg area, where the film was shot. The principal character in that film, Baroness von Trapp, has written her own account of the family's fortunes in pre-World War II days, when the Trapp singing group was first formed and once sang before Chancellor Schuschnigg. The details of the family's escape to freedom from the Nazis are only briefly outlined. The second part of her book moves to the United States where the Trapp singers continue to give concerts and raise money for charitable causes in Austria. The story, like the film, is a touching one and the author tells it with warmth and feeling, supported throughout by her strong religious faith.

705 **Die österreichischen Langfilme, 1946-1971.** (Austrian full-length films, 1946-1971.)
Compiled by Dina Unterkirchen. Vienna: Austrian Society for Film Documentation, 1972. 18p.

A straightforward index of full-length films produced in Austria during the first quarter century of the Second Republic. The titles are listed alphabetically with names of producers and première dates.

Folklore, customs and costume

706 **Folklore Studies in Austria, 1945-1965.**
Klaus Beitl, translated from the German by Dieter Schmölling, Stephen H. Wedgwood. *Journal of the Folklore Institute*, vol. 5, no. 2-3 (Aug.-Dec. 1968), p. 216-35.

Austrian folklore studies, which had been interrupted by World War II, were revived on a country-wide basis in 1945 and were soon flourishing in all the nine provinces. This activities report by the General Secretary of the Austrian Folklore Association shows the position some twenty years later, during which time nearly 250 independent articles or scientific essays on the subject had been published, with thirty trained folklore specialists active on a full time basis in various Austrian scientific institutions. The report lists: various folklore museums collections and documentation centres; publications in regular circulation; and specialist monographs, atlases and topographical works produced during the two decades in question. Although a national folklore bibliography is already in existence, the provinces have begun to set up their own regional bibliographies, Burgenland being the first to do so. A report on the period 1965-1985 is in preparation.

707 **Dances of Austria.**
Katharina Breuer. London: Max Parrish, 1950. 39p. bibliog. (Handbook of European National Dances).

Sponsored by the British Royal Academy of Dancing, this guide gives a brief description of different types of traditional Austrian folk dances, and selects four for wider treatment. The author provides a step notation and music arranged for easy piano-playing accompaniment and there is a useful list of festivals and other occasions where folk-dancing can be seen at its best.

708 **The imperial style: fashions of the Habsburg era.**
Edited by Polly Cone, introduced by Diana Vreeland. New York: Metropolitan Museum of Art, 1980. 166p.

This sequence of ten essays based on the 1979-80 exhibition at the Metropolitan Museum of Art, New York, brings the most fastidious experience to bear on an essential element of Austro-Hungarian Imperial life, namely, the aristocratic elegance of its court dress and uniforms. If anything, the Hungarian styles were more sumptuous than the Austrian, doubtless due to the oriental influences of the Turkish occupation there. Domestic fashions are also displayed to good effect. The essays on the glory of Vienna by Joseph Wechsberg, himself a Viennese, and on the early 19th-century Biedermeier period by Helga Kessler are of particular significance.

709 **Trachten in Österreich.** (Costumes in Austria.)
Rudolf Fochler. Wels, Upper Austria: Welsermühl, 1980. 176p. bibliog.

This collection of costumes, both traditional and modern, displays examples from all the nine provinces. There are numerous illustrations. The text is in German with French and English translations.

710 **The history of research in folk medicine in German-speaking countries.**
Elfriede Grabner, translated from the German by William Templer. *Journal of the Folklore Institute*, vol. 5 (1968), p. 152-57.

Folk-medicine in the German-speaking areas of Europe, including Austria, is a relative latecomer to the world of folklore research, for it was not until the late 19th century that there was any serious folk-medical scholarship and even then the principal investigators were almost exclusively physicians in Bavaria, Hamburg, Vienna and Graz. The author, assistant at the Styrian Folklore Museum, in this short historical review, explains that the first comprehensive and systematic study of folk-medical customs and concepts was published by Gustav Jungbauer in 1934 in Prague (*Deutsche Volksmedizin*) and still remains a standard reference work. For many years both before and after World War II folk-medicine was regarded as a subject of fringe academic interest in folklore studies generally. Recently, however, it has received much more attention, particularly in Austria where the author has been undertaking an overall study of folk-medical research in the eastern Alps for which an abundance of manuscript material is available. According to Grabner, modern scientific medicine in Austria is taking a positive attitude towards folk-medicine, especially in the field of antibiotics, with some encouraging results, while greater collaboration between medical historians, legal scholars and natural scientists has given the subject a wider acceptability and the status of a serious field of research.

711 **Österreichs Sagenschatz.** (Austria's treasury of sagas.)
Karl Haiding. Vienna: Fritz Molden Verlag, 1965. 436p.

This distinguished Austrian folklore specialist spent a lifetime collecting and setting down sagas and folk-tales originating from all parts of his homeland. The present publication contains 328 sagas, related in a simple, easy style, suitable for a young readership and all reflecting the particular landscape in which they are set. An appendix of sources is included.

712 **Tracht in Österreich: Geschichte und Gegenwart.** (Local costume in Austria: past and present.)
Compiled by Franz C. Lipp, Elizabeth Längle, Gexi Tostmann, Franz Hubmann. Vienna: Christian Brandstätter, 1984. 263p. bibliog.

This is a comprehensive and well-documented study of local costume in all its aspects by a particularly well-chosen team of specialists. The older generation are represented by Lipp, keeper of the folklore section of the Upper Austria Museum at Linz, and Hubmann, the doyen of Austrian photographers, who has also selected the excellent illustrations ranging from earlier paintings and sketches to recent photographs. The 'moderns' are represented by Längle, who is engaged in public relations and marketing for the textile industry, and Tostmann, a practical businesswoman who runs a fashion firm. Although the text is in German, with a very full glossary of terms, the illustrations clearly spell the message out to any reader. The history of local costume dates back to the earliest times of an agricultural community; 'Tracht' literally means 'what you wear'. The text threads its way through developments in each of the historic areas and shows how the country folk gradually transformed their working clothes into glamorous versions for festive occasions reflecting individual wealth and status, while townspeople and the aristocracy wore local costume when in the country and out hunting and introduced refinements back at home for 'smart' wear. Even now invitations to official receptions prescribe 'evening dress or local costume'; and 'Tracht' has become an important element of the current fashion industry.

713 **Living country customs in Salzburg.**
Prunella C. Pott-Flatz. Salzburg, Austria: Karl Gordon, 1950. 64p.

The author has contributed some engaging black-and-white drawings as an enhancement to her descriptions of fourteen different age-old country customs, of both secular and religious origins, involving special costumes, processions, dances, songs and games. An index indicates the dates in the annual calendar and places where such festivals are celebrated in the province of Salzburg and other alpine regions of Austria.

714 **Historische Volkslieder von Österreich von 15.bis zum 19.Jahrhundert.** (Historical folksongs of Austria from the 15th to the 19th centuries.)
Selected with a commentary by Leopold Schmidt. Vienna: Wiener Neudrücke, 1971. 87p. bibliog.

This is a novel and commendable collection of fifty folk-songs from all over Austria specifically chosen for their historical interest. There is an introduction to each folk-song which sets it in its context. The songs have been culled from local papers, tracts and archives and celebrate great events, battles, lives and deaths.

715 **Perchtenmasken in Österreich.** (Carved customs masks in Austria.)
Leopold Schmidt, translated from the German by Traude Banndorff. Vienna: Hermann Böhlaus Nachf. 1972. 151p. bibliog.

Mythical ideas from pagan times, Christian customs, and morality plays from the Middle Ages have been some of the influences which have shaped the ritual dances, traditional costumes and the masks of witches and devils which are present-day living manifestations of Austrian folklore, particularly in the alpine regions of Salzburg and Tirol. The author explains this art of masquerade used in plays and processions – which incidentally, are great tourist attractions – and illumines his text with fifty-nine illustrations of different masks worn on such occasions, each representing a different figure or characteristic.

716 **Das grosse Buch vom Wiener Heurigen.** (The big book on the Viennese Heuriger.)
Bartel F. Sinhuber. Vienna: ORAC, 1980. 223p. bibliog. maps.

Nearly every guidebook on Vienna has a section on the Heuriger, the basically open-air pursuit of happiness through continuous intake of young wine sustained by snacks and a small band which plays for you at your table. It is probable, however, that this is the only full-length treatise in any language, and non-German speakers will find it well worth-while poring over the maps, photographs, wine-lists and song scores that accompany this compendium of a peculiarly Viennese cult which has been continuing for over 1,200 years.

717 **Austria folk customs.**
Helmut Steininger. Vienna: Federal Press Service, 1985. 32p.

The author has selected a number of characteristic, colourful and unique examples of folk-customs from each of the nine provinces, all of which are performed in public at different seasons of the year. They include major processions, religious and secular, play acting, dancing and other ceremonies steeped in Austrian folklore. A brief description is given in each case, but since so many of these customs are performed in remote villages, the exact location is not given, interested parties being invited to contact their local tourist office for details. There are thirty-two excellent colour photographs.

718 **Research on folk-music in Austria since 1800.**
Wolfgang Suppan, translated from the German by Eva Borneman. Kingston, Ontario, Canada: *Yearbook of the International Folk Music Council*, vol. 8 (1976), p. 117-29.

This extended article surveys the whole scene and shows how in the late 18th century emergent patriotism and the liberation movement in the Tirol added impetus to folk-music research and practice which reached a peak just prior to the Revolution of 1848. Although standard German folk-music at that time contained much Austrian material, provincial folk-song collections were soon started in Austria itself and half a century later the Austrian Folksong Foundation was formed. Its primary task of publishing a major collection was frustrated by the outbreak of World War II and the Foundation itself was dissolved at the time of the *Anschluss*. It is now flourishing again and the Austrian folk-song tradition has been revived, with research being conducted at various levels on changing fashions and the transition of folk-music to more modern musical entertainment using folk-music sources.

719 **200 Jahre Mode in Wien: aus den Modensammlungen des Historischen Museums der Stadt Wien.** (Two hundred years of Viennese fashion; from the fashion collections of the Museum of History of Vienna.)
Compiled by Herbert Tomoczek. Vienna: Verein der Freunde der Hermesvilla, Lainzer Tiergarten, 1976. 175p. bibliog.

This catalogue of a special exhibition held in the summer of 1976 displaying a selection of 1,062 exhibits from the vast fashion collection of the Museum of the History of Vienna contains fifty-four full page illustrations of costumes, hats, shoes and all manner of accessories covering the period 1794-1976. The foreword is by Robert Waissenberg, the director of Museums in Vienna and two further explanatory essays describe in some detail the development of fashion in the capital. The display is fully representative and the non-German reader will find the excellent reproductions and prints extremely helpful in following, without the aid of the accompanying text, the course of Viennese fashion over the past two centuries.

Spanish Riding School

720 **The Spanish Riding School in Vienna.**
Hans Handler. London: Thames & Hudson, 1972. 215p. bibliog.

The Spanish Riding School, whose beginnings can be traced back to 1565 when performing horses were first shown in a riding track in Vienna, is the oldest of its kind in the world and the only one to teach the classical tradition of horsemanship in its purest form. This beautifully illustrated book, with its 364 plates, sixty-four in colour, presents the school's history and development, explains the art of classical riding, and the breeding and training of the Lipizzaner stallions of

Spanish stock which are a living example of a unique baroque tradition. The author, who was for ten years director of the school, a court appointment which carries with it important privileges, provides an excellent text. A definitive work of considerable merit. Handler's predecessor, Colonel Alois Podhajsky, in a semi-autobiographical account entitled *My horses, my teachers* (Harrap, 1969) concentrates on schooling, the technicalities of dressage and the movements uniquely associated with the Spanish Riding School. Another work of interest by Podhajsky containing over 200 exquisite photographs is *The White Stallions of Vienna* (Sportsman's Press, 1985).

Sport and Recreation

721 **Hochschwab Wanderführer.** (Walking guide to the Hochschwab.)
Günter Auferbauer. Graz, Austria; Vienna: Verlag Styria, 1975. 256p. map.

The Hochschwab massif in Upper Styria, which has interesting historical links with Archduke John of Styria, is ideal climbing and walking country with a very varied scenery and an amazing richness in natural history, particularly bird life and lepidoptera. This compendious guide, after a technical explanation of the area's geomorphological features, describes, with black-and-white illustrations, a number of climbs and mountain walks and assesses the hunting possibilities in this attractive region which is virtually unknown to British tourists.

722 **On foot through Europe; a trail guide to Austria, Switzerland and Liechtenstein.**
Craig Evans. New York: Quill, 1982. 211p.

The executive director of the American Hiking Society spent three years compiling information and walking the major trails described in this extremely useful and practical guide. Almost 25,000 miles of Austria's walking routes and footpaths are marked by the Austrian Alpine Club and there are more than 700 mountain huts available for overnight accommodation. The section on Austria (p. 5-77) contains brief articles on the general walking areas, flora and fauna and climate. It lists walking associations throughout the country, maps, and guidebooks and presents information on mountaineering schools, guides and cross country skiing. The author then describes in greater detail the ten long distance treks which cross the country from north to south and east to west. He also makes suggestions for shorter distance walks in each of the nine provinces. There is a host of other valuable information packed into these pages and although some details will already be out of date, the basic information still holds good. The work is extremely well organized and presented and is a very easy reference book to handle.

723 **Ski Guide – Austria.**
Mark Heller. London: Quartet Books, 1973. 215p. maps.

Mark Heller, the *Guardian* newspaper ski correspondent presents an objective view of the downhill skiing available to all grades of performers in almost a hundred Austrian ski resorts. This is the most comprehensive account since James Riddell published his classic *Ski Runs of Austria* (London: Michael Joseph, 1958) which is now sadly out of date and out of print. All the centres included have been personally researched and skied by the author, who provides some excellent explanatory notes and a table of grading symbols indicating particular characteristics, such as suitability for ski touring, Nordic-type skiing or trekking, family holidays and places offering exceptional value in terms of potential enjoyment rather than price. The list of conventional signs for each run, which is described with a marked diagram, explains the type of terrain, degrees of difficulty, danger spots and suggested off-*piste* routes as well as marked and prepared runs. A first class reliable guide for all standards of skiers which is unlikely to be bettered for some time.

724 **For the record: my years with Ferrari.**
Niki Lauda, translated from the German by Diana Mosley. London: William Kimber, 1978. 222p.

This is a remarkable account, almost a minor epic, of four fateful years in the life and career of Niki Lauda, the Austrian World Championship motor racing driver. In 1976, when driving for Ferrari he was very severely burnt and almost killed in a crash and for months his life hung in the balance. Yet he made an astonishing recovery and in the following year proved unassailable on the circuit and regained the World Championship. The story is one of tremendous courage and the strength of human resources when faced with the ultimate challenge. However, it is not all high drama. There are informal insights into the champion's home life and his other interests, particularly his love of flying. The writing is simple and modest and the reader is left with an overall impression of strong will power, great physical courage, good manners and style.

725 **Interview with Franz Klammer.**
Philippa Le Neve Foster. *Skier*, (Nov. 1984), p. 53-4.

One of the world's greatest down-hill racing skiiers gives his views on competitive World Cup skiing, and describes his training methods and home life and his promotion of Carinthia, his home province, as a tourist attraction. Klammer, who has been in top class skiing for over ten years speaks with charm and modesty and it is easy to understand the enormous popularity he enjoys, not only in his own country, but on the international circuit as well.

726 **Wildwasser – Kurzführer Österreich.** (Short white water guide to Austria.)
Hans Matz. Vienna: Freytag Berndt, 1971. 79p. maps. bibliog.

With its many fast-flowing mountain rivers and streams, Austria offers excellent opportunities for canoeing, which in recent years has become quite a popular sport in the country. This useful guide, with forty illustrations and a number of maps, provides details of 130 rivers and streams suitable for the canoeist, indicating any special characteristics, degree of difficulty, the navigable distance and the best season to tackle the course.

727 **The true origin and development of the Austrian school of physical education.**

Nicolas J. Moolenijzer. *Canadian Journal of History of Sport and Physical Education* vol. 5, no. 2 (spring 1974), p. 48-55.

The author discusses the natural approach to physical education which was developed after World War I by the Austrians Margarete Streicher and Karl Gaulhofer and which was adopted by a number of central European countries. The system was later exploited by the National Socialists in Germany, and to a lesser extent in Austria, for political ends at open air mass youth rallies.

728 **The new national Austrian ski system.**

Translated from the German by Roland Palmedo. London: Kaye & Ward, 1974. 88p.

Austria's national sport is, without any doubt, skiing and each year thousands of winter sports enthusiasts flock mainly to the Vorarlberg and Tirol for skiing holidays. The present Austrian national ski school system has developed since the 1950's and the so-called Arlberg technique has become a household word in the skiing world. This manual, with explanatory diagrams provides information on basic schooling, advanced techniques and how to adapt to different snow conditions. Although primarily containing guide lines for teachers – it is a basic manual for ski training in the Austrian army – it can easily be followed by the enthusiast eager to learn the rudiments.

729 **Salute the mountains: the hundred best walks in the Alps.**

Walter Pause, translated from the German by Ruth Michaelis-Jena, Arthur Ratcliff. London; Toronto: Harrap, 1962. 210p.

Austria features in thirty-nine of the mountain walks in this selection by a distinguished writer on the Alps. The walks are very varied, covering parts of Vorarlberg, Tirol, Salzburg, Styria and Carinthia, and all can be accomplished without a guide, and with one or two exceptions, are graded easy to moderate. Each walk is described with a sketch map and a black-and-white photograph and details of the maps and guides required are provided. The special characteristics of the region are also considered. The ten rules of conduct for summer walking in the mountains in the appendix are written in a personal, but eminently practical style and will repay careful study by anyone intending to use this guide.

730 **Salute the skier.**

Walter Pause, translated from the German by Ruth Michaelis-Jena, Arthur Ratcliff. London; Toronto: Harrap, 1963. 208p.

A companion guide to *Salute the mountains* (q.v.) by the same author. This is a personal selection of one hundred ski runs in the Alps, thirty-seven of which are in Austria. Pause caters for both the *piste* runner as well as the ski mountaineer and has included a number of glacier runs for the more experienced; two in the Ötztal region of Tirol. The general format is similar to that of the earlier book on mountain walking. Some of the better known runs duplicate those featured in Mark Heller's *Ski Guide* (q.v.) but are less detailed and the translation at times appears rather old-fashioned. However, the author captures well the flavour of each ski area described and the book can certainly be recommended for the excellent long shot monochrome photographs.

731 **Stubai alps: a survey of popular walking and climbing routes.**
Eric Roberts. Goring, England: West Col Productions, 1981. reprint. 167p. (West Col Alpine Guides).

Eric Roberts was a remarkable British mountaineer who had already climbed 1,100 summits in the Alps by the age of thirty-three; he lost his life in an avalanche in the Himalayas in 1979. On all his climbs he kept careful notes and diaries and always took his own photographs. These were later arranged into mountain guides, generally commissioned by the United Kingdom branch of the Austrian Alpine Club. These guides included diagrams of different routes with their grading, descriptions of access routes and climbing conditions and also listed mountain huts and peaks. Three key mountain areas are covered by the present guide and its two companion volumes, *Glockner Region*, (1976, 135p.); and the *Zillertal Alps*, (1980, 94p.). The latter was published posthumously with an introductory dedication.

732 **Hunting in Austria.**
Kurt Smolka. *Austria Today*, vol. 6, no. 3 (autumn 1980), p. 50-54.

Although there are over 100,000 holders of hunting permits in Austria, the latter are only issued on very strict conditions and after a lengthy examination. The term 'hunting' has a wide connotation in the country and includes everything connected with knowing wild animals in their natural surroundings, protecting, preserving and observing them, as well as killing them. The author, in this brief illustrated article, provides details of the main hunting animals in Austria, of which the hare, statistically speaking, is the most important, and goes on to describe various hunting methods as applied to typically Austrian species of game, such as red and roe deer, chamois and the rarer capercaillie or mountain cock. He explains that hunting in Austria is not just the privilege of the very wealthy, for probably about three quarters of all permit holders are farmers, small businessmen and others drawn from the professional classes.

733 **Ötztal Alps: a selection of climbs.**
Walter Unsworth. Goring, England: West Col Productions, 1969. 112p.

There are few regions within the Austrian Tirol which have proved more popular with British climbers than the Ötztal, probably because of its easy access, its good and numerous huts and the variety of first-class climbs it offers. The majority of routes are in the easier and middle grades, and although this excellent guide by a very experienced mountaineer is primarily intended for climbers, many hillwalkers will also find it helpful. A general introduction, explaining the topography and giving practical information on maps, guides and grades of climbs, is followed by a section on mountain huts in the region and descriptions of ninety climbs with peaks averaging 10,000 feet in height.

734 **The Vienna Prater.**

Austria Today, no. 2 (1985), p. 52-55.

Once just a collection of islands in the middle of the Danube, then a hunting ground for the early Habsburg rulers, the Vienna Prater is one of the oldest (it was first opened to the public by Emperor Joseph II in 1766) and largest amusement parks in the world. This brief article traces its history and describes with illustrations its principal amenities, with its 150 different gastronomic and amusement establishments, its extensive and varied recreational areas and of course the famous 'Riesenrad' (giant wheel) built by the English marine engineer Walter Basset in 1898 to commemorate the 50th anniversary of Emperor Francis Joseph I's reign.

Food and Wine

735 **Austrian cooking.**
Gretel Beer. London: Deutsch, 1983. 7th impression. 220p. (André Deutsch Cookery Books).

Austrian cuisine today still reflects the multinational character of the Danube monarchy. As the writer, a Viennese journalist long resident in Britain explains in her introduction, it 'derives much of its strength from Moravia and much of its daring from Poland. It knows of the fiery spices of Hungary and the elegance of French cuisine'. This is a deservedly popular cookery book with a wide range of traditional Austrian recipes. It is particularly strong on cakes, pastries and biscuits.

736 **The Tyrolese Cookery Book.**
David Bethel. London: Medici Society. 1937. 45p.

Accompanied by some charming woodcuts of traditional Tirolean kitchen utensils, this collection of recipes was 'hunted in the high Alps, run to earth in the charming cafes, smuggled out of Schloss kitchens or stripped from the poor peasantry'. It was gathered during a year's stay the author made in Tirol in the 1930's to escape the bustle and noise of London.

737 **The Viennese cuisine I love.**
Jules J. Bond. New York: Leon Amiel, 1970. 160p.

The author, a well-known food columnist and gastronomic expert, has written up 150 recipes with clear and simple instructions, concentrating mainly on appetizers, soups and garnishes, and desserts. There are sixteen colour illustrations.

738 **The wines and wine gardens of Austria.**
S. F. Hallgarten, F. N. Hallgarten. Watford, England: Argus, 1979. 339p. maps. bibliog.

The family firm of Hallgarten Brothers are major importers of Austrian wine into Britain, and the two authors, acknowledged experts on wine-growing, have published many books on the subject in a number of European countries. This publication contains an extended history from early Roman times, when vineyards were first cultivated in the Danube area, to the present day, and there are separate chapters on wine categories, classification and labelling. The four maps cover the principal wine-growing areas of Austria: Lower Austria, Southern Styria, Burgenland, and the Weinviertel lowlands bordering Czechoslovakia. There is a good glossary of technical terms and various appendixes. This volume is altogether an absorbing and well-presented production; it is essential reading for the serious wine-lover and a persuasive enticement to anyone venturing on their first tasting of an Austrian wine.

739 **The home book of Viennese cooking.**
Trude Johnston. London: Faber & Faber, 1977. 190p. (Home Book Series).

In this practical cookery book the author has adapted her mother's handwritten recipes to take advantage of modern labour-saving devices while still retaining their traditional authenticity. Apart from certain specialities of its own, such as the Wiener Schnitzel (veal escalope) and Sachertorte (chocolate cake), the Viennese cuisine draws substantially on a number of regional dishes and thus provides a great variety. The preparation of cakes and biscuits and other appetisers in different shapes and flavourings, much relished by Austrians as a tasty accompaniment to a cup of coffee or as an offering on more festive occasions, is extensively covered. The bi-lingual German-English index is useful.

740 **Gourmets old Vienna cookbook.**
Lillian Langseth-Christiansen. New York: Gourmet Books, 1982. rev. ed. 634p.

The charm of this carefully prepared and substantial cook-book, which was first published in 1958, undoubtedly lies in the author's nostalgic evocation of Viennese life in the 1920s when she was studying with Josef Hoffmann, the leading architect of the Vienna Secession movement. Her reminiscences are cleverly interwoven with the practical professional presentation of over 1,200 recipes, many of them traditionally handed down in her family from one generation to another.

741 **The Austrian wine scandal: the sorcerer of the vineyards.**
Special report by Paul Levy, Sue Masterman, Martin Bailey, Charles Metcalfe. *Observer*, (11 August 1985), p. 9.

The Austrian 'wine scandal' which broke out in July 1985 and had widespread international repercussions in the trade centred around a certain Otto Nadrasky, a bio-chemist from Lower Ausria who mixed a toxic product, diethylene glycol, commonly known as anti-freeze, as an additive to good quality wines to improve their sweetness and viscosity. This preliminary article on this damaging affair provides the background to the train of events leading to widespread prosecutions of many respected wine producers and their imprisonment pending trial. Austrian laws on the production and marketing of wines have now been considerably strengthened to prevent a further spread of contaminated wines in Europe.

742 **Austrian cooking for you.**
Elisabeth Mayer-Browne. London: Bles, 1969. 234p. illus.

This book contains traditional family recipes, including many provincial dishes. The menus are imaginative and the section on open-sandwiches is particularly extensive and appetising.

743 **Know Austria by cooking.**
Annitta Moesli. Glasgow: Ossian Publishers, 1984. 171p.

Prefaced with an inspiring foreword by the Federal Vice-Chancellor Norbert Steger and colourfully presented in an original format this is rather an unusual cookbook. The author, a travel and sports writer turned culinary expert, in collaboration with her husband, sets her subject against the historical background of the country as she traces the development of Austrian cuisine through the Middle Ages, and imperial Habsburg times to the present day. The book opens with a lighthearted but authentic description of the Viennese coffee-house and recipes for cakes and pastries normally served there. It continues with a number of tradiitonal 'royal' or 'imperial' dishes dating from Habsburg times which well-illustrate the multi-national character of Austrian culinary achievement; the reader will appreciate, for example, that *Wiener Schnitzel* originated from Milan, that *Apfelstrudel* and *Gulasch* found their way to Vienna via Budapest and that the sweet dumplings which accompany so many Austrian meat dishes were first baked in Bohemia. Regional dishes follow, with indications of their historical and geographical origins, while the two chapters on the Viennese Heuriger and Austrian wines are delightfully written, well-illustrated and informative. The book concludes with another original touch – facsimile reproductions of some imperial Habsburg menus for grand festive occasions, such as State visits by foreign royalty in the late 19th and early 20th centuries.

744 **Viennese cookery.**
Rose Philpot. London: Hodder & Stoughton, 1975. 246p.

Written by a Viennese housewife living in London, this is much more than an ordinary cookery book. Indeed, the author has compiled a short history of gastronomy in Vienna from the time of the early Roman settlements to present day eating and drinking habits. She indicates which hotels and restaurants specialize in certain dishes and where to find a particular confectioner or bakery. There is a concluding chapter on Austrian wines, and the book is of particular importance to visitors through its explanation of the history and rites of perhaps the most famous element in Viennese experience, i.e., the Heuriger or 'this-year's wine' – (which also includes last-year's). This is a comprehensive presentation of wine, food, music and 'Stimmung'-atmosphere: not for nothing did the famous entertainer Hans Moser score perhaps his greatest success with his song of the Viennese reveller who hired a factotum to get him home safely but then found, when it came to the point, that the factotum was even more happily 'under the influence' than he was!

745 **The Viennese pastry cookbook: from Vienna with love.**
Lilly Joss Reich. New York: Macmillan; London: Collier-Macmillan, 1970. 335p.

There is a romantic flavour about both the origins and the contents of this book. The Austrian author, now living in the United States had to leave her native Vienna at the *Anschluss* and took refuge in France, only to be over-run once more by the Germans. She managed to salvage her mother's cookery books, but only put these to practical use after her marriage at her husband's express wish. Those wanting to take up the art of home baking, will find here inspiration, encouragement and practical guidance. There are some useful tips and techniques and lists of essential and make-do substitute equipment, while the recipes are presented in a personal and attractive manner. The range is impressive and covers every type of pastry – those with flour, with yeast, with nuts and no flour, cakes and hot desserts – the whole topped off with decorations, icing and other fillings. A delicious classic.

Encyclopaedias, Directories and Reference Works

746 **European Political Facts.**
Chris Cook, John Paxton. London; Basingstoke, England: Macmillan. 3 vols. 1975-81.

This is a reliable compendium of basic historical data, spanning the 200-year period from the French Revolution to the present day. It is a quick reference source classified for each major European country, including Austria, under a comprehensive range of applicable headings, such as heads of state, ministers, principal battles, treaties, parliaments, political parties, international organizations and the press. The periods covered by each volume are: 1789-1848; 1848-1918; 1918-80.

747 **Current European directories.**
Beckenham, England: CBD Research, 1981. 2nd ed. 413p.

This is a standard guide to international, national and specialized directories, listed by country. The section on Austria (p. 87-97) includes official yearbooks, general trade and professional association directories, gazetteers and specialized directories. Each entry lists the name, address and telephone number of the publisher, the frequency of publication and, where possible, the date and price of the latest edition.

748 **Europa Yearbook, 1985: a world survey. Volume 1.**
London: Europa Publications, 1985. 1,368p. 1926-. annual (2 volumes).

The section on Austria (p. 294-314) includes a useful statistical survey covering: area and population; agriculture; forestry; mining; industry; finance; external trade; transport; tourism; communications and education. In addition there is a most useful and highly informative introductory survey covering Austria's recent history, government, defence, economic affairs, transport and communications, social welfare, education and tourism as well as a directory which deals with a wide range of subjects including: constitution and government; diplomatic representation; the press and mass media; finance; and trade and industry. An authoritative and well-established reference work.

749 **Handbuch Kunst Wien, 1984.** (Handbook of art in Vienna, 1984.)
F. Falter. Vienna: Falter, 1984. 144p.

This is the first in an intended series of annual handbooks on art in Vienna, containing a classified list of museums, galleries, art and antique dealers, leading artists, engravers, designers, picture framers, art restorers, bookshops and publishers, with addresses and brief details. A system of symbols, with explanations in English, is used to denote the various categories and a non-German speaker should have little difficulty in finding his way around this useful reference work.

750 **Handbook of the press, advertising and commercial art in Austria.**
Vienna: Association of Austrian Newspaper Publishers, 1952-. annual.

An extremely useful reference source which lists all the main newspapers and periodicals published in the country as well as: professional yearbooks and directories; press, photographic and advertising agencies; advertising rates; leading figures in journalism and the graphic arts; and the addresses of press and publicity offices.

751 **Industrie-Compass.** (Compass Directory of Industries.)
Vienna: Compass-Verlag, 1902-. annual.

This reference work is similar to *Kelly's Directory* and contains an index of some 18,000 firms in Austria, arranged alphabetically and then by trade and location, not by province. The same publishing firm also produces: *Finanz-Compass*, which provides information about banks, building societies, insurance companies, consumer associations, imports and exports; *Handels-Compass* (trade); and *Personen-Kompass* which lists directors and leading business figures. All are produced annually. A parallel production, *Handelsregister Österreich* (Austrian trade directory) (Vienna: Jupiter Verlag) lists registered firms by province.

752 **Österreich: Daten zur Geschichte und Kultur.** (Austria: dates on history and culture.)
Walter Kleindel. Vienna: Überreuter, 1978. 570p.

This is an unusual but extremely useful reference aid. It is based on a straightforward chronological arrangement of 10,000 dates from pre-history to the end of 1977, but its unique features are the abridged versions of treaties, and other historical documents. In some cases it also provides extracts from specialist articles on important and relevant subjects. The volume contains a complete list of dynastic rulers, as well as cabinet ministers, provincial governors and mayors from the end of World War II onwards.

753 **Politisches Handbuch Österreichs.** (Political handbook of Austria.) Edited by Wolfgang Oberleitner. Vienna: Federal Ministry for Education, Science and Art, 1945-. annual.

By far the most complete directory of Austrian political life to be published on an annual basis this handbook contains lists and details of leading political figures, and members and officials of all political parties, including those no longer in existence at both national and provincial level. Associated bodies are also included.

754 **Österreichischer Amtskalender, 1985-86.** (Austrian official directory.)
Vienna: State Publishing House, 1922-. annual.

This official list of all public bodies in Austria including universities and their senior staff is arranged by authority, or organization, and is sub-divided by place. It incorporates a number of provincial directories compiled on a similar basis.

755 **Österreichisches Jahrbuch.** (Austrian yearbook.)
Vienna: Federal Press Service, 1928-. annual.

Austria's official government yearbook is a valuable compilation and covers the widest spectrum. Federal matters are handled in separate sections on such subjects as: government and politics; domestic and foreign policy; the law; education; social security; banking; economic development; industry; trade; and building. Provincial affairs follow, while the final section provides useful basic statistical data.

756 **Österreichisches Biographisches Lexikon, 1815-1950.** (Austrian biographical encylopaedia, 1815-1950.)
Leo Santifaller, Eva Obermayer-Marnach. Vienna: Academy of Sciences, 1946-. approximately biannual.

This monumental work was first set in train during the First Republic by the historians Bettelheim and Redlich, who contributed essays on prominent Austrians living within the borders of Austria-Hungary from the Congress of Vienna onwards. In 1946 the project was taken over by the Austrian Academy of Sciences, which now publishes instalments of ninety-six pages in length at about six-monthly intervals. The June 1985 issue is up to the letter 'T'. The encyclopaedia is therefore not yet complete, but is regarded as a definitive reference work, containing concise objective and informed entries, with bibliographies covering not only standard but specialist publications as well. A rather more subjective biographical offering and covering approximately the same contents is published by Almathea Verlag under the title *Grosse Österreicher* (Prominent Austrians) and is edited by Kurt Skalnik. This, however, is not alphabetical and appears at irregular intervals, roughly four times a year.

757 **Austria: a chronology and fact book, 1437-1973.**
Robert I. Vexler. Dobbs Ferry, New York: Oceana Publications, 1977. 154p. (World Chronology Series).

This is a chronology of important events in the history of Austria, accompanied by relevant documents, many condensed, in English translation, and a critical but general bibliography. The author's intention was to illustrate the continuous development of Austria from the crowning of Albert V, and the accession of Bohemia and Hungary to the Holy Roman Empire in 1437 to the dissolution of the Vienna Municipal Council in 1973. All the documents reproduced are prefaced by a short explanatory preamble. A useful reference tool for the student of history and the general reader wishing to find his bearings amidst the entanglements of the Habsburg dynasty.

758 **Who's who in Austria.**
Munich: Who's Who Verlag, 1982-83. 10th ed. 1,224p.

This directory, part of an internationally-recognized series, contains more than 5,500 biographies of prominent personalities in Austria and abroad, most of whom have been personally interviewed to ensure maximum accuracy of information. A detailed index lists the names and addresses of the most important national and international organizations in the country and a further section deals with the economic achievements of industrial firms.

759 **The World of Learning.**
London: Europa Publications, 1984-85. 35th ed. 1,853p. annual.

An indispensable reference work which arranges its material alphabetically by country and indexes by institution. The section on Austria (p. 93-112) covers: the Academy of Sciences; learned societies; research institutes; libraries and archives; museums and art galleries; universities; and colleges and schools of art and music. Degrees and other academic qualifications are no longer included.

760 **Biographisches Lexikon des Kaiserthums Österreich.** (A biographical encyclopaedia of the Austrian Empire.)
Constant von Wurzbach. Vienna: Universitätsbuchhandlung I.C. Zamarski, 1856-91. 60 vols. Reprinted, New York: Johnson, 1964.

Something akin to the *British National Biography* but covering only the period from 1750 to the date of publication, this monumental work consists of lengthy biographical articles with bibliographical notes on leading Austrian personalities living in the Austrian Empire between these dates. Each of the sixty volumes contains an alphabetical index of entries which is further subdivided into professional groups and geographical spread by province and state.

761 **Yearbook of international organisations.**
Munich, New York; London: K. G. Saur. 3 vols. annual, 1908-.

Volume 2 of this yearbook, entitled *International Organisation Participation*, regularly includes in its sections on individual countries, lists of international organizations, societies or bodies with which Austria is associated, either directly or indirectly. It also lists the titles of international treaties and agreements to which the country in question is a signatory. The 1984 edition, for example, featured Austria on p. 5,008-40, with 2,166 entries.

Museums, Libraries, Art Galleries and Archives

762 **Der österreichische Museumsführer in Farbe.** (The Austrian museum guide in colour.)
Maria Dawid, Erich Egg. Innsbruck, Austria: Pinguin Verlag, 1985. 452p. bibliog.

The authors' credentials are impeccable: a classical archaeologist and the director of the Tirol Provincial Museum. The two of them have compiled a work of real practical value: the complete list of over 900 museums and collections, grouped alphabetically under location and name, with names of the director, opening details, and an indication of the highlights, often beautifully illustrated in colour. All types of museums are listed, including not only classic indoor collections but open-air displays of historic farmhouses and even a tramway museum. The non-German reader should have little difficulty in interpreting the clearly set-out text with the aid of a dictionary, and no other work provides the same detail. There is a useful glossary of terms and an excellent index of artists, architects, writers, scientists, inventors and historical personalities. An abridged list of some of the principal Austrian museums in English providing very brief details of their contents can be found in *Museums and collections in Austria* (Vienna: Federal Publishing Office, 1978. 33p.) which also includes a number of recommended art tours – Roman, Romanesque, Gothic, Baroque, castles and mansions – a valuable addition and not often found in most guide books.

763 **Dokumentationsarchiv des österreichischen Widerstandes.** (Documentation archive of the Austrian resistance).
Vienna: Federal Ministry for Science and Research, 1982. 60p.

Founded in 1963, the 'DÖW' is an attempt to document Austria's efforts to achieve her own liberation in the light of the Moscow Allied Declaration of 1943 which looked forward to a free and independent Austria. It started as a private initiative but has now been taken over by the government and consists of a number of bodies which form the Commission comprising no less than 160 members, some of whom are Austrians living abroad. This article traces the development and usage of the archive collections which include some 10,000 pamphlets, periodicals, photographic collections, posters, newspaper cuttings, microfilms, cassettes and records. The archive is dispersed throughout the country and various provincial governments are responsible for different holdings.

764 **Informationsführer: Bibliotheken- und Dokumentationsstelle in Österreich.** (Information guide to library and documentation centres in Austria.)
Compiled by the Federal Ministry for Science and Research. Vienna: State Publishing House, 1983. annual.

This comprehensive reference work lists 1,436 entries of Austrian academic libraries, institutes, documentation collections, and technical and professional periodicals. The arrangement is alphabetical and the details include usage, opening times, type and description of contents and numbers of personnel.

765 **Schatzkammer (the crown jewels and the ecclesiastical treasure chamber).**
Hermann Fillitz, translated from the German by Geoffrey Holmes. Vienna: Kunsthistorisches Museum, 1963. (Museum of Art History Guide, no. 5).

The Treasury in the Vienna Hofburg was re-opened to the public after World War II in 1954. This is an abridged and revised edition of a German catalogue compiled by the same author at that time. The Treasury contains a notable collection of treasures, both secular and ecclesiastical, belonging to the Habsburgs, including the insignia, regalia and crown of the Holy Roman Empire dating from the 10th century. The latter has been returned to Vienna from its one-time resting place, Nürnberg in Germany, whence it had been removed by Hitler after the *Anschluss*. The catalogue provides a very clear genealogical table of the kings and emperors of the Holy Roman Empire while the English translation is first-class.

766 **Handbuch österreichischer Bibliotheken.** (Handbook of Austrian libraries.)
Vienna: Austrian National Library, 1971-72. 2 vols.

Volume 1 of this handbook, compiled by the Austrian Library Association, presents under the name of province and town 1,350 academic libraries or archives. In each case the following information is given: address; telephone number; size of stock; special collections; services and names of senior staff. There is an index to subjects and institutions and a brief sketch of the Austrian library system. Volume 2 contains statistical data and lists members of the Association.

767 **World guide to libraries.**
Edited by Helga Lengenfelder. Munich, London, New York, Paris: K. G. Saur, 1983. 1, 186p. 6th ed. (Handbook of International Documentation and Information series, vol. 8).

Austria is featured on p. 3-17 of this handbook which lists over 42,700 libraries in 167 countries, each with holdings of over 30,000 volumes, as well as specialist, government and business libraries with 3,000 or more books. The entries are listed according to type of library and are arranged alphabetically by location: statistical information is provided about each library. The text is in German and English.

768 **Ost- und Südosteuropa-Sammlungen in Österreich.** (East and southeast Europe collections in Austria.)
Compiled by Walter Lukan, Max Demeter Peyfuss. Vienna: Verlag für Geschichte und Politik, 1982. 98p. (Institute of East and Southeast Europe series, vol. 9).

This is a detailed documentation register of 145 institutions in Austria with holdings on academic material relating to east and southeast Europe. The institutions are divided into four categories: holdings in large general libraries; documentation points holding east and southeast European material; research and development bodies of the Slovene and Croat ethnic minorities; and institutions directly controlled by east and southeast European countries.

769 **The Austrian State Archives: its history, holdings and use.**
Rudolf Neck (et al.) *Austrian History Yearbook*, vol. 6-7, (1970-71), p. 3-77.

The Austrian State Archives, which span nearly six centuries, were described as 'the most important archive for German history' and ranked with the French and Vatican collections, when Alfred von Arneth was appointed director in 1868. This centenary article reviews their history, and describes how during World War II they were dispersed in a number of occupied countries and, on their return to Vienna, were completely reorganized. There are at present four main collections: family, court and State archives (established 1749); war archives (1711); transportation (1895); administrative, and finance (1945). The series of five short articles contained within these pages is accompanied by a full bibliography listing works edited and published by the State Archives.

770 **Österreich zur See: Schriften des Heeresgeschichtlichen Museums in Wien.** (Austria at sea: the holdings of the Museum of Military History in Vienna.)
Vienna: Federal Publishing Office, 1980. 190p. bibliog. (Institute of Military Science, vol. 8).

The Austrian Maritime Archives, founded in Trieste in 1884, were transferred to Vienna in 1909 and are now housed with the nation's War Archives. They date from the acquisition of Venice in 1797, while earlier papers on the flotillas of the inland waters form part of the Imperial War Council Archive, held separately. This official publication lists the main collections of the Maritime Archives, which contain over 23,000 fascicules, 3,500 registers, 30,000 technical drawings and sea charts, as well as its stock of 14,000 volumes. The work is preceded by an account of the Austrian Navy from 1848 to 1938, with particular emphasis on its role in the service of science and exploration. The bibliography is extensive but only contains works in German.

771 **Österreichisches Freilichtmuseum, Stübing bei Graz.** (The Austrian open-air museum at Stübing near Graz.)
Viktor Herbert Pöttler. Stübing, Graz: Selbstverlag Österreichischen Freilichtmuseums, 1978. 3rd rev. ed. 224p. bibliog.

Founded as a national institution in 1962 the Austrian open-air museum of historic farmsteads, agricultural implements and household utensils at Stübing, near Graz in Styria, is situated in a delightful wooded valley running east to west. The particular features of this site, in which entire farm buildings reflecting styles and customs from all the nine provinces are displayed, have allowed the arrangement of the seventy-six exhibits to follow the east-west extension of Austria itself. Thus the visitor starts his walk in Burgenland, wanders through the east-alpine provinces of Styria and Carinthia, reaches the Danube basin and then the alpine regions of Tirol and Salzburg before completing his tour in the province of Vorarlberg. Professor Pöttler, the museum's director and the inspiration behind the whole project, has spared no effort in creating a unique and authentic museum with a character of its own. Moreover, he has succeeded brilliantly in his objective of preserving for posterity, in charming surroundings, the heritage of a vanishing vernacular rural architecture. This detailed guide is handsomely illustrated and contains a glossary of technical terms. The abridged version in English translation is a perfectly adequate guide for the general visitor.

772 **The Vienna Dorotheum.**
Egon Reiner. *Austria Today*, vol. 6, no. 4 (winter 1980) p. 32-35.

The Vienna Dorotheum, the largest auction house in Europe, was founded in 1707 as a pawnshop which applied the interest from the loans it granted to charitable purposes. Now completely renovated, and employing 550 full-time staff, it caters for a large number of private clients rather than museums and galleries. However, its historic pawn credit sector flourishes and is still attractive to people requiring short-term bridging loans. This brief article outlines its history with some excellent colour photography.

773 **Behind the scene.**
Franz Scharinger. *Austria Today*, no. 1 (1985), p. 52-54.

The Vienna Clock Museum, of which the author is the director, contains over 3,000 historic timepieces, ranging from sandglasses and sundials to the mechanical masterpieces and precision chronometers of modern times. It was formed largely as a combination of two important private collections, that of the well-known horologist, Rudolf Kaftan, and the distinguished 19th-century writer, Maria von Ebner-Eschenbach. This brief article describes this unique collection which reflects Austria's extremely important place in horological production from the introduction of watchmaking by hand in the 1580's right into the 19th century.

774 **The House of Nature.**

Edward Paul Tratz, translated from the German by Catherine Bernrieder. Salzburg, Austria: Haus der Natur, 1974. 95p.

This unusual museum in Salzburg, founded in 1923 by the author of this guide, has won an international reputation for its imaginative displays and exhibits of the effects of natural phenomena and the early evolution of man. Despite the somewhat quaint translation, this slim volume bears all the marks of authority and enthusiastic research.

775 **The Kunsthistorisches Museum, Vienna.**

Philip Wilson, translated from the German by Elsie Callander, Ilse Seldon. London: Summerfield Press, 1984. 256p.

The great and varied art collections of the Habsburg imperial family were brought together in this magnificent museum which was opened officially in 1891 by Emperor Francis Joseph himself. This handsomely illustrated guide, with excellent colour photographs specially commissioned for this publication, takes the reader through an incredible range of art objects from ancient Egypt and Greece to quite modern times. The accompanying commentary does full justice to the superb quality of the visual presentation.

776 **Wissenschaftlicher Informationsführer.** (Scientific Information Guide.)

Vienna: Institute for Library Research, Documentation and Information, 1978. 341p.

This directory contains 750 entries concerning scientific and related specialist libraries and collections and provides details of their holdings and facilities. The work is arranged alphabetically by location in each province.

The Media

General

777 **The mass media in Austria.**
Franz Grössl. Vienna: Federal Press Service, 1985. 12p. (Austria Documentation).

This brochure lists the eighteen daily nwewspapers which currently appear in Austria and which have a combined circulation of approximately 2.5 million. It briefly describes the most important news and information services, outlines the activities of the radio and television services, and the provisions of the Media Law which came into force in 1982. This law gave journalists greater scope for the exercise of freedom of opinion under the constitution, while at the same time provided the individual with a greater degree of protection from abuses of this freedom. The final section deals with the composition and responsibilities of the Press Council.

778 **Österreichs Presse, Werbung, Graphik, Handbuch.** (Austria's press, advertising and graphic arts, a handbook.)
Vienna: Association of Newspaper Publishers. 1953-. annual.

A systematic list of daily and weekly newspapers, periodicals and trade journals produced in Austria, with details concerning publication and circulation as well as advertising rates. A title index is included.

Newspapers

779 **Arbeiter-Zeitung.** (Workers' Newspaper.)
Vienna: 1889-. daily (except Sunday).

This is the central organ of the Austrian Socialist Party with a long history of publication. It is a national newspaper with a current circulation of about 80,000 copies.

780 **Kurier.** (The Courier.)
Vienna: 1954-. daily.

An independent, popular newspaper which is circulated throughout Austria. It has a circulation of about 428,000 copies on week-days and nearly 690,000 copies on Sundays.

781 **Neue Kronen-Zeitung.** (The 'Coronet'.)
Vienna: 1900-. daily.

The paper has the widest circulation in Austria, approximately 856,000 copies on week-days and about 1.35 million on Sundays. Popular in content and projecting independent views, the paper probably has a readership of approximately 33 per cent of the population during the week and about half the total population on Sundays.

782 **Die Presse.** (The Press).
Vienna: 1848-. daily (except Sundays.)

Represents the views of the moderate right and contains serious articles of economic interest and, from time to time, special reports on subjects of current national and international concern. It is a national newspaper with an average circulation of about 70,000 copies.

783 **Videňnské Svobodné Listy.** (Viennese Free News Sheet.)
Vienna: weekly.

This is the official organ of the relatively small Czech and Slovak ethnic groups in Austria, who live mainly in Vienna and its surroundings. It is published in Czech and contains news of topical and cultural interest.

784 **Volksstimme.** (Voice of the People.)
Vienna: 1945-. daily.

This is the official national organ of the Austrian Communist Party, and the paper has had a declining circulation in recent years. The week-day circulation is estimated at about 41,000 and on Sundays it is close to 75,000 copies.

785 **Wiener Zeitung.** (The Vienna Newspaper.)
Vienna: 1703-. daily.

This is one of the oldest national newspapers in the world, and is the official organ of the Austrian Government. It publishes circulars, proclamations, general legislation (in a supplement), and articles concerning public administration. The paper has a circulation of about 50,000.

786 **Neue Vorarlberger Tageszeitung.** (New Vorarlberg Daily.)
Bregenz, Austria: 1972-. daily (except Sundays).

This is an independent newspaper with a daily circulation of about 42,000 copies, which is considerably less than that of its main competitior, the *Vorarlberger Nachrichten*.

787 **Vorarlberger Nachrichten.** (Vorarlberg News.)
Bregenz, Austria. daily (except Sunday).

This is the most widely-read daily newspaper in Austria's westernmost province, with a circulation of about 60,000 copies. It represents independent views.

788 **Kleine Zeitung.** (Small Paper.)
Graz, Klagenfurt, Austria: 1904-. daily.

Very widely read and popular in content, this independent newspaper published in the capitals of Styria and Carinthia, has a total circulation of well-over a quarter of a million copies.

789 **Neue Zeit.** (New Times.)
Graz, Austria: 1945-. daily (weekdays only).

The leading Socialist Party newspaper in Styria with a circulation of about 85,000 copies on Fridays and approximately 78,000 on other days.

790 **Südost Tagespost.** (South Eastern Daily News.)
Graz, Austria: 1856-. daily (weekdays only).

This newspaper projects the views of the Austrian People's Party, that is to say conservative opinion, in Styria. It has a circulation of just over 50,000 copies on Fridays and about 45,000 on other days. It frequently publishes articles of economic interest concerning the country's southern neighbour, Yugoslavia.

791 **Tiroler Tageszeitung.** (Tirolean Daily.)
Innsbruck, Austria: 1945-. daily (except Sunday).

This independent daily newspaper covers Western Austria and parts of South Tirol, with a week-day circulation of about 91,000 copies which reaches over 100,000 on Saturdays.

792 **Kärntner Tageszeitung.** (Carinthian Daily.)
Klagenfurt, Austria: 1946-. weekdays (except Monday).

Represents the views of the Austrian Socialist Party and has a circulation of about 90,000 copies.

793 **Neue Volkszeitung.** (The New People's Paper.)
Klagenfurt, Austria: 1956-. daily (except Sunday).

At one time this paper was the traditional organ in Carinthia of the Christian Democrats but it now represents the views of its successor, the Austrian People's Party. Its circulation is about 35,000 copies and there are special editions entitled *Tiroler Nachrichten* on Saturdays and *Salzburger Nachrichten* on Sundays.

794 **Slovenski Vestnik.** (Slovene News.)
Klagenfurt, Austria: weekly.

Published in Slovene, this publication caters for the needs of the Slovene minority in Carinthia. It includes articles of topical interest mainly in the cultural and economic field.

795 **Neues Volksblatt.** (The New People's Paper.)
Linz, Austria: 1869-. daily (weekdays only).

An organ of the Austrian People's Party with a circulation of about 31,000 copies on Fridays and approximately 26,000 on other days.

796 **Oberösterreichische Nachrichten.** (Upper Austrian News.)
Linz, Austria: 1865-. daily (except Sunday).

An independent newspaper with a week-day circulation of about 95,000 rising to approximately 136,000 copies on Saturdays.

797 **Oberösterreichisches Tagblatt.** (The Upper Austrian Daily Paper.)
Linz, Austria. daily (weekdays only).

This provincial paper, representing the views of the Socialist Party, has a circulation of approximately 27,000 copies.

798 **Salzburger Nachrichten.** (Salzburg News.)
Salzburg, Austria: 1945-. daily (except Sundays).

This independent newspaper contains general news and articles on politics, economics and cultural subjects. Its circulation is about 65,000 on week-days and well over 100,000 on Saturdays.

799 **Salzburger Tagblatt.** (Salzburg Daily.)
Salzburg, Austria. daily (weekdays only).

The organ of the Socialist Party with a weekday circulation of approximately 15,000.

800 **Salzburger Volkszeitung.** (Salzburg People's Paper.)
Salzburg, Austria: daily (weekdays only).

The official organ of the People's Party with a weekday circulation of about 14,000.

Periodicals

General

801 **Austria Today.**
Vienna: Harald Egger. 1974-. quarterly.

A widely-read English-language magazine which contains articles on politics, economics and industry, culture and travel as well as book reviews. Each issue also carries a number of brief reports on different aspects of modern Austrian life. This publication is illustrated and well-produced.

802 **Austriaca: cahiers universitaires d'information sur l'Autriche.**
(Austriaca: university notes and information on Austria.)
Rouen, France: Université de Haute-Normandie, Centre d'études et de recherches autrichiennes, 1974-. biannual.

A serious journal concerned with political and cultural, mainly literary, issues affecting Austria both in its historical and contemporary setting. From time to time a whole issue is devoted to one particular subject or individual, for example, Ernst Fischer the communist politician, essayist and poet is covered in issue no. 20 (May 1985) and psychoanalysis and the Vienna School of Psychiatry are dealt with in issue no. 21 (Nov. 1985). All articles are in French.

803 **Blick ins Land.** (A View of the Countryside.)
Linz, Austria. monthly.

This is Austria's leading farming periodical and has a circulation of about 320,000 copies. Apart from articles of agricultural interest, it contains a certain amount of statistical data.

804 **Bunte Österreich.** (Colourful Austria.)
Vienna: J. Kirschner, S. Gasser. 1948-. weekly.

A general interest illustrated magazine with an estimated circulation of 143,000.

805 **Der Anblick.** (The Country View.)
Graz, Austria: Styrian Provincial Hunting Association, 1946-. monthly.

A well-established and informative periodical dealing with all forms of field sports and nature conservation in Austria. It has a wide national circulation. The country's game laws have done much to help preserve a number of rare animal species which are almost extinct in other parts of central Europe.

806 **Hrvatske Novine.** (Croatian News.)
Eisenstadt, Austria. weekly.

This is the official voice of the Croat minority in Burgenland and contains articles mainly of cultural, economic and social interest.

807 **National Geographic.**
Washington, DC. 1888-. monthly.
From time to time this international and prestigious publication includes articles on Austria accompanied by superb colour photographs. For example: July 1961 – Tirol; July 1965 – Danube by canoe; June 1968 – Vienna; and April 1985 – those eternal Austrians, with an excellent relief map of the Alps (q.v.).

808 **Niederösterreichische Nachrichten.** (Lower Austria News.)
St. Pölten, Austria: 1864-. weekly.
A well-established journal publishing articles mainly of provincial interest and with a circulation of about 135,000 copies.

809 **profil.** (profile.)
Vienna: 1970-. fortnightly.
An illustrated magazine with a circulation of about 83,000 and containing articles on politics, industry, the international scene and cultural topics, as well as book reviews.

810 **Rendezvous Vienna.**
Vienna: Vienna Tourist Board. 1956-. quarterly.
Published in English, French and German 'for Viennese friends all over the world' this magazine contains articles of general contemporary Viennese interest, particularly in the cultural field. It also includes book reviews and lists forthcoming events in the capital.

811 **Wien Aktuell.** (Vienna Now.)
Vienna: Municipal Press and Information Service. 1956-. weekly.
Compiled mainly for visitors to Vienna, this is a useful guide to forthcoming events in the capital, with articles of cultural and sporting interest, a women's page and, from time to time, a historical cameo. It is published in German but contains English summaries.

Professional

812 **Alte und moderne Kunst.** (Ancient and Modern art.)
Innsbruck: AMK Verlag. 1958-. 4 issues per year (2 of which are double-issues).
Published for the Austrian Museum for Applied Art in Vienna, this is a leading periodical in the art world. It is extremely well-produced, has excellent illustrations, and is not over-techncial in its contents. Special supplements covering major art exhibitions are issued periodically.

813 **Architektur Aktuell.** (Architecture Today.)
Vienna: Oskar Schmid, 6 times per year.,

A professional journal concerned with modern architecture design and building in both the private and public sector. It has a circulation of about 5,000 copies.

814 **Die Bühne.** (The Stage.)
Vienna: Theatre Association of Vienna. 1958-. monthly.

The only periodical devoted to the professional theatre published in Austria and with an international reputation. It includes reviews of foreign plays and from time to time recent record releases. Its circulation is approximately 75,000 copies.

815 **Juristische Blätter.** (Legal Notes.)
Vienna: Springer Verlag, 1872-. fortnightly.

This is the leading journal in the Austrian legal profession and publishes articles, law reports and court proceedings. Twice-monthly fascicules are gathered together into annual volumes.

816 **Österreichische Musikzeitschrift.** (Austrian Musical Journal.)
Vienna. 1946-. monthly.

An authoritative source of information about Austrian current musical life, with articles, reviews and news about musical events, personalities, seminars and courses. A widely-read publication of general musical interest.

817 **Österreichs Wirtschaft im Überblick.** (Austria's Economy at a Glance.)
Vienna: Economic Committee of the Museum of Austrian Demography and Economics. 1956-. annual.

This publication is compiled principally for promotional and educational purposes and is available on transparencies for visual display. It provides an economic survey and includes brief commentaries, comparative tables of economic performance in other European countries, and statistics about international organizations located in Vienna. The 1984 issue had sixty pages.

818 **Österreichische Zeitschrift für Kunst und Denkmalpflege.** (Austrian Journal for Art and Monument Conservation.)
Vienna: Anton Schroll, 1947-. 5 times per year.

An important journal in view of Austria's significant contribution both to the maintenance and restoration of buildings and monuments of architectural and historical interest and to housing renovation schemes.

819 **Österreichsche Zeitschrift für öffentliches Recht und Völkerrecht.** (Austrian Journal for Public and International Law.)
Vienna: 1914-. annual.

The articles in this journal are published in German, French and English and deal with legal and constitutional matters affecting public administration and the international scene.

820 **Österreichische Zeitschrift für Volkskunde.** (Austrian Folklore Journal.)
Vienna: 1895-. quarterly.

The leading journal in this field which publishes articles on both local history and matters of demographic interest.

821 **Trend.** (Trends.)
Vienna: 1970-. monthly.

An independent economic publication for businessmen and financiers, with articles in German, but often summarized in English. Its circulation is estimated at about 45,000 copies.

Scientific and medical

822 **Acta Chirurgica Austriaca.** (Papers on Austrian Surgery.)
Vienna: 1968-. 5 times per year.

The surgical research journal for the Austrian Association for Surgery and Related Subjects. The articles are published in German with occasional summaries in English. It regularly includes abstracts of recently-published works in this particular field from international sources.

823 **Acta Mechanica.** (Papers on the Mechanical Sciences.)
Vienna: Springer-Verlag, 1965-. 18 times per year.

The research journal of the Association of Mechanical Sciences of the Austrian Academy of Sciences. The articles are published in German and occasionally in English.

824 **Acta Medica Austriaca.** (Papers on Austrian Medicine.)
Vienna: Brüder Hollinek, 1920-. monthly.

The research journal of the Austrian and Viennese Associations for Internal Medicine, the Austrian Cardiological Association, and the Nuclear-medical Association for Transplants. The articles are published in German, mostly with English translations.

825 **Acta Physica Austriaca.** (Papers on Austrian Physics.)
Vienna: Springer Verlag, 1947-. quarterly.

The research journal of the Austrian Physics Society. The quarterly issues of various lengths are gathered into annual volumes. This periodical contains articles on physics and nuclear energy and is published in German and English.

826 **Archaeologia Austriaca: Beiträge zur Paläanthropologie Ur- und Frühgeschichte Österreichs.** (Contributions to the palaeontology of the primeval and early history of Austria.)
Vienna. biannual.

This journal is issued jointly by the Anthropological Institutes for Primeval and Early History at Vienna University and is edited by R. Pittioni, an archaeologist of international repute. It contains articles on palaeontology and archaeology with updates on current research in these fields.

827 **Monatshefte für Chemie.** (Chemistry Monthly.)
Vienna: Springer Verlag. 1880-. monthly.

This is the official research organ of the Austrian Academy of Sciences and the Association of Austrian Chemists. Articles are published in German and English. The monthly issues are gathered into annual volumes.

828 **Österreichische Geographische Mitteilungen.** (Austrian Geographical Reports.)
Vienna: Austrian Geographical Society, 1857-. 3 times a year.

A long-established major scholarly geographical periodical, containing articles on all parts of the world as well as book reviews. The abstracts are in English, French and German.

829 **Wiener Geographische Schriften.** (Viennese Geographical Papers.)
Vienna: Geographical Institute, 1957-. irregular, but several issues per year.

Contains mainly research monographs dealing with various aspects of the economic geography of Austria. Includes condensed translations of texts and abstracts in English.

830 **WIFO.**
Vienna: Österreichisches Institut für Wirtschaftsforschung (Austrian Institute for Economic Research). 1927-. monthly.

This review of the country's economy commands considerable respect among economists and businessmen. It includes much statistical data on production, prices and wages, the fiscal situation and the export trade. The text is in German but there is a condensed translation in English of the main contents of the review.

Broadcasting

831 **25 Jahre Fernsehen.** (Twenty-five years of television.)
Vienna: Austrian Broadcasting Service (ÖRF), Co-ordination and Communication Division, 1980. 7 vols. (Reports on Media Research).

The Austrian television service operates on two channels; one containing the traditional mix of news, entertainment, music and general culture; and the other offering an alternative service. The Österreichischer Rundfunk (ÖRF) celebrated its twenty-fifth anniversary in 1980 and to mark the occasion a series of twenty-eight reports (four in each volume) were compiled by a team of specialists, covering a wide spectrum of editorial, production, administrative and technical aspects. Each report was about ninety pages in length and was backed up by an extensive and specialized bibliography and, where relevant, statistical data.

832 **Austria: media dependence.**
Benno Signitzer. *Journal of Communication*, vol. 28, no. 3 (1978), p. 79-82.

The Austrian broadcasting service is an autonomous public body holding a legal monopoly of all broadcasting in the country, yet over 50 per cent of its television programmes are foreign in origin. The author deplores the indifference of the general viewing public to this potential threat to the country's national and cultural integrity. A further article in the same journal, entitled 'Austria: policy-making in a small country' (vol. 30, no. 2 (1980), p. 186-89), examines the structure of Austria's mass-communication system, focuses on the country's lack of an explicit communication policy and deplores its dependence on imported material in the fields of television, press, film, music and publishing.

Bibliographies

833 **The armies of Austria-Hungary and Germany, 1740-1914.**
Compiled by Lázló Alfoldi. Carlisle, Pennsylvania: Carlisle Barracks, 1975. 256p. (US Army Military History Research Collection, Special Bibliographic Series, no. 12).

This monumental work provides a systematic guide to the basic literature on the military history of Austria-Hungary and Germany from the middle of the 18th century up to World War I, as housed in this remarkable collection of some 15,000 documents, books, maps and illustrations, in English, French, German, Hungarian and Russian. A further volume is planned which will extend coverage up to the end of World War II.

834 **Österreichische Historische Bibliographie.** (Austrian Historical Bibliography.)
Edited by Eric H. Boehm, Günther Hödl. Santa Barbara, California: ABC-Clio Information Services; Salzburg, Austria: Buchhandlung & Verlag Wolfgang Neugebauer 1983. 1965-. annual.

This is a compendious bibliography of Austrian studies including historical material interpreted in the widest possible sense. It covers not only books and periodical literature but dissertations, essays and *Festschriften* as well as works of a specialist nature and published only in limited editions. Five-year cumulative indexes of authors, subjects and publishers are also issued. There is perhaps an over-liberal use of abbreviations, which does not make for easy or quick reference, but it is very detailed, and its appearance over the last twenty years has been warmly welcomed by historians, specialists and researchers alike. All annotations are in German.

835 **The Habsburg Monarchy, 1804-1918: books and pamphlets published in the UK between 1818 and 1967. A critical bibliography.**
Francis Roy Bridge. London: School of Slavonic and East European Studies, University of London, 1967. 82p.

The distinguished historian C. A. Macartney has assisted in the selection of works included in this bibliography which is of particular value to the student of Habsburg history in the 19th and early 20th centuries. The work is divided into three parts: general history, with sub-sections on shorter periods; diplomatic and military history; and biography and memoirs of the imperial family and other personalities. There are author and subject indexes and an index of persons. The notes are brief and factual, evaluative comments being kept to a minimum.

836 **Austrian doctoral dissertations.**
Eva-Marie Csaly. *Austrian History Yearbook*, vol. 14 (1978), p. 259-265.

A list of doctoral dissertations, accepted by academic institutions in the United States and Europe, and prepared between 1955 and 1977 covering the history of Austria from 1520 to the present.

837 **Austrian politics 1945-1975: a selected bibliography.**
John Dreijinamis. *East European Quarterly*, vol. 2, no. 2 (1977), p. 247-50.

A useful list of scholarly books in German and English on post-World War II Austrian politics, including general reference works and books on foreign policy and political parties.

838 **A bibliography of stained glass.**
David Evans. Cambridge, England. D. S. Brewer, 1982. 201p.

In this extensive world bibliography of stained glass the arrangement is alphabetical by author. A topographical index lists the countries covered, including Austria (p. 196), which is represented mainly by specialist articles in Austrian art periodicals and dissertations, mostly in German.

839 **Bio-Bibliographisches Literaturlexikon Österreichs. Von den Anfängen bis zur Gegenwart.** (A bio-bibliographical encyclopaedia of Austrian literature from its earliest beginnings to the present day.)
Hans Giebisch, Gustav Gugitz. Vienna: Brüder Hollinek, 1964. 517p.

A well-researched comprehensive encyclopaedia of Austrian authors born before 1900 and resident within the territories of the Austrian Empire, including those who later emigrated abroad, particularly at the time of the *Anschluss*. There are also a few entries for foreign authors who, generally for political reasons, chose Austria as their country of residence.

840 **Karl-Kraus Bibliographie**. (Karl Kraus bibliography.)
Otto Kerry. Munich: Kösel Verlag, 1970. 478p.

An abridged bibliography of Karl Kraus's major writings was published in 1954 but the present volume, by the same publisher, is very much more comprehensive and includes both primary and secondary literary material. It lists alphabetically: the articles Kraus wrote for the journal *Die Fackel* (The Torch); all his writings in book form; his publications in their various editions; his lectures; broadcasts; essays; poems; satires; aphorisms; and theatrical works. The arrangement for the secondary source material is thematic and the volume includes an extensive index of authors, publishers, book titles and periodicals.

841 **The Anschluss movement, 1918-38: background and aftermath. An annotated bibliography of German and Austrian nationalism.**
Alfred D. Low. New York, London: Garland, 1984. 186p. (Canadian Review of Studies in Nationalism, vol. 4).

This bibliography contains 515 entries of books, pamphlets, dissertations, essays and articles, including some Nazi propaganda material, relating to German and Austrian nationalism during the period of the First Republic in Austria. It includes works predominantly in German and English, and to a much lesser extent in French and Italian. An indispensable source reference for students and scholars of the *Anschluss* movement.

842 **Bibliographie zur österreichischen Zeitgeschichte, 1918-1980.** (Bibliography of contemporary Austrian history, 1918-80.)
Peter Malina, Gustav Spann. Vienna: Verlag für Geschichte und Politik, 1980. 3 vols. (Political Studies, vols. 28-30).

This historical bibliography, spanning the period from the end of World War I to the present day, lists handbooks, bibliographical references and general works on Austrian political, social and economic history. Monographs utilizing authoritative sources to explain specialist subjects are also included, with brief annotations.

843 **German language and literature: select bibliography of reference books.**
L. M. Newman. London: University of London, Institute of Germanic Studies, 1979. 175p. 2nd ed.

With 1,000 entries this bibliography, enlarged and updated from the 1966 edition, provides comprehensive and systematic coverage of the German-language areas of Europe in the fields of literature, language and linguistics. Brief annotations outline the contents and value of books listed and link related material. A distinction is made between retrospective bibliographies, which list books and other material published in previous years and current bibliographies which record recent publications and are mainly still on-going. The arrangement also distinguishes between works on specific subjects and those covering all areas, so that bibliographies on the same subject are not always together, though they are linked by references in the notes and the subject index. The work cites a total of sixty-two bibliographies relating specifically to Austria.

844 **Bibliography of English translations.**
In: *Anthology of Modern Austrian Literature*. Edited by Adolf Opel. London: Oswald Wolff, 1981, p. 248-52.

This short, selective but useful bibliography lists books in English translation by Austrian writers published from 1930 up to 1980. It also includes a few major anthologies from the 1960's in which contributions from Austrian writers have appeared.

845 **Österreichische Bibliographie**. (Austrian bibliography.)
Vienna: Austrian Booktrade Association, 1946-. fortnightly.

This classified list of recently published trade and non-trade material is compiled by the Austrian National Library, and contains indexes to authors and titles which are cumulated quarterly and annually.

846 **Bibliographie zur Geschichte der österreichischen Arbeiterbewegung, 1867-1918.** (Historical bibliography of the Austrian workers' movement, 1867-1918.)
Compiled by Herbert Steiner. Vienna: Federation of Austrian Trade Unions, 1962. 316p.

Although written almost a quarter of a century ago the serious student of the Austro-Hungarian working-class movement will still find this an invaluable reference work. It lists all relevant newspapers, pamphlets, official reports as well as books, researched by the compiler in thirty different central European libraries, twelve of them in Vienna alone. In each case the name of the library or institution holding the publication is provided.

847 **Personalbibliographien Österreichischer Dichter und Schriftsteller von den Anfängen bis zur Gegenwart.** (Personal bibliographies of Austrian poets and authors from the earliest times to the present day.)
Edited by Karl F. Stock, Rudolf Heilinger, Marylène Stock. Munich-Pullach: Verlag Dokumentation, K. G. Saur, 1972. 703p. bibliog.

Over 6,000 entries appear in this substantial reference work containing detailed personal bibliographies of Austrian writers from the earliest times to the present. The categories included are those who were born or lived within the Austro-Hungarian boundaries with German as their mother tongue, and those who were born and died in Austria, or who worked for a reasonable period of time in the country. Over one quarter of the work is devoted to the reference books and monographs (international, German and Austrian) from which information has been drawn. Within authors, items are presented chronologically with a contents note but no evaluation. There is even a section on proscribed literature, dating mainly from the 18th century. A good name and title index services this impressive documentation.

Index

The index is a single alphabetical sequence of authors (personal and corporate), titles of publications and subjects. Index entries refer both to the main items and to other works mentioned in the notes to each item. Title entries are in italics. Numeration refers to the items as numbered.

C

D

F

H

I

J

K

L

M

N

Q

R

S

T

U

W

Y

Z